This Is Germany

Edited by
ARTHUR SETTEL

THIS IS GERMANY

Introduction by
GENERAL LUCIUS D. CLAY

WILLIAM SLOANE ASSOCIATES, INC.
Publishers   *New York*

Copyright, 1950, by

WILLIAM SLOANE ASSOCIATES, INC.

Second Printing

Typography and format designed by
LEONARD W. BLIZARD

Manufactured in the United States of America
Published simultaneously in Canada by
George J. McLeod, Ltd.

This book is dedicated to the men and women of the press who are the watchdogs of liberty in an age when this liberty is threatened on many fronts.

Introduction

By LUCIUS D. CLAY
General, U. S. Army (Ret.)

I N MAY 1945 THE TOTAL DEFEAT OF THE GERMAN ARMED
forces by the victorious Allied armies led to the
unconditional surrender of Germany. The American
people had reason to believe that the danger of future aggression in Europe had been destroyed and that lasting peace
would result.

Our government had entered into an agreement with the
governments of France, the United Kingdom, and Russia
for a four-power occupation of Germany. This occupation
was to have as its major purposes the exacting of security
measures, to include the punishment of the Nazi leaders, so
that a recovered Germany would not become again an aggressor nation, while at the same time restoring an economy
which would provide the German people with a reasonable
standard of living, and the rebuilding of self-government
under democratic procedures.

Unfortunately we soon found that all of the four powers
did not interpret their agreement for the occupation of Germany alike. As a result, four-power government failed, and
for many months each of the four powers governed its separate zone of occupation independently. It was obvious that
the complex, closely integrated German economy could not
recover under such conditions. Hence the British and Ameri-

can zones, and later the French Zone, were joined into an economic unit.

Concurrently, our government had offered financial assistance to all of Europe only to have its offer rejected by the Soviet Government and the governments of its satellite states. However, the offer was accepted by the free countries of Europe, which led logically to the inclusion in this economic program of the three Western zones of Germany, represented by their military governments in the co-operative organization which was to develop the program. Thus Soviet rejection of our offer resulted in the division of Europe into two economic groups, with East Germany, under Soviet domination, in the Soviet-controlled economic bloc and West Germany casting its lot with the free countries of Europe.

It was under these conditions that the Soviet Government established the blockade of Berlin by land and water in the attempt to drive the Western powers from Berlin and to create fear and uncertainty in Europe which would retard the progress of economic recovery. The blockade failed because of the successful airlift. However, while it was in effect the three Western powers reconciled their views so that West Germany could be united under its own elected government which, under a liberal occupation statute, would receive a large measure of responsibility. Moreover, this new German government was to continue to receive economic assistance and to co-operate in the common endeavor of the free countries of Europe to re-establish economic self-sufficiency.

The expansion policy of the Soviet Government was stopped although it has resulted temporarily in dividing Europe into two parts. The dividing line was inside Germany, so it too is divided into two parts. While the German people fervently desire a unified Germany under the conditions which pertain to West Germany, it seems clear that the people of West Germany prefer a government of their own for the time being rather than a unified Germany that is not guaranteed the basic rights of a free people.

A divided Europe in which there is a divided Germany cannot offer the stability that would make lasting peace possible. As long as there is division, we cannot call the European problem or the German problem solved. Both remain major questions, to which our statesmen must devote their full attention in the months and years ahead.

There can be no solution of the European problem until there is a solution of the German problem. It is complex, and cannot be reduced to simple terms, and yet the American people must understand it if they are to contribute to its solution. Therefore books which describe the problem are important to its understanding and to its solution.

In spite of its complexity, the German problem can be solved without war if we are both understanding and patient. Our statesmen can succeed in their task if they have the full support of the American people. They can receive this support only from an informed people.

During my tour of duty as military governor I learned to know the journalists and correspondents who have joined together to prepare this book. While I may not always agree with their conclusions, I have respect for their knowledge of their subject, for their powers of observation, and for their objective presentation of facts. To see Germany through their eyes is truly to see Germany.

This is a book written by experts. Moreover, they are experts who believe in the dignity of man and in his right to live as an individual. They know both the value and the importance of free institutions. While their book will necessarily reflect their differences in viewpont, fundamentally they all believe in representative government and in international co-operation. Therefore their differences in viewpoint as to progress in these objectives are stimulating. The reader may have confidence in the facts which are presented by the authors because they are also reporters schooled in the presentation of facts. It is "must" reading for those who wish to understand the German problem.

South Yarmouth, Mass.

Contents

Introduction   *General Lucius D. Clay*   vii

Preface   *Arthur Settel*   xiii

No More Conquerors   *Robert Haeger, United Press*   1

The Man in the Goldfish Bowl   23
     Lyford Moore, American Broadcasting Company

The Germans in the Cold War   40
     Richard Lowenthal, London Observer

Tomorrow Is the New Moon   74
     J. Emlyn Williams, Christian Science Monitor

Education—For What?   *Robert Lewison*   89

The German Guilt   *John Anspacher, United Press*   116

Freedom on the Auction Block   136
     Russell Jones, United Press

"Der Kleine Mann"   *Jack Raymond, New York Times*   149

Candy-Bar Romance—Women of Germany   161
     Judy Barden, North American Newspaper Alliance

Case History of a German Town   177
     Ralph Harwood, Weekend

Germany's Stepchildren   195
     Ernest Leiser, Overseas News Agency

March of Millions   210
     Denis Martin, London Daily Herald

Contents

The Hard Peace 226
David M. Nichol, Chicago Daily News

The Unpayable Debt 249
Joseph E. Evans, Wall Street Journal

Eternal Triangle—The Ruhr 268
Terence Prittie, Manchester Guardian

What Price Co-operation—Resistance and Collaboration in Occupied Germany 293
Peter de Mendelssohn, London Observer

Obituary of a Government—The Story of the East-West Breakup in Germany 309
Marguerite Higgins, New York Herald Tribune

Birth of a State 329
Kathleen McLaughlin, New York Times

Beauty and the Beast—France Takes a Slow New Look at Germany 346
James Preston O'Donnell, Saturday Evening Post

Germany as Seen by Her Neighbors 359
Theodore H. White, Overseas News Agency

Zone of Silence 370
Landrum Bolling, Overseas News Agency

Biographical Notes 415

Preface

THE ANSWERS TO THE GREAT PARADOX OF POSTWAR GER-many are inevitably paradoxical. It is rare to find agreement on any concept relating to this country which, for reasons explained at some length in this book, has brought so much misery upon the world. In the broad field of international relations these differences have split the world in two. On the level of individual criticism no two observers have reacted in a like manner to the German problem or to any of its myriad complexities.

It would be a betrayal of all for which America stands, however, if we were to beg the question by ignoring it. In the four and a half years during which I have served United States Military Government as a public relations officer in the office of the United States High Commissioner for Germany, I have consistently adhered to the concept that impartial observers should be given every opportunity to make their voices heard and their presence felt. The daily newspaper is at best an evanescent medium; some of the best journalism of our time passes into oblivion almost at the very moment of its writing. This is one reason for this book.

But there is another, perhaps even more important. We Americans are privileged to enjoy a free press. In subjecting ourselves to self-examination and self-criticism, we are following an instinct which is inherent in our democratic way of life. In a world a large part of which is under the shadow of tyranny and the heavy hand of dictatorship, this quirk in our character stands out by sheer contrast. It should act as a reminder that American policy in Germany, which is subject perhaps to more public criticism and analysis than the political and economic philosophy of any of the three other occupying powers, has its base in practical realism and enjoys the support of the American people.

I do not say this by virtue of my being associated with the United States High Commissioner. I am the last one in the world to deny that there are imperfections in our German program, or to conceal our errors. I insist, however, that no power is so quick to admit them or so prompt in taking steps to correct them. This is basic to America's efforts in encouraging Germans to follow a democratic concept, extirpate militarism and militaristic nationalism from their way of life, atone for their mistakes, and rejoin the ranks of those who believe in the dignity of man rather than the deification of the state.

In April 1949, while in New York on a special mission for United States Military Government, I was asked whether my job as information officer meant that I was supposed to "whitewash the maladministration, the blundering and the bungling" of Military Government agencies. I said that like all governments, we made mistakes, but unlike many other governments, we don't suppress them. I explained that good public relations and good performance were synonymous, that the function of my office was to advise the functionaries of government when the parallel lines were likely to cross.

Thus, a correspondent in search of the facts, no matter how unpleasant they may be, can get them from the Public Relations Office, subject only to security considerations. As often as not it was the "old man" himself, General Lucius D. Clay, who was the first to come out with the truth in an ugly situation. This is by way of explanation as to why an official of the Commission Government presumes to edit a book by

American and British newspaper correspondents. The writers represented in *This Is Germany* asked me to act as a kind of editorial catalyst because they and I understand each other, and because they were convinced that I would see the project through to its finish. For this implied compliment I am grateful. It must be emphasized that the contributors to this book write as free agents and as they please, and their opinions do not necessarily represent those of the Commission or my own.

Those who may question this point need only read the pages which follow. Here they will find a mixture of approval and reprehension, of reporting and editorializing, characteristic of the ineffable paradox that is Germany in this year of grace 1950. One of the few things which these writers have in common is a respect which frequently approaches veneration for the former military governor, Geneal Clay, who, himself aware of many shortcomings in the policy for which he was the principal architect, agreed to write the introduction. He did this knowing that while the press fraternity admires him personally for his impartiality, his genius as an administrator and negotiator, his astonishing grasp of the German problem, many of them were dubious of his position on many issues.

Most of the attacks on American policy in Germany are predicated upon the fear, certainly not unjustified, that the country's resurgence as the most highly industrialized nation in Europe will result once more in her running amuck in quest of world dominion. The measures taken by authority to insure adequate safeguards in the control of Germany's industrial potential are either ignored or discounted, while steps to restore normalcy, decency, and self-sufficiency in a society of 48,000,000 (the estimated population of Western Germany) are often misrepresented in what has become virtually a cant of despair. In appraising the extent to which we have struck a balance between these two apparently self-contradicting aims, the following considerations must be taken into account:

Relations between the United States and Soviet Russia have forced the pace of the reconstruction program for Germany, with each side vying to influence the thinking of the people occupying the strategic center of the board. A Communist Germany would inevitably lead to a communized Europe, which in turn would bring disaster to the United States.

The governments of the very countries which have been attacked, invaded, and occupied by Germany are at one with the United States in believing that there can be neither security nor prosperity in a world from which the German people derive relief but to which they do not make the constructive contribution which they are capable of making.

In underwriting the cost of its recovery, the United States must assume a great share of responsibility for directing and determining the life of present-day Germany, not only in economic but in political fields as well.

Our stake in Germany has been described in a House Committee report as follows: "Twice in a lifetime, the German people under evil leadership have upset the stability of Europe and the peace of the world. Today the United States has a major responsibility for the political, economic, and social life of 48,000,000 German people in the Western zones. Whether their capacities contribute to world order or world disorder is largely in their hands. We pay the costs of failure, in any case."

It behooves every American citizen to realize the importance of our stake in Germany and to follow the development of our policy in this country. The corps of United States newsmen who cover the German story carry a heavy responsibility: they are the eyes and ears of 150,000,000 Americans who are the final arbiters as to the direction and the tempo of our policy. My own findings during two trips to the United States, one in 1948 and another in the spring of 1949, were extremely disillusioning. I found that there was an appalling degree of apathy toward and ignorance of our objectives in Europe generally and Germany in particular. But the extent of misinformation was even greater. It is difficult to ascribe this to a failure to read the newspapers, or the paucity of interpretive material published on the subject. It surely cannot be explained by any want of thoroughness or diligence on the part of the correspondents, or of Mr. McCloy's office in making available to the public adequate background and progress reports on its operations. Perhaps this book will serve to fill the gap. If it does, it will have accomplished its purpose.

ARTHUR SETTEL

Frankfurt am Main

Chapter I

No More Conquerors

By ROBERT HAEGER

IN THE early days of the Occupation of Germany a wry joke in the form of a rhymed prayer buzzed through American-held Bavaria. It went like this:

God, give us the Fifth Reich.
The Third and Fourth are just alike.

That prayer has been answered.

The New Occupation, supervised by skeleton staffs of Allied officials and backed up only by comparative handfuls of troops, bears almost as little resemblance to the lawless "Fourth Reich" of the Old Occupation as to the Hitler regime.

The vanished rosy optimism about postwar relations with the Soviet Union, the subsequent cold war and Berlin blockade, have put the United States in the position of wooing the German for the future rather than whipping him because of the past. To see just how complete the about-face has been, look back to the tough statements made in the early days of the Occupation by the three generals who ran American Military Government.

As his GI's stormed into Hitler's Reich, General Dwight D. Eisenhower reminded them and the Germans that "We come as conquerors, not liberators." But those conquerors shrank in numbers faster than those of any other nation. They handed governing powers back to the Germans in a hurry. And Military Government courts have ruled that at least one segment of the conquerors, the civilians, is subject to the laws of conquered Germany. When he took over the top job, General Joseph T. McNarney estimated that the Occupation would last at least thirty years. Predictions of that kind were standard then. It was thought that full-scale, long-term methods were needed to keep the militaristic Germans from rising again. Barely three years later tremendous pressure had arisen from the East, from the West, and from within Germany itself to pull the troops out, despite the fact that American military strength in Germany had shrunk to less than 10 per cent of what it was at the time of Mc-Narney's prediction.

In his early sessions with the press General Lucius D. Clay was fond of referring to his administration as "the punitive phase of the Occupation," but even as he spoke those words the United States was pouring hundreds of millions of dollars into food for the defeated. It was rebuilding trade and boosting the productive capacity of the crucial Ruhr. It was pushing for a separate West German government to take over most of Military Government's work. And, while paying lip service to the idea of denazification, it had passed most of that unique task into German hands, where it was allowed to waste away, by-passed by fast-moving postwar events.

As official policy has transformed the German from a near-animal to be shunned and despised into a desirable citizen who should be helped to his feet, welcomed back into the family of nations, and, above all, be kept anti-Communist, it has inevitably curbed the powers and individual rights of the American occupier. The kind of free-swinging in the back-wash of war that makes good material for reminiscing in the

American Legion clubhouse no longer exists. A GI conqueror, class of '45, coming back to Germany would find the details of everyday life turned upside down. "Kraut," his favorite designation for the German, is seldom heard now. American clubs and theaters, formerly exclusively for Allies, unroll a figurative red carpet for the once officially untouchable fräuleins. Hundreds of former GI hotels, clubs, and private homes have been handed back to their German owners. American police can't enter a home in Germany without a search warrant any more than they can in the States. Until recently, no soldier could eat or drink in a German restaurant except as the invited guest of a German. The American can't get into his own post exchange without winning the approval of an eagle-eyed doorkeeper, usually a German.

The days of taking the best and leaving the rest for the Germans are over. Requisitioning of property halted when the Occupation was only a year old, and the pressure now is in the opposite direction, to give back everything that can be spared. The Occupation is one of rules and regulations, most of them designed to protect those who lost the war. It protects some of them to this extent: Standing Army orders are that no German employee can be fired from an American military installation for being insubordinate or drunk on the job just once. He has to commit the offense twice before he gets the sack. And sleeping on the job is not a dismissal offense until the weary one is caught napping for the third time.

It is not only the Americans who have retreated from their whip-cracking positions. The same trend is obvious to varying degrees in all zones, including the Russian, as the three Western and one Eastern powers scramble for the allegiance and friendship of the nation they combined to beat.

The closest parallel to the American course is found in the British Zone. The United States and Britain have worked so closely together that combining their supervisory organizations in the steps toward a West German government was relatively simple. Both nations agreed to get Germany going again and together yielded ruling prerogatives to get that job accomplished. But the economic recovery which blossomed under this policy was so sensational as to leave the uncomfortable British conqueror looking up to his defeated opponent in at least one respect—food. Many British occupiers, bitter opponents of the Labour Government, came here just to get out from under its wing. But some phases of Crippsian austerity have pursued them. Their rations are better than those of their relatives back home but not up to what the German economy is producing. The contrast in quality and quantity has been glaring enough to stir up a couple of near-riots by Occupation wives of the British Zone. In both Düsseldorf and Kiel indignant housewives, spearheaded by some titled spouses of Occupation officials, paraded down the main streets and demonstrated for food at least equivalent to that consumed by the "beaten" Germans. This paradox reached its craziest refinement in a Cologne hotel. Partly requisitioned for British use, its dining room presented an aggravating contrast. On the British side breakfast consisted of such uninspiring items as dried fish; beyond the invisible line splitting the room Germans gorged on bacon and eggs.

No such unhappy situation could have arisen in the French Zone. Of the Westerners they have been the most reluctant to yield the tight rein of control. Off in the Black Forest corner of the country they followed their own tough way of Occupation for a long time after the British and Americans had waived such principles. It was a way calculated to give the maximum return to France and the maximum comfort to the occupier and his family, and sometimes the family reached incredible proportions. The spectacular spa of Baden-Baden was practically transformed into a French resort. Luxury hotels were packed with the wives, children, cousins, uncles, and grandmothers of Occupation job holders, all eager to get out of their hungry home country. Like the Russians, the French had no compunction about living off the land they occupied, and they brought their relatives along to do the same. When the French joined the British-American Ruhr Control Board they sent up eight specialists. With families the new colony totaled more than fifty persons.

While going their own way, the French ate good German food and drank good German wine. They took over industries and set them producing for French benefit and cut a great swath through the lush forests, sending the timber back home or selling it to other countries. Occupation officials were paid out of the proceeds of exports from the French Zone, a policy which was modified when the three Western areas were fused early in 1949.

When they finally chose to go along with the Anglo-American idea of a West German state, the French proceeded slowly, ever watchful for dangers to their own security. With the unhappy memory of their own occupation by Germany fresh in their minds, they were slow to accept the idea of re-creating any kind of government and revitalizing Germany industrially. The first field in which the French were to co-ordinate their policies with the Americans and British was foreign trade. It took them more than six months after the target date on trade to swing into line and they have carried their cautious policy into all related fields.

Always proportionally far more heavily staffed than either of the other Western military governments, the French worked diligently in fields sadly neglected by their co-occupiers, particularly education. Acting on the theory that the only class of Germans that can be weaned away from the

Hohenzollern-Hitler heritage is the very young, they spent hard-to-get dollars to finance a textbook program aimed at putting the school system on a democratic road. The Americans, in contrast, concentrated on economic recovery at the expense of democratization—with former Nazi party members returning to power in many spheres of activity.

Denazification never troubled the Russians. They polished it off in a hurry once they overhauled their ideas of punishment and decided that punitive measures constituted a poor way to win German favor. They simply excused all "little" Nazis, then went out of their way to persuade these millions to get on the band wagon by joining one of the People's Front parties of the Eastern Zone. As the vengeful phase of the Soviet program dissolved, the propaganda guns were turned in a different direction and the approach to the Germans ran along this line: "We can all be buddies together against the monopoly capitalists of the West."

Terror tales from the Russian-held area have dropped off sharply. No longer are bloodcurdling recitals of mass rape by U.S.S.R. soldiers gossiped about on the street corners of Berlin. Stories of mass kidnaping and the disappearance of anti-Communist Germans have tapered off too.

Having decided to cultivate the Germans, the Soviet Military Administration has had to face the unique problem of making sure that the Germans don't turn the ideological tables and cultivate the Russians. They face the very pressing danger of Soviet troops getting fed up with the Communist system and becoming "Westernized" when they get a look at another way of living.

Russian desertions piled up in the early days. The best estimates run from 20,000 to 30,000 during 1946 in Germany and Austria. In the summer of 1947, when the West was on more chummy terms with the Germans, the Soviet administration decreed a stringent new form of nonfraternization. Soviet troops and families were ordered into fenced-in compounds to cut down association with Germans and possible contamination by Western ideas. The powerful conqueror from the East, intent on winning over the German population, had to hide lest the reverse occur.

In contrast to this, the American, both civilian and soldier, has been told by the Army that he is an unofficial ambassador who is supposed to build up good will for the United States and for the democratic system. Having given up his special rights as master of the master race, the American is closer to the German. He plays the part of a somewhat privileged visitor. Being privileged, he can hardly be genuinely popular and is welcome only insofar as he is the lesser of evils when contrasted with the Russian.

The latter-day American occupier is probably no better an individual than his predecessor, but his opportunities for straying off the straight and narrow are far more limited. The big operators who grabbed millions out of the United States Treasury via the cigarette black market have gone on to greener fields. The crazy-to-get-home draftees who racked up the highest venereal disease rate in American military history have been replaced by a smarter, less troublesome Army, many of whose units are publicly advertised as having gone without VD for months on end. The khaki-clad mob on which McNarney had to order a crackdown in 1946 has vanished. In its place is a scattered American community of less than 200,000, about half of them soldiers. According to official figures, it is healthier and more law-abiding than the average Stateside community of equivalent size.

Higher considerations dictated the shift in American policy toward the Germans, but the performance of the old occupiers could have provided reason enough. Newcomers who know only the sedate, relatively scrupulous later Occupation find it hard to believe old-timers who reminisce about the Bad Old Days in Berlin and factual incidents like these:

The GI whose mass-scale cigarette operations were so successful he hired a half-dozen less enterprising fellow soldiers each day to do nothing but sweat out lengthy post-office lines and send home money orders for him. His take was sufficient to allow him to pay each man $100 a day.

The lieutenant who arrived six months after V-E Day with a stated goal of $12,000 profit in the cigarette league. He reached his target in four months.

The soldier who went home carrying $25,000 in money orders, boasting that he had sent an additional $15,000 ahead. He was a private first class; monthly paycheck, $64.80.

The early Occupation units in Berlin, which regularly proved themselves the "thriftiest" in the Army, shipping home more than their payroll each month. The tongue-in-cheek explanation was that they had won it all gambling, presumably with each other.

The Russian general who was arrested by British military police for setting up a sidewalk shop and marketing to tattered Berliners an impressive stock of clothing, not his own.

The visiting congressmen who skipped an important conference with Military Government officials and were missing for hours. A frantic escort officer finally located them on a mass shopping expedition in the blackest of black-market shops along Berlin's Kurfürstendamm.

The distinguished citizen who once held a cabinet-rank job in the United States Government and who traveled here as the Army's guest. A man of foresight, he provided himself with fifty cartons of cigarettes before setting off on his tour of Germany.

The Frankfurt burglar who was repelled from an American home when an object was bounced off his skull. The

Occupation newspaper *Stars and Stripes* identified the missile in dead-pan fashion as a Meissen vase "valued at $600."

All these, plus the fantastic "Tiergarten Tales," in which Americans unloaded dollar watches onto eager Russians for two hundred times their value. The market mushroomed during the brief and expensive period when the United States Treasury was redeeming all Occupation marks in dollars. And the Russians, to whom we had handed the engraving plates, kept their presses hot turning out those marks.

This oblique raid on the Treasury amounted to more than $300,000,000 before the Army called a halt, first with "currency control" measures which ruled that all money transactions had to be recorded in a small printed folder resembling a bankbook, then by issuance of dollar scrip. Even the latter has produced headaches for the military finance experts. Because of alert and able scrip counterfeiters, we have so far had three different varieties of Occupation dollars. And every time anyone breaks a scrip five- or ten-spot, he fills out a form accepting responsibility just in case it turns out to be phony money.

New money cut off Treasury pirates, but it barely dented the still-booming black market. The occupiers' cigarettes couldn't be magically transformed into loads of dollars any more, but they could be and were turned into Rolleiflex cameras, Meissen china, fine linens, sterling silver services, and precious stones. This was the era when the Occupation wife—always categorized merely as "dependent" in official Army lingo—demonstrated that she too was no second-rater when it came to getting something for next to nothing.

The wife came after the easy money days were past, but many soldiers and civilians of the Occupation claim that she was the worst black-marketeer of all. She was often armed with wallpaper marks bought with cheap export cigarettes or coffee and was bent on squeezing every last Leica and onion-pattern dinner service out of the groggy German economy. The bitterness of soldiers and civilians about her probably came from jealousy. With servants provided by the Army and paid for by the German economy, she simply had more time to hunt through antique shops and second-hand stores for bargain treasures. And it must be admitted that no wives took part in the Treasury raid. They hadn't arrived yet.

In the spring of 1947 General Clay dealt the black market a haymaker wallop. He ruled out all further imports of cigarettes and tobacco. The operators who had brought smokes in by the hundreds of cartons were on their uppers— but only temporarily. On the theory that half a loaf is better than none, they found a semi-satisfactory substitute in coffee. Only a few went in for it in the wild fashion of one high-ranking officer who had his sent by the sack direct from Brazil, but there was enough traffic in it so that Army post offices had the pleasant fragrance of an A & P. Finally, in 1949, mass coffee shipments followed cigarettes onto the *verboten* list.

By that time, though, the once-mammoth black market was just a shaky shadow of its old-time self. An all-but-killing blow had been dealt a year before, not by handing down any new orders or prohibitions but by issuing new German money in the West.

This turned the economy topsy-turvy to the benefit of the natives. Money, which had been plentiful but next to worthless, suddenly became the German's rarest and most desirable possession. Herr and Frau Schmidt simply had no wherewithal to buy black; they no longer provided a market for cigarettes, coffee, or much of anything else. German black-market middlemen of years' standing found themselves without clients and were forced to find legitimate jobs.

The currency reform also had a sensational effect on regular German business channels. Caches of goods which had been hoarded during the "funny money" days came to light; food, clothing, furniture, electrical appliances, pots and pans, and scores of other "impossible" items magically appeared on store shelves and counters which had been empty for years.

Prices were high but goods were plentiful enough so that, especially in food items, the black-marketeer actually had to undersell legal sources of supply to stay in business. You can see what happened to the black market by checking the prices of its backbone commodities. In Berlin's palmiest days a carton of Camels brought two thousand marks, then translatable into two hundred good American dollars at the Army post office. Four years later a carton yielded only twenty marks, officially six dollars and definitely not convertible. Coffee tobogganed from ten dollars a pound to one-sixth of that in the same period.

The conqueror's climate of 1945 was favorable to the acquisition of jewels, cameras, furs, watches, antiques, and just about everything else that was portable, from hungry Germans who were in no position to protest. The temptation was great and so was the take, although no reliable estimate as to how much sticky-fingered occupiers got away with has ever been made. The system was simple: Take it, put it in a box, send it home. Overworked postal clerks had no time to verify contents, and American customs regulations were not enforced on the Army in those days.

The biggest known chunk of loot came from Kronberg Castle, the country home of the Hessian royal family just outside Frankfurt. For lifting an officially estimated $1,500,000 worth of jewels, silver, gold, and heirlooms from this gray stone pile which had been taken over as an officers' club, three Americans—Colonel Jack Durant, his WAC wife, Captain Kathleen Nash Durant, and Major David

Watson—were jailed. But even in this case, which made headlines in 1946, the exact amount of booty is obscure. Margarethe, Landgrafin of Hesse and sister of the late Kaiser Wilhelm II, always insisted that only half the family treasure had been unearthed and that actually some $3,000,000 worth had been taken.

There have been scores of smaller but equally unsavory episodes.

A group of paintings which once had hung in a Frankfurt gallery, and which had been tucked away for safekeeping in rural castles at Amorbach and Büdingen, turned out to be not at all safe when American officers located them. Several, including a Rubens, vanished.

The Stauffenberg family, one of whose members deposited the bomb which nearly killed Hitler on July 20, 1944, has formally charged that agents of the American Counter-Intelligence Corps, theoretically a carefully selected group of incorruptibles, looted some $75,000 worth of their jewelry.

Bulk was no deterrent in the days when outbound shipments went unexamined. A disgusted Military Government official tells of the ambitious American officer who carefully packed up and sent home the municipal archives of a Hessian town. Later, influenced either by conscience or by the non-salability of his find, he offered it to the library of his alma mater, a large eastern university. Perplexed college officials communicated with Military Government, then repacked the lot and shipped it back to Germany.

A pair of Army officers, one a chaplain, took from Military Government custody $4,000,000 worth of Jewish books and historical objects which had been looted from synagogues and libraries throughout Europe. Plans to prosecute the pair were dropped when months of investigation disclosed that they had sent the collection to the Hebrew University in

Jerusalem, where Jewish communities and organizations probably would have wanted to ship it anyhow.

Looting was not an exclusively American preoccupation. The other three conquerors were no less guilty. British authorities are still embarrassed about the way a castle near Celle was cleaned out; nor were the Russians and French above helping themselves to what they could find. These two conquerors started with a looting deficit, the Germans having demonstrated that they were perhaps the most acquisitive occupiers of all when war trends were running in the opposite direction.

Fraternization was the word for sex in Germany, and the Army tried to legislate it out of the occupiers' existence in the early days. In effect the nonfraternization rule said: "Talk to Germans only in line of duty and don't ever do more than talk to them." With the policy came the "sixty-five-dollar question," so christened because fraternizers were to be fined that amount.

Loud protests from the GI's forced a quick back-down by the Army. The "off-limits" signs were taken off German girls in the summer of 1945, and in a series of steps the military gradually admitted them to equality under the War Brides Act with the mademoiselles and signorinas the soldiers had found elsewhere in their travels.

The first fräulein, a pretty brunette ballet dancer from Russian-occupied Dessau, made it to the States in September 1946, and after that the big push was on. More than ten thousand German girls married Americans, and late in 1948 a special airlift was laid on to get the last-minute contingent to the States before expiration of the Brides Act. The Army grumpily labeled the ladies' airlift "Operation Crow."

But all the fräuleins who found favor with the Americans didn't make the transatlantic trip. There are uncounted

American-fathered children in Germany's orphanages. And there are uncounted others being raised by mothers who know the fathers will never come back. A popular German saying on this subject is: "Next war just send the uniforms. You left the Army here." This "army" is legally and completely a German problem. The American fathers bear no responsibility for the babies they sired and cannot be held accountable in any way. E. G. ("Red") Valens, former United Press correspondent in Germany, after a detailed study of the legal aspects, came up with this succinct summary: "The fruits of fraternization hang on the German side of the tree."

Tales of Americans in Germany patterning their lives after Oriental satraps, dining off overloaded banquet tables and washing down epicurean meals with the finest of Europe's vintages, have occasionally come out of Occupationland. Most of these came at a time when the German was painfully underfed and given to pointing the finger at the occupier as a callous conqueror gluttonizing in the midst of pathetic want.

At best these stories contained only a grain of truth. However, it is undeniable that in the days before the United States embarked on a policy of rebuilding the German economy, many of the occupiers had an undreamed-of chance to taste a way of living several notches above that which they were accustomed to at home. As the only haves in a realm of have-nots, they started at the top of the social ladder and accumulated such standard European evidences of prosperity as a crew of maids, chauffeurs, gardeners, *et al.*, paid for by German governmental offices.

But with growing solicitude for the German financial position, the Army halted this and decreed that each American family could have only one servant paid for by the Germans. They could still keep the extra servants but had to foot the bill themselves, which only a small fraction were able to do.

This enforced comedown of the would-be social lions keynotes the shift in the role of the new occupier. He is no longer legally given the extras he had in the easy, generous, inexpensive past. Now he's living very much as he would at home.

If the illegal trading of the first days was black, now it has faded to a misty gray. Practically every American—and this goes for the other occupiers too—still dabbles in the illegal market to the extent of his much-curbed resources. In many cases it is still cheaper to tip for services and to buy goods with cigarettes. Coffee, cocoa, and cooking fats still have a slight market, but they're tightly rationed. Instead of a high road to profit, the black market is just a way to get some of the things the Army can't or won't supply in the desired quantities: clothing, toys for the kids, knickknacks, and small luxury items. The profiteers have been wiped from the map of Germany by the new rule of law.

The other extra-legal and shady activities which disfigured the Old Occupation—looting, wild violations of police power, ostentatious living—are as much out of place here as they would be in the United States.

Perhaps to salve his collective conscience about the unpretty past, the American occupier now demonstrates a phenomenal personal generosity toward the defeated German. His government has for a long time supplied half the food eaten by the Germans under his jurisdiction. Individuals and charitable organizations back home have piled gift packages higher in Bremerhaven than in any other European port. But this, the occupier feels, is not enough. Local American charity groups have mushroomed. Wives in scores of Occupation communities have sent back to the States for food packages and bundles of clothing for needy Germans.

The average occupier hands out pounds of coffee and

cartons of cigarettes to his German acquaintances, mostly waiters, employees, and personal servants. Fräuleins with GI boy friends obviously get the biggest slice of the American gift chest, but their kid brothers and sisters get a cut, too, through Army-sponsored youth programs.

Considering all this, it is not surprising that the American occupier is in some respects a popular institution. United States Military Government public-opinion polls show that Germans favor their "masters" in this order: American, British, French, Russian. It is probably not coincidental that this preference conforms exactly with ability, both as governments and as individuals, to contribute tangibly to German welfare.

However, it isn't a desire to help the German or any other altruistic motive that tempts Americans to live in this battered and ruin-pocked nation. Government personnel men used to think that the primary temptation was the chance for adventure. Now that most of the adventure has been erased from the Occupation job, the principal attraction is a bigger paycheck. Overseas, Uncle Sam pays well. The average salary of civilian workers is close to $400 a month.

This hardly permits the twenty thousand civilian employees to indulge in any spending orgies, but it allows them to keep up with Army officers and comfortably ahead of the Germans he is helping to govern, mainly because the Army has brought in Stateside comforts and luxuries. More than any other occupier the American has demanded that his home, or as much of it as can be imported, follow him to Germany. To satisfy the civilian and to keep the professional soldier happy, the Army has struggled to build a Little United States atop its part of Germany.

American night clubs in Occupationland bear such romantic and nostalgic names as the Stork Club, Casa Carioca, Rendezvous, and Manor House, which is plugged on the Army radio network as being "only fifteen minutes from downtown Frankfurt, just off the Wiesbaden turnpike."

Every American community in Germany has its soda fountain, where American-style "super de luxe" malteds and banana splits and the usual list of ice-cream concoctions are dispensed. The highways of the American Zone are dotted with hamburger heavens and lunchrooms fronted by signs echoing from across the Atlantic—Tiny Tim's, Tuxedo Junction, Sunset Inn. Walk inside and you're greeted by the glaring lights and blaring music of a jukebox.

In his passion to create a reasonably accurate facsimile of the homeland four thousand miles away, the American persists in keeping his old habits, doing the same things, buying the same products. Aside from the plentiful Army surplus jeeps, his favorite cars are Fords and Chevrolets. Post exchange sales records show that Luckies are the pet cigarette of the occupier, that he most often brushes his teeth with Colgate's, washes with Lux. He buys 14,000,000 candy bars and 2,000,000 packs of gum in a typical month. To keep him supplied with these and other commodities, to keep his clothes cleaned and pressed, his radio functioning, his watch ticking, and to perform scores of other services, the Exchange Service has established a chain of 1,200 stores, specialty shops, and concessions. The string did an $80,000,000 business in 1948.

The occupier has an almost insatiable thirst. To quench it the Army is in the liquor business to the tune of $10,000,000 yearly. Proximity to the exotic wines and liqueurs of Europe hasn't changed the American alcoholic palate. Seventy cents of every dollar spent for hard liquor goes for whisky and gin. Beer purchases amount to 12,000,000 bottles per month. The soft-drink market is split between two familiar competitors, Coca-Cola and Pepsi-Cola.

What the American eats comes from an Army commissary.

All his canned food and frozen meat comes from the States. The skimpy supply of fresh fruits and vegetables is bought in Italy and other European countries; nothing is taken from the Germans. Persons entitled to buy at the Army grocery store leave $2,000,000 there monthly. The average for a three-person family is $90. And there still is rationing, mainly of butter, coffee, fats, and cocoa.

For years it was strictly taboo to augment the canned-food diet of the commissary with purchases of fresh items from German stores. Now nobody will arrest you for that if you buy your marks legally, but prices are so high that the majority get along with what the Army imports.

The cost of living on the Army economy has risen steadily throughout the Occupation. Typical is the cost of medical service. It costs a privately employed American civilian in Germany $9.75 a day in an Army hospital. In 1948 it was possible to have a baby in the same hospital, from first pre-natal examination through the first week of the infant's life, for as little as $13.60. (I know; the Haegers did it for exactly that.)

Eventually, the civilian segment of the Western Occupation forces will be cut off from military services and stores of all kinds and will live on the local economy just like foreign residents of any unoccupied country. This exclusion process is now under way. Before the United States Government did this about-face the Army insisted that no American could eat in a German restaurant or have a quick one at the corner taproom unless some German had invited him.

The French and Russians could never see any reason for such a rule; the British had one which they ignored. But General Clay issued orders to his military police to see that it was observed to the letter in the American Zone. The official reason was that such practices encouraged black-marketing and snatched food out of German mouths. Nothing was ever said about the lack of sanitary inspections of kitchens and restaurants.

In winking at the rule the British were only accepting the truth that the beaten Germans were dining better than the conqueror from across the Channel. When a Britisher here wants a filling meal, he swallows his pride and, with it, a healthy portion of appetizing wienerschnitzel or sauerbraten in a dining place of the defeated.

But if the American couldn't eat in a German restaurant, he certainly could, did, and still does live in a German house. At this writing he is still savoring the fruits of victory in this respect, dwelling in a house or apartment from which Germans were summarily ejected when the war was still going on. Uncle Sam is the landlord and collects the rent in dollars, lopping them off the paychecks of government workers and married soldiers (unmarried soldiers are quartered in barracks). The owner of the house is paid in Deutsche marks by the local government, which chalks it up to Occupation costs, part of the price of having lost the war. The Army turns the dollars over to the United States Treasury.

Living in requisitioned housing is the single outstanding factor of the Old Occupation that has been carried over to the New. And the latter-day occupier can be grateful to the early billeting officers for having done an efficient job of eviction. Armed with easy-to-get documentation from their headquarters, these functionaries roamed their territories in the spirit of choosy shoppers. Finding a residence in good shape and well furnished, they pronounced, "I'll take that one." A sign was quickly tacked on the door; the occupants were given twenty-four or perhaps forty-eight hours to get out —"Take only clothing and small personal possessions, *versteh?*"—and the job was done.

Just before the first arrival of American wives and children in Germany in 1946 the Army cut out requisitioning entirely and started wholesale returns of property to German owners. So Americans who had left a housing problem back home found another at this end of the voyage. There just isn't enough to go around. Families still spend months in hotels impatiently waiting for other families to go home and make room for the new arrivals.

The tightest housing area of the American Zone has always been the pivotal headquarters city of Frankfurt. Here, instead of picking the best for the victors, the Army executed its requisitioning scheme on a compound basis, with solid blocks of apartments taken over and a nine-foot fence built around the area. The fence is down now, but the district still exists. It was second-rate to start with and there are luxurious German homes within a few blocks of it across whose thresholds no American has ever stepped. This considerate attitude has always been a source of wonder to Germans, who shake their heads over the mystery of these "soft" Americans.

Living almost entirely within this imported super-economy, an American could be effectively quarantined from the Germans. Many rejected this cloistered pattern, but others accepted it. Thousands who spent long periods of time over here never learned any but the most rudimentary of pidgin German, never knew any Germans except those who had been hired to work for him or his Army, never associated with a native except in the master-servant relationship. This now-crumbling segregation system represents a lost opportunity. It is American policy to sell democracy and the "American way," but thousands of potential salesmen on the grass-roots level never went to work. It's extremely doubtful that the American occupier, even the reformed, legal and proper occupier of recent vintage, has been of much value in guiding the German to the path of redemption that the West wants him to follow.

Despite the failure of on-the-spot Americans to serve as an example, some of the most capable Americans who served in Germany are convinced that, under the Occupation, the Germans of the West have started along the road leading to a working democracy. General Clay repeatedly expressed his confidence in the Germans publicly and privately. He backed up his statements with action, giving those under his jurisdiction a free hand to work out their own salvation by rapidly handing back political and economic power. Many of the ranking advisers, the "brain trust" of Military Government, seconded Clay's confidence. John J. McCloy, the first American civilian Military Governor and High Commissioner, has indicated that he feels the same way.

There's plenty of evidence to support this view. For a people cut off from democratic attachments for more than a decade, the Germans have put on a commendable postwar political performance. The valiant and downright dangerous anti-Soviet stand taken by the residents of Berlin in the darkest moments of the blockade was inspiring, and those who live in Trizonia backed up their beleaguered fellow citizens to the best of their limited ability. The Germans of the West have also displayed their own interest in what makes this strange new democracy tick. Although it's only superficial evidence of progress, it cannot be denied that in every election held under the Occupation a far greater percentage of the eligible voters has turned out than for a Presidential contest in the United States.

But has the Occupation yet molded the German into a truly dependable democrat? Look into American Military Government's own files for the answer. Through periodic public-opinion polls, Military Government has found out time and again that an increasing number of the "conquered"—it's now a majority—are sure of this: Adolf Hitler's Nazi system was really a good idea badly carried out.

Chapter II

The Man in the Goldfish Bowl

By LYFORD MOORE

PRESUMABLY at some future date the boundaries of the four Occupation cities that now comprise Berlin will be removed, no matter what sort of government finally rules the area. And when the sector lines are erased perhaps the military governments of the four occupying nations of today will be recalled to their homelands. Then the bomb-gutted center of the city will be rebuilt and the relatively undamaged and now overcrowded suburbs drained of bureaucracies and importance. Berlin *mitte* will again become the heart of the city.

In that time to come, young Germans may wonder why a quiet, leafy street far out in the southwestern suburb of Zehlendorf is called Clayallee. Older people will remember the hard year when this short street, then called Kronprinzen, was the nerve center of three-fourths of Berlin as well as of three-fourths of Germany. In the summer of 1948 it was the most important spot in Europe. It gained its importance from the fact that the headquarters of the American Military Government of Germany during the Russian blockade of Western Berlin was located on Kronprinzen.

That the Georgian name, Clay, is celebrated in a city famous for streets named after the German military great of several centuries is only one of several paradoxes. This is probably one of few times in history when an occupied people has of its own volition, even happily, so honored a proconsul. And Clayallee, though a tribute to Lucius D. Clay, an American wartime general, is named for a man who never saw combat.

Still more paradoxically, Clay, not a combat man, proved to be one of the master strategists of our time. His achievement may outweigh those of strictly military men. He won his victory under duress but without resort to arms.

Shortly before German workmen changed the name of the five-mile-long street, Clay received in his Kronprinzen headquarters a tribute of another sort. At the beginning of his final news conference in the ornate white building that once housed a German *Luftwaffe* establishment, some two hundred foreign correspondents from a dozen nations rose spontaneously and applauded as the slight, very tired general entered the room. And they rose again to applaud as he left it, to return to the United States and retirement.

More than anything Clay had said, more than the end of the blockade itself, this double ovation impressed the many topflight and hard-bitten Washington and London correspondents who had come to the city to report the end of the blockade. In their experience, not even heads of state received such a heartfelt farewell twice.

Shared experience, an intimate appreciation of what the General had faced, and close friendship prompted that tribute from the correspondents who had been in Berlin throughout the blockade. The American sector of the city had been a very small place during the siege.

At the beginning of the Occupation, Clay had announced that American Military Government would operate under a "goldfish-bowl" policy. He and his associates had nothing to conceal, he said, and to the day he left his office door was never closed. Correspondents could and did go to him at any hour when a big story was breaking. They had almost hourly knowledge of his problems and solutions, though often they couldn't write what they knew until much later. They watched him in action day after day when their own freedom and that of their families hung in the balance.

He bore up well under this close and sustained scrutiny. He was a man of integrity and sincerity. He believed passionately in democracy and served it fourteen hours a day, seven days a week. He fought a resourceful and relentless fight against tremendous odds. Without exception, correspondents admired and respected the American Military Governor. For these reasons they appraise his era and his contribution differently from the way it is sometimes appraised in France, England, and to a lesser extent in the United States. There were, for example, four military governors in Germany during Clay's tenure. But as the journalists saw it, the Occupation of Germany has been primarily a struggle between the United States and the Soviet Union, with Russia seeking domination and absorption of the whole country and the United States determined that Germany should not go communistic unless she wished to. Throughout the Occupation the United States has taken the lead in the formulation of German policy for the three Western Allies, and often Clay was actually out in front of Washington. Thus the story of Germany from the war until 1950, as written on the West side of a city where a single street was the border between democracy and totalitarianism, was the story of Clay against the Russians.

Perhaps it will be several years before General Clay's achievement is properly understood in any area that was still free while Communist Russia was at the peak of her postwar expansion. To realize fully what his decisions could have meant for him and for us all one must first realize that a strong and hostile army surrounded him for a hundred miles in all directions when, with a handful of troops and a defenseless people to carry out his commands, he ordered Western Berlin to defy the Soviet Union.

Commonly, in the wake of a change in command, a headquarters is strident with charges of shortcomings in the make-up of the departing commander, of tasks poorly done or left undone. And as John J. McCloy took over his herculean task as United States High Commissioner for Germany, there was considerable talk of Clay's shortcomings—which was, first of all, an indication that the pressure had been eased. It was said that if Mr. McCloy proved unable to cope with the heavy legacy of vital problems left unsolved by Clay, the American Occupation of Germany would turn out to be a calamitous failure.

Chiefly these critics said that Clay was autocratic and too preoccupied with making his own policy in defiance of Washington to implement satisfactorily the specific policies he was sent to Germany to carry out.

His assignment in 1945 as Deputy Military Governor was to implement what he called "the four D's," the demilitarization, denazification, decartelization, and democratization of the defeated enemy. It has been widely charged that he failed to deal adequately with any of these, that in emphasizing the economic recovery of Germany he left an open road for the West German state that he later fathered to negate our basic aims in Germany and adopted policies which could re-create the militaristic Germany of tradition and its forge for war. A British official protested that Clay looked like a Roman emperor "and acted like one, too." Others found his handling of the case of Ilse Koch, the sadistic wife of the Nazis' Buchenwald concentration camp commander, inexcusable. His commutation of her sentence on the grounds of lack of evidence against her was the least important of all the complaints against Clay and caused the greatest furor in America.

But even many of Clay's critics acknowledge that his job was the most complex, responsible, and thankless that could have been assigned to any American. And it should not be surprising that he could not in his two years as Military Governor achieve all that everyone at home and abroad thought he should. As far back as the time of General Eisenhower, the first American Military Governor, it was reported that Eisenhower's chief of staff, Lieutenant General Walter Bedell Smith, said that Eisenhower was being recalled because the job of military governor "will ruin any man's reputation, no matter how good it is." That was a full year before the Soviet plan for expansion in Germany was understood and appreciated.

As Military Governor, Clay was commander of American forces in Germany. It was his job to revive a bankrupt and apathetic people and to instill in them a love of true democracy. He was to restore agriculture in Western Germany, though it had been separated from its "bread basket," the Silesian area which had been closed to the West by the Soviet Union. At a time when the bulk of American personnel was being sent home, he was asked to run a Germany of forty millions without being permitted to use the millions of Nazis who, despite their unsavory background, were the only Germans available with the special skills required. He was expected to restore German industry and simultaneously to dismantle factories for reparations and shut down as excessive and dangerous concentrations of economic power the great industrial complexes that were the strength and substance of the country's existence.

All this was to be done in conformity with the plans and ideas of three other Occupation powers which differed greatly in temperament and approach to the job.

Clay did what he found possible in each of these fields and then finished by doing something which was infinitely more important to the West at the time. It is generally accepted in Germany that by making the decisions he did and insisting on them despite their apparent impossibility until Washington, and still later England and France backed him and them, Clay in 1949 saved Western Europe from communism.

Clay had not had a spectacular career prior to the war. He was a West Point graduate and an Army engineer who performed difficult tasks without wide renown. He was a captain twenty-two years after leaving the Academy, but he rocketed from major to major general in two war years. As director of matériel for the Army Services of Supply during the early war years he tackled bottlenecks in supply and production and did much to aid the arms procurement program. His only overseas assignment prior to coming to Germany was to clear the clogged and desperately needed Cherbourg Harbor in November 1944. He doubled the flow of goods almost overnight and quintupled it in three weeks' time.

This came to the attention of James Byrnes, then director of war mobilization and reconversion and "assistant President," who had Clay assist him for four months at home. As Byrnes' deputy Clay was responsible for the electricity "brownout," the curfew on night life, and the racing ban in the United States in early 1945, which he ordered to conserve power for Army needs.

Clay came to Germany with a government reputation as an ace trouble shooter and with the endorsement of Franklin D. Roosevelt as a "tough-minded soldier." He came at Eisenhower's own request as Deputy Military Governor. It has been reported that Eisenhower selected him for the post because Byrnes recommended him as the "most civilian-minded man in the Army."

On his arrival in Europe to take over the German assignment Clay seemed to be the epitome of American patience and friendship with Russia and of the coexistent American policy of "hard peace" toward Germany. At his first news conference in Paris just a week after the end of the war, the man who was to be in charge of Military Government's policies from the start told correspondents: "If the four nations cannot stick together to govern Germany, what hope is there for any of the things we are trying to do . . . if the people at home will recognize that this experiment of four nations trying to punish and redeem a nation means much to the future of the world, then we have hopes of the future of this job."

At the same conference he also said: "The government we propose to set up in Germany is going to be a military government and the Germans are going to know it is a military government. We have time enough later to consider the long-range terms of Germany and the regeneration of the German people. Our first objective is to smash whatever remaining power Germany may have with which to develop a future war potential. . . ."

The Potsdam Declaration called for accommodation with Russia in promoting unity in and toward Germany, and the American people, still fighting Japan, demanded that highly industrial Germany be turned into a pastureland that could never again endanger world peace. Clay's rigid sense of duty made him follow these policies scrupulously. No one could have been more patient with the Russians, and it took time before he discovered that there were still "some decent people in Germany." But in his year and a half as deputy, first to Eisenhower and then to General Joseph T. McNarney, our second Military Governor, Clay learned that neither policy was practicable under the conditions existent in Germany —the Russians wouldn't co-operate with co-operation and the Germans needed something more nourishing than mere punishment and control.

The story of the Occupation soon became a tale of three

Western powers trying to float a German ship of state, of sorts, despite Russian torpedoes. However much Russia secured by force and by evasion of her own commitments, she always wanted more and went after more with invective and abuse, pressure and strong-arm tactics. Non-Communist nations were enemy nations. Russia persistently blocked both unity in Germany and German recovery at all levels.

It was Clay himself who first deviated from the Western policy of trying to temporize until the ever demanding Russians could be placated. Clay, though famous for compromises like his ancestor Henry Clay, tore a great gap in Western policy when he ended an economics argument with the Russians by ordering an abrupt halt to the dismantling of reparations plants for the U.S.S.R. until she proved more tractable. This was an early example of Clay making major policy, and Washington supported him.

Clay saw early that if Germany were to become truly democratic, Germans must be given practice in democratic ways, not just a conqueror's directive that they embrace democracy forthwith. Six months after his arrival in Germany he decided, again against most advice both from Washington and in Germany, to hold popular elections in the American Zone. Eighty-five per cent of all eligible voters appeared at the polls to elect, for the first time in over a decade, their own representatives to a State Council. The American Zone soon moved far ahead of the other three in political development.

Clay insisted that the sooner governmental authority was returned to the Germans the sooner the objectives of the Occupation would be realized. He brought into being legislatures and constitutions in his three zonal provinces, created a German advisory board to aid Military Government, and instituted other democratic procedures, along with a considerable body of democratic law to safeguard those procedures.

In answer to criticism that he was giving ex-enemies too much power and too many opportunities to tear down his work, he insisted that the Germans "can only become democrats by experiencing the forms of democracy."

Clay was sure that the plan to reduce the German war potential by deindustrialization was unworkable, and by the time he succeeded to the military governorship in early 1947, Washington was torn between the "hard peace" and "soft peace" schools. Guidance often arrived too late, and, as in the case of dismantling, it devolved upon the man on the scene to make many decisions.

Russia was coming up like a storm at sea, and even as he fought the gale Clay had to first formulate and execute policy and then sell it to the cautious British and the reluctant, security-minded French, both of whom feared Germany more than they did the Soviet Union.

Washington permitted Clay to retain the initiative in making policy and thereby gained immeasurably from his ability and experience. This leeway also gave him far more authority than the military governors of Great Britain and France, and throughout his tenure he always seemed to be somewhat ahead of them, chafing impatiently until they came along, which they or their governments nearly always did after Washington had. Clay fully appreciated both his unique power and his unique responsibility.

"Thank God, Washington always backs me up!" he said.

Until 1948 the job of keeping the American Zone alive was a more urgent and difficult problem than dealing with the Russians or democratizing the Germans.

As far as punishment of the masses of the ex-enemy was concerned, the "hard peace" policy called for flogging a dead horse. The Germans were completely inert after the war; they responded neither to punitive measures nor to schemes for industrial rehabilitation. They had time only to search for food and shelter. Democracy did not have a chance on empty stomachs.

Russian intransigence worked an enormous hardship upon the three other Occupation zones, for their bobtail agriculture could not sustain three-fourths of the population of a land which even before the war was required to supplement its food production with imports. Industry, by and large, was destroyed or stagnant. Refugees flooded the Western areas, and millions of Sudeten and other *Volksdeutsche* were streaming back into the fatherland to swell the vast numbers who had no food, no work, and no money.

It fell to the American and British taxpayers to keep the two Occupation zones of Germany fed or witness mass starvation. Prodigious imports of foodstuffs began to arrive from the British Empire and Western Europe, but principally from the United States. Though these supplies were only enough to maintain a minimum subsistence ration for the zones, the cost to American taxpayers alone amounted to hundreds of millions of dollars annually.

Drastic action was called for to circumvent Russian obstructionism. The United States proposed mutual assistance through economic fusion of the American Zone with any of the others. The plan carefully avoided any hint of political fusion or partition, which would have violated the Potsdam Protocol. Great Britain alone accepted the proposal and fused her zone with the American.

Some authorities say that the conception of Bizonia, as the combined area came to be called, was Clay's own brain child. It was at least a codification of plans originated and long advocated by him.

Next a vast export-import program was instituted in the bizonal area. It called for tremendous expansion of production for export of consumer goods in lieu of machinery and other heavy manufacture which had been the mainstay of the prewar German economy and was now forbidden. The plan was designed to relieve the British and American taxpayers and eventually to raise the German standard of living. It envisaged ultimate achievement of a balance between revenues from German production and the cost of food imports.

Meanwhile the alignment of world powers was shifting around prostrate Germany. By early 1948 Russia rather than the ex-enemy had become the villain of the plot. The Soviet was on the march westward. She had gobbled up and was ruling by fear all territory east of central Germany from the Baltic to the Adriatic. She had converted her zone into a police state and wanted the rest of Germany and Western Europe. Western Germans—and Western Europeans all the way to the Atlantic—were terrified.

In February 1948 the Communists seized the government in Czechoslovakia, and the West finally moved openly to stop Soviet expansion. Congress had delayed action on the Marshall Plan for American economic assistance in European recovery, but now the legislation was passed swiftly. The nations of Western Europe formed a political, military, and economic union to counterbalance the Soviet's Eastern European bloc. And, in London, economic merger of all three West German zones was agreed upon.

The West had acted barely in time and still faced a practical and ruthless opponent with no more than paper defenses. The democratic nations were in complete agreement as to what they must do, but for a long time to come none would be equipped to put up any real struggle. Like Germany, the Atlantic nations were still in postwar disorder, nearly impoverished, perfect targets for communization. Elections were coming up in Italy and France, where Communist blocs were so strong that the incumbent democratic governments were very apt to be overthrown. Events everywhere were moving rapidly toward a showdown.

As a Russian answer to the Western agreements Marshal Vasili Sokolovsky, the Soviet Military Governor, walked out of four-power government of Germany. With the exception of the Western island in Berlin, the division of Germany between East and West was complete.

The first effect of this walkout was that Washington canceled plans to transfer authority in Germany from the Army to the State Department on July 1, 1948. And Clay, who was scheduled to retire on the same date, was ordered to continue as Military Governor for the duration of the emergency. Clay sent for his uniforms, which he had already shipped to his son, an Army major, and put away thoughts of an immediate future of catfishing in Georgia.

It was absolutely essential now that Western Germany be sustained as a democratic buffer state between the Atlantic nations and Russia. The work previously and painstakingly done by Clay in conjunction with General Sir Brian Robertson, the British Military Governor, was perfectly adapted to the present need. The fusion of the zones was strictly economic, but it provided a framework upon which a separate West German state could be constructed.

But the Western Germans felt little incentive to become the battleground for the big powers. Western Germany, wanting unification with Eastern Germany and still the apathetic pensioner of the United States—with flowering of the pretentious export plan still years off—seemed more apt to fall to communism than any other of the remaining democratic nations. Germans had little faith that the Western powers would stay and defend them if the war which seemed so close actually came. If Western Germany went Communist, it would be hard to save Italy and France. By the same token, if Berlin went, it would be almost impossible to save Western Germany.

The German currency was almost worthless, supported

only by edict. It would not provide raw materials, incentive to work, nor savings. Here again Russian refusal to reform the currency except on her own terms amounted to keeping the west demoralized as a prelude to Communist penetration. Currency reform was imperative if any of Germany was to be saved for the West, and the Western military governors ordered it, effective June 18.

The next day the Russians responded with the blockade of Berlin. In an attempt to dominate by force, the Russians in a time of peace imposed economic sanctions which it seemed would, if continued for two or three weeks, prove as brutal and effective as any acts of war. By closing a highway bridge for repairs, by discovering a "technical disturbance" along the railway track from the West, by ending barge traffic on canals in their zone surrounding Berlin, and by cutting off food and power supplies from the Soviet Zone upon which the city depended, they *almost* completely blockaded three-fourths of the world's sixth-largest city. The blockaded Western sectors faced starvation, cessation of industry, and exhaustion of water, power, gas, and coal stocks in a month's time. The sole purpose of the siege was to drive the West out of the capital.

Clay's immediate reply—and this was the supreme example of his improvising policy to suit a situation—was that the Americans were in Berlin by agreement and would not leave unless forced out of the city. Iron-willed, nerveless, quite willing to risk severe censure so long as he felt he was right, he issued his defiance and then had to live up to it.

This he did, of course, by creating the stupendous airlift over the Russian Zone to Berlin. At first the airlift consisted of only a trickle of aircraft and seemed scarcely impressive enough to support Clay's conviction that the risk of staying in Berlin was outweighed by the consequences almost certain to follow if we left. As a military proposition, Clay's decision was insane. He became a target of attack at home and abroad, inside and outside of Germany. He was ridiculed in cartoon and editorial, by congressmen in Washington and by members of Parliament in London. But he called for more planes, and the planes came in from American posts all over the world, from Hawaii, Alaska, the States, the Caribbean, Australia. British planes joined the airlift, and then planes of the American Navy. It began to worry the Russians. They showed their concern by talking tough and sending interference that ranged from flak and fighters to parachutists into our air corridors leading to Berlin.

The British and French took a firm stand after Clay had, but it was not until a full month after the blockade had begun that the United States Government officially approved Clay's statement that we were staying in Berlin. Even after that few Germans anywhere thought that the United States either could or would stay.

When the iron curtain thudded down around the Western sectors, no one knew whether or not Russia wanted a war. Perhaps she was bluffing, but Clay would have gained nothing by leaving, and he could have lost Western Europe. Much of the talk in Berlin at that time concerned the possibility that if the airlift really delayed the timetable of communism, the Red Army might quite easily overrun Berlin and in a matter of days continue to the Atlantic Coast. Once there, Russia could have called off her lightning war with the argument that she wanted no more than that and with the knowledge that it would take expensive and bloody years to dislodge her.

It is easy now to underestimate the gravity of that early blockade period. All Russia's moves were military and menacing then. Certainly at the first sign of weakness the already nearly intolerable pressure would have been increased.

In making his commitment Clay realized the full risk, including the fact that it automatically made himself and all other Americans in the city expendables. Asked during this period if he intended to evacuate the American women and children from the city, Clay said he would not, because there were 240,000,000 other families in Western Europe who would also like to retreat to safer territory but had nowhere to go. The times were so tense and European morale and faith in us so low, he said, that he simply couldn't risk sending American women out at the first indication of trouble. In fact he was considerably worried over the possibility that a hue and cry in the States over the danger to American families might lead to an official demand that they be returned home.

The airlift was a well-established operation before even Clay could say that it would be able to keep the two and a half million Berliners in the West sectors alive. I recall two interviews with him, almost on succeeding days. At the first he said flatly that the lift could not bring in an adequate tonnage. At the second conference, on the basis of a new assignment of planes to the lift, he was just as flatly certain that it could.

Later there came a day when we watched the first planeload of coal being off-loaded into trucks at Tempelhof Airfield. The coal was carried in Army duffel bags, but enough came in to keep essential industries going.

Neither the blockade nor the airlift became commonplaces in Berlin, but attention turned to other things. An economic counterblockade intended to deny the Russian Zone raw materials it desperately needed was imposed by Clay. A constitutional assembly began preparing a draft constitution for a West German state, and from across the ocean there came the suggestion for the Atlantic Pact.

The Germans took courage from the spectacular airlift

that was always overhead, and that courage and a concomitant respect for the democracies spread beyond the beleaguered city. Berliners prayed that the airlift would prove stronger than the coming winter and prepared willingly for a winter without coal, light, or adequate transport, and in many cases without work. It became a primitive existence, but they preferred it to Soviet domination.

Russian maneuvering continued through engineered riots, kidnapings, and a terrorist putsch that took over City Hall and split the Berlin government—until Clay and his airlift received a unique vote of confidence from the Germans themselves. Despite all they had been seeing of Russian ruthlessness, and despite the fact that their names would be on record as opposed to communism if the Russians finally did take over the city, 86 per cent of all eligible voters in the besieged sectors went to the polls in December 1948, and voted against communism.

It took almost a year before the combination of the airlift, Western firmness, counterblockade, and the December election forced Russia to call off her hunger blockade. She finally did so in May of 1949, even though it meant compliance with the Western demand that the blockade be lifted before any Big Four discussion of the Berlin and German problems. Russia had insisted that the discussion come first.

The year of the blockade was invaluable to the West, for it meant precious time in which to bring the West German state and the Atlantic Pact into being. And Russia, once forced to abandon her strong-arm methods, would never again have such a chance for easy conquest. By the end of the blockade the Atlantic nations were moving toward preparedness for all contingencies.

The justification of Clay's policy is that it worked, and it is difficult to see what else could have. He, personally, was most happy when the French, British, and American governments resolved all their differences concerning Germany and presented the Western area with an Occupation Statute. This embodied everything that Clay had fought for throughout his stay in Germany. To him it meant a guarantee that she could continue toward a democratic future he had begun charting for her as early as 1945.

Clay's sense of timing held to the end. Months before the New York negotiations that led to the end of the siege he chose the date upon which he wished to leave Berlin to return to the United States and retirement. He selected the fifteenth of May. The blockade was lifted on the twelfth.

He left Berlin at the peak of his career. And as he flew westward along the air corridor from the city, his plane was accompanied by the great silver ships of his own airlift, now multiplied from the first paltry few into hundreds. Unwittingly, still engaged in their job of feeding the hungry, they formed a perfect honor guard for Lucius Clay.

Chapter III

The Germans in the Cold War

By RICHARD LOWENTHAL

THE Germans are once again a factor in world politics. Less than twelve months after the unique national collapse which ended World War II, in the middle of ruin, hunger, and demoralization, the Germans, divided, occupied, and under tutelage, were confronted with the need for a political choice between their conquerors—and made it.

The choice was inevitable because Germany, less than a year after ceasing to be a military battleground between Hitler and the Allies, had become a political battleground in the cold war between the great world powers, the United States and the Soviet Union. It was the beginning of a process by which the Germans ceased to be mere numbed objects of Allied policy and themselves began to influence the outcome of the struggle for the future shape of the world.

That is the central fact of German postwar politics. Many Westerners deplore it because, as they see it, "Disunity between the Allies has made yesterday's common enemy the arbiter of their dispute." Many Germans deplore it because, as they see it, "Disunity between the Allies has delayed German reconstruction and made the division of Germany permanent." But deplored or not, the cold war dominates the German scene. It is the central formative experience by which the outlook of the new political forces is being shaped.

It has opened to Western Germany the chance to recover statehood, to participate in Marshall Plan aid, and to become a partner instead a pariah in Western Europe.

Many who are fascinated by the spectacle of German economic and political recovery already see another German threat to world peace developing. That, I think, shows a defective sense of proportion. Germany will never be a major power again—not because the Germans have changed but because the proportions of world power have changed. There is no uranium to be found in the Ruhr. There is no chance for even a united Germany to match the resources of the major powers of the new age. Germany now can only play the role of a member state of the Western or a satellite of the Eastern bloc, or possibly of a minor buffer state trying to maneuver between them, but not that of a power in her own right.

Yet much may depend on which of these roles the Germans eventually choose. To my mind it is the one big question about Germany today. I am not attempting to give a dogmatic answer. I merely offer, as a contribution toward it, the story of the choices actually made by the Germans in the first four postwar years, of the factors that determined them, and of the new leaders and political forces that emerged in the process.

The outstanding broad fact here is this: In a starving country studded with ruins and crowded with refugees communism has proved much weaker than even during the most prosperous and stable times of the Weimar Republic. This is in contrast to the general development in Western Europe, where communism emerged from World War II stronger than ever before—not only in France and Italy, where at times it was able to make a serious bid for power, but also in comparatively stable countries like Belgium, Holland, and Denmark.

This striking difference of development in Germany is not due to Allied pressure. It has been almost forgotten that Communists sat in the first postwar governments of nearly every West European country liberated by the Allied armies. The Allied-appointed first governments of the West German states were no exception, while the first Russian-appointed city government of Berlin was clearly Communist-dominated —not unreasonably, since the Communists had been Berlin's strongest party from 1926 right up to the end of the Weimar Republic.

Yet when the first elections came around the Communists received less than 10 per cent of the votes in Western Germany as a whole, less than 15 per cent in North Rhine–Westphalia, which includes the Ruhr, and less than 20 per cent in Berlin. In Essen, capital of the Ruhr, a British-appointed Communist mayor was defeated by a Christian Democrat, succeeded by a Social Democrat at the following election. In the entire heavily industrial area from Düsseldorf to Essen, where the Communists consistently had been the strongest party in Weimar days, they retained this position only in the twin steel-finishing towns of Solingen and Remscheid, and even there lost it in 1949. In the first West German general election, the Communists failed to win a single seat in direct election by a plurality of votes; the 15 out of 402 seats they now hold in the *Bundestag* have all been obtained by proportional representation in four of the eleven West German states, while in the other seven the Communist vote was left out of account, having failed to reach 5 per cent of the total. Not a single industrial trade union fell under Communist domination; even among the miners, where Communist influence was strongest, the anti-Communists had a two-thirds majority by the end of 1948.

There are, of course, no comparable figures available from the Eastern Zone, where elections were permitted only after the Social Democrats had been compulsorily fused with the Communists, and the middle-class parties were largely deprived of independent leadership. But even here the Socialist Unity party failed to gain an absolute majority precisely in those big cities and industrial areas which had traditionally shown Socialist-Communist majorities. The works councils were abolished for the same reason the Nazis had abandoned them after one year: Too many "nonparty candidates" were elected in defiance of the official list.

Finally, the "elections" to the "People's Congress" held in May 1949, on the basis of a single list and in the form of a plebiscite for "German unity and a just peace," resulted in so many "no" votes that the organizers, after considerable delay and consultation with the Russian authorities, admitted an opposition of one-third of the voters. Local counts in places where reliable informants sat on the polling committees invariably showed an absolute majority of protest votes.

What are the reasons for this astonishing eclipse of communism in a war-devastated country? The lingering effect of Dr. Goebbels' propaganda against "Asiatic Bolshevism" has been suggested as an explanation. But this seems to exaggerate the possible effect of propaganda in a manner that only propagandists can believe in, and it conflicts with the comparative failure of Dr. Goebbels in arousing hatred of the Western invaders, to which every Tommy and GI who entered Germany under General Eisenhower's command can testify. The failure of German communism is due to deep-seated fear and hatred of Russia, but the truth of the matter is that these emotions were created not by the assiduous efforts of the Propaganda Ministry but by the experience of a national clash between Germans and Russians of truly horrifying intensity and scale.

That clash began when German armies invaded Russia and discovered the poverty and primitive living conditions of the Russian peasant. It was intensified when German soldiers, by either witnessing atrocities committed by the SS against the Russian population, participating in them, or at least hearing of them, acquired a feeling of guilt and a fear of retribution which were no less powerful for being repressed. The fear was kept alive by Russian partisan action behind the German lines; and it was fully confirmed when the first Russian troops entered Germany, raping and pillaging as they went. Finally, the national experience was rounded off by the picture of the first prisoners of war who returned, emaciated and in rags, from the Soviet Union.

I know of rigidly high-principled German Communists whose abstract faith survived the raping of their own wives by drunken Russian soldiers. In general, however, the practical encounter with the Russians fixed a gulf between the former Communists who had served in Hitler's army and their former leaders who, in the concentration camps or as emigrees, continued to dream of liberation by Russia. Every American or Britisher who had to deal with German prisoners of war is familiar with the type of decent-minded German Communist who, drafted to the Eastern Front, was equally unwilling to fight the Russians and to surrender into Russian hands, and finally wangled a transfer to the West only to surrender happily to the Western Allies. These people were good antifascists; they rarely remained Communists.

Only one stratum of German society has remained partly untouched by the emotional shock of this national clash: the technical and "managerial" intelligentsia, including the officer corps. They were taught that in *Realpolitik* you must not be sentimental. They found much to admire in the institutions which enabled Russia to hold out despite enormous losses of blood and territory. The SS paid some of these institutions, including the political commissars, the compliment of imitation. Above all, some were attracted by the power of the Soviet official and officer to enjoy unquestioned privileges and unquestioning obedience, to "get things done" without democratic impediment. What they have seen of Russian living conditions only strengthens their hope that in an alliance it would soon be German efficiency that held the reins; and it pleases them to think that such an alliance would be in the tradition of the most successful among the creators of German power, Bismarck and Frederick II of Prussia. Behind the appeal to this tradition lurk the two most powerful baits to any German nationalist, the hope that Russia might in a new partition of Poland return to a friendly Germany the lost provinces east of the Oder-Neisse line, plus the lure of economically "organizing" the semideveloped territories of East and Southeast Europe which are now part of the Soviet sphere. As every German economist and businessman knows, trade with these countries is vital to German industry. Is it not in Russia's power to open or close the door to trade with them?

This attitude is by no means general among the technicians of production, warfare, and thought control who flourished under Hitler both inside and outside the Nazi party. But the argument is certainly thoroughly familiar in these circles, and they are the only ones with whom Russia has made new "moral conquests," compensating in part for the loss of most of her former hold on the working class. Russia knows it and is increasingly appealing to them, without trying to turn them into Communists. The National Democratic party in the Eastern Zone, whose organizers are Communists delegated for the purpose but posing as pro-Russian nationalists, was especially designed to rope in those elements and to exploit their links with the Western zones. In the spring of 1949 the "bloc of democratic and antifascist parties and mass organizations" in the Soviet Zone was rechristened the "National Front." For the first time those former leading members of the wartime National Committee for a Free Germany and German Officers' League who had been successfully indoctrinated in Moscow were permitted to come forward publicly as political leaders. At once they started a recruiting campaign among ex-officers in all zones, stressing the point that a Nazi past need no longer prevent an efficient man from playing a role appropriate to his talents and that this was the time for good patriots to volunteer for dangerous work.

This appeal has had a definite though limited success. In contrast to the constant flow of refugees from the East to Western Germany, estimated at 300,000 during 1949 and representing all strata of society, there has been a trickle of a few hundred officers and military technicians from West to East during the same period. This "Plebiscite of the Feet" probably offers the fairest balance sheet of the attraction and repulsion exercised by the Communist system on the Germans today.

Even so the Russians have not been able to exploit the nationalist appeal consistently. Regard for their Polish and Czechoslovak allies has forced them again and again to discourage German nationalist hopes by insisting on the finality of the Oder-Neisse frontier. At the Foreign Ministers' Conference in Paris last June, Vishinsky refrained at the last moment from playing the German nationalist card and came out as a champion of strict Allied control. The campaign to eradicate "Titoist" tendencies from the German as well as other Communist parties, conducted as a struggle against "nationalist deviations," must have been an eye-opener to many who had hoped that a Germany moving into the Russian orbit would still find scope to advance her own interests. The periodic purges of officials and industrial managers for alleged sabotage are a constant reminder to the ambitious of the intense personal risk which forms the reverse side of the alluring

career prospects in a totalitarian state. Thus the rigid central-
ism of the Russian planetary system and its sudden incalcu-
lable changes of political "line" and personal fortune may in
the long run prove as powerful a barrier to allegiance for
Germany's nationalist would-be elites as the low standard of
living, the lack of personal freedom, and the memories of war
and postwar experience are for her "toiling masses."

The Germans, then, have overwhelmingly rejected communism because it is identified with Russia. The one organized force in German political life which has openly and
consistently sided with the cause of the Soviet Union has
turned out a powerless minority wherever the vote was free,
and has not been able to win the semblance of wholehearted
popular allegiance even where it wields dictatorial power.
But while the Communist attitude to Russia is known as an
integral part of the Communist faith, that of the other political forces emerged only gradually as the issues of the cold
war defined themselves.

By now, politically articulate non-Communist Germans
have developed four main basic conceptions in foreign policy.
First, there are the advocates of a political counteroffensive by
democracy against Soviet totalitarianism; this group looks for
the restoration of German and European unity without war
by the collapse of the Communist satellite regimes east of the
Elbe. Second, there are the supporters of Western self-sufficiency, prepared to put up for an indefinite period with a
truncated Western Germany, speed up its integration into
Western Europe, and come to terms with the East Zone of
Germany in what is virtually foreign trade. Third, there are
the apostles of "neutrality," who hope that the Western
powers and Russia will one day agree to evacuate Germany
and that the difference of regimes will somehow disappear,
if only the Germans get together and pledge themselves never
to join either the Western or Eastern bloc. And finally, there

are the advocates of a restoration of German might by a military alliance with the West against the East, to be concluded on German terms.

Though none of these conceptions is confined to any one party, class, or group, the first is dominant among the Social Democrats, the second most strongly supported among Catholic political leaders and the moderate and democratic elements of the middle class, while the third and fourth are hotly disputed among the traditional Protestant Right, the gradually politically awakening front generation of World War II, and in the new militant nationalist groups.

The Social Democrats were the first to develop a clear-cut attitude on these issues, under the impact of the compulsory fusion imposed by the Communists on their organization in the Russian Zone. Despite the bitter struggles between the two parties in the Weimar Republic, of which the Social Democrats were the chief pillar while the Communists were its implacable enemies, the common origin of both from a labor movement that once was united had not been forgotten; and when the most active survivors of both parties emerged from the underground circles and concentration camps in 1945 many of them hoped that the time had come to let bygones be bygones, that Socialists would henceforth be militant and Communists democratic, and that confident co-operation in common tasks might result in speedy reunion. In fact the first-hour offers of fusion came in many places from the Social Democrats, and it was the Communist leaders returning from exile in the wake of the Red Army who turned them down, insisting on reorganizing their own centralist party machine first.

When a few months later, shocked by the weakness of the Communists in the November elections in neighboring Austria, the Russians began to insist on immediate fusion, much had changed: the Social Democrats had, to their surprise, turned out to be much the stronger party everywhere; they had had their first taste of Soviet rule and of new Communist methods; and the veterans of the concentration camps had been given time to absorb something of the experience of the Russian system which the rank and file had gathered in the meantime. Above all, the Social Democrats in the Western zones, much hampered by the slower pace of the Western powers in admitting German parties, had meanwhile succeeded in setting up a provisional center at Hanover under the leadership of Kurt Schumacher. Hence when the East Zone Social Democrats demanded that fusion be decided only by proper democratic procedure, they meant that they wanted first to call a national party congress and to hold it outside the reach of Russian bayonets.

At this point the Russians dropped the mask. Joint meetings of Social Democrats and Communists were suddenly called all over the Soviet Zone, and in the presence of Soviet officers were asked to vote, by show of hands, on fusion resolutions poorly translated from the Russian. People who objected were invited again and again to endless nightly "discussions" with the local Soviet commander or political officer, never knowing whether they would be allowed to go home in the morning. Dozens soon found themselves back in the very same concentration camps from which the Allied armies had liberated them only a few months before. Town by town, village by village, "fusion" was carried out "according to plan." By the spring of 1946 the East Zone Social Democratic leaders, pressed hard not to abandon their followers who had joined the new party, and lured with the prospect that creation of "unity" would mean the end of Russian dismantling and a new chance for Germany, surrendered and agreed to fusion without a party congress. The Russian aim seemed achieved—when the rebellion of a few dozen young men in Berlin changed everything.

They had belonged to the last generation of the Socialist youth movement before 1933. In their twenties they had experienced the collapse of German labor before Hitler's onslaught, had started to work underground against the Nazis, and had sooner or later ended up in their prisons. Now they felt that it was all happening again, the same totalitarian terror, the same *Gleichschaltung* of the labor movement. They determined that it should not. Their decision was the first free choice made by any group of Germans after the war. It was the beginning of the resistance of Berlin.

Abandoned by their official leaders, these young people got the Berlin Social Democratic district chiefs together. They pledged themselves to stand by their demand: no fusion without a party congress. They got it adopted by a district conference. The fusionists expelled them and tried to appoint a new Berlin district executive. The opposition replied by calling a secret ballot of the entire Berlin membership. The Russians banned it in their sector. The Western Allies permitted it. The fusionists were overwhelmingly defeated. On the morrow of the ballot a Social Democratic party organization stood in Berlin, right in the heart of the Soviet Zone, proclaiming to the world that the fusion was being forced, that the Social Democrats in the Soviet Zone would have rejected it if they had been free, and that democracy east of the Elbe was dead.

These first steps of resistance to totalitarianism were taken in the face of pronounced Western skepticism. A small band of British and American officials and pressmen familiar with the labor movement helped as best as they could; most of the prominent Allied representatives were then still convinced that communism was bound to advance to the Rhine. (As if it would have stopped there!) Yet the success of this first plebiscite had a great effect on Western Allied opinion.

The facts of what had happened in the Eastern Zone began to reach the world via Berlin.

One result of the Berlin events was to make Kurt Schumacher uncontested leader of the Social Democratic party. He had gone to Berlin at the height of the struggle; the reorganized party there had immediately acknowledged him. The one-armed man, who had endured ten years in a concentration camp and nearly lost his eyesight rather than buy his freedom by signing a declaration in conflict with his convictions, now turned the blast of his invective on the new totalitarianism. The Social Democratic party in the Eastern Zone, he announced, had not merged with the Communists. It had been suppressed by the occupying power. He would not ask again for its admission there while the present police regime lasted. There could be no compromise with that regime for democrats, any more than there could have been compromise with Hitler. There could be no joint democratic body representing both the Western and Eastern zones so long as the official spokesmen of the Eastern Zone were not representatives of its people but their jailers. With the same stubbornness with which he had, at great cost to himself, said no to nazism, he now said no to every proposal for "national unity" with the Communist regime.

Now the Social Democrats are Western Germany's second main party, forming the official opposition in the Federal Republic and leading the government in five of the eleven West German states. At the general election of August 1949, they polled 6,800,000 votes and gained 131 seats—400,000 votes and 8 seats less than the Christian Democrats. As the traditional party of German labor, they dominate the outlook of the trade-union movement even though the unions contain Catholic and Communist elements as well and maintain strict official neutrality toward political parties. Through their delegation in the Bonn Constituent Assembly of 1948-9, brilliantly led by Carlo Schmid, the Social Democrats' impact on the "basic law" of the new Federal Republic has probably been greater than that of any other party. Their leadership of the resistance of Berlin, confirmed when the West Berlin electorate returned the Socialist city administration with an increased absolute majority in the midst of the blockade, has won recognition throughout Western Germany. Their strength as a parliamentary opposition has forced the anti-Socialist government of Western Germany to consult them on major questions of international policy, and to make special efforts to proceed in agreement with them on East German questions. The Socialists' strict and consistent refusal to have any dealings with the present East Zone regime has therefore been a major factor in Germany's postwar development.

Yet the Social Democrats have by no means turned their back on the Eastern Zone. A constant stream of underground reports reaches their headquarters from beyond the Elbe, and their West German policy is more deliberately framed with an eye to the East than that of any other party. Saxony, Thuringia, and Saxony-Anhalt, three of the five states in the Eastern Zone, are traditional labor strongholds, and Schumacher has remarked that while they are not free, his party is "breathing on one lung only." How, then, do the Social Democrats imagine that they can regain the use of their other lung —that is, restore German unity on a democratic basis?

The answer was given to me, during the 1948 party congress, by Berlin's mayor, Ernst Reuter. This man, whose cool courage, steady judgment, and quiet humor became symbols of the spirit of his city during the year of the Russian blockade, said without the slightest hesitation that the only road to unity in liberty was incessant political warfare. He is convinced that the Communist regime in Eastern Germany, as indeed in Eastern Europe, can be made untenable without war, i.e., without a "shooting war." For that, three things would be necessary on the part of the Western Allies: an openly proclaimed determination to achieve the liberation of Eastern Europe from Communist rule and to make this achievement the chief aim of Allied political strategy; a systematic support of the anti-Communist forces there by all the well-known methods of political warfare; and a continued effort to build a united, stable, and prosperous Western Europe. On the German side, this requires that Berlin be maintained as the "show window of freedom" for Eastern Europe, that the West German state be formed rapidly and effectively without regard to Soviet protests, and that the state be constructed in such a way as to leave the door open for the adherence of an unfettered Eastern Zone, making it as attractive as possible for its inhabitants.

That is a program for fighting the cold war without truce or quarter, a program for an all-out counteroffensive of Western democracy. It was in the same spirit that Dr. Schumacher proclaimed, on the eve of the Paris Conference in May 1949, what he termed the German democrats' conditions for German unity in liberty: freedom of party formation in the Eastern Zone, applying not only to his own party but to the "unfettering" of the middle-class parties from the tutelage of the "bloc policy"; free elections under inter-Allied guarantee; reduction of the East Zone "people's police" in size, armament, and powers to the Western level.

The Western powers actually entered the Paris Conference with a very similar program, designed to meet an expected Russian initiative for German unity without democratic safeguards. But when Vishinsky proposed a simple return to strict four-power control, which could easily be rejected as impracticable, the Western powers did not press their ideas of democratic unity but willingly accepted the "modus vivendi" between the two different regimes in Western and Eastern Germany as a compromise.

I believe that at that moment—immediately after the failure of the blockade of Berlin, with the East Zone still reeling from the effects of the counterblockade and the Western zones at the peak of recovery following the currency reform, with the West German constitution just ratified and the Eastern state not yet founded—the Russian position in Germany was weaker than ever before or since. Then, if ever, there was a chance to restore unity on Western terms. The attempt was not seriously made. Four months later, the West and East German republics had been formed. Another two months, and the chancellor of Western Germany was publicly discussing remilitarization.

The Paris Agreement between the Western powers and Soviet Russia to consolidate the partition of Germany—for that is what the "modus vivendi" amounted to—has made much more difficult the position of those Germans who believe in restoring freedom East of the Elbe without war. The Social Democrats lost the initiative in international policy even before they lost the general election. The supporters of Western self-sufficiency on one side, the advocates of a "neutral" buffer state on the other, came to the fore and finally the debate on West German remilitarization was started not by the Germans themselves, but by a number of leading military men of the Western world. It found the German Socialists in strict opposition. Erich Ollenhauer, Schumacher's deputy in the party leadership and probably the party's coolest and most balanced politician, put it that the Socialists regard the security of occupied Western Germany as solely an Allied responsibility, and consider that German democrats should fight for their ideas with the moral weapons which Berlin has shown can be used with such effectiveness. Any talk of Western remilitarization, he claimed, could only destroy the last chances of restoring unity in freedom.

Since then, these chances have been even further reduced by the steady tightening of the East German police regime and by the attempts to "invade" Berlin by the Communist-kept youth group, the *Freie Deutsche Jugend,* at the end of May, 1950. The Socialists themselves cannot now be sure how long Berlin can be defended by moral force alone. There is no doubt that in the face of armed aggression, they would be willing to fight for freedom. But to restore freedom to those Germans who have lost it, they still rely on political rather than military means. They want to fight the cold war, but to keep it cold.

The other parties were not so quick to come into decisive conflict with the Soviets. For one thing they were later in trying to organize themselves on a national scale, so that events in one zone did not immediately affect organizations in the others. Moreover, the East Zone Communists made no attempt to swallow the "bourgeois" parties wholesale as they tried to do with the Socialists; they merely put pressure on them to support Russian policies and change recalcitrant leaders. It is ironic to recall that Dr. Andreas Hermes, who later played host to the Bad Godesberg talks between West German politicians and businessmen and former Ambassador Rudolf Nadolny, was removed from the East Zone leadership of the Christian Democratic Union at the end of 1945 under Russian pressure for opposing land reform, and that Jakob Kaiser, later West German minister for all-German affairs, was then Hermes' Soviet-approved successor.

For two more years Kaiser pursued his sincere though illusory attempt to preserve a measure of independence for his party by supporting those measures of Soviet policy which he regarded as genuinely progressive, and to maintain equal good will toward Russia and the Western powers. When he embarked on the experiment the cold war had not been declared, and official British and American policy highly commended his "statesmanship" as against the "sterile doctrinaire," Schumacher. When he in turn was removed by the Russians for refusing to join the "People's Congress" movement he entered the Western camp with an immaculate reputation but very little following—a general without an army.

Meanwhile the last attempt to devise a common four-power policy for Germany had failed, the Anglo-American "bizone" had been formed, and the West German Christian Democrats had become the dominant party in its economic departments. That meant little enough in the beginning; it was going to mean a great deal once currency reform was carried out and the Marshall Plan got into its stride. To go ahead first with the bizone, then with separate Western currency reform, meant to embark on the road to a West German state; you could not co-operate in these measures in the West and, in the name of one and the same party, join the "People's Congress" started to oppose them in the East.

The time of decision for Germany's middle-class parties had come. They, too, decided for the West wherever they were free to choose—in the West itself and in Berlin, with many leaders from the Eastern Zone crossing over as soon as they got a chance, and many others prevented from doing so only by arrest.

The choice of 1948 marks the second great stage in the Germans' alignment in the cold war. In the West it was primarily an economic choice before it became a political one. It was implicit in the administration of the bizone and the co-operation in preparations for currency reform; it was implicit also in the German administrators' agreement to Germany's joining the Marshall Plan, though the decision itself was taken by the military governors. It became explicit when the agreement on the creation of a West German state, reached in London by the three Western powers, was submitted to the West German minister presidents, who after some hesitation decided to call a constituent assembly on the terms laid down in London.

The full story of the protracted birth pangs of the West German state is given elsewhere in this book. Here it must suffice to say that the initial qualms shown by some of the minister presidents did not refer to the substance of the decision that had to be taken, only to its form. There were doubts whether an administration formed under alien occupation in only a part of Germany should be called a state. There were doubts whether a provisional charter ordering the functioning of such an administration should be called a constitution, and the assembly charged with drafting it a constituent assembly. There were doubts whether the detailed terms laid down by the Allies were acceptable.

But there were no doubts, among either the minister presidents or any other politicians then in responsible positions in Western Germany, that it was urgent that a single, democratically elected parliament and government should be created as soon as possible for the three Western zones with as much power in its internal affairs as the occupying powers would concede. There was also unanimity in the belief that, while the new structure should be kept open for the East, it should not wait till agreement with the East was reached. Even the formal reservations that were made came largely from the strongly anti-Soviet Social Democrats, and not because of hesitation at taking responsibility for one-sided Western action—"Western counteraction to Russian action in setting up a totalitarian regime in the Eastern Zone," Schumacher called it—but from fear of giving the names properly belonging to a democratic state to institutions which still very imperfectly deserved that name.

Not one of the Western leaders has ever claimed that in laying the groundwork for the new state he was acting unwillingly under pressure of the occupying powers. On the contrary all have rebutted the Communist charges that they were carrying out Allied orders by claiming to act with the mandate and in the interests of the German people. The real pressure was that of the circumstances: the need to give the reviving German economy a sound political framework, the urgency of overcoming the isolation of the French Zone and ending its very special type of Occupation regime, the wish to take advantage of the offer of greater self-government after three years of military rule, the hope to form institutions which could speak on behalf of German interests to the outside world. But the West German leaders knew, and were constantly reminded by the Communists, that in putting these considerations ahead of "unity" with the Eastern Zone they were making an option for a divided Germany that might have lasting effects.

To those who watched the decision take place, the Christian Democratic leaders, who had longer maintained official relations with the Eastern Zone, seemed now even more determined than the Social Democrats to complete the breach. No doubt this was partly due to the direct responsibility of the CDU for the economic administration of the bizone, where with the help of the Liberals it maintained a free-enterprise majority in the Economic Council. But it is probable that it was also much influenced by the specific Western outlook of the most important single force within the ranks of this highly composite party, political Catholicism.

The Christian Democrats are not a party of old tradition. They were founded in Berlin in the summer of 1945, in that honeymoon of Soviet liberalism when the Russians went out of their way to get ahead of the West in according freedom of expression to all nonfascist political tendencies. But they have a solid traditional core, German political Catholicism. Before 1933 that found its expression in the Center party, formed in opposition to Bismarck's Reich and later the most stable partner of social democracy in governing and defending the Weimar Republic. After 1945 political Catholicism merged with Protestant conservatism, most of whose forces had supported the nationalist Right during the Weimar period, in the Christian Democratic Union; only an insignificant portion joined the new Center party in parts of the British Zone. But the Catholics quickly gained control of the party machine not only in the predominantly Catholic but also in the mixed areas. Konrad Adenauer, the chancellor and the party's undisputed leader since the period of the Constituent Assembly, is a Catholic; so are all the five Christian Democratic minister presidents of West German states; so was Doctor Hermann Puender, who headed the bizonal administration of the U. S. and British zones before the federal republic was set up; so were even the party's first two leaders in the predominantly Protestant Eastern Zone, Doctor Andreas Hermes and Jakob Kaiser; so are seven out of eight Christian Democratic ministers in the federal government. Only in some of the purely Protestant provinces of northern Germany have the Protestants in the CDU provided their own leadership. As a result the Protestant middle class in such mixed areas as Hesse and Württemberg-Baden has tended to leave the CDU and join the Liberals.

Now political Catholicism is one of the most undeniable Western forces in the world of today, but in Germany at least it is Western in a very different sense from that described in the case of the Social Democrats; one might almost say that the Western outlook of the German Catholics is of a less crusading kind. Kurt Schumacher, born in the province once called Western Prussia and now Pomorze (a province with a traditional Polish majority, awarded to Poland in 1919—not only after the mass expulsions of 1945), is as much at home in Eastern Germany as in the West, where he has lived since the First World War. Dr. Adenauer, who for decades was mayor of Cologne, has never ceased to look with a certain distaste on the trans-Elbian lands whose soil was never trodden by St. Boniface. Speaking to an American, he once listed as his chief national dislikes "the Russians, the Prussians, and the British"; he prefers the French and the Americans. That dislike of Prussia, or what is now Eastern Germany, is not uncommon among West German Catholics, many of whose leaders feel that their cultural ties with the Latin Catholic countries of the West are closer than with their own kinsmen East of the Elbe.

Today powerful practical considerations are reinforcing this emotional outlook. Western Germany is easier to integrate into Western Europe than the whole of Germany would be. Politically, admission of a Western Germany of 48 millions as an equal partner encounters less resistance among the nations of Western Europe than would that of a united Germany of 66 millions. Economically, reunion with impoverished Eastern Germany would immediately lower the West German standard of living. The need for capital, already scarce in the West, would be enormously increased if the ravages of Russian dismantling were to be made good, and Marshall Plan aid could hardly be expected to increase in the same proportion. There has been much grumbling in Western Germany, not always confined to the man in the street, about the cost of aid to Berlin; the Catholic minister of finance of a South German state who, in one of the first committee discussions on the subject, expressed the opinion that "the Americans should pay for their own cold war" may not really have meant that the cold war was not his concern, but he certainly did mean that the defense of Berlin was more expensive than its value to Western Germany justified. If that view is possible about Berlin, even though only in committee behind closed doors, the attitude of the same group of people to the much larger cost of restoring German unity on democratic terms can be imagined.

Finally, no Catholic politician can be indifferent to the fact that Catholic influence in Western Germany is much larger than it would be in a united Germany, and that it will be a very powerful factor in a united Western Europe bounded by the Elbe. The preferences of German Catholic politicians coincide closely with those of their French co-religionists. Catholic influence in West German education has increased by leaps and bounds since 1945, and the policy of the French Occupation authorities, concerted in some cases directly between the Quai d'Orsay and the Vatican, has been an important factor in this direction. Even beyond the sphere of direct Church interests, French policy in recent years seems to have aimed at a "little Europe" which, but for British membership, would be almost identical with the traditional conception of the "Catholic West," and Western Germany fits well into this pattern.

This outlook has eminently fitted the Christian Democrats, and the Catholic core of their leadership, to become the leading party in the first government of the West German Federal Republic. At the August 1949 elections, it obtained 7,200,000 votes and 139 seats—one independent member has since joined the party's *Bundestag* delegation—and in the government, formed by coalition with the Free Democrats and the German party, it furnishes, apart from the chancellor, eight out of thirteen ministers. The five state governments under Christian Democratic leadership include the two largest ones, North Rhine Westphalia and Bavaria, and there are only three states without Christian Democrats in their government, two of them the city states of Hamburg and Bremen. The party has no mass membership like the Socialists, and can therefore afford to be loosely organized on federalist lines, a fact which seems to make it easier to harbor simultaneously a wide range of social, cultural and regional interests. Doctor Adenauer and his ministers of finance and economics, Doctor Fritz Schaeffer and Professor Ludwig Erhard, are outspoken conservatives in economic policy; but Karl Arnold, minister president in the Ruhr state of North Rhine Westphalia and president of the *Bundesrat* (the upper house representing the state governments), is a Catholic trade-unionist of socialist inclinations. In the party's *Bundestag* delegation, steel industrialists sit side by side with a miners' leader, Catholics with leading Protestant laymen, Bavarian federalists with former Prussian officials, bankers with leaders of farm co-operatives. This composition alone obliges the party to steer a course near the center, and internal trouble develops whenever its coalition partners try to drag it too far to the right.

One of the Christian Democratic government members is Jakob Kaiser, the former East Zone leader, who now holds the ministry for all-German affairs. This ministry has been created to maintain contact with Berlin, which under an Allied ruling is not allowed to be a direct member state of the federal republic, and with the people—not the government—of the Eastern Zone. In practice, aid for Berlin is a responsibility of the government as a whole; it is being given less speedily, and more sparingly, than the Berliners (and sometimes also the Allies) would wish, but it is nevertheless real and vitally important. The government's attitude to the Eastern Zone is complicated by the fact that it does not wish to recognize the Eastern Government, but needs the interzonal trade; the dilemma was straddled in February 1950 by negotiating a commercial agreement not between the governments but between special trading organizations whose heads, though in fact officials, signed on behalf of their "currency areas" and not of their states. Under the circumstances, the possibilities of direct political warfare by the government are naturally limited.

The Christian Democratic party as such has long avoided denying officially the legitimacy of the party that bears the same name in Eastern Germany. Joint meetings ended when Jakob Kaiser was deposed in the East and came to the West, but the Western party made no formal denunciation of his successor as a usurper. A number of individual leaders in the West, chiefly those interested in expanding interzonal trade, have used this situation to maintain personal contact with East German Christian Democrats, and after the 1949 Paris Conference, Bavarian Deputy Premier Josef Mueller even propagated the creation of official joint economic organs linking the Eastern and Western governments. In the end, it was the behavior of the Eastern regime that completed the breach: the new ruthless purge of the remnants of the bourgeois parties in the Eastern Zone, prosecuted during the early months of 1950, caused the West German Christian Democrats to appeal officially to party members in the Eastern Zone to resist the purge and retire from public activity rather than follow the new "leaders" appointed by the "National Front" at the behest of the Russian Occupation authorities.

The only other party of major importance in Western Germany, the Free Democrats (frequently described as "Liberals"), have followed a road similar to that of the Christian Democrats in defining their Western orientation, but at a somewhat faster pace. During the period of the Berlin blockade, they underlined the formal breach with their former sister party in the East by choosing "free democrat" rather than "liberal democrat"—the label of the Eastern party—as the name for their unified West German organization. Today, based chiefly on the Protestant middle class in religiously mixed areas, the West German Free Democrats have attracted two widely divergent elements. In Württemberg-Baden, and to some extent in the Hanse ports, they continue the best traditions of old German liberalism, splendidly embodied in their former party leader Doctor Theodor Heuss, the West German president; in Hesse and some parts of Northern Germany they are simply the respectable section of the nationalist right. Their official policy on the East-West issue is that of the government.

The limit of any purely Western policy is of course the need for trade with Eastern Germany and with Eastern Europe in general. The more West European production increases and the more the Marshall Plan proceeds, the more acute becomes the problem of export markets. Every German economist and businessman who looks ahead to the time when Germany will no longer be able to live on subsidies is haunted by the specter of cutthroat competition between Britain and Western Germany, those two highly industrialized countries both dependent on large-scale imports of food and raw materials, with Britain still in the position of an occupying power. The result is not only extreme sensitivity toward both real and imagined cases of British policies dictated by competitive interests—there can be no doubt that both sorts exist—but also a widespread conviction that the opening of the Eastern markets is the only way out. That conviction is not confined to those advocates of "neutrality" who believe that the opening of trade channels should be bought by political concessions to the Russians. It goes as frequently with the purely Western political outlook just discussed. Once you have drawn a clear borderline across Germany and silently accepted it as final, you may then develop "foreign" trade across the border without political inhibitions.

A widely publicized secret meeting took place at Bad Godesberg between Rudolf Nadolny, former German ambassador to Moscow, and a number of leading West German conservative politicians and businessmen. They had been invited by Doctor Andreas Hermes, the former East Zone Christian Democratic leader and head of the West German farmers' unions. The presence of Nadolny, whose traditional good relations with high Russian officials were known, and the secrecy of the preparations for the meeting gave rise to the suspicion that pro-Soviet elements had gathered here to harmonize a policy for preventing the creation of a West German state; yet a glance at the list of participants, which included the bizonal chief administrator, Doctor Hermann Puender, as well as Professor Ludwig Erhard, who subsequently became minister of economics, should have been sufficient to discredit that view. The best information available at the time indicated that Nadolny was not then acting on Russian instigation, and that Berlin industrialists interested in getting East-West trade were partly responsible for initiating the meeting; furthermore, the program with which the organizers faced the press a few weeks later excluded any opposition to the Western state or dabbling in international policy, confining itself to the suggestion that economic co-operation between East and West Germany, and possibly co-operation in other non-political fields, should be developed despite political separation. On this platform, the "Godesberg circle" has since constituted itself as an association of the "Friends of German Unity," but with the emphasis clearly on interzonal trade.

That is not to say that such a group is entirely without political significance. It is apparently without political ambition. Its persuasion is that one should do business with the Eastern Zone, and through it with Eastern Europe, whatever the politicians and the Western powers might say to the contrary. The volume of "black" trade across the Elbe border, the smuggling of Western steel products in exchange for Eastern sugar or tax-free coffee, often tolerated and encouraged by the West German provincial authorities, is a measure of the importance of this tendency. Another yardstick is offered in the fact that, although Doctor Adenauer has publicly appealed to all Christian Democrats to withdraw from the group, a number of prominent party members, including ministers in state governments, have defied his advice. In the end, it has once again been Eastern policy which condemned the group to futility by suddenly turning against it and denouncing Nadolny and Hermes as "American agents." But the tendency of West German business circles to trade with the East without political interference has, of course, remained and will again come to the surface whenever political tension relaxes.

The underlying political conception of this business circle and others like it is that of the "cold truce" through which runs the hope that the border line in the cold war will trade across it. It is quite distinct from that of the genuine advocates of "neutralization" who hope to end the cold war and to restore German unity by an agreement on the withdrawal of all occupation forces and by setting up a "neutral" German buffer state with inter-Allied guarantees, without specific conditions regarding the internal regime of such a state. The advocates of "neutralization" form the first non-Communist political current in Western Germany that could be systematically exploited by Russian diplomacy and propaganda. It has never crystallized into an organized movement or taken hold of one of the major parties, but during its peak period in 1949 it gained a considerable following among the inarticulate mass of the people in Western Germany, and therefore its history furnishes valuable indications for the kind of hidden reserves Russia might be able to mobilize west of the Elbe in an emergency.

The "neutralist" tendency first emerged early in 1949, when the Russians were preparing to abandon the Berlin blockade and were feeling their way toward a four-power conference. The program of neutralization worked out by the

"Nauheim circle" of Professor Ulrich Noack was then given wide and favorable publicity in the controlled East German press. Its central argument to which the Russians never committed themselves, but to which they gave the widest possible circulation, was that the Russians were not primarily interested in having a Communist Germany, but in preventing a rearmed anti-Communist Germany allied to the Western powers. Once the West agreed to withdraw its occupation troops simultaneously with the Russians and join with them in guaranteeing the permanent disarmament and neutrality of Germany, theoretically there would be no longer any serious obstacle to German unity.

The Nauheim circle consisted largely of intellectuals without an established position in West Germany's political life. The only politician of standing who at one time maintained some contact with it was August Hausleiter, then deputy leader of the Christian Social Union (the Bavarian branch of the Christian Democrats) and now founder of the "German Community" which aims at welding the various provincial organizations of the bombed-out and expellees into a nation-wide new party. A Protestant from Franconia in his early forties, Hausleiter is also one of the founders of the "Deutsche Union," an organization appealing to young people of all parties and for a program of presidential government, party reform, and plebiscitary democracy not unlike that advocated by General de Gaulle in France. In fact, the advocates of neutrality found their response less in the established parties than in the undergrowth of West German politics where "circles" and "cross-contacts" pullulate—above all among active Protestants dissatisfied with the strength of Catholic influence in Western Germany, and among the young "front generation" with its strong distrust of the official parties and politicians.

There exists also a militantly nationalist version of the "neutrality" idea, represented for instance by the followers of

Otto Strasser, the former Nazi follower who rebelled against Hitler and is at present prevented by the Allies from returning from his Canadian exile. For Strasser and his friends, any German who co-operates either with the Russians or with the Western powers is equally a "quisling" and a "mercenary." They regard a third world war as a certainty and advise the German people not to allow themselves to be used as "cannon fodder" by either side, but to insist on an army of their own, which would then become the basis for restoring German greatness by independent maneuvering between the blocs. One of the new nationalist parties of the extreme right, the "Socialist Reich Party" headed by Doctor Fritz Dorls and former General Otto Remer (who foiled the 1944 conspiracy against Hitler by going over with his key battalion to the Nazi government) advocates similar ideas.

The bulk of the West German "neutralists," however, are attracted by anti-militarist rather than warlike ideas. That goes, above all, for a large part of the young generation; they may be "nationalist" in the sense of distrusting all foreign powers and their ideas, but they have absorbed the lesson of the ruins among which they live and they genuinely loathe the idea of further fighting. When early in 1950 the echoes of the international debate on German remilitarization at last reached Germany, and Chancellor Adenauer gave his famous interview to John P. Leacacos of the *Cleveland Plain Dealer* on a possible German contribution to Western defense in the form of a German contingent in a European army, the first reaction among the young generation was almost unanimously negative. *"Ohne uns"*—without us—became the most popular slogan wherever young people talked about it. People felt that they were being asked to fight "other people's war"; they also felt that they would have to fight their own kinsmen east of the Elbe—and the word "kinsmen" must be taken literally, as millions of families in Germany are today split by the iron curtain. So the first immediate result of remilitarization talk was a strong increase in "neutralist" feeling.

It was at that moment that "neutralism" acquired its most powerful spokesman yet—Pastor Martin Niemöller. The former U-boat commander who had defied the Nazis for spiritual reasons and spent many years in Hitler's concentration camps is without question the strongest personality in German Protestantism today. He is not its recognized leader; he always goes his own way and frequently embarrasses the official church organization. He has never learned to weigh his words. He zealously speaks out whatever his conscience dictates him, and the result is usually as striking as it is liable to misunderstanding. But he always taps sources which the more conventional leaders of German public life ignore. Whenever he speaks, he uncovers, in however one-sided and unbalanced fashion, some important undercurrent of German opinion. Now he suddenly came out against the idea that Germans should fight Germans in the service of the present "pseudo-states" of Eastern and Wesern Germany. The partition was a disaster, he said, a general disaster for all Germans and a special disaster for German Protestants who, in the West state "conceived in the Vatican and born in Washington," now found themselves under Catholic rule. He did not wish unity to be restored by a Communist assault, but if it came, West Germans should rather submit to force than fight their own kin. Was there not a peaceful way to heal the breach, by the powers' agreeing to leave Germany and hand the Occupation over to a contingent of the United Nations?

The echo of Niemöller's statements was considerable. The West German minister of the interior, Doctor Heinemann, himself a leading Protestant layman, wrote him and asked for an explanation. Niemöller replied. The highest organ of the Church made it clear that Niemöller's personal political views had not been expressed in its name, and that it was undesirable that clergymen should venture so far into political controversy. But a large, hitherto inarticulate section of German opinion felt that it had for the first time found a spokesman.

And then the Russians, once again, destroyed it all. In mid-January 1950, the most far-reaching purge yet descended on the remnants of the non-Communist parties in the Eastern Zone. Their most important provincial leaders were deposed or driven out; their local organizations were merged into new, compulsory local groups of the "National Front," leaving the central party chiefs as figureheads without an organized following. One of the principal reproaches leveled against the victims of the purge was that they had advocated "neutrality," instead of calling on the people to rally to the side of the Soviet Union in view of the imminent danger of Western aggression. The Russians themselves broke the weapon of neutrality propaganda at the moment when, for the first time, it seemed to have hit an important target in the West.

Meanwhile it turned out that the response to the idea of remilitarization in the West was not entirely negative. Like a stone thrown into a pool, it gradually had started widening circles among the traditional nationalist right. Today, these circles have found a new topic for discussion: the terms on which they should agree to furnish troops for a Western army. For in contrast to some of the "National-Bolshevik" groups mentioned before, the bulk of Germany's old-time nationalists and militarists would be prepared to join the West—on terms.

The "German Reich Party," led by jack-booted, Mosley-mustached former Sudeten schoolteacher Doctor Franz Richter, has five members in the *Bundestag*. It lives by attacking all the Allies on all occasions; but like its model, it is prepared to offer the West an alliance against the East in return for the Reich frontiers of 1937 and a plebiscite in

Austria. Its leaders love to talk of their European outlook. European fraternity is also the main theme in the official statements of the *Bruderschaft* (Brotherhood), that new freemasonry of a self-appointed elite of which General Hasso von Manteuffel, former Nazi *Gauleiter* Kaufman, and former departmental head in the SS security office Franke-Kriegsch are leading members. Manteuffel is the author of a memorandum, receipt of which was acknowledged by Chancellor Adenauer in March 1949, suggesting a German contingent in a European army of up to 30 divisions with German leaders to the corps commanders, but without a navy, air force, or armament industry of its own. Other and larger groups of former senior officers are preparing to send assurances to Adenauer's government that they are without any political ambitions of their own but will be loyally at the disposal of the legitimate government when it needs them.

I have tried to sketch the constantly changing picture of German attitudes to the cold war. What are the permanent features? What is the long-term importance of the various tendencies described? What are the lessons for Western policy?

I think the first permanent feature is the absence of any serious political attraction by the East, either by Communist or "National-Bolshevik" propaganda. In the record of five postwar years, I can find no evidence that Russia is willing or able seriously to "play the German trump card." Russia is growing more rather than less committed to the Oder-Neisse line, unacceptable to German nationalists or even German patriots, as time goes on. The East German regime is becoming more narrowly and openly Communist, not more broadly national, under the slogan of the "National Front."

The second permanent feature of the cold war does not come out clearly in an account of the programs and actions of political groups because it is essentially inarticulate though of vital importance. It is the prevalence of fear and cynicism among large numbers of ordinary Western Germans. The danger to the West in Germany is not the few people who sympathize with the East, but the many who are unwilling to fight it because they are afraid to be overrun, and because they are too tired and disappointed to take any new risk for the sake of the idea. There is a story of a German driver who told an Allied officer frankly why in case of war he would join the Russians. "If I fight on your side and get captured by the Russians, they will kill me," he said. "If I fight on the Russian side and get captured by the Allies, they will give me a job."

Given these fundamentals, the relative importance of the various tendencies described will largely depend on Allied policy. "Neutralism" in particular is little more than the articulate form of the fear and cynicism described—an attitude not uncommon in some other West European countries as well. It will be smallest when the West shows that it is taking every possible initiative to restore German unity on democratic terms, as was recently demonstrated by High Commissioner John J. McCloy's appeal for all-German free elections. It will be largest when the West gives the impression of being indifferent to German unity, and interested solely in integrating Western Germany into a military alliance.

From this, there follows in my opinion one main lesson for Western policy: There is a job of political consolidation to be done in Western Germany, which must have unquestioned priority over any military plans. By an accident of history, Western Germany has become the Eastern march of Western democracy, and democracy must defend its marches. But Western Germany is still far from being a well-founded democracy herself. That is the immense difference to Berlin— there, democracy has real roots, and the airlift has made it possible for the island city to hold out. In a real emergency, it would be possible to arm the people of Western Berlin and tell them to defend their freedoms. That is not the position of Western Germany today.

At the present time, if Western Germany were asked to furnish a number of divisions for Western defense, there would be two calamitous effects inside Germany, quite apart from the repercussions in other European countries: there would be a great increase in anti-Allied "neutralist" feeling, and the worst nationalists and reactionaries would be the first to volunteer to bear arms. Many decent and well-meaning people would be driven on the wrong side, and many of the most dangerous elements would gain positions of power.

The conclusion is not, in my view, that German defense must be abandoned as a bad job, or that its burden must fall on the Western nations alone for an indefinite time to come. The conclusion is that, to consolidate its Eastern march, the West must create there the same kind of positive confidence in its cause that exists in Berlin. The aid given to Berlin did much to create that confidence also in Western Germany. Constant stressing of Western proposals for democratically achieved unity, such as the effective plea made by John J. McCloy, is a step in the same direction. But one more thing is needed to eliminate the position of cynicism and nationalism. Beyond the formal integration of Western Germany into the Western community, practical proof must be given of Allied willingness to treat the defeated and occupied country in current economic and political issues not merely as an object of Allied solicitude, but as a genuine partner. To mention the recent cases where that willingness was lacking would be to tell another story. But one thing is certain—to divide Germany as a military partner of the West before she has truly become a political partner would result in the rearming of German nationalism and the disarming of German democracy.

Chapter IV

Tomorrow Is the New Moon

By J. EMLYN WILLIAMS

THE Nazi period of "closed thinking," along with totalitarian war and catastrophic defeat, left Germany morally, intellectually, and materially poorer than she had been for centuries—even after the Thirty Years' War. Those who entered Germany with the occupying armies were appalled by the colossal property destruction. They later discovered that the political, social, and economic chaos was even greater.

As one watched Displaced Persons trudging homeward along the highways, followed later by thousands of *Volksdeutsche* seeking new homes and, still later, by thousands of prisoners of war returning from the various battle fronts, the unspoken question was, What is the future of this country? To these human tragedies was added the splitting up of Germany into four occupied areas in which each of the Allies tried to introduce her own ideas of government and culture. Since the Western democracies differed little in their basic outlook on life, the real division of Germany was along the river Elbe between the Soviet and Western zones.

Under conditions which prevailed after the collapse four years ago, economic necessity compelled the Germans to concentrate upon the problems of food, shelter, and work. This applied to all sections of the community. As for the in-intellectuals, they seemed glad to be saved from the necessity of having immediately to explore the reasons for Germany's cataclysmic defeat. "Unconditional surrender" had its advantages. It could be interpreted to mean unconditional responsibility of the victors for dealing with the existing abnormal conditions.

No section of the community failed more miserably under the Third Reich than the intelligentsia. At first the intellectuals disdained their Führer and his program. Later the majority of them either fled or capitulated. In 1945 the foreign observer was struck by how little German intellectuals knew of the outside world. Some of the older generation, who retained memories of pre-1933 foreign contacts, either had been compulsorily retired by the Nazis or were in minor positions. Most of those in prominent public office were tainted with nazism and had been ousted by the Occupation authorities.

For the first three years after the collapse there were few evidences of constructive German thinking. At that time German war guilt was so obvious that the matter was not even disputed. It was simply accepted. However they may have regarded it in victory, the vast majority of Germans, including the intellectuals, were so tired of nazism in defeat that they were disinclined to do more than condemn it. The needs of everyday life were too pressing.

In those years few books were published. Most discussions on cultural issues were confined to the newspapers, which appeared under the license of one or the other of the four occupying powers. Outstanding among such issues was the problem of Germany's collapse. "Why," Moeller van den Bruck had asked years earlier, "are the Germans a people born to trouble others?" "Why," asked the postwar Germans, "did we allow Hitler to go so far? He did a lot of good things for us, but why didn't we stop him before the rest of the world could have such an undisputed right to interfere?"

The German attitude has undergone a marked change since 1945. A former active admission of guilt and willingness to atone have faded into the background. This was to be expected, but the process was made easier by the emphasis in some Allied circles on collective guilt. The Germans pointed out that this looked very much like adopting Hitler's racial theories.

The verdicts of the International Military Tribunal were received by most Germans as a necessity of defeat but by others as a purge of their moral responsibility. The troubles had come, they seemed to argue, from their leaders, from men like Göring and Ribbentrop. The leaders had deceived the nation; therefore it was right that they should pay. But as for the average German, he should not be confused with his leaders. *Die ganze Richtung hat uns nicht gepasst* (The whole line did not suit us) appeared to sum up the final judgment of nazism as far as many Germans were concerned.

Their defeat was and still is interpreted by many Germans as due not to moral default but to the enemy's better technical and psychological equipment. Unfortunately many discussions of the *bessere Gesellschaft* turn less upon why the Germans themselves had done so little to bring about the overthrow of nazism than upon why other nations had not done more.

Two facts about the Nuremberg trials puzzled most Germans. Why should any of their leaders have been found guilty of the crime of preparing aggressive war when the Soviet Union, a partner to the nonaggression treaty of August 23, 1939, was among the judges? Further, most of the prisoners in all these trials offered the same defense: they were carrying out the orders of their superiors. This principle of blind obedience is so deeply rooted that even today few

Germans understand why members of their armed forces, their diplomats, or their civil servants should have been expected to behave otherwise. An interesting development from this attitude is that each individual appears to be satisfied that in this way freedom from responsibility was established not only for himself but for his class or profession.

An impression of a similar sort is left after reading former Chief of Staff General Franz Halder's pamphlet on *Hitler as Military Commander*. All that this distinguished soldier has to say about the failings of the Führer as a military leader is convincingly set out. At the same time Halder appears to be seeking in this way to exonerate the General Staff of responsibility for military defeat. He omits even a passing reference to the fact that the General Staff was only too willing to follow the Führer in the days of his successes.

One of the main sources of moral support for thousands of members of the intellectual classes in the early years after the war was the memory of the revolt of July 20, 1944. It was surprising how many Germans claimed to be directly or indirectly implicated, partly as a means of ingratiating themselves with the Western Military Government authorities. An impartial examination of this revolt has yet to be written. What is certain, however, is that the memory of this sole example of an anti-Nazi rising in Germany during the war had an encouraging effect during the first year of contact with the outside world. The revolt was often interpreted as a first step toward emancipation from totalitarian control.

Through their own propaganda both during and since the war the Western occupying powers have concentrated so much upon the fact of membership in the Nazi party that many Germans feel the Allies have tended to play down the historical factors which made Hitler possible. When the incoming victors made membership in the party almost the only standard by which to judge the Germans after the war, they adopted a policy which was uniform and easy to apply but which took little account of the abnormal conditions existing under the Third Reich. Therefore, since the end of the war little attention has been given to the close and direct connection between nazism and earlier Germanic ideas, especially militarism.

Today the question is not whether a new Nazi party will arise but whether the old militarism still exists. It is sometimes forgotten that German militarism was a danger not only because the Reich had a large army; equally important was the fact that the civilian population had become dependent upon the army for its ideas. The kind of independent thinking that democracy assumes could not function where the officer class determined what was *anständig* (good form). Because of this lack of individualism there was much truth behind the apocryphal story attributed to Goebbels that the answer to the question of how long the Nazi party would survive was *Nur solange die Affen parieren* (Only so long as the apes obey)!

Pan-Germanism supplied the false belief in German racial superiority. Hitler's *Mein Kampf* and the party program contained few basic ideas which were not derived from pamphlets of the Pan-Germans before 1914. The Germans lost their freedom by not destroying Prussian militarism. In the end it destroyed them.

It was therefore not surprising that after 1933 many Germans saw no alternative to nazism except a withdrawal into themselves. Their resistance to tyranny and terror was not the struggle for freedom but an outward acceptance accompanied by an inner rejection. This is the same attitude which, with more justification, is generally adopted toward the Occupation.

It is a great temptation to establish a theory and then

make the facts fit. One such theory, which the Western world is fond of preaching today, is that nationalism is or should be dead. The fact is that nationalism is by no means dead in Europe, and it can be argued whether or not it should be. Everything depends upon the ends to which it is directed.

Germany has not fully realized herself as a nation. Yet only when she has done so will she make her proper contribution to world progress.

Thirty years ago the Western world was enthusiastic about the theory of self-determination. A German once said, "Between the two world wars, *you* had the minority complex and *we* had the inferiority complex." Today everyone in this imperfect world knows that self-determination can be carried to absurd extremes. Many of us have reacted by going to the other extreme of assuming that nationalism should be annihilated. Obviously the important thing is that this nationalism shall be kept within bounds. Bismarck linked it to Prussian absolutism and we have seen the disastrous results. The question now is not whether there will be a nationally conscious Germany tomorrow but whether Germany will be linked with progressive forces in the interests of peace and prosperity.

German nationalism in the past few generations has shown a form of egotism that led to an overrating of German power. German philosophers did not set a limit to the legitimate self-assertion of the nation. Political and cultural leaders too often accepted their premises and attempted to lead their followers far beyond the realm of the rational and possible. In politics the German will is honest in blindly following its own line, and it is not surprising that even today Germans are shocked that the unbridled expression of some of their aims has led to opposition in the outside world; e.g., their *Lebensraum* theory disregarded entirely the claims of other peoples.

The natural tendency in German writing and speeches now is to stress antitotalitarian views. How much the change is real and how much due to opportunism is hard to judge. The sense of nationalism is growing. Through its growth the Germans are regaining their self-confidence, but nationalism will have to grow within a larger unit for the Germans to realize their duties as well as their privileges. Unless they begin from within and consolidate themselves there is a great danger that they may give lip service to the cause of Pan-Europe without understanding what such participation will demand of them.

German cultural and political development has not been the kind to encourage a belief that this country will soon become "democratic" in the Western sense of that term. The period of Occupation is still too short to have brought about such a fundamental change. Even if the soil were suitable democracy could not have been so quickly transplanted. And it has not been suitable. Foreign occupation and scarcity can lead to the uprooting of democracy before it has had a chance to live.

Institutions can foster but cannot create the spiritual foundations of true democracy. Germans look back with little pleasure to their own experiences in this form of government. The Reichstag before 1933 had become a kind of "talking shop." The violent criticisms of "decadent" Western democracy by the Nazis were accepted by those of the older generation who were tired of what they saw going on around them. The younger generation, which knew only the Nazi dogma, has been influenced by Goebbels clichés more profoundly than we care to admit.

Today the average German sees democracy as the refuge of a conquered people, a system decreed by the occupying powers. Gradually Germans are more and more coming to say that they see around them the same bureaucracy applying the same regulations as before 1945. This leads subconsciously to a vindication of what the Nazi regime did. Many Germans say that Hitler was:

> "A tyrant, but our masters then
> Were, at least, our countrymen."

It is often forgotten abroad that Germany never really gave parliamentary democracy a chance under normal conditions. Such experiments as were tried failed very largely because they were made under the shadow of national defeat. The Revolution of 1848 did not achieve democracy. The Germany which fought in two world wars was essentially that of Bismarck, and one of its early triumphs was the Battle of Königgrätz, in 1866, in the Austro-Prussian War. "The Gordian knot of the German situation cannot be unraveled by a friendly consent of the parties but must be cut with the sword," said Bismarck. Obviously justice and tolerance played little part in his conception of internal political development.

Some of the most honest and able Germans still reject the Western conception of democracy as unsuitable for their country. They maintain that in its present stage of political development Germany needs a system in which individual leadership can play a much greater part.

In addition many Germans are tired of hearing the very word democracy. "If you would only find a new word for the system you want us to adopt, perhaps we might be interested," a German professor said recently. This is understandable since the term has come to mean to the average German a justification of almost any action by the occupying powers, and the German Communists have used this term to cover all kinds of totalitarian activities.

At times every criticism made against the occupying powers ends in being a criticism of democracy. As they read of the dismantling of industrial plants, many German business-men would remark, "That's democracy. If we have more of it, we shall go over to bolshevism."

Actually this is probably the last thing that will happen. The Soviets, by their actions in Germany and Eastern Europe since 1945, have lost their chance. Soviet policy has made it transparently clear that its aim is to extend totalitarian imperialism directed from the Politburo. This does not, however, preclude the possibility of German-Soviet cooperation under certain conditions.

As for the future German system of government, it will probably be based upon a fusion of ideas from West and East, with emphasis upon the benefits of order and organization. Private enterprise will probably not receive the deference given to it in the American system. The German is more likely to embrace some form of radical socialism.

In 1933 a substantial number of Germans believed that Hitler was taking over dictatorial power to deal with a crisis their parliamentary democracy could not solve. They did not believe it was for the purpose of imposing his ideology. The majority of them considered Hitlerism too irrational to be taken seriously. The failure of the Weimar system, largely because influential sections of the population were determined to make it unworkable, gave Hitler his chance. It is still too early to tell whether the Germans have learned one of the basic arguments for democracy—that only the wearer knows where the shoe pinches.

Germany has not yet found a political rhythm which suits her. The belief that Western Germany is on its way to democracy simply because certain parliamentary institutions have been created is naïve. A future Führer could "democratically" remove the safeguards in the Bonn Constitution which theoretically prevent his seizing absolute power. Can anybody imagine that the occupying powers would again take over complete control of Germany in order to prevent it? This could not be done even today without great opposition here and at home, still less in a few years' time.

The difficulty in attempting to interpret postwar thinking in Germany lies in the fact that the great upheaval of the years 1933 to 1945 split the nation from top to bottom. In addition, the entry of millions of Germans from territory now occupied by Poles, and of *Volksdeutsche* from Central and East Europe, has also created a situation in which further unpredictable influences will react upon German life.

The majority of young Germans have known practically nothing except Hitlerism and the war. Their views about what was wrong with nazism are confused. They bitterly resent the fact that their teeth should be so much set on edge by the sour grapes which their fathers have eaten. At the same time the majority would probably not completely accept the opinion that the twelve years of the Third Reich were nothing more than an epoch of madness in German history. Some still look back with pleasure on their years of comradeship in the Hitler Youth Movement and their *Fronterlebnis* in the war. The majority are disillusioned and bewildered about what has happened. Thrust into adulthood through exceptional emotional strain and bitter disappointment, the younger generation seems to regard developments at home with inner alienation rather than with real interest. They are looking for peace and security but are suspicious of foreign remedies.

The dilemma of many students of the new era is that which Hartmann, the young *Luftwaffe* officer, presents to General Harrass in a popular postwar German play by Carl Zuckmayer. "In the *Ordensburg* [the special Nazi training institution for the future elite] they told us that we were crusaders of the new era," Hartmann says. "The old, the Christian [era] had had its two thousand years. The new should be built according to our plans. A Reich of strength and majesty in this world. I believed all that. It inspired me. But how should there be something new, something strong and good, when it began with the unleashing of the lowest and the basest in mankind? How can we bear the new era when it opens with nothing but murder?" It is doubtful, however, that these same students would accept Harrass' reply: "New era—that is something which does not exist. Time—that is always the same. Great—unaffected. Without beginning and end. Where, however, a man is renewed—there a world will be newly created."

Although the vast majority of students are concerned mainly with qualifying for their future jobs, it would be idle to deny that chauvinistic tendencies have shown themselves among certain groups in some universities. Every incident is unfortunately seized upon by some observers as conclusive evidence of a widespread chauvinism, even if it is due to only a small rowdy element. Anti-Semitism is not dead among those students who consider themselves the heirs of the former aristocratic student corps, nor is the feeling that a national resurrection must follow the old chauvinistic lines. Some seem to long for a Führer in whom are "the roots of our world," as Baldur von Schirach once wrote.

Too often during the Occupation it has seemed that many well-intentioned educational advisers from abroad have expected the impossible of German youth, especially the students. "They have no clear conception of a life purpose. There is spiritual confusion," a prominent United States educator told me some time ago. He had not noticed a similar condition among the academic youth of the United States and Britain. The utter intellectual chaos of army life following the Hitler Youth period makes concentration upon higher issues almost impossible for the majority of students today.

The last great period of university history in Germany was begun when the new model University of Berlin was opened a century and a half ago. Reform is certainly necessary today, but it should be a grafting of new life on the old. It is essential because Germany will have to rely more and more upon her universities for leadership.

If we look at literature and the arts, there is little which can help to form a conclusive judgment on basic trends in German thought. The creative arts must always depend upon spiritual forces in the social environment, and German society is still uprooted. The bourgeoisie as it existed in 1933 is dead. It will probably be resurrected but in a modified form, depending upon the new economic changes.

Much has been written by the Germans themselves about the problem of Germany, but it is inconclusive. During the first two years after the collapse there was a surfeit of explanations in the press. Some writers condemned the German weakness for blaming others for what had happened. They pointed out the danger of becoming pharisaic through concentrating on the mistakes made by the occupying powers. They also pointed out how much of Germany's economic recovery is the result of outside help for which the Germans themselves are paying very little.

But as long as control of the press was in the hands of the occupying powers no true idea of what the Germans were actually thinking was possible. Even today, when editors and writers have almost complete freedom of expression, observers are only looking "through a glass darkly."

There was a great hunger for any kind of printed matter at the end of the war. The shortage of newsprint, however, restricted the output of books and newspapers. Preference was given to translations of many works considered valuable from the viewpoint of their democratic influence. Many German writers who might have given a clearer insight into the thinking of their people were prevented from doing so because of their former connections with the Nazi regime.

A number of memoirs and diaries dealing with the revolt of July 20, 1944, have appeared, but there is no evidence in any of them of a properly organized or a well-directed resistance against the Hitler regime. In some cases the reader is left with the impression that if only some of these authors had been given positions in the later Nazi period they would not have been in the revolt at all.

Few novels or poems of outstanding value have been written by German authors at home. The younger generation describe only their wartime experiences, and there is little demand for such books today. The civilian population had its war at home too and is uninterested in mere descriptions of horrors and sufferings.

The outstanding works have been written by German émigrés. Chief among them has been the Zuckmayer play already mentioned, *Des Teufels General,* the story of General-of-the-Fliers Ernst Udet, which gives one of the best descriptions of German reaction to Hitlerism.

Basic new trends in German literature have not yet appeared. Cultural rebirth, according to some observers, will require a re-forming of the language of German writers. It was deformed and devalued by the Nazis, and some critics say that even the language of Goethe and Schiller can express only a part of the reality of the recent catastrophe.

Writers like Ernst Juenger still appeal strongly to some Germans. It is doubtful, however, whether they can inspire the next generation to higher aims. As one critic of Juenger's new book *Heliopolis* wrote recently: "We have learnt that the world is not an ideal place. But we wish to strive for the possible. Here Juenger cannot help us, since all he has to offer is a flight from reality."

In the summer of 1945 it seemed easy to draw final conclusions about the Germans and to know how to "treat them." Today foreign observers are admitting that it is essential to appreciate more fully the historical background of the *Weltanschauung* which led to 1933 and 1945.

In addition, it is often forgotten now that Hitler's confidence in January 1933 was based upon the assured support of the industrial and financial interests of the Ruhr-Rhineland. Without it he would never have dared to introduce so quickly the terrorist campaign which was to give the Nazis complete control of their country. This fact is especially significant in connection with the future ownership of the great Ruhr-Rhineland industrial area. Already there are indications that many American business experts would be prepared to solve this problem solely on the basis of efficiency without giving much thought to its social implications. The interests of peace and progress demand that preconceived notions about private enterprise and socialization shall not be the determining factors.

The Western military governments have already done much to aid recovery in their zones of Occupation, but still more remains to be done. Whether the Germans will have the patience to work out their own future in a rational way remains to be seen. Their present political, economic, and cultural leaders lack experience in self-government and will soon be faced with tremendous problems.

We are going to be seriously disappointed if we expect the Germans to behave more rationally and more prudently than we ourselves. There will be upheavals which will be the despair of even their best friends. The new nationalism which has already awakened has yet to produce leaders who can show real statesmanship in setting their country on the road to healthy co-operation with the rest of the world. National prestige will demand that the Occupation (even in its present supervisory capacity) cease, the whole country be politically unified once more, and the Oder-Neisse frontier be revised. German statesmen will seek to evolve an international policy which aims at benefiting from Germany's geographical position between West and East. They will probably try to find a compromise with the Soviet Union. This is understandable. Everything will depend, however, upon how this is reached. The attempts hitherto made by some groups of Germans show more regard for expediency than for the basic principles of democracy.

The old idea so prevalent in 1945 and 1946 that a war between the Western democracies and the U.S.S.R. could only redound to Germany's benefit is dead. In its place some groups, like the "Nauheim Circle," would seek to make Germany a neutralizing factor between West and East. But it is difficult to see how such an idea can be effective until Germany is strong enough to become the arbiter between these two opposing sides—if she ever is. In these days of marked ideological cleavages, inside this country as well as out, the result might well be either civil war or some form of totalitarian dictatorship.

The Western powers cannot give Germany more than a start on the road to material and cultural recovery. How quickly advances will be made no one can judge. All we can hope is that no German statesman of the future will have to repeat Gustav Stresemann's words, in April 1929 (to a British journalist): "Well, nothing remains now but brute force. The future is in the hands of the new generation. And the youth of Germany which we might have won for peace, and for the new Europe, we both have lost. . . ."

Chapter V

Education——For What?

By ROBERT LEWISON

ARLY in 1950, after five years of trying to reshape Germany's schools into democratic instruments, American officials in Germany summed up their problems
in a confidential report to the State Department in the following words:

"For generations the schools and universities of Germany
have been a breeding ground of nationalism. Glorification of
the state rather than the free development of the individual
has been a major goal of the education system. Despite the reforms enacted in the days of the Weimar Republic and since
the fall of Hitler, nationalism, authoritarianism, and tradi-
tionalism pervade the German school system. . . .

"Thus far, German politicians, educators, and others with
influence in the field of education have been able to resist
basic school reforms . . . Despite the strongest kind of
pressure from U. S. officials, the entire school reform program is dragging its feet."

This private admission by the United States Military Government, and by its successor organization the United States
High Commission for Germany, indicates failure in a task
perhaps more important than any other undertaken by the
Allied Occupation of Germany, the task of educating a new

generation of Germans in a new way. Unless redressed rapidly, it is a failure of which the democratic world will hear much more in decades yet to come, as the well-scrubbed, well-disciplined youngsters now sitting, good as gold, on school benches throughout Germany emerge as adults to take over the job of running Europe's most powerful industrial nation.

To see what Germany's new generation is like, and how it is being educated, the writer visited numerous German classrooms and talked with students, teachers, and Allied educators in all three Western zones of Germany. The dominant impressions with which I returned were these:

1. Nationalistic ideas are being taught openly in Germany's schools. Nazi schoolteachers, once ousted, have been returned to their jobs. At least six out of ten German youths are being taught by former Nazis. Others have non-Nazi teachers who are scarcely less nationalistic. There is a growing danger that Germany's new generation will be educated much like the generation that backed Hitler.

2. As after World War I, hatred for the Allies is being encouraged among West Germany's eight million students. Resentment of Allied "injustices" is being built up. The generation that will supply Germany's future leaders is being taught to blame all of Germany's difficulties on other countries rather than on the Nazis who led Germans into aggressive war.

3. A widespread belief that nazism was not a bad idea but a good idea badly carried out is being reinforced among older students, many of who were indoctrinated thoroughly during the Nazi period. The same thought is being siphoned into the minds of school children under fifteen, three-fourths of whom escaped membership in Nazi youth organizations.

4. Once again the new generation is being taught that

Germany must struggle to regain lost populations, lost territories, and added *Lebensraum,* the three nationalistic desires that brought Hitler the most support in his rise to power.

Some observers feel that the revival of nationalism is only natural in a defeated country under a military occupation. Others argue that Germans cannot learn democracy under Allied controls which by their very nature are undemocratic.

It is evident that the Western powers cannot withdraw so long as there are Russian troops in Germany. But apart from this, some Germans feel that their chances for survival would be slim if the Allies were to leave now. Genuinely democratic Germans are still a small minority in Germany. They could be overwhelmed quickly.

Communists have been losing strength steadily in West Germany since the day the Russians started their blockade of Berlin. In the general election of August 1949 the Communists polled only 5.7 per cent of the vote. But nationalist elements seem to be gaining strength even more rapidly than Communists are losing it.

The Allies are going ahead in the belief that Germans eventually will accept democratic principles after practicing them under Allied supervision. But the re-education of Germans for democracy seems to be losing rather than gaining ground.

Nazi thinking in Germany is returning to the schools through the influence of the older generation. The transmission belt is made up of parents as well as teachers. The ideas taught in the schools are held by a majority of German adults. These nationalistic ideas were widely held before the Nazis' rise to power in 1933, and they have not been abandoned since 1945. Nationalism was submerged until recently by more pressing concerns over food and shelter and by fear of Allied punitive measures. Economic recovery and the softening of Allied policy in Germany have cleared the way for the old ideas to come out from underground.

Germany's political leaders of all parties are appealing more and more to nationalist instincts in their search for votes. Their appeals are further reinforcing the grip of nationalism on the German mind. Several new political parties with neo-Nazi programs came out into the open in 1949. The two smaller of the three parties that constitute the Bonn Government coalition are dominated by ultra-nationalists of a neo-Nazi type.

Despite Allied reprimands German newspapers are turning increasingly to nationalistic themes. Banned pamphlets are reappearing surreptitiously. A crack-down has even had to be enforced on the German-language newspaper published as the official organ of United States Military Government; it was found that German staff members were slipping old familiar propaganda into news and editorial columns.

Authoritarian ideas are coming into the open alongside the revival of nationalism. Undemocratic practices by Germany's state governments are being defended more and more openly in the face of Allied demands for change. Many Germans are saying that they prefer their own kind of "efficiency" and "order" to Allied ideas of democracy. Reform measures are being resisted bitterly or sabotaged after enactment. Democratic guarantees in state constitutions are openly violated.

German police in the American Zone make four out of five house searches without the search warrants required by law. Discriminatory taxes on newspapers, which courts in the United States hold contrary to freedom of the press, are upheld by German courts in the face of constitutional guarantees. Legislative committees in many German states continue to do their business in secret instead of in the open as prescribed.

Land-reform laws, enacted by German states at American insistence, largely have been ignored, although the laws are on the books. German legislatures have refused to pass civil service reforms. Military Government was forced to issue its own law in an effort to eliminate a "caste system" and take the civil service out of politics, but the law is not being carried out by German state governments.

Developments of this kind are convincing American officials that it will take a long time to make democrats out of German adults. But plans to educate a new generation along different lines also are running into snags.

One difficulty is that the Allies cannot educate German youth directly. The United States, Britain, and France are forced to rely on some hundred thousand German teachers to do the educating for them. Germany's teachers are no more democratic-minded than other Germans. In some ways they are even less so. In fact their percentage of membership in the Nazi party was more than three times that of the population as a whole.

Germany's teachers are products of a caste system in education. This caste system preceded Hitler's rise to power and helped pave the way for the Nazis. It still obtains in most of West Germany's schools. It separates an "elite" from the common folk at the age of ten and determines, at this early age, the position most Germans are to hold later in life.

The "elite," about 12 per cent of the ten-year-olds, are selected largely on the basis of their families' wealth and social position. They are sent to expensive schools for eight or nine years and then a fourth of them go to universities. Secondary schools and universities are financed entirely from public funds, but they charge steep tuitions. Here the "elite" are trained for the professions, for government, and for positions of leadership generally in Germany.

The other 88 per cent of Germany's children are limited to

four more years of elementary schooling of an inferior quality. At the age of fourteen they are apprenticed for vocational training. They are taught to be unquestioning followers.

This system of education is one reason German youths very frequently follow in their fathers' footsteps, with the sons of miners becoming miners, officials' sons officials. It has helped to keep German society a warren of layers and strata much as it was in the Middle Ages, a society based primarily on order and discipline in which everyone is supposed to know and keep his place.

As members of the elite, Germany's teachers are among the most stalwart defenders of this kind of society and of the educational system that helps to maintain it. Most of them prefer an educational system that turns out what Germans call "bicyclists," people who bend their backs to those above them and step hard on those below, and which produces youths who feel uncomfortable and confused if they don't find a leader.

When the Allies ousted Nazis from the schools in 1945 they eliminated about 70 per cent of Germany's teachers. Some teachers had joined the Nazi party early, preferring Hitler's promises of "law and order" to the unsettling effects of freedom. Others had climbed on the bandwagon later. As educated men in small communities, many rose to dominant positions in local Nazi hierarchies. Germans say that as a group few Nazis were more fanatical than the schoolteachers.

In 1945, however, the Allies, were confronted with a shortage of teachers. New ones could not be trained overnight. The French made a beginning, revising thoroughly the methods of teacher selection and training, but in the American Zone few teachers are being trained, and even those few are selected and taught by other Germans much as before. The shortage of teachers in all zones has been "solved" by taking back the Nazis.

Two Allied amnesties for "little" Nazis enabled some Nazi teachers to return to their classes. A somewhat larger number of "bigger" Nazis then were tried by denazification courts run by Germans under Allied directives, and most of the teachers in this group were fined small sums or reduced in pay grade, then sent back to the schools to teach.

In Hesse, in the American Zone, about 7,000 of the state's 10,000 elementary schoolteachers today are former Nazis. In Württemberg-Baden about 10,500 of the 18,000 teachers in the school system are listed as having been incriminated under the denazification laws. In some states, like Bavaria, the percentage is even higher. In others, like Bremen, it is lower. Over-all, in the three Western zones, at least 60 per cent of the teachers now at work are former Nazis.

Beyond this, a study by the French in their own zone indicated that many of the non-Nazi teachers are just as nationalist in outlook as the Nazis. Close observation of German teaching since 1945 has convinced French educators that some of the most reactionary teachers in their zone are those who stayed out of the National Socialist party because it was "socialist" as well as nationalist.

A number of German teachers in all German states are co-operating with Allied attempts to change Germany's school system, but the large majority are resisting fiercely, openly or behind the scenes. They are being supported in most places by the parents of their pupils and by the state officials who run the schools.

A typical reaction was that in Bavaria when American officials suggested that whipping be outlawed in elementary schools. "How can a school be run without whipping the disobedient?" German teachers asked in dismay, slapping their palms with the official wooden ferrule like cavalry officers with riding crops.

The Bavarian Minister of Education, a nationalist with an anti-Nazi record, led the opposition. He sent out questionnaires to parents to prove that whipping was popular. It was. A public-opinion poll taken by American officials verified his results. Two out of three parents in Bavaria favor whipping in the schools, and whipping continues.

Pupils are taught to learn by rote, to repeat their lessons after the teacher. Classes are centered on the teacher or on the subject, rarely on the child.

An Allied educator who studied German schools before the war visited four hundred classes before he heard a pupil ask a question. Then the question was something like "May I leave the room?" The same approach is still in vogue.

I asked several German school principals, one of whom recently had visited schools in England, what they thought of the idea of "teaching the child instead of the subject." Their answers all were the same: "German mentality is different," they said. "We have no time for such methods. German pupils must work hard to learn their subjects and pass their examinations." The school principal who had visited England added, "After all, England is a rich country. They have colonies. We are being kept poor by the Allies."

When a visitor enters a German classroom the children usually jump to attention, stiff as soldiers. There are no smiles, no giggles. At a command, they sit down. When a German child passes his teacher on the street, he tips his hat in a gesture that Allied psychologists feel is closely related to the soldier's salute to his officer. "The trouble with our schools," one democratic German educator told me, "is that they resemble barracks, both in discipline and in the relation between teacher and pupil."

"It is not a question of teaching politeness or respect for

elders," an Allied educator said. "These attitudes can be taught in other ways. I would a thousand times rather see American children with their spitballs, note passing, and whispering. At least they are developing as individuals."

Courses of study in German schools are organized to produce narrow specialists. Few students get the general education needed to understand the modern world. Elementary and vocational schools turn out skilled carpenters and mechanics. Secondary schools and universities turn out legal experts and trained engineers. Few German schools attempt to educate the "whole man" for citizenship in a democratic society. German youth get little or no education in the basic elements of social living or of international understanding and co-operation. Attempts by the Allies to introduce courses in the social sciences, such as politics, economics, and sociology, have been resisted by German educators at all levels.

"We have practically given up trying to change the German university," said one American educator. "It is hopeless."

The French have had the same experience in their zone. Their answer has been to open a new German university at Mainz, now the third largest in Germany. They have brought in a substantial number of professors and students from other European countries to leaven the thinking of the university's Germans.

Secondary and elementary schools in all zones are under Allied pressure to introduce a course in social science similar to high-school citizenship courses in the United States. But most German schools have yet to comply. They prefer to compel nine years of Latin study and seven years of Greek, to "strengthen the mind."

"Most German teachers think of the mind as a muscle which can be strengthened by exercise," said an Allied educator. "They see no need for teaching that leads youngsters to understand their world and think for themselves."

Even when civics courses are introduced, the results are not always favorable. "Most of the civics teachers in my school are former Nazis," said a teacher in a Frankfurt secondary school. "When the students come to my class in German literature, their comments show that they are learning little about democracy. On occasional social evenings, after a few beers, many of the older ones complain about the dullness of life. They talk nostalgically of the exciting days when they were in the *Wehrmacht*. They are yearning after a new adventure, more successful than the last."

New textbooks have been published by all the Allies in an effort to eliminate racist, militarist, and nationalist doctrines in German schools. German teachers have no objections to new texts in science or to new arithmetic books which substitute apples for guns in addition exercises. But they find many excuses to avoid the use of books that challenge traditional social thinking.

Allied experience with history books is typical. When they entered Germany the Allies found that not only Nazi histories but those published before 1933 could not be used. German history books played up battles, idealized autocrats, and colored historical events from the viewpoint of German nationalism as far back as Caesar's time. One leader of a primitive German tribe, for example, was treated in most books as though he were the monarch of a united Germany more civilized and more powerful than the Roman Empire. Actually he was a minor Roman puppet. At the same time Germany's strivings toward democracy, such as the Revolution of 1848, were usually ignored.

These history books and 80 per cent of other German texts were ground into pulp and converted into writing pads for school use. Replacing them, however, turned out to be more difficult. German historians were urged to write new books, but all those submitted turned out to be just as bad or worse.

The French brought in German-language history books used in Swiss public schools. They spent scarce dollars to buy publishing rights from a New York publisher for a series of history books written by German scholars in exile. The largest printing house in the French Zone was put on a twenty-four-hour schedule to bring out these and other textbooks.

At first German teachers sabotaged the plan by "forgetting" to distribute the new history books. One teacher claimed he was lecturing out of a new book. But he said he was afraid the students wouldn't listen closely if they had the book themselves. Today the books are well distributed, and the French believe that German youngsters are reading them. But there is evidence that many teachers are ignoring the new approach to history in their lectures.

Two high-school principals whom I interviewed in the French Zone admitted that their history teachers made no use of the new books at all. They write their lectures from books in their private libraries, books usually barred from the schools by the Allies. Outlines of these lectures are mimeographed for the students, who are encouraged to use the outlines instead of the approved books. "We take our lectures and outlines from the same book I used in school," one teacher said. "We can't use the new books. They are not adapted to the German mentality. There is too much discussion of ideas, not enough dates. Anyway, we don't feel that the new books are objective."

The same technique of lectures and outlines is used by most history teachers in the United States Zone, but with more excuse. No history textbooks at all have been published there. American educators are having new books prepared by German scholars and teacher committees, a lengthy process. They hope that these books, when ready, will gain more general acceptance then those in the French Zone. But they are not sure that this will happen.

"We can only wait and see," said one German educator who is working on the project. "We tried this before and it didn't work. After the First World War the Weimar Republic prepared new history books, which were not as nationalistic as the books in use before. But many teachers taught their pupils from outlines taken from books of the Kaiser's time."

When new textbooks actually are used, German teachers can manage to do interesting things with them. In one classroom the teacher proudly showed a wall exhibit made up by her pupils to illustrate a story they were reading. The story itself was a simple tale of a boy's wanderings in the countryside. But the exhibit had nothing to do directly with the story. It had to do with the author's birthplace, which by chance, it seemed, happened to be East Prussia.

The father of one of the children, a German refugee from East Prussia, had provided all the photographs and prints. They showed scenes of cities like Königsberg and Danzig, which are now, with American and British agreement, part of Russia and Poland respectively. Asked what she told her students about East Prussia, the teacher replied, "Why, the usual things. I tell them this is German land, which must come back to Germany because Germany needs more *Lebensraum*. I tell them that many Germans were driven out of East Prussia and want to go home. I tell them about the suffering of the Germans who remain in East Prussia now."

That teacher was not an ex-Nazi. Her record, in fact, showed some resistance to the Nazi attack on the Catholic Church. She had once spent a few days in a Gestapo jail. She had no idea that anyone could consider anything wrong with her wall exhibit. She showed it with pride. She had merely forgotten, as most Germans have, that Hitler's effort to regain Danzig was the immediate spark that set off World War II.

Despite conscious and unconscious sabotage by German teachers, Allied educators are convinced that new textbooks are vital. Destruction of old books has left a vacuum that new books must fill. The new books give pro-democratic teachers a useful tool. There is evidence, too, that they put questions into the minds of students whose teachers are not democratically inclined. That is one reason such teachers try to get around the use of the new books.

The United States is lagging far behind the other Allies in the textbook field. In 1947 a study showed that for each 100 school children in their zones, the French had published 800 textbooks, the Russians 700, the British 400, and the United States only 150. The American Zone was still last in 1949, with 700 textbooks per 100 students, compared with 1,300 in the French Zone, which led the rest.

American efforts to catch up have been hampered primarily by a shortage of funds for education in Germany. This fund shortage has crippled seriously not only the textbook program but the entire American effort to educate a new generation of Germans as democrats.

American policy in Germany, until recently, has given education one of the lowest priorities among Occupation tasks. United States appropriations for "prevention of disease and unrest" in Germany for 1947, 1948, and January to June 1949 were: $1,009,819,691 for food; $113,541,468 for agricultural supplies; $66,625,760 for petroleum, oil lubricants; $58,018,875 for pay of civilians; $176,690,937 for transportation of goods; $2,172,909 for travel; $5,279,228 for incidental operating expenses; and $17,597,756 for "reorientation and education." On the other hand, the French have given education one of the highest priorities. American educators are now trying to overtake the French, but they still have too few resources.

United States policy in Germany has concentrated on revival of Germany's economy. A secondary policy has been the construction of governments with democratic constitutions and free elections. French policy has concentrated first on developing Germans who could be trusted.

"What good is a democratic structure built with Nazi bricks?" a high French official asked. "If Hitler were to come back to life today, he would walk away with a free election. We first must educate a new generation of Germans that would laugh at a Hitler and insist on governing itself in a democratic way."

In their zone the French in mid-1949 employed 560 French educators for the supervision of German schools. There are 800,000 students in the French Zone. The United States, with 3,000,000 German students to educate, employed 140 American educators. This means that the United States employed one educator for every 20,000 German students, while the French employed fourteen. And the United States staff steadily is being reduced. By the spring of 1950, the number of American educators had been cut back to 82, or one for every 37,000 German students.

The United States today is spending about $8,000,000 a year on education and reorientation in Germany, including all varieties of cultural relations and exchanges. This is about 1 per cent of the American Occupation budget.

Until 1948 education was not even given the status of a division in Military Government; it was lumped together with miscellaneous activities such as roads and communications. Protest resignations by some of the most talented American educators helped bring about a change and a separate division was set up for education activities in 1949. The Superintendent of Education for the state of Connecticut was brought to Germany to direct the program. The education budget was enlarged and the staff increased. But the total effort was still ridiculously small. The new Director of Education had a staff of 150 in Connecticut, as compared with 140 to supervise the education of an area with ten times the population of Connecticut, not to mention a background of miseducation. And later in 1949, the trend was reversed again. The arrival of a civilian High Commissioner, John J. McCloy, to replace the American Military Governor, General Lucius Clay, brought promises that education would play an even greater role in United States operations. On the contrary, one of McCloy's first moves was to divest education of its status as an independent division. Staff cuts of more than 40 per cent were ordered. Director of Education Alonzo Grace resigned quietly, too weary even to make a public protest.

With little staff of their own, American officials are forced to work almost entirely through German authorities. They can give support to such democratic Germans as they find. They can run occasional conferences and one-week "training" courses for a few German teachers. They can send a small number of German teachers to the United States for brief periods. But all in all their influence on German education is minute.

In reaching Germans on the city and county level United States educators must rely on American resident officers in each *Kreis,* or county, who have no background in education and have precisely 103 other functions to perform, ranging from intelligence work to approving marriage licenses for German war brides.

The French, in their zone, have smashed the caste system of teacher education. A large-scale program has been launched to produce teachers willing and able to educate

German youngsters as responsible and democratic citizens.

Sixteen boarding schools of high-school level have been set up to prepare students for seven new teacher-training colleges. Tuition and books as well as board and room are free at both the high schools and the colleges. Students are selected primarily on the basis of ability, but evidences of liberal orientation are also taken into account.

The schools are run by the German states, but they are supervised closely by the French. Half the pupils in these schools are selected from elementary-school graduates, who would otherwise have been apprenticed to a trade. Youngsters enter the special high schools at the age of fourteen and remain for four or five years, living away from home in a new kind of atmosphere. Upon graduation they get two years of college study in a similar environment, then two years of practice teaching. One out of five graduates of these special colleges is sent to a Swiss teachers college for a further year's study free of charge.

Classes at the high schools and the teachers colleges are kept small. Emphasis is put on discussion techniques of teaching instead of lectures. Discussion evenings are staged. These forums are often led by outstanding men from various walks of life, such as political leaders, trade-union officials, university professors, and businessmen.

There are now 3,400 students in the twenty-three teacher-training schools and colleges in the French Zone. This is more than twice the number of new teachers now being trained in the state of Hesse, which has a school system roughly the size of that in the French Zone.

Every fourth teacher trainee in the French Zone spent several weeks last summer in a free vacation camp in the Black Forest with an equal number of French, Swiss, Belgian, and other foreign students. International good will, instead of hatred, is being cultivated.

For each ten German teachers at the teacher-training schools, there is one French *lecteur,* or instructor, whose primary task is to teach the French language and literature. There is also a French *lecteur,* at least part-time, in almost every secondary school and college in the French Zone.

These *lecteurs* are young university graduates who have obtained their doctoral degrees. Many of them come from Alsace-Lorraine and other areas bordering Germany. All speak fluent German and are skilled in modern educational methods. The *lecteurs* submit a written report to the French High Commissioner every six months. The reports mention no names, and the information is used carefully to keep from embarrassing the *lecteur's* relationship with his students and his German colleagues, but the education division of the French High Commissioner can keep close tabs on what is going on. Most important, the *lecteurs* organize cultural evenings, movie clubs, and hiking groups in their spare time. In classes they encourage free discussion and independent thinking. Once the students get a taste of this, they rebel against the discipline of their German instructors.

The twenty-three teacher-training schools and colleges contain two hundred German instructors. These teachers have been carefully selected to screen out former Nazis and present-day nationalists. The idea is that over a period of years the new schools will turn out enough new teachers to replace in large part the twelve thousand men and women now teaching in German elementary schools in the French Zone.

In other words, with the aid of less than 2 per cent of the teachers in their zone the French are creating a completely new corps of teachers for the future. One indication of the difficulty all the Allies face in re-educating Germans can be seen from the fact that even among the two hundred normal-school teachers, presumably the best 2 per cent, there are some who have been unable to break with traditional ideas. But the French say they are pleased over-all with the way the students are turning out.

At one teacher-training college the students recently got together and adopted a resolution criticizing some of the methods used at the schools. The teachers were incensed. The state minister of education immediately outlawed all student meetings. The students protested without avail, and the French had to intervene to get the order relaxed.

At another school, newly opened, a visiting French educator gave a talk to a group of German students and teachers on modern educational methods. Some of the teachers complained that discussion methods were encouraging the students to doubt what their teachers told them. They said they could not understand how this would help the students to learn their subjects. The Frenchman quoted a paragraph from a French teachers' manual: "The teacher will see the first evidence of his success when his pupils show that they are beginning to question what he has been telling them." The German teachers shook their heads sadly at this. But the students applauded enthusiastically.

"Some German youngsters are beginning to rebel against the traditional ideas of their elders," a French educator told me. "One of our most important jobs is to prevent them from being slapped down by their teachers and by reactionary government officials."

Though the French get the compliments of most other Allied educators in Germany, they themselves feel that they are only at the very beginning of what must be achieved. They point out that it will take fifteen years before the new teachers now being trained begin to predominate in the school system. As for German youth, under the French time-table it will be sometime in the mid-1960's before a new kind of German school graduate is turned out in any numbers.

What French educators fear most is the threat that their program will be interrupted before it can produce this final result. They know, from the resistance they have met, that the whole program would be wiped out if the Allied Occupation were ended.

Allied creation of a West German government is endangering a crucial part of the whole education program in West Germany, the school-reform laws. The Occupation Statute drafted by American, British, and French diplomats eliminated Allied authority to issue directives to German state governments in the educational field. Allied educators now are authorized only to "advise, observe, and assist." Actually this has been the practice for about three years in all three zones. But German officials previously were under pressure to take Allied "advice," knowing that otherwise a directive could force them to comply.

School-reform laws designed to eliminate the caste system in German education may never be enacted in most German states now that Allied directives are ruled out in this field. The new laws are intended to provide equal educational opportunities for all German youth. Compared with public education in the United States, only moderate changes in the German system have been asked.

The system requested by the Allies would give all German youngsters a common education for six years, instead of four as at present. It would then, when they were twelve, separate them according to vocational choice. But instead of only 12 per cent, it would send all children to a high school of one kind or other. All high schools would teach a similar core of general subjects, including the social sciences.

Academic high schools would provide six- or seven-year

courses leading to the university. Other high schools would provide three-year courses of compulsory education. No longer would there be two qualities of education after the age of ten, one for the elite and one for the followers. Instead, all children would get two "layers" of education, identical for all to the age of twelve and roughly similar to the age of fifteen.

Children who were not placed in academic high schools at the age of twelve would have an opportunity, now impossible, to cross over later and go to college anyway. Free tuition and books would be established at all secondary schools and colleges. Choice of students for college training would be made on the basis of ability rather than social status.

Although these reforms have been urged by the Allies for more than three years, only Bremen, the smallest of the eleven states in West Germany, has enacted them fully. The population of Bremen is about 1 per cent of the total in West Germany. Another state in the American Zone, Hesse, has instituted free tuition and books. Bavaria (American) and Schleswig-Holstein (British) have reduced tuition fees, looking toward their gradual elimination in several years. The other states, which contain more than 60 per cent of West Germany's school children, have taken no action at all, despite repeated prodding.

With one or two exceptions all the West German states have been considering school reform for two years or more. But the laws they have submitted for Allied approval have been designed to maintain rather than to eliminate the basic caste structure in the schools. These laws, with the exception of those in Bremen, have had to be rejected by the Allies. Bavaria's proposals have had to be rejected four times. In Hesse a law was not prepared until Military Government threatened to draft one itself.

Until recently Allied educators felt that they could wait

out this filibuster. They have set the principles for the new laws, but they have wanted the individual state governments to fill in the details themselves. Allied officials have been unwilling to issue their own laws. They have wanted education to be handled locally. Moreover, they have felt that Military Government or High Commission laws could not be enforced in this field.

As long as the military governors had the power to issue such laws, Allied educators felt reasonably sure that the German states eventually could be forced to act. Now that the Allies have relinquished this power, the odds are that the German filibuster will thwart real reform in most states.

In the opinion of Allied educators the threat to school reform is matched by another danger. Germany's older youths, who will provide the next generation of German leaders, have been educated largely in Nazi schools. Unlike some youngsters under twenty, who are rebelling against their elders, particularly in the French Zone, older students everywhere seem to be adopting their parents' ideas. Few are branching off in a democratic direction. Many German youths between the ages of twenty and thirty seem to be waiting for a new leader to appear. Others want to see which way the wind blows before making a political choice. Brought up in a one-party state, they find the conflict of political parties distasteful. No party permitted by the Allies appeals to them. They are in the market for a new party yet to appear.

To get one measure of the political leadership for which German youth is waiting, I went to one of the two teacher-training colleges in the state of Hesse, the Weilburg Pedagogical Institute. In a seminar room I talked around a long table with a score of students, men and women, ranging in age from twenty to twenty-eight.

Although tuition is free at this teachers college, the students were all members of the educational elite, since they were all graduates of Germany's traditional secondary schools. Typically, they were all opposed to school reform. Some of the students were familiar with the new ideas of education favored by the Allies, but it turned out that they themselves had few courses in social science. Neither political science nor economics was taught at their college. Nor were there courses in international relations. There was one course in sociology, but it was optional, and few students had time to attend, they said.

All the students said they favored discussion methods of teaching. But during three hours of "discussion" with this correspondent, no student ever took issue with another. Remarks made by professors in the course of the evening were not challenged. No one spoke without first raising his hand for the rector's permission. Most instruction at this college is given in lecture classes where no questions are asked by students.

As for political views: "We are not interested in political parties," said one young man. "We have been burned once."

"We're waiting for a party that will oppose all the other parties that are now doing so much talking," said a *Wehrmacht* veteran. "Or else a party that will combine all the parties into one."

One question stumped all the students at first. They said they had never thought about it before. The question: What was there about German education before 1933 that led a generation of Germans to follow Hitler?

It wasn't education that was at fault, said one student. The foreign bankers who financed Hitler brought the Nazis to power. How could the German people be blamed for backing Hitler, asked a second student, when foreign countries came to Germany for the 1936 Olympics and gave the Nazis the stamp of approval? A third student said Hitler came to power because there were too many political parties. A fourth blamed the depression.

"There were many good things about Hitler's program," said a woman student. "The things Hitler wanted were the things the German people wanted."

"We must not educate German youth to be pessimistic about Hitler," said another. "What if an honest Hitler should come along?"

They all insisted that the German people did not realize Hitler's rule would result in a disastrous war. Anyway, they said, Germans never were as enthusiastic about this war as they were during the First World War. "Even after the fall of Paris in 1940?" I asked.

"Well, wouldn't the French have cheered if they had captured Berlin?" one student countered. "Why should Germans be punished for that?"

"All countries are nationalistic," said another. "German nationalism is no different from that of any other country. It was nationalism that started the war. Other countries were jealous of Germany. Don't tell me the United States entered the war just to punish evils in Germany. The United States had economic objectives, to destroy German competition."

"We can see that now," said a young instructor. "The Allies are using the war as an excuse to steal Germany's factories for their own use. The Allies are trying to keep Germany down because they are afraid of German competition."

"We can't tell yet who was responsible for the war," said one of the older students. "It's too early. What the Allies tell us, we don't think is objective. I was just reading an article the other day that said Poland started the war. It was a very objective article."

"We are blamed for not speaking out against the Nazi

concentration camps," said a young girl. "But now the Russians are putting Germans in concentration camps. The Russians are holding a big part of German territory. East Prussia and Silesia are German lands."

"Yes," said a slender youth, "there is a lot of talk about a united Europe. But what good is a united Europe? It won't get us back our German territory in a hundred years. What's more, the Western powers are now taking the Ruhr and other sections of land away from Germany."

"Would German youth go to war to regain East Prussia and Silesia from the Russians?" I asked.

"I would fight tomorrow to free those lands," said one *Wehrmacht* veteran.

"What would you do if the Japanese had occupied half of the United States?" countered another.

A young woman hinted that Germany might turn to an alliance with Russia to regain lost territory. This is an idea, coming down from Bismarck, that is widely held by right-wing Germans as well as by the Communists. "Everybody knows," she continued, "that Germany could not exist in the small territory she now has. Germany must have more land."

After the discussion was over the youth who had said he would "fight tomorrow" received a few sharp words from the college rector. He came over, clicked his heels, bowed sharply from the waist, and apologized.

"I didn't really mean it," he said. "I fought in Russia. I would rather go into the Soviet Zone with a white flag in my hand than with a gun."

The rector, an astute professor who had selected the group for the evening's discussion but evidently not carefully enough, asked this correspondent to excuse the "slips" some of the youths made.

"You know," he said, "we Germans do not have a democratic tradition."

The ideas emerging in this discussion with students undoubtedly will be taught to German children next year when these students become primary-school teachers. They show some of the areas of thought in which Allied re-education evidently has had little effect.

The ideas of war, dictatorship, one-party state, and Hitlerism are by no means as repugnant to German youth as to the Allies. Among the nationalistic ideas which Hitler exploited before 1933 to win power, those of regaining lost territories, lost populations, and *Lebensraum,* have as much or more attractiveness to Germans today.

"Some people," said an Allied official who had studied this problem closely, "may be inclined to think the Allies are to blame for this revival of nationalism. It is easy to say now that we should not have detached German territory, or taken reparations, or that we should have made Germans prosperous sooner. But the real problem of German nationalism lies elsewhere. Germany never was as prosperous as she was when Hitler started the war. Germans then were easily aroused over such tiny bits of land as the Polish corridor and the Czech Sudetenland. There are more excuses now than then on which German nationalism can feed. But the real roots of German nationalism lie deeper, in the kind of education Germans get from their earliest childhood."

German attitudes generally, as reported by United States Intelligence agencies in Germany and by public-opinion polls, support the conclusion that Germans of all ages have made little progress toward democratic thinking. Some polls indicate that democratic ideas are losing ground.

An Allied Intelligence officer who has studied German attitudes since the war believes that one idea more than any other is the base on which most nationalistic attitudes are built, the idea that Germans were not responsible for the war. Polls at intervals since 1945 always have brought in similar results on this query.

Between 70 and 80 per cent of the Germans interviewed answer no when asked whether the German people as a whole are "responsible for the war because they let a government come to power which plunged the whole world into war?" Only 20 to 30 per cent of the Germans interviewed ever say yes.

The Intelligence officer believes that the dominant German thought pattern can be outlined as follows: "Other countries are more responsible than Germany for the war. Anyway, the German people gave over all authority to the Nazi leaders. Therefore the German people cannot be blamed for the war. As a result, it is unfair and unjust for the Allies to make the German people repair the damage done by German armies in other countries. The Allies are using this as an excuse to keep down the Germans, who they know are more efficient and more cultured than they are. But some day Germany will come back and show the world."

A study by Dr. Alonzo G. Grace, former director of education in the American Zone, emphasized that Germans generally have not yet lost "their reverence for guns and military glory."

"With generations of training and indoctrination in the nationalistic spirit," Dr. Grace said, "one would be fairly naïve to expect a people to change in the space of three years."

What this means was stated clearly by General Clay, toward the end of his tour of duty, in a talk to a closed meeting of United States educators in Germany. "We are knowingly restoring into German hands an industrial potential that is larger than any industrial potential in Europe," he said.

"There is no alternative. They must be given an opportunity to live.

"What they do with that potential depends on what is in their hearts and what is in their minds. On you lies the responsibility to see that their hearts and minds use it in the common good and not as it has been used in Germany so often in the past, for aggression. You are only now at the beginning of what you can accomplish in this field."

All in all, the assertion by General Clay that re-education of Germans was merely beginning, four years after the war, underlines two conclusions reached by most observers in Germany.

The first conclusion is that Germans will hardly become "democrats" without continued Allied supervision. The second is that Allied supervision will not make "democrats" out of Germans unless, over a long period of time, a vastly greater effort is made to educate a new generation along new lines.

Chapter VI

The German Guilt

By JOHN ANSPACHER

THE defeated Germany of 1945 presented a problem which history had never before faced. The war had left upon millions of individuals all over the world the imprint of a symbol, a political caste to which could be traced the responsibility for the war's havoc. To establish that responsibility, and to make it plain that the war and the inhumanities which accompanied it were to be considered criminal acts, it became necessary to root out and to punish those individuals and groups within the framework of the German society through whose efforts National Socialism had become the scourge of modern civilization.

Broadly speaking, the four-power Allied Control Council recognized this need in Directive No. 24, issued on January 12, 1946, calling for the removal and exclusion of National Socialists and militarists from public administration and other positions. In the ACC concept, "Everyone who is responsible shall be called to account . . . At the same time he shall be afforded opportunity to vindicate himself." The United States Military Government decided that the German people would share responsibility for carrying out the Law for Liberation, as it is popularly known, which had four objectives:

1. To provide just and effective procedures for judging every individual according to the degree of his responsibility for the wrongs committed by the Nazi regime.

2. To impose upon those found responsible definite sanctions designed to eliminate their influence in the community and to bar them from public office and positions of responsibility in important private undertakings.

3. To provide opportunities for rehabilitation through probation for lesser offenders.

4. To remove disqualifications from exonerated persons and from followers (nominal Nazis) who have paid their fines and against whom no employment sanctions have been invoked.

By far the most challenging aspect of this task was to determine the difference between offenders and major offenders, probationers and activists, followers and contributors. Captured records showed that there were thousands upon thousands of them. The sorting out, the searching out, and the early trials began almost immediately in each of the four zones of occupied Germany. The military governments themselves conducted the proceedings until sufficient German jurists could be cleared to do the job, and in all parts of the vanquished state the "little men," as they almost all professed themselves to be, began to move through the legal mills.

The police, whose own denazification had to be a top-priority project in 1945 to insure a modicum of public safety, saw to it that no one was overlooked. Germans streamed into the courtrooms. From their testimony and from evidence gathered by special investigators, there were found to be "major offenders," "offenders" (activists, militarists, and profiteers), "lesser offenders" (probationers), "followers," and "persons exonerated." The guilty were sentenced to prison terms, loss of civil rights, or expulsion from their chosen professions for varying periods of time. From the ranks of those cleared of major responsibility for the Nazi crimes came the petty officials who in one degree or another are now conducting the affairs of the several German *Laender,* or states.

One by one the Germans appeared in their home states before a court of their peers, to be charged with crimes against victims or opponents of National Socialism, treating foreign civilians or prisoners of war contrary to international law, committing excesses, plundering, giving "major" support to Nazi tyranny, participating in killings, tortures, etc. The courts reached into every imaginable social stratum and occupation; the baker, the butcher, the candlestick maker, the professor, and even Anton Lang, portrayer of Jesus in the Passion Play, all went through the final purge of justice. Some served prison sentences; others paid fines; others went about their business with a little slip of paper attesting to their "denazification."

Superimposed upon this painstaking process were three sets of relatively high-powered legal proceedings designed to establish and publicize, by trial and conviction, the Nazi criminals. In order of scope they were:

1. The International Military Tribunal, a combined Russian-American-Anglo-French court which heard the Allies' case against Nazidom's principals, the men who created the party's policies, guided the German ship of state through preparation for war and war itself, and determined the means of insuring the dictatorship's longevity.

2. The so-called subsequent proceedings against top-drawer Nazis who had been moving forces in the execution

of the party's policies. These trials were conducted at Nuremberg, based on a four-power agreement.

3. The American trials of common war criminals at Dachau, site of the notorious Nazi concentration camp. These were conducted by the Judge Advocate Division of the United States Army.

As the trials progressed, the Germans, like the Americans, began to tire of the incessant documentation of crimes, and they made loud and frequent protestations of their innocence. Thanks to American supervision of the German press, the newspapers were encouraged to give their readers as complete a treatment of the trials as space allowed. The German answer to these stories was the inevitable attitude of shocked surprise. Undoubtedly there were details of the conduct of the concentration camps which may have escaped their attention, but since so many of them claimed impressed service in the armed forces and so many others complained of their own treatment at the hands of the Nazis, it was hard to believe that the Nazi methods were entirely unknown.

The fallacy of feigned ignorance plus the far too recurrent sentiment about Hitler's program for the extermination of Jews—"a job he should have finished"—strengthened the impression among American authorities that the Germans as a people were far from guiltless. Such thinking can hardly be eradicated simply by legal process. It is even today among the deepest roots of the Occupation problem in Germany, despite efforts of military government over the past few years to minimize its consequences.

Political manifestations in recent months have revealed that even the best efforts of the American and German authorities have not been a guarantee against Nazi outcroppings. On at least two occasions only the intervention of an American military governor of a *Land,* or state, prevented the election to public office of men whose National Socialist principles were obvious. Yet the German denazification boards in those communities had "cleared" the individuals in question for public officeholding.

At the outset denazification determined only whether or not an individual had been a member of the Nazi party, and if so to what extent he had participated in its activities. These standards were considered high enough to sift out from among the German people those whose political background and professional qualifications warranted almost immediate assumption of low-echelon administrative functions.

Later, however, when denazification became a German rather than an American responsibility, the courts began to take judicial notice not only of the findings but of the evidence and arguments in the international war crimes trials at Nuremberg. By this time the crimes of the Nazis had been defined, and a German found to have been a member of the party automatically became suspected of participation in the party's malpractices as well.

United States Supreme Court Justice Robert H. Jackson drew the pattern of this malpractice when, as United States Chief Prosecutor, he opened the case before the International Military Tribunal in Nuremberg in November 1945. He charged the twenty-one defendants (and the two million Germans on the rolls of the seven Nazi organizations indicted at the same time) with conspiring to wage aggressive war; planning and waging that war; committing common-law crimes against prisoners protected by international covenant; and committing similar or worse crimes against civilians not at all involved in the military conduct of the war.

Jackson appeared, he told the court, not only as counsel for the Allied powers, but for the entire civilized world whose long-standing international agreements had been violated by

Germany's prosecution of an aggressive war. "The real complaining party at your bar," he submitted, "is Civilization. In all our countries, it is still a struggling and imperfect thing."

His reference was not only to the Kellogg-Briand Pact and the Hague Convention but also to the acknowledged Grotian concepts of international law and the irrefutable progress through the centuries of common law known to all nations. "When the law evolves by the case method," Jackson charged, "as did common law and as international law must if it is to advance at all, it advances at the expense of those who wrongly guessed the law and learned too late their error."

In support of this contention the court held that "the [London] Charter is not an arbitrary exercise of power on the part of the victorious nations . . . but it is the expression of international law existing at the time of its creation."

Under the terms of the charter the Allies had charged that Germany, having signed the Kellogg-Briand Pact of Paris in 1928, was bound by its provisions, which "condemn recourse to war for the solution of international controversies, and renounce it as an instrument of national policy in their relations with one another." Almost a year later, the tribunal held, in its judgment, that ". . . the solemn renunciation of war as an instrument of national policy necessarily involves the proposition that such a war is illegal in international law; and that those who plan and wage such a war . . . are committing a crime in so doing."

Counsel for the defense protested that the decision to wage the war, and responsibility for its planning, could be attributed to only one man: Adolf Hitler. The defense rested on the principle of the Führer's "oneness." His will, said counsel, was supreme and all else subordinated to it. But at least one witness, Hans Heinrich Lammers, head of the Reich Chancellery, weakened this position when he testified that "willingness to bear responsibility, aggressive energy, and real authority—these are the qualities which the Führer demanded first and foremost of his subordinated leaders."

In its opinion on this significant point the court held also that the Germans themselves had set a precedent for individual guilt at the Leipzig trials which followed the First World War. There a German court had convicted twelve Germans of war crimes perpetrated in the name of the state.

The responsibility for aggressive war was clear. Despite Hitler's supreme command over the Nazi party and its administrative functions in all of Germany, he was surrounded by men whose positions of real importance involved them in the guilt for violating known and agreed-to covenants for the maintenance of peace. But counsel for the defense went back over this same ground in its pleadings to the accompanying charges of crimes against prisoners of war and crimes against civilians. The defendants took the witness stand themselves to deny all responsibility. They claimed never to have heard of the wholesale murders, beatings, tortures, concentration camp gassings, genocidal eradication of whole communities, and the killings of surrendered Allied soldiers, which the prosecution specified. They greeted each new piece of evidence to support these charges with "incredible . . . shocking . . . unheard of."

It was a demonstration of a striking inability to share responsibility in collective guilt—but the documents in evidence proved themselves. They were dated, addressed, signed, and sealed with Berlin's stamp of officialdom. Denial of the deed was impossible. There was no question but that the crimes committed at home and abroad by the Nazi hordes were born first of National Socialist philosophy, second of the Nazis' aggressive war, and third of the national character of the Germans. One need only trace the development of the super-race theory from *Mein Kampf* down to the establishment of the SS "Race and Resettlement Office," under whose aegis members of the SS were encouraged to breed in and out of wedlock. The SS chief, Heinrich Himmler, boasted that "in twenty to thirty years we must be able to present the whole of Europe with its leading class. . . . We shall in twenty years push the national boundary 500 kilometers to the east."

This was no haphazard fury that was unleashed upon millions of defenseless souls who had been classified as "substandard." It was an obsession of long standing, a conviction that the German people were, are, and always will be far superior to any human race the world may ever create.

Having failed to establish "ignorance" of what had been going on in Germany, the defense pleaded that every crime perpetrated in the name of National Socialism was committed "under orders." Duress or resistance to these orders was never proved, but the accused protested that all of these crimes had been conceived and directed by higher authority, as part of national policy, and that they had been powerless to resist.

To this the court in its finding replied succinctly that the law does not protect a wrongdoer simply because he pleads he was acting in someone else's behalf. The agent of the state, said the court, is as responsible as the state itself for crimes of such magnitude.

Here was the key to concurrent and subsequent denazification proceedings. By due process of law the Nazi policies had been proved criminal, and a decision had been rendered making even lesser characters in the plot responsible for their crimes. German denazification tribunals have not always given due consideration to this judgment, but the weight of evidence pointing to the participation in, or cognizance of, the Nazis' crimes has strengthened the wide-spread conviction that the mass of the German people were guilty of criminal practice in world society.

The echeloned program of war crimes trials dropped one level after the completion of the international trial and in dropping broadened its scope. The subsequent phase was based on the London Agreement and Allied Control Council Law No. 10, organized by the Department of the Army and directed by Brigadier General Telford Taylor. It concerned itself with bringing to justice the evil managerial geniuses of the criminal policies adopted in Berlin, and with reading into the record of history the unbelievable accounts of horror, terror, and inhumanity which the Germans had managed to accumulate in the twelve years the Nazis were in power.

Probably the most striking aspect of these proceedings was the breadth of their indictments. They reached into the fields of medicine, law, agriculture, industry, science, journalism, finance, civil administration, diplomacy, and professional militarism. They left little doubt that the masses of Germans could not help having been affected by, or at least cognizant of, the heinous crimes being committed in their name. Damning evidence of malfeasance in these otherwise normal fields of social and economic endeavor in a modern nation was sufficient to brand the two hundred-odd accused in these trials as perhaps the larger criminals, in the common-law sense, although they were certainly much smaller fry in the Nazi party and government rolls than their predecessors in the International trial.

Such a cross-sectioning of German society was the beginning of the long road to complete "denazification," if such there would ever be. While the Germans consistently denied all knowledge of the concentration camps and of the Nazi "People's Courts" which sent victims there, it was extremely unlikely that the business practices of I. G. Farben, the world's largest chemical cartel, or of Krupp A. G., could possibly have been ignored. The fabulous Farben empire spread its tentacles into every portion of Germany's and the world's economic pie. Krupp enterprises, whose wealth put Hitler in power and whose industries rearmed the Reich, were just as extensive in their field. Farben and Krupp officials helped plan and wage wars of aggression, plunder and despoil the countries invaded by the *Wehrmacht,* exploit slave labor, and abuse prisoners of war. The evidence submitted in the trials of the twenty-four Farben executives and the twelve Krupp defendants provided undeniable proof to thousands of Germans, when they took the trouble to read even the skimpy newspaper accounts, that their entire society had been rotten to the core. Tens of thousands of their neighbors had been involved almost as deeply as the men in the dock at Nuremberg; they simply weren't big enough fish to be caught up in the War Crimes net. They were left to "denazification."

In his indictments General Taylor specified basically the same charges against his defendants that the four Allies had listed in their proceedings before the International Tribunal. Because of the strict hierarchy, however, little of the responsibility for aggressive war filtered down to the level of these defendants, with the exception of the case against the Nazi diplomats of the Wilhelmstrasse. In the other cases, the bulk of the evidence had to do with crimes against humanity and war crimes. The specifications of murder, torture, and inhumane treatment of prisoners of war and "captured" civilians were sufficient in most cases to send these men to their death or to prison terms.

When the trial of I. G. Farben directors and managers opened it became apparent almost immediately that the "aggressive war" charge was loaded with much more than its legal ramifications, especially in the light of recent changes on the international scene. The records of the cartel's affairs prior to and during the war revealed that unusual agreements had been made between Farben and business interests of similar scope in the Allied countries.

In influential circles at home the Farben charge sheets created considerably more unrest than had previous cases. The specification cited such firms as DuPont, Standard Oil, Agfa Ansco, and Bayer in America, and others in Allied nations, and it appeared from reports reaching Nuremberg that the executives of these firms were identified uncomfortably closely with the accused men in the war crimes dock. No concerted pressure was brought on the United States Government to dismiss the indictment, but the three justices appointed to hear the case were left in no doubt that American big businessmen took a dim view of aggressive war charges against industrialists anywhere, no matter what their politics.

Out of context such reaction might be of only passing interest and, under the circumstances, could be classed as exceptional. But the context, the state of international relations everywhere at the time, was an important factor in determining the intensity of this reaction.

This was the fall of 1947. The best-laid plans of Yalta and Potsdam were going awry. United Nations meetings had become harangues lasting for months. The spirit of trust and friendliness between the Soviets and the Americans had begun to weaken perceptibly, and much of the friction was arising from Germany. The finality of a West German government, the blockade and the counterblockade were yet to come, but the Allied Control Council in Berlin was finding it difficult to discover grounds for common agreement on many of its most pressing problems.

Naturally, such a turn of events encouraged the I-told-you-so factions to clamor for attention, especially in the recently isolationist United States. Both military and industrial circles in America began to "take the long view," and the government's policy on Germany was inevitably affected.

In a sense such an adverse reaction to war crimes trials was a natural phenomenon brought on by the trend of international affairs. It might have been avoided at Nuremberg by a faster-moving program, but current events caught up too fast. It was a serious factor, however, in the pursuance of America's original Occupation policy, of which denazification and the war crimes trials were cornerstones by inference.

At about the same time there was, of course, an accompanying shift in the American approach to decartelization and deindustrialization. Military and industrial interests in the United States began to look to Germany as a nation of possible strategic importance which could not remain a distressed area. Soviet activity east of the so-called iron curtain naturally strengthened such a view in the United States, and when the Farben indictment specified serious charges against top-flight German technicians and businessmen who had once been allied with their American counterparts in a commercial way, the interests at home were quick to show their discomfort.

In retrospect, and taking note of such incidents, for example, as the blatant but unsupported charge by a Michigan congressman that the chief prosecutor of the Farben case was a Communist, it is evident that the change in American opinion was simply a tip-off to what might be expected of United States policy with respect to denazification vis-a-vis the mounting East-West tension. A clear pattern of the change is available in a study of the decartelization program, including dismantling and reparations, but it was not without considerable effect on the war crimes program and denazification as well.

As a result there was some skepticism surrounding the "subsequent proceedings" at Nuremberg. In addition to the trials' longevity, which had begun to cost patience and money, American political attitudes toward Germany were shifting. The hard and fast approach to denazification began to weaken. It was not yet time for this change to take effect in the German denazification courts, but it became more evident in Nuremberg as the Farben proceedings gave way to those against Alfred Krupp von Bohlen und Halbach. Alfred and eleven of his codirectors of the Krupp steel combine appeared as defendants; the senior Krupp, old Gustav, was declared too ill to stand trial. Joseph E. Robinson, an American attorney, was granted permission to represent young Krupp. Although two earlier applicants had been denied, he became the first non-German attorney to speak for a Nuremberg defendant.

It is significant that no provision in either the London Agreement or the Allied Control Council law, under which the "subsequent proceedings" operated, forbade non-German attorneys to plead for the defense. Nor had there ever been any objection to the admission of German Nazi lawyers for the defense. In fact throughout the trials several of the defense counsel were under indictment in their home state denazification courts.

In the final trial on Taylor's program Robinson's precedent was followed by the appearance of Warren F. Magee, of Washington, as counsel for Baron Ernst von Weiszaecker, leading man in the case against the Nazi ministries. This case against the "gentlemen of the Wilhelmstrasse," Berlin's Pennsylvania Avenue, brought to trial twenty-one Nazi cabinet members, diplomats, and key economic officials of the Hitler government. They were charged with having applied the bizarre credos of National Socialism, including racial superiority and aggressive war, to such activities as governmental finance, agriculture, propaganda, and, of course, foreign affairs. Baron von Weiszaecker was probably the most prominent of Ribbentrop's state seecretaries. He was his deputy from 1938 to 1943, and German Ambassador to the Vatican until the end of the war.

It must be said that some of the attention paid by several influential friends of the former Ambassador to the Vatican was not construed by either the prosecution or the bench as interference. This was the first time that any outside party had injected itself into the prosecution of German war crimes to such a degree. It was an unmistakable sign that the prosecution of war crimes was becoming somewhat unpopular in certain circles. This attitude was hardly noticeable during the international trial, except in the case of an American admiral who sent encouraging notes to Raeder and Doenitz in the dock, but it grew to real proportions during the Farben, Flick, Krupp, and Weiszaecker cases.

By the time "subsequent proceedings" closed in April 1949 with eighteen convictions in the Weiszaecker case (including five for aggressive war), more than two million Germans had been affected by the high-powered legal machinery at Nuremberg.

But America's task was not yet done. Concurrently with the "subsequent proceedings" under General Taylor, the United States Army's Judge Advocate Division conducted the series of war crimes trials at Dachau, just a few miles west of Munich.

One of the principal aims of the entire denazification program was to impress upon the German people the collective guilt of the nation in supporting a criminal government for thirteen years. The legal proceedings had proved the Nazis' crime. The eighty million people of Germany who had, wittingly or not, accepted the Nazi government could not plead complete innocence. But according to General Clay, to prosecute the lowest form of Nazi war criminal at Dachau was to overshadow the impression of guilt with one of sacrifice and, in some instances, martyrdom. Toward the end, American criticism of the Dachau trials encouraged German sympathy for the defendants and for their ideology. To the German, Dachau was likely to become a hallmark of injustice instead of a symbol of Nazi criminality.

Unlike the proceedings at Nuremberg, these Dachau trials made no effort to pin the responsibility for aggressive war or its execution, or of crimes against humanity or war crimes, on the defendants. The American prosecution at Dachau indicted several hundred concentration camp guards, trusties, wardens, medical technicians, and Nazi ward bosses on the simple charge of murder. Their means of killing ranged from cold-blooded shooting of Allied prisoners of war, many of them disabled flyers who had bailed out of their aircraft, to the traditional rubber-hose beatings and pursuit of "escaping" prisoners, forcing them into high-voltage barbed-wire fences.

With one or two exceptions the Dachau proceedings became routine after the first two trials. The court was United States military; the prosecution was United States military; and for the most part so was the defense. The indictment of a German prince named Josiah von Waldeck und Pyrmont created a small stir in the German press, where his name at least was known, but only two of the trials achieved any prominence.

One was that of Ilse Koch, whose exploits as wife of the commandant of Buchenwald camp were documented by testimony concerning lampshades made of human skin. The account of her participation in the inhumanities practiced at Buchenwald was sufficient to convince most observers of her responsibility in the Nazi era of crime, but after she had been sentenced to life imprisonment, the American authorities stirred the embers of the case again by reducing her prison term to four years, most of which she had already served.

The Koch case raised a provocative question about the conduct of the war crimes trials in American public opinion. The United States Army's review of the judgment fostered a feeling that the evidence had been "stacked." There seemed to be no concrete, undeniable proof that Ilse had indulged in interior decoration of her Buchenwald home at the expense of human lives. The lampshades had been there, and medical testimony upheld the theory that the shades had been made of human skin. But there appeared to the reviewing authorities no hard and fast connection between these facts and Ilse Koch.

Violent reaction to the Army's decision to free Ilse Koch within a year had not even died down before another Dachau trial created a similar flood of comment, first on a principle of right, and then on the manner in which the prosecution was conducted.

Seventy-three German officers and soldiers were convicted, forty-three of them sentenced to death, for their part in the murder of American infantrymen who had surrendered at Malmedy during the Battle of the Ardennes Forest in 1944. A good many American veterans of combat wondered about such a finding—wondered whether the colonels and majors on the bench at Dachau had been completely oblivious of the tendency of American troops to dispose of prisoners of war by somewhat the same methods. There were never any specifications of American or Allied activities in support of this doubt, but thoughtful combat veterans and a certain faction of American public opinion reacted along just such lines to the final judgment at Dachau.

Far more significant, however, was the allegation by American critics that the prosecutors had intimidated witnesses and defendants prior to their trial to obtain confessions of guilt or damaging testimony which made such a finding almost a certainty. Investigations of pre-trial interrogations, they said, brought to light such practices as "mock trials" and solitary confinement.

One aspect of the proceedings, however, became a target for particular emphasis, tending to discredit the war crimes trials and the denazification program all over Germany. Elements of American public opinion began sharply to criticize the conduct of the prosecution by a small number of Americans whose citizenship dated back no further than ten years. This was part of the hue and cry raised against recently acquired citizenship throughout the entire Military Government establishment and was based on the loyalty scare in Administration circles as well as the revival of nationalism in Germany.

Critics of the Dachau trials selected as their specific targets the members of the prosecution teams who had emigrated from Germany before the war and who, it was charged, were biased in their conduct by a "vengeance" motive toward the Germans. The word "Communist" did not appear in these attacks, but the implication was that in the eyes of their critics at least, the loyalty of these refugees to American interests was "in doubt." The critics were not afraid that these refugees might be particularly "pro-Nazi"; they had fled Germany ostensibly because they were violently and outspokenly opposed to the regime. But the time had apparently come when *anti-Germanism,* in almost any form, was almost more suspect than pro-nazism.

At the same time, within Germany at least two political parties had achieved some prominence on the grounds of their admitted adherence to National Socialist principles. Encouraged by open chanting of nationalist anthems, they have catered successfully to the young postwar element in Germany which boasts that "if real free elections were to be held in Germany, 90 per cent of the electorate would favor a return to National Socialism." (United States Military Government Opinion Surveys Branch found in a poll taken in December 1945 that more than 50 per cent of the Germans questioned regarded National Socialism as a "good idea badly carried out." In January 1949, approximately the same results were obtained.)

Military Government now claims that these political movements are "under surveillance," but their continued existence, and perhaps increasing numerical strength, may well show denazification to have been a failure.

Ostensibly the leaders of some of these parties have been "denazified." So have Baumgartner and Loritz in Bavaria. But at one time or another each of them has been termed a potential dictator in his own political sphere by both his followers and his bitterest enemies.

Three former defendants at the international war crimes trial at Nuremberg, although acquitted there, have also been subjected to denazification proceedings by the Germans. Franz von Papen and Hans Fritsche are languishing in jail, but Hjalmar Schacht is living in northern Germany a free man. The courts convicted him first, but he won his appeal and has never been molested since, although one German denazification minister is anxious to confront him with "new evidence." Schacht is out of the jurisdiction of the interested German authorities, and no one, least of all Military Government, will expedite his extradition.

Military Government in the Western zones managed to squeeze out of most of the tight corners on denazification by claiming "no jurisdiction." Denazification became almost wholly a "German problem." Yet as Military Government proclaimed the virtual completion of the German denazification program, it became patently evident that men of Nazi or fascist sympathies were holding jobs within the several German state administrations. In the all-out drive to "rehabilitate" the country, for political and perhaps even military-strategic reasons, the Occupation authorities in all zones left the question of a man's ideological fitness for office up to the administrators who were faced with the monumental task of forming a government. These men were aware of the change in attitude toward Germany; they had seen the handwriting on the wall and acted accordingly. They were aware of the "loyalty check" within the United States Government, and they were quick to realize its significance.

This is not to predict a resurgence of nazism in Germany, neither encouraged nor admitted by the government established at Bonn. But the rules of the game have obviously been loosened considerably. British authorities have freely admitted that the coal and steel trustee boards would permit *"one or two members with a Nazi taint, but no more."* The fact of the matter is that almost all of the board members were prominent industrialists in the system of cartels which existed before and during the war.

Even at its best, denazification alone cannot stop that. The real fact is that the entire concept may well be considered hollow. It is simply a set of legal procedures imposed by the Allies to comply with the provisions of "unconditional surrender." As an ex post facto principle, established to do away with an accepted fact or to destroy a faith, denazification means little or nothing.

The German, like any nationalist, is hard to convince. He may pay the penalty of error imposed by the righteous (and victorious), but can such penance eradicate the faith? If one acknowledges the error of his ways and turns to another, perhaps ethically superior faith, all well and good. But the efforts of Military Government to provide that faith, in conjunction with the denazification program, have been pitifully inadequate. The branches of the Occupation administration concerned with education and information have been severely crippled by inadequate funds and personnel.

While there was no letup in respect to the policy of demilitarization, denazification was turned back to German supervision. With the end of the denazification program there was scant attention paid to the provision for a new faith. Reeducation was relegated to a lesser place in the economic revival of Germany. But the authorities have insisted until now that a legal procedure called denazification be applied to the German people, creating at best a vacuum in the national *Weltanschauung*. What have we done to convince them of anything but the criminality of nazism? The efforts of the Military Government to create a "true democratic spirit" have been overshadowed by the top-priority program of industrial rehabilitation which has casually overlooked the "Nazi taint" in hundreds of minor and too many major instances. Denazification, to all intents and purposes, is at an end, but it did not, because it could not, attain the goal set for it by the policy makers in Washington and at Potsdam in 1945.

Chapter VII

Freedom on the Auction Block

By RUSSELL JONES

THE uprooting of Nazi influence and militarism in German life is one of the major objectives of the American Occupation. This resolve was based on the unprecedented decision of the four major conquerors to punish all Germans who were in any way responsible for the rise of nazism or who in any way benefited through it. Not only were those in the driver's seat to be punished; the humblest party official and the pettiest civil servant who had taken part in the great conspiracy were to pay for the crimes committed in the name of the German people.

The entire success of the four-power control of Germany would have seemed to hinge on the ability of the victorious states to rid the defeated nation of its deeply fixed totalitarian impulse.

That was the reason the Allied Control Authority implemented its decision to cleanse Germany politically by promulgating a Law for the Liberation from National Socialism and Militarism, which established categories into which offenders were to be placed and the penalties to be exacted. There were to be four classes of chargeable crimes, the least severe of the punishments to consist of a fine or, in the case of civil servants, demotion or retirement. Those convicted in the higher categories were to be permanently barred from public service, either elective or appointive, and sentenced to jail.

What happened? The plain truth is that the denazification program, well intentioned though it may have been, is an almost complete failure; the German mental attitudes which made possible the acceptance of the Hitler philosophy still exist; the plan for weaning Germany into the paths of democracy and away from militarism has miscarried, and, in the opinion of most of us who have been on the spot, we are just where we started in 1945.

Perhaps this is just as well. It may be that the men who set the original course for the Occupation were too deeply affected by the passions of war and confused retribution with re-education. Perhaps it was political expediency to promise to punish all the guilty even when the promisers knew the program was unworkable. But whatever the cause, denazification as defined by law and as understood by those who fought the war against Hitlerism has not been carried out and probably never will be.

The American denazification chief of Hesse, one of the three states which make up the United States Zone, says flatly, "We are building democracy with Nazi bricks." Just how right he was is shown by figures compiled by American and German denazification experts. For a few examples: More than 50 per cent of the "high" and "higher"—top brackets of German civil service—officials in Hesse are former Nazis; 80 per cent of the Nazis originally ousted by the Americans from government positions in Bavaria have been reinstated; 60 per cent of the Bavarian judges and 76 per cent of the prosecutors were tried by denazification courts and now hold office; in Württemberg-Baden 20 per cent of all the city, township, and county officials served under the Nazis; 70 per cent of Bavaria's teachers were incriminated; and throughout the zone as a whole more than 50 per cent of private industry is estimated to be in the hands of former Hitlerites. These figures, shocking in themselves, take on added significance when it is recalled that membership in the Nazi party was awarded only to the most deserving and that party strength never exceeded four million.

Rheinhold Maier, now minister president of Württemberg-Baden, was a member of the Reichstag in 1933 when it voted to hand over the government to Hitler. He said at that time: "We feel ourselves as one with the views expressed by Hitler here today." Joseph Baumgartner, American-appointed minister of agriculture for Bavaria, repaid this mark of esteem by declaring at a secret meeting in 1948: "Today only third- and fourth-rate Americans are here in Germany. . . . Everywhere . . . the majority of important Americans consists of Freemasons and Jews." Baumgartner is now head of the *Bayernpartei,* probably the most rabidly nationalistic of all political groups.

Perhaps Maier has had a sincere and honest change of mind and heart since 1933, but it seems doubtful in the light of the fact that it was in Württemberg-Baden that a former Nazi campaigned for the mayoralty on an anti-Semitic platform and defeated his half-Jewish opponent by three to one. It was also in Maier's territory that a man who complained of the activities of some public servants in an American-sponsored town meeting was fined for his criticism.

And it was in Baumgartner's Bavaria that a man ran for public office—and won—while being held in an internment camp as a major Nazi offender. Another Bavarian got himself elected by charging his opponent, a *Spruchkammer* (denazification court) official, with being an "informer."

These are not isolated instances. The whole trend in Germany, among Germans on all economic and social levels, has been toward the individual and collective arrogance which made possible the acceptance of Hitler and the Nazis. A Military Government report released at the end of 1948 records how German attitudes swung from "exaggerated desperation" in 1947 to a "national egotism." The period covered by this report, incidentally, was that during which Western Germany made its astonishing economic recovery, engineered to a great degree by the Americans.

This report defined "national egotism" as "the overrating of its own interests, its own power, and its own material resources." It cites the instance of a former German officer who had been captured by the Americans and had been chosen to attend the United States Army's school for democracy: "They talked to me about democracy, and I kept my mouth shut in order to get home quickly. I'll show them what I think of their dirty democracy. What we need is a couple of SS divisions. They would have their own way of dealing with these swine [the occupying powers]."

In the years since the law of denazification was promulgated every survey and intelligence report I have examined shows high percentages of Germans who think National Socialism was a "good idea badly carried out" rather than a "bad idea." By early 1948 more than 55 per cent of those in the American Zone thought that, as well as more than 70 per cent in Bavaria. Concurrently more Nazis were returning to high government and business positions.

What happened? Are the Germans unteachable or did we go about it in the wrong way?

A good many Germans certainly are incapable of understanding or appreciating democracy, and our efforts at educating the rest have been, at best, a hit-or-miss proposition, with no clear idea of what things come first. One official, who asked to be unnamed because his thinking was no longer popular, explained it this way: "Only about 3 per cent of the people in Germany have popular-leadership qualities and believe in democracy. Perhaps another 17 per cent have the qualities but don't believe in democracy. The rest can be led either way. Obviously we should have taken the 3 per cent and backed them to the limit. As for the others, we should have made it impossible for them ever to hold office or positions where they could exert economic or political pressure. Our basic mistake was that we did a little of each but not enough of either."

The drive for economic recovery and for advantage in the cold war was too important to allow a political concept to interfere. The natural result was that democratic-minded Germans were blamed for the hard times immediately following the war while former Nazis, already benefiting from the nostalgia for the "good old prewar days," were on the rebound just in time to be credited with the industrial recovery which came to Western Germany in 1948.

Blame for the fiasco is not traceable solely to the men who considered economic recovery more important than political purification. Much of it must fall on those who in their hatred of the Hitler state and their desire to see that the guilty were punished burdened the denazification plan with unworkable details. Under the provisions of the Law for Liberation one out of every three or four Germans could expect to be tried. In Bavaria 1,500,000 out of 6,000,000 adults were charged, while in Hesse almost 900,000 out of 3,000,000 were "affected" or chargeable. This was a little too much to ask even of the Germans.

"The result," says one disillusioned American official, "was obvious. First we started out by trying everyone in sight; then, after the little fellows were convicted, the policy was modified so that the big fry got away. Now most people are tired of the whole unsavory business."

Official Military Government reports bear out this pessimistic view. One says: "The widespread conviction that the

Nazi return to power is inevitable is inhibiting potential witnesses against the majority offenders and intimidating *Spruchkammern* officials." Another is more frank: "A deep-rooted conviction that it is dangerous to testify against the formerly powerful Nazis has rendered prosecutors almost helpless."

The end of America's denazification program was the signal for a fresh wave of revulsion by the Germans against their fellow countrymen who had carried it out.

A cold boycott was applied to former *Spruchkammern* judges, prosecutors, and witnesses, barring them from jobs in the *Reichsbahn,* the federally operated post office, and even industry. German legislation making it mandatory to give employment preference to ex-denazification officials was ignored. A Bavarian newspaper, the *Süddeutsche Zeitung,* reported that it was easier for former "P.G.'s," *Partei-Genosse,* to find jobs without the help of the Labor Exchange than it was for ex-denazification officials with the aid of the Exchange. The situation became so dangerous that the director of Military Government for Bavaria, Murray D. Van Wagoner, felt obliged to issue a stern warning against the practice of dismissing non-Nazi government officials to make way for denazified civil servants.

The feeling of the general populace on the denazification program was expressed in the *Bayerische Bundeszeit.* After quoting General Clay to the effect that the German people were "not so much the supporters of Hitler, but his tools," the paper describes the purification policy as being "without a moral, juridical, or political basis . . . denazification was an act of self-righteousness of the victor and his demands for reprisal . . . it created mass injustice . . . defamed all Germans."

At the same time democratic-minded Germans were disheartened by a cynical demonstration of the fraternity of arms among professional soldiers. From the millions of German soldiers who surrendered, several hundred former *Wehrmacht* General Staff officers were rounded up by the United States Army and put to writing their own versions of the history of their side of the war. In return for their services, which were legitimate war booty, they were given far greater privileges than allowed common prisoners; and although the law—remember, it is for liberation from militarism as well as National Socialism—specifically stated the accused were to be tried in their home towns, special *Spruchkammern* were set up for these men in their camps. Although the favored few included most of the top strategists in the *Wehrmacht,* not one was found to be a "major offender" by the hand-picked courts. General Franz Halder, onetime chief of staff, head of the history writing project, indicated his own conversion to democracy by stating in a pamphlet that he and his fellow Prussians could have won the war if only Hitler had kept his hands off the army.

Booksellers attributed the success of Halder's book to the fact that a picture of the Führer appeared on its cover. The sales value of pictures of Hitler, banned for use as ornaments, or on postage stamps, was demonstrated earlier when the American-owned magazine *Weekend,* featuring a picture of the Führer on its cover, was sold out within hours of the time it hit the newsstands. Since then other magazines have boosted their German circulation by publishing stories about Eva Braun, Otto Skorzeny, and other Nazi figures.

Skorzeny, who as an SS lieutenant colonel rescued Mussolini from the Italian partisans, is in Argentina, having escaped from the Darmstadt internment camp. He writes for a German-language magazine called *Der Weg,* dedicated to the "perpetuation of the Führer's ideals." Smuggled into Germany, this offspring of Julius Streicher's *Der Stürmer* sells for the highest black-market prices.

The failure of denazification spread its evil into the all-important Ruhr industries when it was decided that European economic recovery required high-level production by this great industrial area. Although the Krupps and Thyssens had been removed, the men who were on the operational level, and had learned their business—and politics—from the Krupps and the Thyssens, were moved to the top.

When General Clay was asked about the presence of this type of man on the international board of trustees for the Ruhr, he is reported to have answered, "We must have men who know their business or we'll have a hell of a mess." A logical answer, perhaps, for a man whose main job seemed to be the revival of German economy so that it could help European recovery, but hardly a guarantee that the German trustees had been disabused of the kind of thinking that had led to their positions under the Nazis and to the formation of the great industrial combines which had contributed so much to Hitler's success.

Perhaps it is reasonable to forget the war-making record of a soldier who can tell us how to fight a battle on the Russian steppes—just in case we may have to—or to forgive a Nazi who can produce more steel than an anti-Nazi. Probably it would make sense if the forgive-and-forget policy stopped right there. But it didn't. The situation was a vicious circle: the more Nazis were set free, the more there were to frighten people into freeing others who could frighten them more.

The freed Nazis pursued a policy of nepotism. In some cases officials were known to have created new places for the anti-Nazis while holding open the actual positions until the former holders could take them. Then the new offices were abolished and the anti-Nazis lost their jobs. Reports show that the influence of former Nazis on both public and private employment is so great that most Germans preferred to be found guilty as "followers," the lowest category of offenders under the denazification law, than to be completely exonerated. "They want to be sure people know they were 'one of the boys,'" an official explained to me. "They would rather take a small fine or even a short sentence than be labeled anti-Nazi." This is borne out by examination of trial records. According to the denazification law, members of certain organizations such as the SS or the Gestapo automatically fell into the top brackets, while others were chargeable according to their individual actions. Nevertheless, many high-ranking officials in the Bizonal Economic Administration, the highest governing body prior to the establishment of the Federal German Republic, were former SS officers.

One would think there would have been no difficulty in understanding the law and little possibility of evading it. But the record of one series of trials showed that of fifty-nine Gestapo men in Bavaria, all of whom had worked in concentration camps, fifty-five were charged as "major offenders" but only two were convicted. Thirty-one were found to be "followers" and seven exonerated because of lack of evidence. On an over-all average in Bavaria during 1948, only 5 per cent of those charged in the top three brackets were convicted, while 95 per cent of those tried as followers were convicted.

The German share of guilt for the failure of denazification does not fall on the conservatives and right-wingers alone. Every German party from the Communists to the most extreme nationalists has sponsored former Nazis in election contests.

A poll conducted by *Der Spiegel,* a top-selling news magazine, showed that Germans rated Hitler as the "fourth-greatest statesmen in history." Above him they put Winston Churchill and Gustav Streseman, the fumbling chancellor of the Weimar Republic, and, on top, Prince Otto von Bismarck, creator of the German Empire and Greater Reich.

Obviously a Nazi background is no handicap to a political aspirant.

The Germans are not alone in thinking that having been a Nazi is not necessarily bad. Murray D. Van Wagoner, once governor of Michigan and more recently director of Military Government for Bavaria, told a correspondent: "There's been a lot of talk about whether Nazis who have been in camps should be able to run for office. I don't know—but prison records aren't always bad politically. I know that in the Polish section of Detroit, if you've been in jail a couple of times, it helps a lot if you're running for office. And for that matter, look at Curley."

Not even the Nuremberg trials made a dent on the German mind. Brigadier General Taylor has written: "If Germany again falls victim to the delusion of anti-Semitism and militarism and the mirage of dictatorship, it will be because the lesson of Nuremberg has not, even yet, sunk in. The resurgence of militant German nationalism tends to take shape as justification, sometimes sly and sometimes brazen, of the events of the Nazi era."

The real danger is that the Nazis have demonstrated to the country's youth that democracy doesn't pay. While former party members try actively to further Nazi ideas, reports show that younger students are more apt merely to stick together and passively resist Military Government policy and objectives. An official who made a study of schools in Hesse stated in a report to Military Government that, while the teachers don't yet dare to praise nazism, "they sneer when the word 'democracy' is used. The children know what they mean."

A good deal of emphasis has been placed on the town meetings in which Germans are encouraged to call their officials to task or interrogate Military Government officers. The idea behind the program is to impress the Germans with the concept that officials are servants of the people, and, as such, are accountable. But things don't always work out that way. For example, at separate town meetings two American officials were asked the same question: "What about the Negro problem in the United States?" One replied, "That's a Communist question," and refused a more direct answer. The other said, "There isn't any."

In any case, despite town meetings, Germans have to be extremely careful of what they say about their officials. The man in Württemberg-Baden who was fined under a 1931 law for "criticism of officials" at a town meeting was told by the Americans that as long as the so-called "insult law" was on the books, nothing could be done. They suggested that he campaign for the repeal of this pre-Nazi regulation but offered no advice about how to do it without being fined for more criticism.

The fact that Russian, British, French, and American definitions of the word "democracy" differ widely makes it even more difficult to find a workable formula for the political purification of Germany. The French, perhaps the most realistic of the Western powers, have never relinquished control of the officeholders in their zone, thereby avoiding the pitfalls which lay in the path of their American colleagues. The French were quite willing to blink their eyes at a Nazi background if the individual's value to their national effort made it necessary or desirable to use him. The British, too, were inclined to justify the means by the end to be accomplished. With the vastly important Ruhr area under their exclusive control during the first years of the Occupation they were faced with the problem of using the wartime industrialists—almost all Nazis—or having a stagnating industry. They chose the easiest course.

The Russians, who have the greatest reason to fear and

hate the Germans, were the most hypocritical. The state police force set up by the Soviet Military Administration to control their zone was organized largely by men who had performed the same functions for Nazi regime, and the Soviets used the "harshness" of the American denazification program as a propaganda weapon to impress the Germans in their zone with the benefits of the Russian brand of "democracy."

The net result of this divergence of aim and treatment was the spectacle of the occupying powers in a series of wrangles which must have made Hitler shake in his grave with laughter. Never did Goebbels' predictions seem to be more justified. In the American Zone any German coming from the Soviet-controlled area was ordered subject to "re-denazification" by an "unbiased" court. The courts of the British Zone refused to approve the extradition of Hjalmar Schacht, although "America's Germans" said his acquittal had been "fixed" and the prosecution wanted to try him again. At the time of this writing he has been tried, in person or absentia, seven times. This lack of unity in political action even resulted in the Americans and British disagreeing on Max Reimann, Communist leader in Western Germany. Reimann broke parole in the British Zone and went to the American area. Although he appeared publicly in Frankfurt and other cities, it wasn't until he tried a secret trip to the British Zone that he was picked up again.

Naturally the only winners in this game of political blindman's buff were the Nazis. The anti-Nazi Germans were sold out as soon as the conquerors decided that the new enemy—to the East or the West, as the case might be—was more dangerous than the old.

What will fill the vacuum left by the destruction of the National Socialist party, as such, only history will tell, but it seems fairly certain that it will not be any of the parties presently tolerated, or even a democratic movement sired by the United States or Britain. The strongest appeal made by any party—and all must make it if they are to stay in business —is that of militant nationalism. In the struggle for Germany all the great Powers have permitted this appeal to be made, within limits. Once the Occupation is over the lid will be off and the real fireworks will begin. The cry for *Lebensraum* will be heard again and the old slogans will be dusted off and the people will heil their new Führer.

Few if any potentially great leaders have come forward since V-E Day. The simple reason is that no German with political ambitions can afford to identify himself as a collaborator. Once this collaboration is no longer necessary, a truly dynamic leader of the type Germans have always loved will surely emerge to lead Germany back to her lost greatness and recover her lost glories. Who he will be none can say, but he won't get far if he believes in democracy.

Chapter VIII

Der Kleine Mann

By JACK RAYMOND

THE first Germans I ever knew were all villains. They were characters in the movies, wore spiked hats and monocles, and stamped noisily in and out of doorways. They were always satisfactorily dead by the end of the picture.

Another German I knew as a youngster was the big fat Bavarian janitor of the apartment house next to the one in which I lived. He wore a rope around his bulging middle, in lieu of a belt, chased all the kids away from the front of his house (we were marking the sidewalk with chalk), and, of course, he owned a huge German police dog.

We played a game called "Three steps to Germany," the idea of which was to run across the street without being tagged by the "German" who was "it." This was obviously the first American experiment in nonfraternization.

The man who ran the corner delicatessen was a German. Max Schmeling was a German. The refugees who came to New York were Germans. The people who populated Yorkville were Germans. There seemed to be quite a lot of Germans everywhere. Finally, one even studied German in school because it might turn out to be "useful."

The first Germans I met overseas were prisoners. In fact the first individual German I talked with was a young blond Teuton who had been sniping at a group of us from a tree on the side of an Italian mountain.

When the boys in the outfit caught him he started to cry, saying he was only eighteen years old and please don't kill him, he wanted to study to be a doctor to help the human race. One of the boys in the outfit, himself only eighteen, grabbed the medical aspirant by the collar and demanded, "What made you think we'd kill you? Is that what you do with your guys?"

After the war, as a correspondent, I visited a political meeting in Leipzig in the Soviet Zone. The Congress Hall was crowded with about three thousand people. The speeches were harangues for unity. Unity! Unity! Unity! All those in favor, raise your right hand. With one motion three thousand arms were stiffly aloft. The Communists had gone into action.

In Greifswald, also in the Russian Zone, I asked a group of women shoppers congregated outside a small hotel how things were going. It was the terrible winter of 1946.

"We are hungry," said one of the women, the others nodding assent. "The Russians take everything. We wish you Americans were here. We hear you bring in food."

"The Russians have no culture," said another.

Just then my Russian companion joined me, and the women backed away and scattered. A few minutes later I was standing alone again and one of the women returned.

"Do you have any cigarettes?" she begged.

I was sorry but I did not.

"Are you really an American?"

"Yes," I said.

"Then you must be a Communist. How can you associate with those filthy Russians?"

On May 8, a couple of years ago, my housekeeper asked, "Today's a holiday for you, isn't it? An American holiday, right?" It never occurred to her that the end of the war in Europe could be anything but an American holiday.

On June 6 of the same year a Berlin newspaper carried a lengthy feature story on the anniversary of the "landing"— the landing of Chamberlin and Levine, who flew to Germany from the United States June 6, 1927. The paper carried no reference to June 6, 1944.

I am going to turn this chapter over to an average German, so as to give you an idea of what he does and what he is like. Before doing that, however, here's a popular story among Americans who have lived in postwar Germany a number of years: It seems Hitler was found dead, lying in a Munich street. His fist was tightly clenched. His fingers were pried open and a piece of paper was found in it. On it was written, "I was never a Nazi."

Now meet *der kleine Mann,* whose views, of course, are entirely his own. He's going to take you with him through a typical working day. He wears neither monocle nor spiked hat.

At 5:30 the alarm rings; the night is over. My wife is already in the kitchen preparing the breakfast. I wash and dress hurriedly. It doesn't take long because in summer drawers and undershirt are unnecessary. Every morning I have two slices of bread and marmalade. For the second breakfast, which I eat in the shop, my wife prepares two lard sandwiches and a bottle of coffee. I would prefer a good piece of sausage but at present prices this would be an expensive luxury. In less than an hour I leave the house and walk to the streetcar line, which is only five minutes away.

I am a mechanic, forty years old, married, with two children, a seven-year-old boy and a four-year-old girl. My name is Hans Durchschnitt. That means average. Or, as we Germans say, *der kleine Mann*. The little fellow. In actual size I am tall, and as a youngster I played a good deal of soccer. During the war I was a sergeant pilot in the *Luftwaffe*. Six years. I shot down many an American plane. That's over now. Luckily I was not hurt. I have a place to live. I have a job.

The war still has memories for me, but lately they are becoming fewer. Once, in April 1945, I was nearly captured by the Americans. I was on leave. My home city had already fallen, so I went to visit my father in Zerbst. One hardly knew where the front lines were. In Berlin I had heard the Amis were near the Elbe, but I did not realize they had already scaled the river.

I looked for the house of my old father and mother, just off the market place behind the gabled *Rathaus*. Mother greeted me at the door with tears in her eyes.

"Your father is wandering around town in his uniform," she cried. "The Americans will be here any minute."

"That's silly," I assured her. "There is no fighting around here. I was not even asked for a pass."

"Pass? Who thinks of them now?" she wept. "I tell you the city commander is fleeing and he is abandoning us to the Amis. Who knows, maybe there are Russians with them."

I looked out the doorway down the street and, sure enough, our people were in flight. I went out to search for father, a man well over eighty, who had fought at Mézières and Belfort, Mons and Ourcq in the First World War and was still tough and unafraid. I found him standing placidly in front of the Church of St. Nicholas. He smiled as he greeted me.

"Look at me," he said, "back in the army."

Der Kleine Mann

He wore a huge greatcoat that nearly touched the ground, and a small overseas cap, the *Schirmmütze,* with a button on the front. On the sleeve of the greatcoat there was an arm band. The thought struck me that my father was blind or crippled and that he was wearing the ochre band with three black balls on it worn in Germany by mutes and the disabled. But, no, it was the insignia of the *Volkssturm.*

"Come," I said, "you must go home."

"No," he insisted. "I want to stay here and watch our conquerors come in. They will not trouble an old man. But you must go," he continued, "you have yet some duties to your country and your comrades."

That was true, and I knew I could not dissuade him. So I left him in the street, rushed to a hurried good-by with mother—she died recently—and sought to join some outgoing troops. As I turned a corner I saw two Americans. Then two more. Soon the column was moving toward me.

It would have been easy to give up right there and then. My wife and baby were in Frankfurt, which had already been captured by the Americans. But I had a duty. I knew the old city. I ducked into a house. It was the home of an old bus driver I knew well. It was empty. I made my way through the gardens and back alleys of the streets and then to the countryside. Within two days I was in Berlin. The Russians were besieging the city. I rejoined my outfit for those last terrible days.

At the streetcar stop I now see the same people every morning. About ten or twelve of them, also workers. We know each other, say *Guten Tag* and discuss the weather. There is not much more to talk about because we are still sleepy. After a half-hour's ride I leave the streetcar, hurry a few blocks to my shop. I put my work ticket in the time clock and press the lever to punch it. In the dressing room I change to my work clothes, then I take my place at my workbench.

This is in a big room with many machines and tool cabinets. My fellow workers are standing in small groups, smoking cigarettes or their pipes. I remember when we shared the butts picked up from the street. Tobacco is more plentiful now. We are discussing an accident one of the men saw this morning. This leads to a discussion of bad drivers who think they are masters of the road. The worst drivers are Americans, we agree. Now it is seven o'clock. The bells and sirens sound the beginning of another day.

My comrade and I must finish a job we started yesterday. We have to replace a bearing of a lathe. The parts are heavy and we must move them, and this causes us to sweat freely. We do not talk much, for we concentrate on our task. We have been working together for years and we know how to co-operate.

My comrade was not in the war. He has had a lame leg from birth, although this does not prevent him from doing his job. He has powerful shoulders. My comrade was close to being an important Nazi. He had a good job in the *Kreisleiter's* office for a couple of years and then he got into a fight with the *Kreisleiter*. It was over a girl. My friend then went back to being a mechanic.

When he had to be denazified two years ago he called upon me as a character witness. I have known him since we were schoolmates. I testified for him and it helped him get off with only a fine. I myself was not a Nazi. But I think we should do everything to end this stupid denazification business. My friend and I get along very well, although we do not visit with each other in our homes. He is still a bachelor and runs around nights. I have my family to think of.

At 9:30 the bells toll again. Fifteen minutes' rest for the

second breakfast. I eat my two lard sandwiches and drink my coffee, then I light my pipe. My comrade and I talk about the repair of the machine. Perhaps we could install an additional spare part. Now it is time to continue our work, and we try to put into practice the ideas we discussed. At 11:30 the young office clerk, neat in his starched collar and pressed trousers comes around to notify us we can collect our pay at lunch time. That will be 12:30. We used to get paid monthly, but money is short and the workers demanded weekly wages.

I queue up with the others outside the office. I sign the payroll and receive my money. The gross pay for a forty-five-hour week is sixty-seven Deutsche marks and fifty pfennigs, half the cost of a good suit of clothes. Sixteen Deutsche marks and twenty-two pfennigs are deducted for taxes and insurance. That leaves me with fifty-one Deutsche marks and eighty-eight pfennigs. For a married man with two children that is not much. It might buy my wife a new dress but not a pair of shoes in the same week. Every time I get my pay I think about this—but only to myself. It is not correct to grumble. As my father said, *Ich bin nur ein kleine Mann.*

There are some grumblers in the shop. They complain about the politicians and about the union leaders. Also about the Amis. Nothing suits them. Of course there is often a lot in what they say, but I don't like their type. There is an apprentice who works in the shop who had a job with Americans. He used to go around to people's houses and ask them what they think about things. It was for public opinion polls.

One day, he told me, he climbed a flight of steps to the third floor of a house and knocked on the door to ask an opinion. A man opened the door and threw the young opinion taker bodily down the stairs, without even asking him who he was. The boy just quit his job and started to work in our shop. I guess he has learned not to have a job to mind other people's business.

I wash my hands and go to the mess hall. I have a mess card which entitles me to five meals a week, for which I must pay four Deutsche marks. Of course we always get soup. To-day it is barley broth. There is enough soup and it is warm. Everyone agrees the diet is monotonous, soup all the time, but most of the workers eat here in order to get something warm in the stomach. After I have eaten I sit in the yard and enjoy the sun.

It is nice in the summertime. One can lean back against the warm brick wall and doze a bit. The *Meister* comes by to chat and to ask me if I would sign a paper for him. He has four children—his wife was killed in an air raid—and they live in a single room outside of the city. He wants to move into the city near the shop, but he needs permission from the local housing office. They told him to prove it was necessary for him to live near the shop. He brought them a letter from the shop owner but this is not enough.

The housing official is a Communist. He said it was not enough to have such a letter from a capitalist. The *Meister* must bring at least fifty signatures from workers in the plant. This would also show whether the workers like the *Meister*. I sign the paper. The *Meister* goes off to collect more signatures.

At one o'clock the work continues. Our stomachs are full and our minds more at ease. We begin to talk a little more readily as we work. We chat about the soccer tournament. We also agree that it's about time it rained because we hate to water the garden. If God is kind to us, we won't have to. Time goes a little faster today.

One of the men is bragging about the fine catch his daughter made. There will be a wedding soon and the young couple will go to the Argentine to live. I know the girl. She and my sister-in-law were in the *Bund Deutscher Mädchen* together. I have some relatives in the Argentine also, but I have not heard from them since before the war.

The *Meister* comes by and gives me a new job for tomorrow. At last it's 4:30 and the day's work is done. The washroom is crowded. Everyone wants to leave as quickly as possible. The young apprentice tries some horseplay with me, but I tell him I'm in a hurry. He goes off to tease someone else. The workers from out of the city are in the biggest rush because they must catch their trains. At 4:35 I punch my work ticket and walk to the streetcar stop.

Now the streetcar is crowded and the ride is not very comfortable. I must stand all the way. Some other standees complain about the crowded conditions.

"Do you know," a stranger says to me, "the Amis are using the streetcars for artillery practice in maneuvers?"

"No, I did not know that."

"Yes," he continues, "they take streetcars from each city and scatter them around the countryside in Bavaria. Then they shoot at them for gunnery practice." His cousin wrote that to him the other day, he said.

The streetcar lurches suddenly. A woman screams. I cannot see her, for she is in the front part of the trolley. We are squeezed so together I can smell the nasty breath of the man who told me about the artillery practice. There seems to be a hush. "You stepped on my foot," I hear the woman say. There are some titters, and I cannot repress a smile. When a woman screams it sounds as if the world is coming to an end.

At 5:15 I arrive home. We have three rooms in a partly bombed building that is still unrepaired. We are one of two families occupying the premises. On the ground floor a whole six-room apartment is intact, but eighteen people live in it. In my apartment there is only my own family. The toilet has been rebuilt against the kitchen wall in order to take advantage of the pipes.

My wife joins me in a cup of coffee and a few slices of bread. We and the two children then go to the garden. It is a rented plot about four hundred yards from the house. In summer, I go there every evening. There is always something to be done. The children play and do not quarrel. They are good, handsome children and we love them above everything in the world.

"When you are older," I tell my young daughter, "I hope you will have such nice children as you and your brother."

"I don't want children when I am older," she says very seriously. "I'm going to have automobiles."

"You've got to have children," the boy assures her. "Automobiles are something else. Women always have children," he says. "Isn't that so?" he asks.

My wife assures her offspring they will have both children and automobiles.

My wife is thirty-three. She is still quite pretty, although she has worked very hard all her life. Until recently she took in sewing, but I told her to stop because she had no time for it. She helps with the gardening. Mostly she waters the plants.

She tells me about the refugees from Czechoslovakia who live in the next house. The man does not work and he and his wife had a noisy quarrel again today. We do not like them. The man is a glass blower by profession and he does not think it worth his while to find other work. So he sits around at home all day and agitates for a pension of some kind.

He seems to think we Germans owe him a living. The other day his wife told my wife that the Sudetens sacrificed themselves for the Germans and for Hitler and now we don't appreciate it. I told my wife not to pay any attention to her. If the Führer had won, they would probably demand special rewards.

At seven o'clock my wife and daughter go back to the house. The little girl must go to bed. My wife must prepare supper. The boy and I continue to putter around the garden. He has a new friend, he tells me. His father has that new shop on the corner. It is a wooden stand built in front of the ruins of the old department store. It has small household articles for sale. The owner is a Jew.

I do not say anything to my little boy about his friend being Jewish, but I wonder if many Jews will move into the neighborhood. I don't mind them, the German Jews. It's the Polish Jews, the Displaced Persons, who are obnoxious. I wonder if the German Jews will come back. My son likes his friend, who shared a chocolate with him. I resolve to treat my son to a chocolate tomorrow so that he can reciprocate. At 7:30 the boy and I walk home.

We clean up and have supper. Tonight we have noodles and fruit. The fruit is from our garden and was canned last year. My wife is saving a piece of ham for Sunday. The boy sits on the kitchen floor, turning the pages of a picture book. I read the newspapers. My wife sews my jacket, which I tore on a protruding nail in the hallway. It is an old flying jacket which I had dyed. It is five years old but still wears very well.

I am reading the serial first. It is an interesting novelette about the war of 1870. Wars were more gracious in those days. Then I read the general news and the headlines. There is an investigation about a man who was supposed to be an agent for the Gestapo and now he has an important post in the Chancellery. But I am not much interested in politics.

Before the war I followed Centrist. My family are Catholics. My father was a mechanic also and he mixed a little in the trade unions. We were not interested in Hitler at first, but one must concede Hitler had some good ideas. National Socialism was not a bad thing in some respects but the wrong people ran it.

But that is no longer important. National Socialism is dead. Germany itself is practically dead. Perhaps now there will be some kind of world government. But that is the millennium. Who will force Stalin to join it?

I only want to work and earn money in order to feed and dress my family. The representatives and politicians promise much in the newspapers and over the radio—my radio is broken, and I must fix it tomorrow. They cannot keep their promises. I guess it does not make much difference whom I shall vote for in the elections. Today I cannot spend so much time with newspapers, for I must write a letter to my father in Zerbst.

He's having a hard time of it, but it is better that he stays where he is. I have no room for him in my house. I send him a small package every now and then. So does my brother who lives in Hamburg. My father says the Russians don't bother him. He lives with an old woman he met recently, a friend of his family. They do not bother to get married. He feels it is too late for such nonsense, as he puts it, and he hopes the Lord will forgive him as he goes to church regularly but skips confession.

It is getting late now. My son has long since gone to bed, and I write by lamplight on the old desk I salvaged from a bombed-out house. It is eleven o'clock now, and I must go to bed for tomorrow I must get up at 5:30.

Chapter IX

Candy-Bar Romance—Women of Germany

By J U D Y   B A R D E N

M Y FIRST encounter with German women in the mass, so to speak, was with a group of *Blitzmädels,* similar to our WAC but in job only, who had been captured just outside Munich.

They were being marched through the streets by a few uncomfortable and tired-looking GI's who obviously thought it pretty silly to keep a gun trained on such a beaten-up crew. The *Blitzmädels* were filthy. Their uniforms were torn. Many were without caps or stockings and many were limping badly, but they held their heads high. They were the counterpart of their Nazi brothers, arrogant and disdainful.

While with many this attitude lends a certain amount of dignity, it did just the reverse to these maidens. They were dumpy, bulging in all the wrong places, and exceedingly fat. There was something pathetically stupid about them as they spat between their teeth and glared at the crowds of Americans and Germans watching them. Eventually they were housed in a camp, given some soap and delousing powder, and told to get on with the job of cleaning themselves up.

Then the fun started. They vied and fought with each other for the attentions of the embarrassed American guards. There were hair tearings and face scratchings and the inevitable denunciations. They were without any moral sense at all, sun-bathing in full view of the public in filthy bits of underwear, offering themselves to any American who happened along.

That was over four years ago, when Americans were hating everything German except cameras. The *mädels* got nowhere, though they must have swung their incredibly large hips into a state of exhaustion trying.

At the time I told myself all German women couldn't be as bad as these. These were what the *Wehrmacht* had produced; there must be women who had stayed at home and retained some decent instincts. If there were, I wasn't meeting them.

As we captured town after town the same things happened, women offering themselves and denouncing each other. It became a sickening business to see one's own sex fallen so low. It was usually a woman who would come crying into Military Government with some secret information about her neighbor who was hiding a German soldier in the cellar. It was usually a woman who, after a German had been screened and given a job, would come cringing into the office with some damaging information about his past. In this way they hoped to ingratiate themselves with the Americans. They gave Intelligence a hard time tracking down the various leads with the denouncements of their onetime friends.

Never having known the same fear these women knew, nor ever having been as hungry as they, I tried not to judge too harshly. But somehow I didn't believe the French women had acted as badly when the Germans occupied their country. Neither could I believe the American or British women would behave this way if placed in a similar position. The German women just seemed to have no sense of loyalty.

All over Germany at this time, the most beautiful hospitals flew a white flag with a red spot in the center. These flags denoted maternity hospitals for unmarried mothers. They were filled with girls of seventeen to twenty-five. I visited one of these institutions in May 1945. It was an exquisite place built on the lines of an exotic Swiss chalet. Young mothers nursed their babies in the sunshine on the verandas. Other mothers wandered around chatting happily with the nurses and with each other. I was unwelcome.

The things I thought these mothers would fall for, like glugging over their babies, admiring their hospital, showing sympathy for them, fell as flat as a Russian promise. In fact my attitude of sympathy was obviously resented.

A few candy bars and liberal handing around of cigarettes eased the tension somewhat, and as it slowly penetrated that my skin was like that of an elephant and I intended staying no matter what their attitude, they thawed out.

Their stories were stark and shattering.

I remember wanting to write them for the *Sun* and then deciding against it. They were just too much in the raw. The *Sun* would have been horrified and even its most broadminded readers could not have understood the attitude of these girls.

Their aim in life was to propagate the species. They were hand-picked specimens who had originally volunteered for the job. Once they had passed the tests of health, beauty, and curves, they were dispatched to various Officers' Leave Centers where they stayed until they were pregnant. It was as simple as that.

Once they became pregnant they were treated with every luxury left in Germany. The care they received was far better than that of the average mother having a legitimate child. They were helping to build a strong Germany. They were proud of their "career," indifferent to the fact that they didn't know the fathers' names.

I asked one of the girls how she intended to take care of her child now the war was lost for the Germans. She gave the baby, a gorgeous infant, a casual look, and said, "Somebody is bound to turn up who will look after it."

All these mothers appeared to feel the same way. They had been indoctrinated. They had learned to love their carefree existence and the baby figured as a handicap in their future life. The state had promised to look after these children. Now all that was changed and most of the mothers felt irritable and let down. They didn't want the responsibility.

This was during the nonfraternization period. The war was over and thousands of Americans were wandering around basking in the luxury of baths and no bullets. They had little to do and it didn't take the average fräulein five minutes to realize that they were lonely for a woman's company.

In a climate where neither one is necessary, the fräulein wore the shortest skirts and the lowest necklines I have ever seen outside the "Follies." They lay around provocatively in the sun wearing beach suits which would have been banned on any beach. They treated all American women with contempt and all American men as gods.

American women didn't look too smart in those days. Our uniforms reeked to high heaven of gasoline in which we had dunked them for months, our hair was revoltingly "home done," and the only thing we had to offer was the language. The fräulein offered everything but the language. As one GI remarked, "Well, who wants to talk?"

As always, however, the things you can't have you want most. When the ban on fraternization was lifted, most of the soldiers lost interest in their temporary girl friends. There was talk about going home on a point system. The GI who had slipped a bit hated the thought of facing mom and pop.

He compared his hard-to-get American sweetheart with his German fräulein. Manlike, he wanted something that wasn't so easy. Fräuleins began to be out of date.

But things had progressed. Fräuleins flew to officers saying they were pregnant. Others declared they had been raped. There must have been many a good Joe whose life was spoiled by his first encounter with a German woman. Many kids who had left the States at the hand-holding stage quickly learned what life was all about by being chased into a bush and taught by experts. If there was any rape, it certainly wasn't necessary.

In the big cities old women hired out their bedrooms for the use of GI's and their fräuleins. I went on one night police raid in an apartment building of about thirty families. Seven old fraus were sleeping on chairs in their kitchens while their own rooms were rented.

The old and young women alike appeared to see nothing wrong in their actions. The GI's, mildly uncomfortable, dressed and went to the police trucks with heads down. The fräuleins screamed insulting remarks at the MP's. They were anything but penitent as they were carted away to the police station.

I arrived in Berlin in October 1945 with a pretty bitter opinion of German women, every German woman. Berlin at first did nothing to sweeten my impression. The same boldness, the same cheapness, the same old routine I had seen right through Germany. Necklines dropped lower, skirts grew shorter, and 90 per cent of the females went blond. In the film *A Foreign Affair,* Marlene Dietrich portrayed faithfully the average life in those early days of a fräulein who had secured for herself an American, any American.

I had been in Berlin three months when I met Gerda. She was the first "good girl" I had encountered. Twenty-four, pretty as a picture, she had been a junior officer in the *Bund*

Deutscher Mädel, another of Hitler's movements to control all youth. She wanted a job and I wanted to employ her. She was the only girl I had met so far whom I could tolerate.

She explained how, against her parents' wishes, she had joined the movement at the age of twelve because by so doing she could continue horseback riding. This was her favorite pastime. She said she had no other motive and I believed her. Against the rules I employed her.

Through Gerda I met Inge and many other good German women of all ages. I was told the reason I hadn't met any such women before was that they had stayed at home. Tired of war and the fearsome aftermath, they had locked themselves in and awaited their fate. I soon discovered that all German women were not as bad as I had thought. Hitler had done his best to lower the social standards of living, but in many families mothers and fathers, while unable to revolt openly, had retained some influence over their youngsters.

This had been one of the most difficult problems for them to face. If a mother told her child she didn't want her to join a youth group, that child might innocently repeat this at school. Such a confession could result in the arrest of both parents. They could be sent to a concentration camp for three months to learn "obedience."

There were many mothers who had made this slip and had been so punished. Where most children in the world have their own imaginative little secrets, these children were growing up with real fears. Heavy responsibilities were placed on their shoulders. Parents would whisper in front of them. Then, afraid that the whisper might have been heard, they would threaten the heavy use of the hairbrush if the child should repeat what he had heard at home.

It is no wonder that German women of today, who were teen-agers and less under the Nazis, have a different approach to life from the American girl. It is no wonder they are slow to voice an opinion and slow to form any women's groups. Anything organized smacks to them of the ugly "compulsory" days under Hitler. They want to stay out of trouble.

The Nazis had done everything to attract youth. It was then as it is now in the Soviet Zone of Germany. If children wanted any sports or fun, they had to belong to one of the movements. Mothers, unable to bear the thought of what that one word "no" might mean, gave in. Thousands of girls and boys came to believe more in Hitler than in mom. Germany's future womanhood was growing up under a dictator instead of a mother's love.

All these things I began to learn as I settled down in Berlin. Mothers came to me asking if I could help their daughters. When I suggested that they go to one of the many Americans who might need a secretary, nothing more was heard. They didn't want their daughters associating with our men. It wasn't that they liked me better, but that I wouldn't be likely to lead their daughters astray.

Of course there were still the many cheap fräuleins hanging around. But now I could see the difference. The comparison was between those girls who wanted candy bars and cigarettes for their souls, and those who wanted to work and earn them.

Great women who had spent years as political prisoners in concentration camps began to return to Berlin. Among these was Luise Schroeder, who is regarded as the first lady of the land. She is sixty-one years old, has the appearance of a lamb and the courage of a lion.

From 1946 until after the beginning of the blockade she was acting mayor of the whole city. Never before in German history had a woman been mayor of Berlin. Her gentle smile and iron will resulted in a fan mail larger than Frank Sinatra's. She is attacked constantly by the Communist press. If the Russians ever had a free hand in Berlin, her lot would be the salt mines, but she cannot be intimidated. She believes all women must take part in the reconstruction of Germany.

Another notable character is Annedore Leber, forty-one-year-old head of the women's department of the Social Democratic party in Berlin, whose name is a household word. Her husband was one of Hitler's worst enemies. He spent four years in a concentration camp and eventually was hanged in 1945 in connection with the July 20 revolt.

After her husband had been executed Frau Leber spent three months in a concentration camp because she tried to tell her people something of the freedom of other countries. This woman has had many offers to leave Germany but she says, "I saw my people were lost. They were helplessly looking for an interpreter of their needs. Somebody must stand fearlessly against any new injustices. I decided to stay." In sessions of the city parliament she represents the needs and the worries of the Berlin housewife.

As one of three licensees of the newspaper *Telegraf,* Annedore Leber plugs away for equality for women. As mother of two children she lends an ear to every mother's worry. But this overworked little woman surprisingly enough has a hobby. She explains that she wishes to educate German women in charm, graciousness, and chic. For this purpose she started a magazine for women in 1947. In her few spare moments she sketches, showing how to make two "old looks" into one "new look" garment. By now many magazines have copied her. There has been a great increase in "women's pages" and special articles of interest to the distaff side in the press. Mixtures of international style in clothes are shown, with American and French predominating.

These two women are not alone with their difficulties. All women in Germany have tremendous problems to face, chief of which is the shortage of men. At the present moment there are 124 women for every 100 men. For every 100 men between 20 and 30 years of age, there are 171 women; for every 100 men 30 to 40 years of age, there are 153 women; and for every 100 men 50 to 60 years of age, 133 women. This result of two wars means that German women have a great potential power of which so far they have not made much use. Of course they can scarcely be blamed for not seizing what to most women would be a golden opportunity. Although they were legally permitted to take important roles previously they were discouraged from so doing. The end of the war found them completely bewildered.

A peculiar kind of lovelorn column broke out as a regular feature of the daily press. Women advertised themselves for marriage both in newspapers and on notices tacked to trees in their neighborhood. The approach was in the best tradition of salesmenship, the women stressing what they had to offer in terms of household equipment and living space. On the Kurfürstendam, Berlin's Broadway, three little kiosks opened as "human libraries." These "libraries" insisted on a photograph of the woman "for sale." She paid fifty marks to enter the race and two hundred and fifty if she won a man. Men paid fifty marks to have a look and two hundred and fifty if a marriage took place. In those days two hundred and fifty marks amounted to one month's salary for a laborer, or two packs of American cigarettes on the black market.

Most of the women who wanted husbands were those who had children, or were lonely war widows. Three-quarters of them ranged between fifty and seventy years of age. Most of the interested men were returning prisoners whose wives had vanished and whose homes had been destroyed by bombs.

The success of these "libraries" produced a glut of small matrimonial agencies in which couples could meet. Swiftly on their heels came an invasion of fortunetellers. These two ran in competition. The most tragic cases they had to handle were women who didn't know whether they were widows or not. Tens of thousands knew only that their husbands were last seen fighting on the Russian front. The soothsayers were confronted with such pathetic questions as, "Tell me, is he still alive?" "Is he a prisoner?" "Does he still love me?" "Shall I wait for him?"

Women's minds were in a turmoil. They had no time or inclination to think about professions or politics. Those about forty were the worst off. They worked amid the ruined cities while their youngsters ran wild in the streets. They earned only sufficient money to keep body and soul together. Women who in the past would have insisted on their children attending school found themselves encouraging their youngsters to pick up cigarette butts which could be sold at the end of the week as pipe tobacco. They were desperate and out of their desperation grew defiance.

When husbands did return home, expecting love, sympathy, and a chance at a new existence, they found instead hunger, suffering, and destruction. Bitter quarrels would result, and despite the shortage of men the divorce rate soared. Women told their men that the home front had been tougher than the battle front. They were no longer the quiet little mice the men had married. Belief in their own importance made marriage to the disinherited soldiers of a defeated army an intolerable thing.

I remember sitting one night in a German club in the Soviet sector of Berlin. In a smoky underground room the house light went down and the spotlights came up on to a girl dressed in rough working clothes. Her blond hair hung in streaks. Her face was smudged with rubble dust. She sang a plaintive, bitter song. The gist of it was this: Men, get wise to yourselves. Stop acting like busted heroes. Help us build something new. Remember we housewives in Berlin went through more than any of you. You had your drink and your

Blitzmädels, your officers' clubs and your medals. We had the American Air Force by day and the Royal Air Force by night, a cold air-raid shelter in which to live and very little to eat.

When the singer finished there was a hush, then almost hysterical high-pitched applause from the women in the audience. The cabaret turn had scored a hit with her own sex. She had given the men something to think about.

This attitude is not shared by girls between the ages of seventeen and twenty-five. Their problem is different but equally as difficult. With men at a premium and with those who are around unable to earn enough to support a wife, or for that matter to buy a girl a cup of ersatz coffee, many of the young girls had given up all thought of marriage. "Our men are becoming accustomed to being chased. They are conceited and apathetic," said one girl. "They are too complacent to fall in love. Who wants a man who is all but asleep when being kissed?"

Another girl asked, "What's the use of thinking about marriage? All the men I meet are either married or expect me to pay the bill. I prefer to take myself out."

So girls go around in pairs. They dance together, picnic together, go to the theater and cinema together. Quite a common sight in Germany today is two girls over twenty years old walking hand in hand or with their arms around each other's waists.

One thing, however, stands out among the German girls of today. They are the least catty of any women I have ever met. They are the first to admire genuinely each other's acquisitions. In a society where a food or clothing package from America is a gift from the gods, there is almost no jealousy. They are the first to congratulate each other on their good fortune.

Before the Hitler regime German women could almost be

included in the inventory of the house. They were almost but not quite on a level with their Moslem sisters in this respect. They were not unhappy, never having known any other way of life. They devoted their whole lives to fulfilling their husbands' desires. But now German women are learning the meaning of independence. It is a strange new world to them, and nobody can say they take to it like ducks to water, but they are making an effort to stand on their own two feet. Girls do secretarial jobs during the day and thousands have begun to study for the professions. This would be quite normal to an English or American girl, but to the German girl it is a revolutionary change.

In the Berlin elections in 1949, although the day was cold and wet, vast numbers of women turned out to vote. It couldn't be said that all of them knew what they were voting for, but they did know what they were voting against. The fact that they themselves made the effort to vote is a long step forward. The past would have seen them voting or not as their husbands or fathers dictated.

Frau Doktor Klaje, a fifty-year-old Berlin woman, is proposing to go even further with women's independence. She maintains that in such times as these, with so many surplus women, marriage is unnecessary and that it is unfair for women to go through life without giving birth. She is appealing for a law which will permit temporary husbands. A man will live with a woman until she is pregnant and then take his love elsewhere and make another woman happy. If this is too broad-minded an approach, then the Frau Doktor suggests that a form of marriage be allowed on the understanding that a divorce will be granted as soon as the woman has her baby.

Oddly enough, these suggestions did not meet with a storm of protest. Many women have already acted quietly on the temporary marriage and divorce scheme. Those who did not agree were not shocked by the idea. They merely thought it wouldn't work. Those who did agree suggested what they thought to be improvements.

The newspapers were inundated with letters from women who had jobs. They wanted to form what they called a "mother family." Under this scheme employed mothers would alternate in staying at home to look after the children and do the shopping and the housework.

Possibly this is a modification of the Nazi concept coming back, but my belief is that it is not intended merely to build up population. Germany already has enough mouths to feed. The plan is aimed at staying the growth of illegitimacy and at the same time satisfying the maternal instincts in women.

In Berlin there are six times as many applications for adoption as there are babies to go around, but mothers who have had babies sired by the members of the Occupation forces—there are tens of thousands of them—usually will not part with their children even though there is no obligation, according to existing military law, on the part of the soldier to support either of them. In some districts the number of illegitimate children has reached 25 per cent of all births, but still the number of babies offered up for adoption is small. Women struggle along with only the money they earn themselves. Pensions are granted to them when they are sixty, two-thirds incapacitated, or have two children under eight years of age.

Each of the four occupying powers has a different policy in dealing with women's problems. Although the British were the first to lift the ban on marriage between their troops and German girls, in 1945 they were violently opposed and sentenced one tommy to 112 days' detention for kissing a fräulein in public. A staff major in Herford is reported to have told the press, "What we need here is cricket bats, not fräuleins."

Today, however, the British tommy can walk down the street holding his fräulein with one hand and saluting his officer with the other. In fact the British are officially encouraged to fraternize with Germans as much as possible. One soldier said dryly, "What 1950 will bring we can only guess. Probably we will be penalized for not fraternizing and those seductive cricket bats will be banned as hindrances to the spread of democratic ideas."

The United States Military Government was the second to allow marriages between fräuleins and American forces. In the first year after the lifting of the ban, 1,211 applications out of 2,650 were approved. The French never made much of an issue of anything in connection with fraternization. (Theirs is the only zone that does not have any women in public office.) Their barriers to marriage with Germans were low but few French soldiers availed themselves of the opportunity.

For the Russians fraternization is still taboo. They still maintain their original "pay as you frat" policy which carries a system of fines for any Russian GI caught making eyes at a German girl.

But the German women in the Russian Zone are far better organized than in any of the other three zones. Maybe "far better" is the wrong term, but the Russians certainly have them under control. During the first year of occupation, when Western German women were bewailing their lot, Eastern Zone women organized five thousand neighborhood clubs. This they did voluntarily. Any individualism or freedom they may have had then is now a thing of the past. They have become one single unit under Communist control.

In the Eastern Zone women aren't asked, they are told. Probably they are not enjoying their enforced independence, but they are learning that they can be the equal of men and can earn the same wages. Equal pay for equal work is an attractive proposition to women who have always been considered chattels.

Berlin girls tell lurid stories of how they were treated by the Russians when the latter entered Berlin, and the only reason they hate communism is because "all Russians are Communists, therefore communism is to be avoided." Neither do they have a clear comprehension of the meaning of democracy, but they have learned to use its parlance. They are willing to play along with their foreign mentors, provided they don't have to join anything and get their names "on a list." They reason that if the Russians or the German Communists ever gain control of Germany, they will be subjected to a denazification program in reverse.

With few exceptions, West German women long to visit the United States. They are fascinated by the shiny American cars which roll along the *Autobahns* of Germany. They are intrigued by the newspapers and magazines filled with advertisements for glamorous clothes and food. They are incredulous over the number of American women in public life. But most of all they wonder that men are seemingly not masters of their own kingdoms.

I have received many letters from German girls who are now living comfortably in the States with their ex-GI husbands. These girls invariably marvel over the treatment accorded to women there. Today in Germany women work in the fields, clean up the rubble, and run the machines in factories. Only a small minority hold positions in public life.

A few German women have realized the importance of a political education and are endeavoring to persuade teenagers to join various groups. They wish to train them and give them experience in group activity in an effort to promote democratic government. These are women who learned what it means to shirk their responsibilities. They are anxious to teach the girls of today that each individual has a responsibility to herself as well as to her country. They look for American help and guidance. They are like children learning to walk. They are goaded by the feeling that they are and will probably remain on their own. Recently they have been insisting on an opportunity to learn a profession which will earn them sufficient money to keep them in their old age.

If the German girl ever emerges as the confident, efficient counterpart of her American sister, it will be because she gazed into the crystal ball and saw a grim future ahead, a future which she can now alter to her own advantage.

Chapter X

Case History of a German Town

By RALPH HARWOOD

WHEN the Allied armies surged eastward from the Rhine in the spring of 1945 in their pell-mell rush to meet the Russians and wrap up the war, few of the overrun towns in what was left of the dying Third Reich retained any identity for the racing troops. Here was none of the bitter fighting that had so indelibly marked dates and place names in the Hürtgen Forest, the Vosges, up in Hollandor, down in the Palatinate. One Neustadt or Steinberg or Gerbersdorf was about like another now—an hour or two's delay, perhaps even a day lost waiting to go through, but surely not enough trouble to worry about remembering an awkward name like, say, Buchen im Odenwald.

Colorless faces peering out of windows draped with bed sheets, symbol of surrender, or red feather ticks taking the air; old men anxiously trying to get someone to listen to their denunciations of Hitler; children, caught between fear and curiosity, straining for a better look at those odd monstrosities, tanks and jeeps; a fräulein's furtive smile—these were the impressions that stuck in soldier minds, and they did not vary from town to town. The impressions of Buchen, certainly, were no different.

It mattered little to tankmen of the Seventh Armored Division approaching the town that in winding along the narrow forest roads north of the Neckar River valley they had sliced through sixty miles of the very heartland of old German history and Teutonic legendry. An occasional student of Wagnerian music or epic poetry may have been set to thinking at the glimpse of a *Rehbock* springing away in alarm, or of *Wildschwein* routed from the deep wood by searching infantry. It was here in the Odenwald that the mighty Siegfried was murdered by Hagen while quenching his thirst after a hot chase, and the saga of the *Nibelungenlied,* which every German child for centuries has had to read and recite, begins to unfold in classic tragedy.

Or someone who stayed with Latin long enough to get Caesar out of Gaul may have realized that this same forest was a bastion of the Roman legions in an earlier occupation that lasted three hundred years, and that their main defense line, where it cut across country from the River Main to the Danube, still was discernible but a few miles away. And even the name, Götz von Berlichingen, immortalized by Goethe, may have rung a bell with some of the Americans who first came upon it along the Neckar or in the high fastnesses of the Odenwald. It was in this area that the ill-tempered baron with a fondness for smashing tables with his cast-iron fist, whose name was to become synonymous throughout Germany with the rude but popular invitation, "kiss my behind!" took advantage of the general unrest stirred up by Martin Luther and rallied the local farmers in an abortive revolt against the feudal minions of the powerful Bishop of Mainz in the sixteenth century.

Stadt Buchen, county seat of *Landkreis* Buchen on the southern edge of the Odenwald, first showed up in American ground force reconnaissance glasses on the morning of April 2, 1945. From the cover of near-by beech-clad hills, from which town and *Kreis* derive their name, the knot of twisting streets and sagging sixteenth- and seventeenth-century houses was cautiously observed. The place lay in a saucer; it would be a simple matter to sit back and knock it to pieces with tanks from the surrounding high ground if resistance appeared.

But there was no sign of activity in the streets or on the half-dozen roads reaching out of town, and the *Bahnhof* seemed as empty as the sidings along the single-track railway curving in to touch the northern edge of the community. The ancient gate tower which, together with the Catholic church steeple, dominated the medieval cluster of red-tile roofs, gave no hint that it was being used as an observation post. The lesser cupola—that would be the Lutheran church in these parts—seemed equally deserted.

Still, even though it was militarily a sitting duck, this Buchen was a *Kreisstadt,* a local political center, and the ways of the SS were not always easy to figure. The men of the Seventh Armored who remembered St. Vith and Stavelot back in Belgium were not inclined to do anything foolish. Somewhere in one of the three columns of tanks and half-tracks now converging in a semicircle an order was given.

Seven shells in rapid succession screamed into the center of the silent town. Minutes passed, and then the clock in the old tower banged out a hoarse, sad acknowledgment of the American calling card. Pieces of white cloth began to appear at windows. There would be no resistance; apparently the SS who were reported to have been in the place only a few hours before had decided not to stick around for a last-ditch affair.

As distant flashes in the night sky had moved steadily closer to Buchen, finally to assume their belated accompaniment of dull reports, rumor ran wild among the townspeople. For several days a heavy-jowled Father Heinrich Magnani had had trouble with his flock. He was convinced they did not mean to be disobedient, but there was no denying they were distracted by the very substance of their prayers. Would the SS insist on defending the town at any cost? Would the American Negroes rape the women? The white troops would be bad enough. Would party members be rounded up and summarily shot?

It was difficult to persuade even the most disciplined of the faithful to seek peace from such thoughts in selfless, humble supplication, exhort them as he would.

Father Magnani sighed heavily as he looked out over the all-too-few bowed heads dotting the gloom of the nave. He would ask God again, he decided, that the town be spared violence. As the priest formulated his prayer he found himself wondering, as he had many times before throughout the day, if American troops respected church property. Perhaps the commander of the approaching unit might even be Catholic. Father Magnani prayed.

In the *Gasthaus* Zum Löwen on the edge of Buchen, a small group of middle-aged and elderly men listened in glum silence to the rumble of the approaching tanks. Theirs was not the numb apprehension that had succeeded frenzied fear throughout the rest of the town; it was, instead, a feeling of frustration, almost shame. For months and years they had been meeting in this same café, when it was safe to do so, to trade bitter, low-pitched denunciations of Hitler and all National Socialism. To a man they hated the Nazi regime, and had hoped earnestly for its defeat and an end of the war.

For some days now the whispered conversations at the Lion had grown more excited, and not alone because the hour of deliverance for anti-Nazis was at hand. One of the group had boldly suggested that they seize *Kreisleiter* Adalbert Ullmer, his strong-arm assistant from Alsace, Albert Hof, and the rest of the abominable party staff up the street, and deliver them bodily to the first Americans who entered the town.

Carried away by the fervor of their thoughts, the little group hatched his idea into a plot. They would need to bide their time carefully. The SS were still about, speaking more loudly then ever of the Führer's secret weapons, and ready to interpret as treason the slightest questionable act of a townsman. They would have to wait until these fanatics had gone—at the last hour, perhaps—but then they would move swiftly!

And now the little group sat in glum, middle-aged silence in Zum Löwen; the only sound was made when one of their number arose from a creaky chair to see if American armor had yet appeared around the bend in the Hettingenbeuren valley road. Ullmer was gone by several hours now, the drunken swine. Together with Hof he had bundled his coterie of close henchmen and hand-picked secretaries into a couple of automobiles, stopped long enough to requisition at pistol point the stock of a local tobacco merchant, and then had fled southeast out of town "on secret orders" before the American ring had been completely forged. Only then had the last SS pulled out of Buchen, too. So it was no one's fault that the plot had failed to materialize, but there was a tired futility in the measured puffing of pipes in the Lion the afternoon of April 2, 1945.

Perhaps if the little group could have known that Adalbert Ullmer and most of the others were to be apprehended and brought back to Buchen almost two years later to stand trial for their crimes, they would have been consoled. Perhaps not. "Here they come!" said the pharmacist Balkenhol, and then, as the others crowded to windows, he added, "Who is that man in German uniform on top of the first tank? I think I recognize him."

Alfred Netter, proprietor of Zum Löwen, looked hard and

swore softly. "Don't you know him?" he asked. "That is our brave town hero, Otto Egenberger, the swine. He's the man who didn't really desert the *Wehrmacht;* his unit just fell apart! Remember? And only two days ago the big brute beat up a man half his size for making what he called a defeatist remark. Look at him now! He's waving to the people in the windows, taking bows for delivering the town safely! I hope the Americans will not be fooled by the acting of this pig."

The little group of middle-aged men turned away from the windows, muttering, just in time to face three other men— young men in grimy green twill with rifles in their hands, who had come bursting through the door. For a moment the two groups surveyed each other tensely. Then the silence of the room was broken by one of the newcomers. "Hey, Joe," he said to the man at his elbow, "ask these old bastards where they hid the likker!"

Nonfraternization had scarcely begun to break down in occupied Buchen—girls and youngsters were still having trouble with such names as Hershey, Chesterfield, and Wrigley—when Captain John A. McGuinness moved in with some twenty officers and men of Military Government team I-3-E-2 and set up headquarters in the erstwhile offices of *Kreisleiter* Adalbert Ullmer.

McGuinness, who was to be only the first of several Military Government officers who have had a hand in the postwar affairs of Landkreis Buchen, could see at a glance that he had inherited a mess. The situation would take a bit of studying before he could hope to bring any sort of order out of the confused scene.

Scattered over the more than eight hundred square kilometers of *Kreis* Buchen were eighty-two *Gemeinden,* only three of which had populations above three thousand. At the last census, in 1939, the entire area had counted only 45,162 residents, but there was no way of telling how many evacuees from Mannheim, Würzburg, Stuttgart, and other hard-hit industrial centers had, by the war's end, taken refuge in this most rural and out-of-the-way area in southwest Germany. Certainly it was more than the meager agricultural economy of the place could accommodate. Already refugees and expellees were beginning to drift in from Eastern Germany, Sudeten Czechoslovakia, Hungary and Austria, an influx that was to continue until, in 1948, when the census was finally taken, the swollen population of the *Kreis* numbered 69,464.

The residents of Buchen alone had increased from a normal 2,500 to some 4,000 during the war years and in the months immediately following. To top this situation, the American Army decided to billet 3,000 troops in the town during the summer of 1945. But this was at a time when requisitioning of property involved little more than issuing a brisk order, with small regard on the part of the conquerors for the consequences. This was an attitude and a system which was to change completely, and far more quickly than the Germans had a right to expect.

There was no question of helping the people of Buchen to rehabilitate industry, for manufacturing enterprises have never been an important factor in their economy. The furniture factory founded in 1892 by Franz Fertig remains the only business of any importance in the town, employing some two hundred workers. And throughout the *Kreis* the picture confronting Military Government was much the same: here and there an occasional small brick works or ceramics plant, or more frequently a wood-processing enterprise eking out an existence from the beech and pine of the Odenwald.

The reason for industry having shunned Buchen as it has few places in Germany was readily apparent to the mass of Americans who were stationed there in 1945. They soon discovered that there was scarcely enough water to go around for domestic purposes among the normal population, let alone enough to supply commercial power or, for that matter, the normal demands of several thousand soldiers.

Alarmed upon learning that fifty natives had succumbed in 1942 to a typhoid epidemic which swept the town, army engineers examined the municipal supply system. They found that two relatively small springs in the hills outside of town were the sole sources of water in the area. While they concluded that the system of purification and careful utilization in force was about all that could be expected from an engineering standpoint, they could also see that Buchen was a rather poor place in which to anchor a large segment of the American Army while awaiting redeployment home.

After re-establishing communications between *Kreisstadt* Buchen and the eighty-one other *Gemeinden* of the county, McGuinness set about appointing temporary burgomasters, a provisional county government, headed by *Landrat* Oskar Haug, a former teacher, and the restoration of a police force. But necessary as these measures were, it was obvious from the beginning that the most urgent problem in each village and town of the overcrowded *Kreis* was the shortage of food.

Fats and proteins constituted the primary diet deficiencies of the people of Buchen, as, indeed, was the case throughout most of Germany in the early postwar years. Livestock populations had been dangerously depleted in the area during the war, and the tiny farms clinging to hillsides about the town were for the most part in root and bread-grain crops. So little of their produce reached the food shops in town that scores of housewives walked or bicycled daily into the countryside in order to supplement their families' meager rations with bartered "luxuries" such as eggs and meat.

But even with all these efforts, the diet of the townfolk dropped steadily until the spring of 1948. While it did not reach the level which obtained in large cities, it was nonetheless a good day when the average citizen of Buchen could treat himself to a piece of meat and a soup to wash it down.

Farmers, by and large, were unwilling to part with their produce for reichsmarks, at least for legal prices. Cattle and swine were slaughtered surreptitiously in forests and remote fields in the night, the carcasses to be carted off before dawn to the teeming cities where they brought fantastic sums on the black market.

For nearly three years one of the biggest headaches of Buchen's succession of Military Government officers was to see that available food in the countryside was channeled into legitimate supply outlets for equitable distribution. Hundreds of barns and cellars and cribs were inspected during this period, and a system of crop sampling was instituted to force recalcitrant, hoarding farmers to report their yields.

But with the reluctance of Local German authorities to crack down on farmers, Military Government fought a losing fight. It would have taken an army of inspectors to get all of the foodstuffs in. Not until currency reform in the summer of 1948 was the situation to be corrected.

When the first weeks of American Occupation came and went in Buchen and the widely anticipated terror had not developed, the townspeople began to relax. These soldiers were not so bad. They were especially kind to children, and no one was being mistreated except for the property requisitioning. Military Government had already given evidence that it was going to try to straighten out the more immediate problems in the town and county. Gradually the Bucheners warmed up to their conquerors. All was forgiven. The war had been a sad mistake; Hitler, the pig, was but a bad memory.

Then it began. Counter Intelligence Corps agents fanned out over the *Landkreis* with lists drawn from the records of the former *Kreisleiter*. Thousands of Nazi party members were picked up in arrest sweeps and bundled off to hastily erected internment camps in the area. In the strongly Catholic town of Buchen proper, there were 260 names on the list.

Stunned and frightened by this seeming about-face on the part of the Occupation authorities, the good citizens scrambled to extricate themselves from the suspect group. As the demand for questionnaires followed upon each other in quick succession—for the CIC, for Military Government, for trade and industry boards, and, finally, for the German denazification boards (*Spruchkammer*), a thriving business in sworn statements was struck up among the people. Affidavits were exchanged in a system of mutual protection and were sold for a few cigarettes. And, conversely, bitter denunciations and false accusations flew thick and fast. Signed and anonymous, they flooded into Military Government headquarters daily as people sought to whitewash themselves by blackening others, or simply to wreak vengeance on old enemies. It was a familiar theme of treachery for the Germans—a page that might have been torn from the history of the Nazi regime.

Disillusionment and disappointment grew in Buchen as denazification proceedings dragged on month after month, through 1946 and into 1947. "The big ones are getting off lightly, and the little people are being stuck," was the common cry. It was obvious that the authors of the Law of Liberation had not understood how the National Socialist had functioned, how it was practically impossible for many a little man to avoid becoming a nominal member. As for Germans sitting on the local *Spruchkammer* in solemn judgment of these little people—well, how about old Max Deggelmann? A pious man and a good Christian Democrat, to be sure, these days. But why did he find it profitable or necessary to sell in his bookshop *Mein Kampf, The Myth of the Twentieth Century,* and the rest of the Nazi literature?

Why did *Ortsbeaustragter* Lauer get off completely unscathed, becoming a member of the Buchen town council after the war? Everyone knew that, but a short time before, his title had been *Ortsbauernführer,* the go-between of the local farmers' association and party officials. He had been a man of so much influence that to refuse to co-operate with him (to the extent of delivering butter and eggs and fresh meat for his bosses) had meant ruling oneself out of consideration for participation in the National Socialist's Farmers' Debt Elimination Program.

Would Herr Kiesling, proprietor of the largest grocery in town, get off as well? He argued that he could hardly have refused the important position of *Ortsgruppenleiter.* To have done so would have invited a boycott of his store by the wives of all the party members in the area. Could he help it if, on the other hand, lesser functionaries, SS people and ordinary SA members, found it pleasant to become his customers? And August Breunig, the tailor—was he to be punished or not, because he joined early so as to be able to share in the uniform-making boom?

Arguments raged nightly over water-beer in the White Horse, the Lion, and the rest of Buchen's dank *Wirtschaften.* Opinions were passed freely as to the innocence or guilt of someone about to be spruchkammered, but invariably the discussions devolved into the question, "What's the matter with the Americans? Can't they see what is happening? Why don't they change the law so that more of the big shots are really hurt and not so many of the small fry are ruined? Look at the bastard Stock—he is the one who denounced old *Landrat* Werber back in 1939 for making an antiwar remark and now he is back practicing law in this town. And then look at poor Joseph Kaiser—can't even keep his job as a postal clerk because he had to be a simple party member. What sort of democratic justice is that?

Joseph Kaiser had been wondering the same thing since the day late in 1945 when the CIC had summoned him. He had reviewed his life openly at that time. Born a farmer, he had grown up in the poverty and inflation Germany knew after the First World War. When the National Socialists came to power, it seemed to him that they were living up to most of the promises they had made to the farmers, so he joined the party. When the war came, it never occurred to him to question the wisdom or authority of the government. Of the 190 men from Buchen who served in the *Wehrmacht,* he was one of the first to get into uniform.

Joseph had been wounded before Moscow, wounded so severely that it was the end of the war for him, or almost, anyway. "What do you mean, almost?" the CIC agent asked. So Joseph, afraid for his job now, told him. He had been in the country outside of Buchen the day of December 31, 1944. There were many bombers overhead that day. Apparently they had raided some city to the north and were on their way back to their bases in England.

Suddenly he had heard a terrific explosion in the air not far away, and he guessed that two planes had collided. Quickly assembling what few men were in the vicinity, he had organized a search through the forest for survivors. Sure enough, they found an injured American officer, and when a young soldier in the search party had wanted to kill the man on the spot, he, Joseph Kaiser, as an old veteran of distinguished service, had stepped between the two and ordered the soldier away. Then the rest had carried the flier to the road and gotten him transportation to the hospital in town.

"He has sent my family three packages from America," Joseph said, "and last week I received this." He drew an envelope from his pocket and handed it over. Enclosed was a notarized statement attesting to the story Joseph Kaiser had just related. It was signed by First Lieutenant Lawrence Adler, USAAF.

The CIC agent finished reading and returned the paper. "But you were a party man, weren't you?" he insisted, and then added, "I'm afraid this won't help you much. Dismissed!"

The town of Buchen is governed, like most German towns, by a *Stadtrat*—in this case a community council of twelve members directly elected on secret ballot from party tickets for a term of six years. This group is headed by a burgomaster who is supposed to give business advice, supervise policy, and represent the city in all its external dealings in the *Landkreis* or beyond.

Since Buchen is 85 per cent Catholic, the postwar Christian Democratic Union—just as the pre-Hitlerian Catholic Center party always had—easily won the bulk of the twelve council seats in the first election after the war. From the city of Mannheim the council promptly imported for the job of burgomaster a rising CDU stalwart and ex-trade-school teacher, paunchy, dynamic little Franz Xaver Schmerbeck.

Casting about for a scheme to put Buchen on the map and incidentally enhance his position politically, Schmerbeck got wind of a proposal to build a tuberculosis hospital which, its sponsors contended, would attract both praise and business to the town. The new burgomaster fell in with the plan wholeheartedly and succeeded in talking the city fathers on the council into underwriting the project to the extent of a hundred thousand reichsmarks.

The hospital, a converted dormitory, was eventually completed, although at a cost considerably above the original estimates, and to an ever rising chorus of grumbling on the part of Bucheners in general. With the people of the town living in antiquated quarters at a ratio of more than three to every two rooms, and the situation getting worse by the month with the endless stream of refugee *Volksdeutsch* from the East, it seemed to many that this money might have been more wisely spent. Perhaps their doubts were well founded. To date the new hospital has not begun to pay off, or at least not to the town. As for the enterprising Schmerbeck, by mid-1946 he had gained enough of a name to be elected to the bigger job of *Landrat* of the *Kreis*.

Walter Kaiser, also a minor CDU party wheel from Mannheim, was the next man to take the municipal helm of postwar Buchen. Although his tenure of office was brief, it is quite likely that he will be remembered in legend long after many another burgomaster of the little community on the fringe of the Odenwald has become nothing more than a forgotten signature in musty records at the *Rathaus*.

A family man with two teen-age daughters and a devoted wife, Kaiser was the epitome of German Catholic correctness in his early months in his new home. He made a particular issue of public morals, even succeeding in having mixed bathing banned at the local swimming pool.

But before many months elapsed, whispers were heard that the burgomaster was believed to be carrying on a liaison with a certain young woman. The rumor was spread carefully at first; burgomasters of small German towns are powerful individuals, and slander of public officials is a serious offense. If Kaiser knew of these stories, he refused to heed them. But he should have.

One midnight in late autumn, 1948, the town's housing director was making his way homeward after working especially late at his hopeless task in the city hall. As he rounded a corner on the way, he observed first the legs and then the posterior of what appeared to be a rather stout man emerging from the side window of a house against which a ladder had been propped. Horrified, the housing chief watched for only a moment before giving the alarm. There would be no such thing as housebreaking in Buchen if he could help it. There was enough trouble in the overcrowded town without thievery. Seconds later, with windows clattering up all about, the two men stood face to face at the foot of the ladder. One of them was a very flustered and red-faced burgomaster named Walter Kaiser.

Burgomaster Kaiser belligerently refused to quit his office for some weeks after the incident. By then the story of the philandering mayor of Buchen had spread far and wide throughout the *Landkreis* and beyond, and the natives, tired of being ribbed, were demanding his removal forthwith. Eventually the embarrassed Christian Democratic party command prevailed upon their wayward son to withdraw from the political scene "for reasons of health."

Not until late in the spring of 1949 was the vacant burgomaster's chair filled again by the voters of Buchen. In the interim a citizens' group had prevailed upon August Schmitt, who had been relieved of the same job by the Nazis back in 1933, to return to town and stand for election to the mayor's post once again. Doctor Schmitt won handily as an independent with no party affiliation. The CDU could thank Kaiser for their defeat.

Old-timers in Buchen looked to the future optimistically with Schmitt back in the driver's seat. They remembered him as a man of integrity and enterprise and intelligence. He had given them good municipal government before; it was to be hoped he could do it again.

Perhaps Schmitt, given time, could restore the financial position of the town to where it was before the introduction of the Deutsche mark all but wiped out depository funds, while leaving public indebtedness at one reichsmark to one

Deutsche mark. Admittedly it would be a tough job with annual tax revenues at about 170,000 marks, with 80 per cent of this earmarked for the maintenance of public utilities, parks, schools, hospitals (two of them, now), salaries, and so on.

If the good doctor could reconstruct the sewage disposal system, improve water purification facilities, construct a morgue and a slaughterhouse, build a new trade and an agricultural school, rebuild the secondary school, and attend to the badly needed repair of roads and lanes, the townspeople would be grateful to him.

But first of all, if he could do something about the housing situation caused by the 1,300 expellees and refugees in the town, they would more than appreciate it. The twelve new houses going up on the edge of town under the auspices of *Neue Heimat,* the privately sponsored settlement association organized by Father Magnani, were fine, but only a drop in the bucket compared with the need. Besides, few of the 174 families in quest of decent quarters could afford the three hundred marks needed to become eligible for a new home.

Easily the most popular of the Military Government officers who have served in Buchen since the war is thirty-year-old, redheaded Marshall Prentice, who resides in the fine house that once belonged to Dr. Karl Holzwarth, the SS *Parteiarzt* who committed suicide when Americans occupied the town. Holzwarth's principal official function during the war had been to insure the sterility of the numerous Middle-European slave laborers who were assigned to farms and homes in the region. Once ousted from this role, he could see no reason to face the future or the Americans, and so did away with himself.

Prentice, a former officer in the parachute troops, knows his Germany well. He was captured in Holland where he had dropped with British forces in September 1944, and thereafter had the privilege of marching twice across the Third Reich. Far from being embittered, although his health was nearly ruined by the experience, he believes that he gained an insight into the German character.

The thing that endeared Marsh Prentice everlastingly to the people of Buchen occurred not many weeks after he had arrived in the town in January 1949. It was *Fastnacht,* pre-Lenten carnival time, which to Bucheners, as to the natives of many towns in Germany, is the high point of the year. Unlike his predecessors, Prentice not only gave full approval to the traditional celebration, he participated in it. He allowed himself to be made an honorary member of the "Board of Eleven Fools" which runs the town for the duration of the festivities.

The Buchen carnival had been suppressed by the Nazis to a point where no attempt was made to keep the five-hundred-year-old tradition from 1938 onward to the end of the war. Adolfus Hemberger, high president of the "Board of Eleven Fools," and his fun-loving colleagues could not bear to see the affair given the political slant without which it was unpalatable to the National Socialist authors of "Strength through Joy."

Carnival in Buchen was officially sanctioned by the Bishop of Mainz in 1447 to celebrate the completion of the summer home he had had erected there, a Roman-Franconian-Gothic structure which still stands and is used as the town museum. Sometime thereafter a second celebration which related to the successful defense of the town when it had been besieged by neighboring communities was incorporated with the religious holiday into one hilarious demonstration.

During carnival time Buchen is referred to as the *Blecher-stadt,* or displayer town. Set up in the center of town is a huge papier-mâché nude human figure straddling a stone block, with its rear higher than its head and with its tongue sticking out in the 1382 equivalent of a Bronx cheer. This attitude of bawdy derision, according to legend, was actually struck atop the town wall by a loyal lady of Buchen during the siege—an act which is alleged to have so shaken the spirit of the attackers that they gave up and went home. The original stone statue, much smaller, rests in state in the museum.

Naturally the time-honored custom of Buchen is to force all strangers to plant a kiss upon that part of the *Blecher* which is most prominent. When Prentice complied with a flourish as hundreds of onlookers chanted the traditional *Hinne Hoch!*—Keep your tail up!—he was "in" with the natives, although he had some explaining to do to his superiors later.

Within hours after having made this politic public gesture, the personable young Military Government officer received no less than twenty-eight house keys, handed to him by various members of Buchen's fairer sex in what is another time-honored tradition of the *Blecherstadt*'s carnival. "Without question," says Prentice, "it was the biggest trial of my life. I had to return each *Schlüssel* graciously and properly before midnight the following Tuesday!"

Ash Wednesday dawned cold and gray in Buchen. The bells in the church tower shattered great, jagged holes in the aching haze created by four solid days of cheap white wine. Slowly the people of Buchen crawled from under their feather ticks. It was the knell of reality calling them, and there was no escape. They were facing another long year of heavy burdens and small rewards—the staid, meager life a small postwar German town has to offer.

Chapter XI

Germany's Stepchildren

By ERNEST LEISER

T HE summer sun pounded down on the bleak and dusty flatlands of Dachau. From the sprawling barracks, where once the inmates of the grimmest murder mill of them all had been concentrated, streamed a throng of shabby men and women.

As they crossed to the wide square opposite the gray building which had housed the gas chamber their faces were intent and angry. They pushed together, squeezing and shoving as close as possible to the platform on which a burning-eyed man of fifty was exhorting them with the controlled rage of a practiced orator.

"Let them remember," he shouted in a German which had the thick accent of the Sudetenland, "that we are German too, that German blood runs fiercely through our veins. Let them not dare longer to treat us as aliens in an alien land. When the might of the Fatherland was marching in triumph, we marched along. Let them care for us now in defeat." As the twenty thousand men and women in the square roared approval, the hard-faced speaker waved for silence. "We must not let them provoke us to violence," he said in a lower, caressing tone of voice. "That's what they want—to break and destroy us.

"Yet I tell you this," and again his voice rose to its trained frenzy, "When they say to us, 'We have no money to care for you,' we must demand that they find money. When they say, 'There are no jobs, no homes,' we must reply, 'Find jobs, find homes or we will rise in our righteous might.'

"And if," he shouted, "the German treasury cannot provide for our needs, let the Americans take care of us. They are spending billions in preparing to start the next world war. Let them take that money to feed and clothe us."

He continued for an hour, ranting on against the German and Occupation authorities. He interspersed his harangue with appeals to "remain calm" so deftly needled that they only incited the crowd to noisier anger. By the time he had finished, in a screaming crescendo of denunciation, his twenty thousand listeners had turned into an uncontrollable mob. They stormed out of the camp armed with clubs and stones, and before police could quell them they smashed the surrounding area in a fury of vengeful destruction.

The man who could stir his auditors to such frenzy is Egon Hermann, the "demagogue of Dachau," something of a man of mystery. He arrived at the former concentration camp in June 1948, having just been expelled, he said, from Prague. Investigation, however, indicated that he and his wife had left Czechoslovakia in 1946 for Russia's zone of Germany and had been able freely to return to Prague, where he lived and worked intermittently until May 1948.

Dynamic and ruthless, Hermann has been called a neo-Nazi and an agent of the Soviets. His own words would offer some justification for both accusations. He admits, with notable pride, that he was a Nazi. He says he is not a Communist but "of the Left" and adds that his "political conviction is the color of my heart's blood." He shouts that "the day will come when we shall take what we want."

Whatever his political coloration, his political ambition is plain. He aspires to be the "Führer" of Germany's expellees and, through them, perhaps of all Germany. He has been sentenced to a year in prison for inciting his followers in Bavaria to riot, and he has privately compared his sentence to that of Hitler in Landsberg Prison. "My sentence is a badge of honor," he has said.

Although Hermann himself may be a mysterious figure, there is no mystery about the "expellees," the people to whom he has made his primary appeal.

They are the Germans and peoples of German origin who since the end of the war have been kicked out of the countries of Eastern Europe and kicked into a "Fatherland" which has no room, few jobs, little understanding, and less hope for its wandering children.

There are 9,000,000 or more of them; no one knows just how many there are because most of them arrived too late to be included in the census of 1946. About 2,500,000 were booted out of the Sudetenland and elsewhere in Czechoslovakia. Half a million came from Hungary, some from Rumania, half a million from Yugoslavia, more than a million from Poland proper. The rest—nearly half—came from the German territories east of the Oder-Niesse line. These include the rich Silesian lands which Russia handed over to Poland in exchange for the Soviet seizure of eastern Poland, and East Prussia which the Russians and Poles divided as the spoils of war.

Most of this latter group first went to the Soviet Zone. Under the Potsdam Agreement those Germans expelled from Silesia and East Prussia were to be settled in Eastern Germany. However, when they were drafted for labor in the uranium mines, or treated as second-class citizens by their countrymen, or fitted into the pattern of Soviet Germany's "new democracy," hundreds of thousands moved on to the Western zones. An estimated 30,000 to 50,000 are still coming across the zonal border to West Germany monthly.

This mass of 9,000,000 displaced Germans—badly adjusted to a strange and often hostile environment, placing heavy burdens on an already overburdened society, resentful and deeply resented—constitutes the gravest menace to the development of democracy in Western Germany today.

Propertyless, afire with bitterness at expulsion from the lands which had been "home" for a lifetime, they are dangerously vulnerable to the importunities of a new demagogue-dictator. At the same time their unwilling and unwanted presence in every city, town, and village of the Western zones is an inevitable cause of conflict among the native Germans and of incitement to a new war to win back the "lost territories" of the Fatherland.

On August 2, 1945, when Harry Truman and Clement Attlee signed the Potsdam Protocol with Joseph Stalin, they reluctantly agreed, at the latter's insistence, that "the transfer to Germany of German populations, or elements thereof, remaining in Poland, Czechoslovakia, and Hungary will have to be undertaken." However, they insisted that any transfer "should be effected in an orderly and humane manner." Not only did expulsion come from countries other than those envisaged at Potsdam, but it was anything but orderly and humane. With the bitterness and vengefulness that only a previously conquered and oppressed people can know, the Czechoslovakians, Poles, Yugoslavs, Bessarabians, and Hungarians threw the Germans and racial Germans out.

From the Sudetenland they were given only a few hours to cross the borders. They had to leave their valuables behind, getting out only with what they could carry on their backs or in their suitcases. From Yugoslavia they were often not even permitted to take extra clothes. From Silesia they had to travel by foot across the new Polish border to the Russian Zone of Germany.

The Potsdam signatories had requested the Czechs, the Polish Provisional Government, and the Allied Control Council in Hungary to suspend further expulsion until the distribution of the expellees could be worked out and facilities found for them. That plea was generally observed in the breach.

Nor was the welcome which met the refugees on their arrival in the "homeland" much warmer than the farewells of the governments which had expelled them. In every community where they sought refuge there was inadequate food even for the natives; people were already crowded together in the ruins left by Allied bombs and shells; there weren't enough clothes or jobs to share, nor was there money to care for them until they could make some kind of readjustment.

When they reached Germany the *Flüchtlinge* were herded together in camps and barracks, many of which had been quarters for the *Wehrmacht;* many others, like Dachau, had housed the laborers brought from conquered Europe to slave for the Thousand-Year Reich.

The camps were unbelievably crowded and often filthy. The *Flüchtlinge* had brought with them the diseases of exhaustion and undernourishment. There were frequent epidemics, and, especially among the old, the death rate was high. When the refugees first came on the scene their German racial cousins were struggling for survival on fewer than fifteen hundred calories a day plus what they could scrounge from their savings on the black market or in the countryside. In most cases the expellees had not even the savings to afford the black-market supplementaries. They were forced to live off the legal ration.

In theory the refugees were to stay in the camps only until the local labor offices could find work for them and until the local housing bureaus could squeeze them into someone's lodgings. That, however, was only theory. In practice, their weeks at the camps often lengthened into months, and sometimes the months dragged out into years before they could be "placed" in the community.

Even today, in the barracks and shanties of the camps, there are nearly a half-million men, women, and children crowded together, several families to a room, sharing the meager food and the primitive facilities.

Whatever the location of these camps—in southern Bavaria where more than 2,000,000 expellees have settled among the clannishly hostile natives or in northernmost Schleswig-Holstein where the 800,000 refugees are nearly half the entire population of the little state—they have a common denominator in the misery and discomfort of their inmates. Some of the camps may be cleaner than others, some more humanely administered, but at best they are all dreary and deeply depressing breeding places of unrest.

In a camp outside of Ludwigsburg, in Württemberg-Baden, I listened to a story which is typical of these forlorn wanderers who once were proud cousins of the mighty Germany, whom Adolf Hitler insisted were his charges, no matter where they might live.

Two families, eleven persons in all, were squeezed into a single barracks room. The air was heavy with the odor of stale straw from the mattresses and the unwashed bodies of the inhabitants. As I came into the room all conversation ceased, and the head of one family approached me eagerly.

"You are the man from the district labor office?" he asked eagerly, in a heavy Slavic-tinged German which bore little resemblance to the slurred local Swabian dialect.

When I answered with an apologetic "no," he found it impossible to conceal his disappointment. "But the *Kaserneleiter* told us three days ago, once more, that the representative of the labor office would come to us with our job assignments this week, so we would be eligible for rooms," he cried. "And he made the same promise last week."

He introduced himself as Herr Mannfried Abusch and pointed out his wife, Gunda, her mother, a wrinkled, eighty-three-year-old wraith of a woman, and his fourteen-year-old twin sons, Horst and Helmuth. Theirs were the five beds in the one half of the room, he said. Across the aisle, the six beds were occupied by the family of Herr Arthur Koeppler, his wife, seventeen-year-old daughter Irme, two younger sons, and his brother. The brother, a deaf mute, was lying asleep on the bed. Herr Koeppler was in Stuttgart looking for odd jobs. The rest of both families gathered around me.

They had all been expelled from Yugoslavia in early 1946, although their families had settled there before the turn of the century in the days of the Austro-Hungarian Empire. The Koepplers had owned a tinware shop at Samobor, a village near Zagreb, in Croatia, and Herr Abusch had owned a sizable farm near by on which he had four tenant families.

Herr Abusch said that he had been conscripted by the German Army when it swept across northern Yugoslavia and had later served in Greece and Italy. He was captured there and released four months after the war ended. Herr Koeppler was too old to be drafted by the Germans, and he was careful to mention that he had taken no part in local political activities.

When he returned home, Herr Abusch said, he found that his entire farm had been confiscated, one of the tenants executed as a collaborator, and the property divided among the other three and the local chairman of the "People's Front." Herr Koeppler's shop was confiscated in February 1946, and a month later he and his family, along with three other families of German origin in the village, were ordered to leave the country. To make sure they got across, soldiers conducted them all the way to the frontier at Maribor in a truck, then to the Austrian border post on foot.

Both families went to a camp at Graz, in Austria, where they
stayed a month, then made their way to Innsbruck, where an
Austrian cousin of Herr Koeppler lived. There, with the
cousin's help, Koeppler found a job in a cheese-processing
plant, and Abusch got temporary work as a common laborer.
However, two years later the cousin had died and Koeppler's
job was taken by a native Austrian. Unable to get more work,
both men had been notified that the local *Wohnungsamt*
(housing office) was withdrawing their right to be domiciled
in Innsbruck.

In a curt notice to all the expellees in the area, the
Innsbruck labor office said that henceforth priority in job
openings would be given to Austrian citizens and that, since
there was limited employment available in the country, the
Flüchtlinge could not count on finding work again.

Out of work, out of their lodgings, the Koeppler and
Abusch families were then brusquely notified by a local
official that it might be better if they left the country altogether. After all, he said, they were Germans, not Aus-
trians. Why did they not go "home"?

In desperation Herr Koeppler remembered another relative, a great-uncle in Stuttgart. He recalled him as a prosperous man. Perhaps he could help. So once again the two
families picked up the handful of belongings they had accumulated in Austria and trudged over the hills into Upper
Bavaria, dodging the border police because, like most of the
refugees, they had no entry permit.

For six weary days they walked and hitchhiked toward
Stuttgart, sleeping at night in woods or barns. By the end of
their journey the mother of Frau Abusch was barely able to
walk, and lack of food had made them all weak.

Then, when they finally arrived in Stuttgart, another blow
fell. The house of the great-uncle had been destroyed during
the war, and no one in the neighborhood knew what had

happened to him or any of his relatives. Destitute, the Abusches and Koepplers had no choice but to report to the local refugee authorities and throw themselves on their mercies.

Those mercies were not conspicuously tender. The official to whom they applied for help sent them to the camp at Ludwigsburg only after violent abuse for their illegal entry into the country. There were nearly three-quarters of a million refugees in Württemberg-Baden already, he said. How did these migratory idiots think the citizens of Germany could continue to support this never-ending influx? These *Flüchtlinge* were not real Germans; they were alien trouble-makers. Why didn't they go somewhere else?

The Koepplers and Abusches took the abuse, and they took the single room in the stone barracks which was made available to them. There they had been ever since, waiting for the local authorities to find them work and a few rooms in which to live.

Uprooted, penniless, almost hopeless, these eleven people by now had two driving compulsions: First, an animal determination to find, once more, enough to eat and a place in which they could have some privacy; and second, a formless desire for revenge on the Yugoslavs and all the others who had deprived their lives of all stability and promise.

Multiply the Abusches and the Koepplers by a million and you have in essence the staggering problem of the expellees in Western Germany today.

In fairness to the state governments in the Western zones it must be reported that most of them have made genuine efforts to meet that problem squarely. Although in the time-honored tradition of German bureaucracy many refugee officials have been more conscious of their dignity and authority than of their enormous responsibilities, the governments themselves have taken every step possible to receive, process, and rehabilitate the expellees. Practically every state has either a ministry or a state secretariat for refugees. In some cases the administration has been entrusted to men who are themselves expellees. Their main job has been to distribute the new arrivals as equitably as possible, settling them where they will cause the least social and economic dislocation and where there is the most room.

It has been an enormously difficult task. Even in Bavaria, the richest and most nearly self-sufficient of all the states in Western Germany, there are two persons assigned to every habitable room. There simply has not been space available to absorb the expellees without sharply increasing dislocation.

The endeavor of the refugee offices has been to place expellees on an equal footing with the rest of the population in allocation of housing space. In practice this has rarely been done. The most accurate estimates available indicate that in the spring of 1949 there were nearly four refugees to a room throughout Western Germany, and that did not include those in the camps, where, of course, the figures were far higher.

The second major task of the refugee administrations has been to find work for the new arrivals. Again, the theory has been that job allocation would be made equally and with no discrimination between the native population and the expellees. Again, in practice that has proven impossible.

Hostility of the local citizenry has made the work of refugee officials enormously difficult from the beginning. However Hitler regarded the *Volksdeutsche,* most of the German people after the war regarded them as aliens. So when the expellees were dumped unceremoniously into a war-shattered, poverty-stricken, and truncated Germany, there was little neighborliness or sympathy shown them.

Egon Hermann could demand that the Bavarians "care for us now in defeat." He could not, however, eliminate the prejudice the Bavarians showed for anything foreign, nor the undisguised antipathy they indicated to the "squatters" in their midst. Fights between the expellees and the Western Germans have been frequent; efforts of the local populations to squeeze the refugees out of jobs and out of their communities have been repeated.

To a slight but perceptible degree, the conflict between the *Flüchtlinge* and their unwilling hosts was resolved during 1949, the year of decision. Generally improved economic conditions and growing normalcy somewhat smoothed over the rough points of friction. Yet although the number declined, there were still 40 per cent of the refugees who, when asked in the spring of 1949 if they were satisfied or dissatisfied with the treatment given them by the indigenous German population, answered in an angry negative. And aware though they are of the Communist rule in their various homelands, 85 per cent of the expellees told United States Military Government opinion analysts that they would go back if they could.

In a camp at Kiel, one refugee explained his reasons to me. "I am no politician," he said. "The politicians are all dishonest, no matter what side they represent. All I want is to be left alone, to work in peace and to have a home of my own. Today when I look for a job I am always asked where I come from. When I tell then Silesia they say, 'We haven't enough jobs for our own people. We will not give you work.' When I look for a room I am told, 'You refugees have taken all our housing already. There is no space.' That's why I would go back, if they let me, no matter who rules my town."

On the heels of an economic boom, brought about by ECA aid and currency reform, Western Germany has been cursed with its largest-scale unemployment since the war. The total of jobless in the summer of 1949 hovered at the million and a quarter mark. The acuteness of the task of finding work for the refugees can be seen from the fact that they comprised an estimated two-thirds of the unemployed. Hundreds of thousands of others found only casual or part-time jobs and had to be partially supported by the German state governments.

Even among those lucky enough to have found work the standards of wages are much lower than among the local population. At the end of 1948, 37 per cent of the refugees quizzed in a Military Government survey reported incomes ranging *downward* from 100 Deutsche marks monthly, a wage barely adequate to keep body and soul together. The comparable figure for the German population was approximately 19 per cent, half as many in the lowest brackets.

Not surprisingly, there are many more broken homes, many fewer living "normal family lives" among the refugees than among the native Germans. Often when they were expelled families were forced to separate. Or on arrival in the Western zones they were compelled to part in order to find work or housing.

As a result a survey showed that, while nearly three-fourths of the married Germans were united with their families, only slightly more than half of the expellees who were married were living family lives.

The problem of the old people among the refugees has proven most difficult of all. Uprooted from their homes after a lifetime of relative stability, they have been totally unable to adjust to their strange new surroundings and their bleak poverty. Their children and grandchildren found adaptability to life in Germany difficult; the elders found it impossible. Homes for the aged and the sick, already jammed as a result of wartime dislocations, have been taxed still more to care for the weak and old among the refugees, with the consequence that inmates of these homes often live in squalor at a bare subsistence level.

Grim as the problem of the expellees is there have been a few bright spots. Included among the millions of refugees were many of great professional knowledge, technical ingenuity, or high craftsmanship. The universities of the Western zones have benefited from the influx of refugee scholars. Industries have been given a boost by specially skilled laborers. And various new handicrafts have been developed.

Near the Bavarian resort town of Garmisch-Partenkirchen, in the winter of 1948-49, refugees put on a handicraft exposition. Given the limitations of material and money under which they had worked, it was an impressive show. A former Messerschmitt airplane engineer had designed a chromium-ribbed umbrella with a four-color Pliofilm top which could be changed in a few seconds to match the costumes of its carrier. There were platters, coffeepots, pitchers, and even jewelry beaten out of the brass castings of *Wehrmacht* shells and cartridges. There was fine Bohemian glassware. A man who had fled Hungary two years previously with only one extra shirt had a prosperous-looking exhibit of fine leather shoes and purses.

But although a few of the refugees have prospered in Germany and some others have made positive contributions to the economic or cultural life of the Western zones, the vast majority have constituted a knotty problem and a threat to the peace.

It is a burden which the politicians of Western Germany have sought to lighten not only out of humanitarian motives or for reasons of civic responsibility. They realize just how potent a political force is this bloc of nine million persons—nearly one-fifth the total population of the Bonn Republic. Men like Eugen Gersteinmaier, the shrewd, tough head of the Evangelical Relief Organization for Germany who has virtually made a career of caring for the refugees, believe that anyone who can swing the expellee vote can rule the Western German state.

On the other hand, the politicians realize that the 9,000,-000 intruders can be an element sufficiently disruptive to bring the new state into political and economic collapse—and either communism or a new fascism. Yet most of all they realize that the expellees are a problem which the Germany of today cannot solve by itself, no matter how determined, intelligent, and even unselfish the approach.

Eleven years ago Adolf Hitler began his march to conquest under the banner of *Lebensraum*. Little justified as the cry was then, even those bitterly hostile to Germany cannot deny that the remaining German territory is desperately over-crowded now. Today forty-six million people live in an area which before the war supported thirty-eight million, an area in which a third of the dwelling space has been demolished. The density of the population in trizonia today is an estimated 568 persons per square mile, more than three times as high as France and higher than any nation in continental Europe except Belgium and the Netherlands.

Inescapably the shortage of space and the inadequacy of the economy to provide for its crowded millions will lead—as soon as Germany's voice is heard again in the councils of the world—to new troubles. The powerful expellee minority, led by its Egon Hermanns, will demand that the Fatherland regain for them their lost lands and lost homes. Nor will they be squeamish, in their deep-rooted bitterness, about the means used to get them back. Under the circumstances the only healthy solution was one suggested, ironically enough, by France. At the conferences of foreign ministers held in Moscow and in London in 1947, Georges Bidault, then French foreign minister, warned the other powers that the future of these evicted millions must be dealt with carefully and sympathetically if a peace treaty with Germany was to have meaning. Bidault proposed an international agreement to sponsor large-scale German emigration, not of the kind by which Hitler infiltrated his victim countries but of a nature which would make possible genuine assimilation of the *Volksdeutsche* in countries sparsely enough populated to absorb them.

No action has been yet taken on the French proposal, nor has any other solution been offered by the world's great nations. Yet day by day, month by month, the influx of refugees continues, and the problem becomes more acute.

Dr. Wolfgang Jaenicke, state secretary of refugees in Bavaria, and himself an expellee from Silesia, told a reporter recently, "We know that it was the mad policies of Hitler which set in motion the horror which led to this enormous reshuffling of peoples. Yet we cannot see how Germany alone can ever cope with a mass of more than 9,000,000 people, evicted from their homes and deprived of their property.

"I suppose," and he smiled wryly, "you could call the *Flüchtlinge* our German war surplus. We cannot convert them to peacetime use within the borders of our own shrunken country. And there is little demand for them elsewhere. The human markets of the world are already glutted with refugees; people who have been driven from so many places, for so many reasons."

Chapter XII

March of Millions

By DENIS MARTIN

RECORDED history knows no precedent for the vast tide of uprooted humanity that flowed, with its undercurrents of potential unrest, economic chaos, and social upheaval, into the prostrate Germany of the Potsdam era. And so great was the confusion that historians and students of tomorrow will never be able to establish how many of the participants in this calamitous pilgrimage died on the way, became separated from their families or were irretrievably lost in the human maelstrom of postwar Germany.

These estimated 12,000,000 refugees left behind them rich and developed territories settled by Germans for centuries in East Prussia, the "New Poland," Czechoslovakia, Hungary, and even the distant Ukraine in the Soviet Union. This was the main stream of derelict humanity which threatened, in the early postwar months, to engulf the rest of Germany, itself on the brink of disaster. Now, four long years later these millions are proving themselves vital in the reestablishment of the German labor force and the recovery of Western Europe.

There were, of course, other movements of Germans back into the truncated Reich from Austria, Denmark, and the

Low Countries, but these resettlements were not of such profound historical importance, nor, being much smaller, were they destined to exercise so great an influence on the social structure of the German people. I refer, in this chapter, for the purposes of convenience, to the Germans drifting from the East as refugees, not only because the "orderly and humane" expulsions laid down in the Potsdam Agreement were rarely observed east of the new German border but because the term "refugee" is universally accepted and used in German today to describe all categories of *Ostvertriebenen*.

Bereft of hearth and home, shorn of all economic resources and social standing, the new masses paid to the full the terrible penalties of the aggressive and inhuman war waged by the Third Reich. The Germany of tomorrow, quite apart from the over-all effects of the war, the social cataclysms that took place independently of the migrations, and the surgical operations of the victor powers on the geographical face of the country, is destined to feel the impact of the refugee millions for generations and, perhaps, centuries to come. The already overcrowded zones of Occupation administered by the United States, Great Britain, the Soviet Union, and France had to accept the refugees, while at the same time suffering the loss under the Potsdam Agreement of 24 per cent of the former German territory and 28 per cent of the previously available arable land. Of grave significance for what remained of the Thousand-Year Reich was the fact that the farmsteads of the "separated areas" from which a high percentage of the destitute and hungry refugees were coming had previously provided a quarter of the prewar German food production. The hulk of the new Germany, with its bomb-torn cities and industries, its paralyzed railway systems, and its worn-out agriculture, was in no position to withstand the further shock of millions of men, women, and children who almost without exception arrived with the last assets of civilized people—a certain amount of knowledge and a pair of hands with which to work. The refugees left behind them 16 per cent of the prewar German production of hard coal, 17 per cent of the lumber output, 19 per cent of the paper and pulp manufacture, and 20 per cent of the alcohol production. Before the war their farms grew 26 per cent of Germany's bread grains, 32 per cent of its rye, and 30 per cent of its barley and potatoes. More than 20 per cent of the prewar German population of cattle, hogs, and sheep was located in the "separated areas."

However much deserved, the tragedy would have been all the more immense had it not been for the unstinted aid provided for Western Germany in the form of food and essential supplies by the peoples of the United States and Great Britain. The eight million refugees now in the United States, British, and French zones—roughly one in five of the total population—could never have survived except for this assistance from the major victor powers. It is a little-known but interesting fact that one dollar out of every ten in the huge loan granted by the United States to Great Britain after the war went to the upkeep of the German people. Thanks to these sacrifices, still being made years after the war is at an end and still placing considerable burdens on the American and British taxpayers, Western Germany has turned the corner, and the refugees, more securely integrated in her communities, are playing an increasingly valuable and co-operative part in the national recovery.

The stark contrast between what is known in Germany as the "Golden West" and the decaying economy and culture of the Soviet Zone has, however, produced still another phenomenon in this nation of nomads. The stream of westward-bound settlers never ceases. Germans are still pouring across the iron curtain border from the Alps to the sea, and by no stretch of the imagination could one claim that the migration is coming to an end. More accurately it is in the second phase, the phase of continued resettlement from the police state of Soviet Germany to the territories of the West German Federal Government. The general principles for the main movement of Germans into the shrunken Fatherland of 1945 were agreed between the Soviet Union, the United States, and Great Britain three months after the end of the war.

In the humid, thunder-filled atmosphere of Potsdam on August 2 of that fateful summer, Premier Joseph Stalin, President Harry S. Truman, and Prime Minister Clement Attlee signed their names to a historic declaration. The relevant extracts affecting the population of the separated areas of Germany and the German communities outside the frontiers of the pre-war Reich are as follows:

Königsberg for Russia:
"The Conference examined a proposal by the Soviet Government that, pending the final determination of territorial questions at the peace settlement, the section of the Union of Soviet Socialist Republics which is adjacent to the Baltic Sea should pass from a point on the eastern shore of the Bay of Danzig, north of Braunsberg-Goldap, to the meeting point of the frontiers of Lithuania, the Polish Republic, and East Prussia."

"The Conference has agreed in principle to the proposal of the Soviet Government concerning the ultimate transfer to the Soviet Union of the city Königsberg and the area adjacent to it as described above, subject to expert examination of the actual frontier."

"The President of the United States and the British Prime Minister have declared that they will support the proposal of the Conference at the forthcoming peace settlement."

Polish Claims in the West: Settlement Deferred

"The Conference considered questions relating to the Polish Provisional Government and the western boundary of Poland. In conformity with the agreement on Poland reached at the Crimea Conference, the three Heads of Government have sought the opinion of the Polish Provisional Government of National Unity in regard to the accession of territory in the North and West which Poland should receive. . . . The three Heads of Government reaffirm their opinion that the final delimitation of the western frontier of Poland should await the peace settlement."

The "Big Three" then set out in detail the new Polish-German frontier known now as the Oder-Neisse line, a bone of contention among the refugees who have moved westward from these areas in the years since the Potsdam conference. They then came to the point with their decision on the transfer of the German populations. The agreement stated:

"The Conference reached the following agreement on the removal of Germans from Poland, Czechoslovakia, and Hungary:

"The three Governments, having considered the question in all its aspects, recognize that the transfer to Germany of German populations, or elements thereof, remaining in Poland, Czechoslovakia, and Hungary will have to be undertaken. They agree that any transfers that take place should be effected in an orderly and humane manner.

"Since the influx of a large number of Germans into Germany would increase the burden already resting on the occupying authorities, they consider that the Allied

Control Council in Germany should, in the first instance, examine the problem with special regard to the question of the equitable distribution of these Germans among the several zones of Occupation. They are accordingly instructing their respective representatives on the Control Council to report to their Governments as soon as possible the extent to which such persons have already entered Germany from Poland, Czechoslovakia, and Hungary and to submit an estimate of the time and rate at which further transfers could be carried out, having regard to the present situation in Germany.

"The Czechoslovak Government, the Polish Provisional Government, and the Control Council in Hungary are, at the same time, being informed of the above and are being requested meanwhile to suspend further expulsions pending the examination by the Governments concerned of the report from their representatives on the Control Council."

So much for the Potsdam Agreement and its obvious indications that the "Big Three" in their sealed-off conference room were already well aware that all was not well in the German world outside. The fact is that long before the ill-starred Potsdam document began its brief course in history the millions were already on the move, surging west from the territories conquered by the Red Army or moving blindly in the bombed-out wildernesses of the industrial areas of Western Germany. In a fantastic and unbelievable manner they were milling around even before hostilities ceased, inextricably tangled up on the one hand with the millions of slave workers then trying to move east to freedom, and on the other hand with the dispirited formations of the defeated and leaderless armies. They had already become an aggravating factor in the serious situation, a direct result of

American and British bombing, which, because of the wartime dispersal of industries and the labor force in general, had already scattered hundreds of thousands of German families from their traditional homes and work places.

Making their journeys in terrible and primitive conditions and carrying all their remaining possessions in bundles of ragged and verminous bedding, the refugees contributed materially to the mass misery. They accentuated the catastrophic food shortages and increased the demand for nonexistent accommodation and the meager reserves of the most elementary necessities of life. These were days of looting, of crime and violence, a jungle-like existence in which only the fit and resourceful could expect to survive. These were the days when the diseases of social distress made deep inroads into the ranks of the German people. Venereal disease, scabies, tuberculosis, rickets, diphtheria, and typhoid increased on an alarming scale. Hospitals could no longer cope with the flow of patients, paper bandages were the order of the day, and drugs of all kinds were in desperately short supply. These were the days when the words of a distinguished German historian, Doctor Friedensburg, writing of the state of the German communities at the end of the First World War, had a prophetic value. If his statement exaggerated the conditions of the time about which he was writing, it was completely true of the refugees after the Second World War. "This was the time," he said in his work on the Weimar Republic, "when a telegram arrived later than a letter, when soap was a luxury, when the worn-out locomotives came to a halt on the open tracks, and when a mother was glad to have a newspaper in which to wrap her newborn child."

In Berlin in the early postwar days a veritable army of despair swarmed into the refugee centers and emergency medical stations of the capital. In that grim autumn of 1945 I reported back to London: "Outside the Lehrte railway station, refugees awaiting onward transport to the west are camped out in waiting rooms, on the platforms and on the waste ground facing the station. Pots and pans project from the bundles of dirty clothes and bedding for all the world like the malignant fruit of some evil and unknown growth. Ersatz coffee boils over the crude fireplaces pieced together from broken bricks and paving stones. Nondescript washing flutters from lines slung between the bent and rusted lamp posts. Although the next train is not due to leave for twelve hours, hundreds of these anonymous and hopeless people have been here all night. Only a few hundred yards away, in one of the former German military prisons, a small team of Red Cross workers and three German doctors are trying to deal with a flow of 2,500 people daily, most of them women and children and each and every one of them in urgent need of delousing and medical attention."

These early movements, frightening and unsettling as they were, proved to be only the forerunners of the unparalleled migrations that date from the Potsdam Agreement. The four military governors on the Allied Control Council were able, by November 1945, to produce a plan of agreed proposals for the gradual resettlement in the four zones of Occupation of approximately 6,500,000 "expellees" from the "New Poland," Czechoslovakia, Austria, and Hungary. Under this plan the Soviet Zone was to receive 2,750,000 Germans, the British Zone, 1,150,000, the United States Zone, 2,250,000, and the French Zone, 150,000. Even if it had not been painfully obvious before, it was apparent from the start of this mammoth operation that the Potsdam Agreement for "orderly and humane" transfers was being flagrantly ignored. It was also quite clear that Germans vastly in excess of those envisaged in the agreement were being turned out with a ruthlessness amounting almost to savagery from the territories ceded to Soviet and Polish administration. It was the same story, too, in the mountainous Sudeten areas of Czechoslovakia, where skilled workers and their families fled to the greater tolerance of the Bavarian provinces of the United States Zone, bringing with them their centuries-old tradition of craftsmanship which, in the years since, has stood them in good stead.

By April 1946 the British Control Commission, after unsuccessful attempts at the four-power level to remedy what was rapidly becoming a weight on the conscience of civilized communities all over the world, was obliged to report back to its government that the "conditions of movements were not being satisfactorily observed." The report to London said, "A high proportion of sick expellees is being included in the trainloads arriving at the frontier posts. Both on the trains and after arrival there have been a number of cases of deaths of people too old or too ill to stand the journey. Many are so ill that they have to be taken straight to hospitals. Women nearing confinement are being dispatched and births have occurred on the trains or in the reception camps."

The British report was a masterly and calculated understatement of the horrors suffered by the refugees in the dirty cattle trucks with their total lack of toilet space and of heating and the crude straw bedding. It pointed out that the Germans were not given sufficient food and that many would have "suffered greatly" if the Russians had not provided some further rations during the westward journey. The Polish guards were not effective, failed to stop people leaving the trains, and worse still, in days of open daylight robbery, did nothing to prevent unauthorized persons from getting on board. A very high proportion of the human cargo shipped to Western Germany, said the Control Commission, consisted of very old, weak, and sick people, and less than 8 per cent were men. And of these men an even smaller percentage were males fit for work.

This biting indictment—never seriously challenged by the Polish authorities—continued with its major charges: "Thus it would appear that what the Polish authorities are transferring is not, as was agreed at Potsdam, the entire German minority population, but a selection of it with the purpose of moving into Western Germany the 1,500,000 sick and otherwise less useful part of the community. In addition to the above matters which have been verified, the expellees make allegations that the conditions of expulsion are not human. These statements may be exaggerated to support their accusations that insufficient notice of eviction is given. It is evident that many of the Germans have been robbed of their personal possessions on the way."

In hundreds of thousands of cases the refugees moved from bad to worse. It was not surprising. Lack of food, lack of shoes and clothing, lack of a room or even a bed were commonplace in the threadbare social structure of what was left of Germany at the end of the war. A new proletariat was being born overnight.

Side by side with the "legal" refugees, that is to say those Germans moving west under the four-power operation of resettlement agreed by the Allied Control Council, floods of illegal settlers were trekking west as best they could. It has taken years of patient research to discover exactly how many Germans moved into the postwar Reich. The problem, ever since the resurgence of Western Germany as an economic power in Western Europe, has been complicated by the secondary migration between the Soviet Zone and the West. By the end of 1948 the provincial governments of Western Germany and the experts of the Western powers agreed that some eight million excess Germans had arrived in the three Western zones. Figures for the Soviet Zone are not available but it is almost certain that Eastern Germany houses some four million refugees and that the over-all total of newcomers is, therefore, in the neighborhood of twelve million. The migration has produced a startling paradox in Western Europe. After one of the most terrible wars in history, in which millions upon millions of people were killed and murdered, the defeated Germany, as consituted at Potsdam, emerged with a population increased by some six million persons.

Any apparent advantage in this unique situation is, however, illusory. The preponderance of females in the postwar resettlements, coupled with extremely heavy war casualties among the male community and the unknown fate of millions of men classified as "missing" on the Soviet front, left the sex ratio badly unbalanced. Within a year after the end of the war it was apparent that the sociological makeup of the German people was undergoing a radical change. In all areas of the country, and particularly in the big cities and industrial concentrations, women outnumbered men on such a scale that females emerged as an important factor in the available labor force.

For the first time in a country in which the dead dictator had inculcated the doctrine that the German woman was dedicated to the home, the procreation of children, and obedience to the state, the women of postwar Germany found the door open to professions that were formerly the domain of males. The shortage of men brought a sensational boom to the divorce courts, radically altered previous standards of moral conduct, and even produced a crop of new schemes for the legal standing in the new state of the unmarried mother and the illegitimate child. Economists were fascinated and worried at the new balance between the sexes and estimated, on the strength of all available figures, that it would be twenty to twenty-five years before the sex ratio could be reestablished on its prewar basis.

It is now necessary to digress for a moment into yet another human problem deeply affecting the lives and outlook of the Germans today, the problem of the prisoners of war. It is a commonplace assertion that the slow return from the Soviet Union of prisoners and the deliberate retention of others is having a grave effect on a country topheavy with females and with its families mixed up on a scale not known in Europe since the Thirty Years' War.

As late as January 1949 the governments of the United States, Great Britain, and France asked the Soviet Government for a statement on the return to Germany of prisoners held in the Soviet Union. Mr. Molotov, then Soviet Foreign Minister, indulged in some remarkable arithmetic at the 1947 Foreign Ministers' Conference in Moscow and said that only 890,532 German prisoners remained in Russia. Very few people outside the Soviet Union and still fewer in Germany placed any credence on this statement. Soviet war communiques claimed 3,730,995 prisoners and the records of the Four-Power Repatriation Committee in Berlin showed that only 252,395 of these had been sent back to Germany by March, 1948, just one year after Mr. Molotov's arithmetic juggling at the Council of Foreign Ministers. Mr. Molotov was, in fact, claiming that 2,840,463 Germans had arrived back in the Reich by March 1947, a calculation made ridiculous by the records in Berlin, to which, as documents of the Allied Control Council, the Soviet delegation had set its signature.

The uncertainty as to the fate of millions of the German armed forces in the Soviet Union has created unrivaled problems in postwar Germany in all matters of marriage settlements, wills, and property. The situation is especially tragic for wives, particularly those in the widespread and powerful Roman Catholic communities, who have had opportunities of remarriage but who, four years after the war, are not certain whether they are widows or not.

Very large numbers of the returning prisoners arrived back in the same position as the refugees from the East. Hundreds of thousands of them came home completely unaware that their birthplaces and settlements in the East were no longer German and without any real knowledge as to where their families were. Throughout the length and breadth of Germany information offices set up by political parties, religious, social, and welfare organizations are still at work trying to unite these scattered family units and to obtain information from returning soldiers about their "missing" comrades. There are numerous recorded cases of prisoners returning to find their wives "remarried," or, as is more frequently the case, settled down with men who can help to maintain a home and support the children. A high percentage of the early prisoners sent back by the Russians consisted of sick, crippled, and morally broken men. These were the fearsome figures, a common sight in German cities as the Occupation began, of human scarecrows, their army uniforms in rags, their sunken faces unshaved, their eyes apparently not seeing whatever was in front of them and their feet shod with wooden clogs or sacking. Like their refugee brethren, these men were merely an additional burden on the collapsed economy of the postwar Reich.

A good example of the confusion arising from the influx of refugees into already overcrowded areas is provided in the great industrial complex of the Ruhr. By late 1948 the refugee population had reached 1,000,000, or one in nine of the indigenous population. But under the bombings the Ruhr lost 40 per cent of its available housing space and 3,200,000 habitable rooms disappeared in piles of rubble. According to a recent report from the German Ministry of Social Affairs in the Ruhr, 23,000 refugees are living in 300 camps and 140,000 are housed in conditions "which can hardly be called decent." With the upward trend of West

German industrial production, the Ruhr Valley has been able to absorb considerable amounts of skilled labor. But the refugee community is not always fitted for this work, and even if it is the great industries, all of them priority air-raid targets, probably lie in the middle of the zones of highest housing destruction. Moreover, refugees arriving in Western Germany were dispersed without regard to labor supply. This was inevitable because the officers of the Western powers in charge of resettlement could consider only available accommodation and not personal qualifications. This frequently resulted in industrial workers settling in rural areas and farmers going to the big cities.

Refugees, in their own interests, organized themselves at all levels of civic life in the new Germany. In some areas they were powerful enough to exercise considerable influence on the course of local and provincial affairs. In the province of Schleswig-Holstein in the British Zone, for example, the city of Lübeck has doubled its prewar population with the influx of refugees. In all areas refugee committees were set up and international organizations such as the Red Cross together with religious, social, and welfare bodies have worked day and night to help the new settlers. Lack of housing space and consumer goods, hardships accentuated by the currency reforms in Eastern and Western Germany, constitute a permanent danger to the stability of the refugee population. Moreover, the demoralizing effects of low-standard communal life in camps have frequently brought about an apathy toward the future and a tendency toward crime and vagrancy in the adolescent groups of the refugees. However, the tide is turning and there is every hope that with the formation of the new Federal Republic of Germany the cause of the refugees will be pleaded by German voices in addition to the appeals so often made by the less influential welfare and religious organizations.

There can no longer be any doubt that thinking mankind has become intensely alive to the significance of future social changes in the structure of the German people. Of particular interest just now is a new scheme which has been put forward by leading refugees with a considerable amount of political backing. Principal points in this refugee charter are: 1. Improvements in the amenities of refugee camps. 2. An over-all stimulus to provincial and federal housing programs. 3. Practical and effective land reforms. 4. A new deal for those industries, particularly handicrafts, in which refugees are more than usually skilled. 5. Free meals at school for refugee children. 6. Refugee co-operation in the administration of reforms. 7. An allocation of Marshall Plan aid to the German authorities to be earmarked for refugee relief. This is one of many schemes, and it is typical of the efforts now being made to raise the refugee problem to national and international understanding.

The experience of the refugees since the Potsdam Agreement might lead one to wonder whether or not the grapes of wrath that undoubtedly flourish in their ranks might yet produce another and more vitriolic vintage of Teutonic revenge. I do not believe this to be the case.

There are many signs that the refugee is beginning to take root in the communities of the new Germany, and beyond all doubt his children are well on the way to acclimatization in their new environment. The refugee shares with his kinsmen a developed capacity for organization and an antlike industry that, in a world of industrial disputes, has been one of the brighter aspects of the postwar German economy. He has found a foothold in the trade unions and political parties and, although at heart an Irredentist, he has responded moderately well to the challenging problems of the new Germany.

His greatest need is for a more liberal policy in refugee

legislation by the provincial and central authorities and international recognition of his still sorry plight. There are indications that these needs will soon be appreciated, and should this be the case the natural yearning for the lost homes might well be sublimated into the wider desire to reconstruct a new and peaceful Germany, a Germany offering her people another, and perhaps a last, chance to redeem themselves.

Chapter XIII

The Hard Peace

By DAVID M. NICHOL

JAMES F. BYRNES, as Secretary of State, sweltered through the Foreign Ministers' Conference in Paris in the summer of 1946, and then went to Stuttgart in Germany to let off steam. Among other things, he told his listeners that the Americans had "long since ceased to talk of a hard or soft peace for Germany."

There was a good deal of wishfulness in the Secretary's pronouncement. His Stuttgart speech was to become one of the most notable in the postwar history of the United States and Germany, but not for the accuracy of this particular bit of reporting.

At that time Americans had been arguing the case for two bewildered years, and the dispute has continued ever since. It will go on so long as there are history books and people to read them, and in one way or another it affects almost everyone in the world.

Much earlier than most people thought, and to a much greater degree than they realized, the course was fixed in the first months of the Occupation. The wisdom and skill with which it is pursued will largely determine how we get along with the Soviet Union and, eventually, whether we must fight another war.

Once it was high policy that Germany should become a giant "cow pasture." Now at least two-thirds of it bristles with smoking chimneys and hums with turning wheels. The "punitive" stages of the Occupation lasted two years longer than was planned originally, but they definitely are at an end.

The long-term implications of this change are not difficult to grasp. But if, for one instant, you believe this a distant and impersonal affair, you need look only as far as your tax bill. By 1952 the United States will have spent almost four billion dollars in a direct effort to pick up Europe's two-time bully, dust him off, get his habits in order, and start him along the road to useful citizenship. To carry the analogy further, this is the bully's second chance. Innate viciousness on his own part, plus the indulgence of his sponsors, let him get away with murder on his first. As social experiments go, this new one is a peach.

The plan to give Germany another opportunity came into being less by plan than by accident. It was a desperate effort to save the peace which the world saw slipping again through its fingers. It was a compound of frustration, and compromise, and flashes of brilliant statesmanship. It came too soon to be capital punishment and too late not to leave ugly scars.

The "hard" peace, the capital punishment which was abandoned, is associated most generally with Henry Morgenthau, Jr., President Roosevelt's secretary of the treasury. How Morgenthau's duties came to include this phase of postwar policy has never been explained satisfactorily.

Morgenthau writes that he had "devoted a good deal of thought and study to the subject" and that shortly before the Quebec Conference in September 1944 the President "asked me to outline for him a program for the treatment of Germany after her defeat." There is a different version which says that Morgenthau squeezed in ahead of the existing Allied planning machinery which had been functioning in London since the beginning of that year. Specifically, Morgenthau was said to fear that the State Department was going to be too "soft," and was determined to prevent it.

Harry Dexter White, an assistant secretary who was later to be questioned by the House Committee on Un-American Activities, was put in charge of the Morgenthau project. The result, when it reached the Hopkins desk in the White House toward the end of the summer, was one of the most startling programs of a far from ordinary period.

There was no nonsense about provincial borders or levels of industry or categories of offenders or any of the myriad other problems which have harassed the occupying forces. White drew boundaries the way the czars built the Moscow–St. Petersburg railroad—in a straight line. If there were mountains in the way, then move them!

One line on White's map began on the Baltic, at Kiel, and cut almost directly south to the Swiss border in the vicinity of Lake Constance. To the west of this arbitrary division lay the entire Rhineland valley, the industrial heart of Germany, half a dozen of its principal cities, eighteen millions of its people, and about one-fourth of its territory. In this western slice fires were to be drawn, factories destroyed, coal mines flooded, and the people moved to the east.

The original plan proposed vaguely that this desert in the heart of Europe should be placed under "some form of international control." Shocked experts pointed out that land itself was immensely valuable in the crowded continent.

"Then," was the bland reply, "we will move in some Italians."

Why Italians, and what would they have done? No one knows. Perhaps, as was suggested wryly, they would grow grapes. The Rhine and half a dozen of its tributaries are famous for their vineyards.

To the east of the arbitrary border another line was drawn, cutting Germany squarely into north and south halves. These were the dual "cow pastures." Their original inhabitants and the eighteen million migrants were to produce 95 per cent of their own food requirements. There would be enough exports, it was argued, to pay for fertilizers and to buy the 5 per cent of their food they couldn't grow themselves.

In these two experimental farms, for they would have been little more, the Allied armies were to carry out additional reduction of industries and a rapid and sweeping purge of the Nazis and the soldier caste. Then—and this is one of the most remarkable features in the light of postwar history—the Americans were to wash their hands of the entire affair and go home. It is not difficult now to see what would have happened.

This fantastic program never was presented at the Quebec Conference. Experience has since shown how completely impractical it would have been from every standpoint. Besides, the United States was committed to quite different arrangements.

The little-known European Advisory Commission had been set up by the 1943 Foreign Ministers' Conference in Moscow. It had drawn and agreed on the outline of the control machinery and the boundaries to separate the zones of occupation. Except for the inclusion of the French, these underwent only minor changes on paper until the arrival of the Western Allied high commissioners in 1949. Only the boundary agreement ever worked in practice, and that against the other Allies.

But Morgenthau's efforts were not finished. Instead of a detailed plan, the Quebec Conference produced a short memorandum. It included the famous quotation that "Germany should be turned into a region primarily agricultural and pastoral." In itself that was a sweeping commitment. Former Secretary of State Hull says that Churchill was persuaded to initial it because of Morgenthau's promise of postwar lend-lease aid to Great Britain, a guarantee which Morgenthau had no authority to make. Those who have seen the memo say that Roosevelt also initialed it. However, he changed his mind and subsequently denied that he had approved the program. Nevertheless the Morgenthau thinking remained the basis of official United States policy for the next two years.

The scene shifts now to the warm and lovely Black Sea city of Yalta. There, in February 1945, Roosevelt, Churchill, and Stalin solemnly subscribed to a document saying, "It is not our purpose to destroy the people of Germany," but setting out at the same time their determination "that Germany will never again be able to disturb the peace."

What they didn't do was far more important and was to contribute as much as any other single factor to the breakdown of four-power control in Germany. The Russians proposed that Germany should pay the astronomical sum of twenty billion dollars for the damage it had caused the world. The Soviet Union would take half. The Western leaders recognized Germany's obligation "to make compensation for the damage in kind to the greatest degree possible," but shied away from any final decision. The frustrations of the next four years were already shaping up.

By the spring of 1945 American policy toward the almost defeated enemy had been reduced to a single document bearing the unwieldy title of "Joint Chiefs of Staff Memorandum No. 1067/6." The geography of Germany was left unaltered in the West, but for most practical purposes this was still the "Morgenthau Plan."

The memorandum is an austere, Draconian pronouncement filled with phrases like: "Germans cannot escape responsibility . . . firm and aloof . . . no action will be taken . . . consumption held to the minimum. . . ." American aid would be extended, it said, only in amounts sufficient "to prevent starvation or widespread disease or such civil unrest as would endanger the occupying forces." From the vantage point of today the document reads like something from another world, certainly from a different war.

Probably no one outside the Soviet Army has seen the directives under which it proceeded into Germany, but of the three Western Allies the policy of the United States was by far the most vengeful and severe, at least on paper. Nonfraternization didn't work because the GI's and German girls had too much to offer each other. Denazification was to prove hopelessly impossible on the scale it had been conceived originally.

But by and large JCS 1067/6 was applied rigorously as the Americans advanced into Germany and was still in effect when Truman, Stalin, and Churchill and Attlee met at Potsdam, on the outskirts of Berlin, in July. The "cow pasture" by that time lacked only the cows to make it a reality. Its industries were operating at something like 10 per cent.

The Potsdam Declaration, or Berlin Protocol, as it is sometimes called, retained many of the punitive features of the American program and added some of its own. Germany was to be disarmed and stripped of its armaments industry. It was never to be permitted to build an army or navy or air force or to support such an undertaking industrially. It was to be cleansed of every taint of National Socialism and Prussian military spirit. The provisions of the declaration were so broad that small boys were forbidden subsequently to play with toy gliders. Frederick the Great became Frederick II, and his colossal, boxed-up equestrian statue in Unter den

Linden was converted to a giant billboard for the Communist party.

For the purposes of this account, however, three other provisions are more important.

One says in black and white, so simply it seems there could never by any dispute: "During the period of occupation, Germany shall be treated as a single economic unit." Resources and industrial capacity were to be pooled throughout the stricken country.

The second was more open to interpretation, although it still seems relatively clear. It said that sufficient peaceful industry would be left to Germany to meet the requirement of the occupying powers and the millions of displaced persons, and "to maintain in Germany average living standards not exceeding the average of standards of living of European countries." Britain and the U.S.S.R. were excluded specifically from the calculations. In other words, Germans were not to starve or go without homes or clothing, but they were to be no better off than the peoples they had robbed and murdered and tortured for almost ten years. The war industries and all that remained of the peacetime industries above the minimum level would be removed and used to pay off at least some of the damage the Germans had caused.

The Soviet Union would skim this surplus from its own zone in Eastern Germany and would receive, in addition, one-fourth of the equipment removed from the three Western zones. For a portion of this it would pay in raw materials.

Eighteen other nations, organized as the Inter-Allied Reparations Agency, or IARA, in Brussels, were to share in the division of the surplus from the three Western zones of Germany.

Experiences after World War I, so the Western powers thought at the time, had demonstrated the futility of trying to collect war debts in cash. The Soviet Union insists it never agreed to this. It has been siphoning off cash, in the form of current production, ever since.

The arrangement was like a wonderful sausage machine. For three years, until East-West trade broke down completely, the Americans poured some $700,000,000 a year into one end of the country while the Russians took $500,000,000 out of the other. It was not surprising that the Soviets wanted it continued, or that the Western powers opposed it violently.

From the standpoint of this account, the third important Potsdam provision was the decision which turned over to Polish administration that fourth of Germany's entire territory lying east of the Oder-Neisse line. The area included a third of Germany's prewar farm lands, and one of its richest industrial centers, in Silesia around Breslau, or Wroclaw. The "cow pasture" had shrunk to a point where Germany must export industrial products to live. There wasn't enough land to feed its people.

These, then, are the principal components of the "hard" peace. If there were doubts as to whether or not it would succeed, they were less serious as to its application in Germany itself than as to the co-operation the Western powers would receive from the Soviets in implementing its delicately balanced program. Serious, thoughtful men believed it would work.

Allied officials then talked of a "long Occupation." Twenty-five years was often mentioned as the period during which close control of German affairs would be retained. But at the same time the Potsdam program of punishment and reparations was to have been completed in no more than thirty months, with drastic political and economic surgery. However, there was no intention that the patient should die under the anesthetic. An early convalescence was expected.

The first six months were to be devoted to stocktaking,

during which the four Allies were to decide jointly what Germany's living standard would be and how much industrial machinery was required to meet it. All of the excess was to have been removed in the succeeding two years, by February 1948, by which time a peace treaty would have been signed. Germany was to be watched but otherwise was to be free to evolve its own peacetime economy. Not one of these things happened according to plan, and most of them haven't happened yet. In this sense, and in some others, the peace has been much "harder" than even its most extreme architects intended.

Problem No. 1 appeared simple enough on the surface. If Germany was to be no better off than its neighbors, it was essential to discover how the neighbors were getting along. Once it was determined how many shoes and coats and how much food would be allowed each individual, the figures could be multiplied by the number of persons in Germany. It was that easy!

The four-power committees went to work in the big Allied Control Authority Building which once housed Berlin's highest court. Almost immediately snags began to appear. They have been turning up and growing ever since. It was not even possible for the four Allies to agree on how many people would live in the new Germany. The Soviets, for example, believed their wartime communiqués, which put the figure of dead on the Eastern Front alone at 7,500,000 men. Thus they estimated that there would be only 62,000,000 persons in Germany. The United States' estimate was 69,500,000, a difference that could upset any scale which might be imposed.

In at least one meeting the Soviets argued that the language of Potsdam meant that anything up to the average living standards of the rest of Europe would be satisfactory. German standards might just as well be lower, they said. In another meeting they insisted on including a figure for "rabbit meat, nuts, and berries" in the food calculations. In another area the gyrations of all four delegations in arriving at a figure for permitted steel production would in themselves fill a volume.

On March 28, 1946, a four-power document covering "reparations and the level of postwar German economy" was finally evolved. The agreement proposed that by 1949 German peacetime industry would operate at about half of its 1938 figures. A number of industries were forbidden altogether, and important limitations were placed on others. The Allies already were eight weeks behind schedule.

By now the plan has practically nothing except historical interest. Long before it could be applied the entire four-power system had been shattered. The Soviets and, to a lesser extent, the French refused flatly to treat Germany as a "single economic unit," without which the plan could not possibly be made to work.

A number of interesting points appeared during the negotiations, however. The 1946 plan was stringent, yet it foresaw a German diet of almost 2,700 calories a day. In spite of the various relaxations that figure has only recently been achieved in practice.

The plan provided about eighteen pounds of textile fibers for every person in Germany each year. Yet eighteen months later, an enterprising official in Münster, in the British Zone, calculated that at the rate at which winter coats were being distributed in his city, it would be 516 years before there was one for each man.

It was proposed at first that coal for German homes should not be limited. Living standards, it was felt, would be low enough without the additional hazard of freezing. Yet in the second winter of the Occupation people burned park benches and anything else they could cart away in a desperate effort to provide a little heat. There was no coal at all and only irregular light.

The attitude of General Clay during this period will come as a surprise to many. Before he resigned in 1949, Clay was to be identified more than any other single person with the effort to restore German economy. Yet officials who worked closely with the General in this formative stage say he was a stickler for the most rigid interpretation of the Potsdam yard-sticks.

At one point he said flatly that the United States had under-taken to guarantee no standard of living for the Germans; if Germany's war potential could not be destroyed otherwise, then the standard of living must suffer. He urged that Germany be left only enough equipment to produce 20,000 automobiles a year. Even the Russians thought this too low. Two years later, Clay agreed readily to a level of 160,000 for the two Western zones alone.

Underlying all this was the dawning realization that the Soviets and the Western powers were poles apart in spite of the signed documents. The 1946 program could be made to function only by the most careful regulation on a four-zone basis, and the Soviets and the French had no intention of permitting that. The United States and the British were to support Germany so that the other two Allies could drain it.

The British seem to have been the first to grasp the im-plications of the policy. While the negotiations for the 1946 level were under way, General Sir Brian Robertson, who was to become British Military Governor, was called to London. When he returned to Berlin he spoke with the full and ex-plicit authority of his government. Britain, he said, would not permit the Germans to be condemned for all time to starvation and slavery.

The arguments that followed were long and bitter. The problem became not only one for the experts but a public issue as well. The British wanted enough steel capacity left in Germany to produce 9,000,000 tons a year. The 1946 agreement provided only enough to produce 7,500,000 tons, and production was originally to have been limited to 5,800,000 tons—unless an increase was authorized by the Four-Power Control Council.

Looking back, the lengthy arguments over the British proposal seem to have been futile. The present level for the three Western zones is 11,100,000 tons, not quite twice what had originally been planned for all of Germany. For their part, the Germans are pleading that they must have more.

Doubts about the early plan were not confined to the British delegation, however. The list of plants which would be available for reparations was based on the original four-power standard-of-living agreement. Six weeks after it had been announced General Clay ordered a halt to factory demolitions in the United States zone until such time as Germany should be administered as an economic whole. The question has never yet been resolved.

During the Foreign Ministers' Conference in the summer of 1946 Secretary Byrnes did everything in his power to reassure the Soviets. He offered to join in a twenty-five-year guarantee of German disarmament, and he pleaded for a joint economic policy by the Allies, but he got nowhere.

So his Stuttgart speech in September was at once an argument and a threat. "The American Government," said Mr. Byrnes, "is unwilling to accept responsibility for the needless aggravation of economic distress that is caused by the failure of the Allied Control Council to give the German people a chance to solve some of their most urgent economic problems." If economic unity couldn't be achieved, he said, then as much as possible of Germany would be brought together and the economic program would be revised to make the area self-sustaining as soon as possible.

Byrnes's idea flourished. Four months later the American and British zones were unified economically. Alternately pushed and persuaded, and baited with special privileges in the Saar, the French threw in their lot two years later.

The Morgenthau Plan was dead.

The decision had not been an easy one for the Western Allies, and was not taken lightly but was made in full awareness of the dangers it involved. Secretary of State Marshall warned his colleagues at Moscow in 1947: "If Germany is divided, each half will require strengthening to exist independent of the other. Two strong halves of Germany may then emerge, later to be fused into a revitalized and militant Germany. The permanent partition of Germany is dangerous to the peace of Europe and of the world."

But the only alternative was even more dangerous. To use Marshall's description again, it was the creation at endless expense to the American taxpayer of a "congested slum or an economic poorhouse" in the center of Europe. The impact of this thinking on Marshall himself was so powerful that it produced the idea for the European Recovery Program.

This awkward choice once made, the problem became one of putting the new program of aid to Germany into effect. Quite obviously, the original instructions to the American Military Governor were as out of date as preatomic weapons.

In July 1947 Washington sent a new "directive" to General Clay replacing the stern provisions of JCS 1067/6. By comparison, the new order was filled with sweetness and light. There were no more thou shalt nots. Instead, Clay was told to "permit," to "guide," and to "assist" the Germans.

The United States, it said, believed lasting peace could be achieved "only if conditions of public order and prosperity are created in Europe as a whole." It set forth that a "stable and productive Germany" was essential. It reiterated that war industries should be destroyed and that Nazis and war criminals should be punished, but it said nothing about the guilt of the German nation as a whole. For the first time in postwar history it spoke of "cultural objectives" and of the "spiritual value" of German traditions.

One month later, in August 1947, a completely new level of industry was agreed for the American and British zones of Germany. By its terms living standards for Western Germans would be about one-third higher than those of the original four-power program.

More important, the peacetime industries of Western Germany would operate approximately at the 1936 level. Emphasis would be primarily on goods for export. Cut off from its normal granaries in Eastern Germany as well as from the areas under Polish administration, Western Germany would have to buy and import about a billion dollars' worth of food each year. Another billion dollars in raw materials must be brought in annually to keep the machines running to buy the food. Increases of 10 to 50 per cent over the original plan were permitted in almost every category of industrial activity.

Even then the German economy was slow to begin rolling. German money was worthless and had to be replaced. When the Soviets walked out on these discussions the Western Allies again had no choice but to go ahead on their own.

Currency reform in the summer of 1948 supplied the necessary transfusion. Blood began to flow for the first time in the new Germany's industrial arteries, and an upward trend was started which has continued ever since.

In the whirl of activity in the spring of 1949, a three-power agreement was signed by the Western Allies on prohibited and restricted industries in their zones of Germany. For example, it permitted Germans to produce limited amounts of aluminum and ball bearings, which until then had been proscribed. It allowed some building of ships. Above all else, it fixed a base below which German industrial capacity would not be molested. It represented what the British called "very substantial concessions." Four years after the end of the war, Germany at last had a foundation on which it could build. The uncertainties had been removed.

Haunting the Allies at every step was the question of reparations. Each time Germany's standard of living was revised upward it meant that more of Germany's original industrial capacity must be left intact. Less and less was available to pay the damages which Germany had inflicted on the rest of the world.

For the Germans the dismantling of their industrial plants is the most tangible measure of their punishment. Because they can see it and feel it, this is the feature which annoys them most. For almost everyone else it has been the subject of more misunderstanding and dispute than any other phase of Allied Occupation.

The Soviet Zone is a special case, but in the three Western zones about 1,600 factories were scheduled originally to be removed. Even before the lists were complete, a hasty survey was conducted under the expressive title of "Operation RAP" (Rapid Appraisal of Plants), and the tearing-down process began.

But by the spring of 1946, in the confusion over Soviet policy, the process of dismantling was halted. Before it was resumed on any scale the Western Allies had discovered that they must make their own way with Western Germany and that much more of the industry would have to be left. By 1947 the dismantling list for the three Western zones was reduced to about 900 plants.

About this time the paradox of modern Germany began to impress itself on outsiders, particularly Congress. Why, congressmen wanted to know, were industrial installations being destroyed at the same time that the United States had committed itself to an extensive program of rebuilding the country?

One belligerent group of senators led by H. Styles Bridges of New Hampshire swirled into the theater and announced that dismantling of all kinds must be halted at once. In Frankfurt, before they had talked with Military Government experts, they seized on a particularly unfortunate example.

Here was Germany, they said, which hadn't washed its face properly for ten years. Yet the Allied were tearing down soap factories. Why?

I was with a cluster of officials and reporters who waited the next day at Tempelhof for the senators to arrive in Berlin. Pacing the broad apron was a disturbed and perplexed officer.

"How can we explain to these people?" he said. "Those plants can't make soap because they can't get the ingredients. There isn't any chance they'll get them before the machinery has rusted into worthless junk.

"I guess they forget," he added savagely, "that we've stopped grinding up Jews for raw materials."

In any event the plants had not been making soap under the Nazis. They had been producing glycerine for explosives. The senators were somewhat chastened but not entirely convinced when they left.

Once the European Recovery Program was under way, it opened new avenues for German exports and new possibilities of obtaining raw materials. A third review of the reparations program was begun with the aid of American production experts. By the spring of 1949 the list of plants to be removed from the Western zones of Germany had been cut to 741. By way of comparison, Germany in 1936 had 19,000.

Of the 741 there are 336 out-and-out war plants. None of the revisions so far has proposed that they be left. The delinquent isn't ready to handle guns yet. Of the others 239 are heavy engineering concerns which could be geared to war production overnight. The machinery will be placed in more trustworthy hands.

By this time, however, the Germans were feeling some of their new-found influence and authority. Synthetic fuels are thoroughly uneconomic in Germany, and most of the plants date only from Hitler's frantic efforts to prepare for war, yet Belgian troops had to seize one Rhineland plant forcibly before it could be torn down. The Communists, with a blind eye toward Eastern Germany, have been screaming "Loot!" ever since.

Reparations and the living standards on which they depend are not the only measures of the peace. Almost every other phase of the Occupation has undergone successive similar revisions in favor of the former enemy. It is ancient European custom, for example, that the victors should take some territory and all the art works on which they can lay their hands. Except in the Soviet Zone and except for those items which the Germans themselves stole during the war, the art collections have been preserved for the future Germany.

Two determined grabs have been made at German territory. One was by the Poles with the support of the Soviets. The other was by the French and geared the industrial Saar into the economy of France. But these were to have been only the beginning.

Each of the Benelux countries and the French asked additional areas. The Americans and the British had agreed in advance to consider these border changes. Reluctantly they followed through, but agreed to what were no more than token alterations. In the end there were thirty-one "minor rectifications" which included only fifty square miles, less than the area of Des Moines, Iowa, and only 13,500 people.

This is only one example of the watering down of the peace settlement. There are others.

Personal relationships between the Allies and the Germans have altered inevitably. It is a far cry from nonfraternization to General Robertson's gentle reminder three years later that Germans for the most part are Christians and should be so treated. Americans have not gone quite so far in encouraging social contacts officially, but some of the barriers have been removed. Clay told the Berliners at the end of the blockade that they had earned the right to freedom and to be accepted by free peoples throughout the world.

Some features of the original program, like the punishment of war criminals, languished less by plan than for lack of vigor and imagination.

American judges at Nuremberg took a few hesitant steps toward a completely new system of international law in which aggressive war would have been defined and its planning and execution made criminal. But long before the series of trials had been completed it became apparent that a single beating or murder was much more incriminating than the plotting and preparation of a war in which millions were killed.

From the high point of the International Military Tribunal which tried Göring and the other top Nazis, the system ran down like an old clock. The steel man, Friedrich Flick, was convicted, not for using slave labor, but for asking for more than the Nazis assigned to him. Eight Nazi generals were found guilty, not of shooting hostages, but of shooting too many. Forty-three SS butchers were sentenced to death for the Malmedy machine-gunning of unarmed American prisoners. The number was first cut to twelve, then to six. By the time two committees of the Senate had raked over the proceedings, the villains in the piece were the American investigators.

Some of the assorted "de's" of the occupation have been carried through completely. For example, demilitarization reached the point of blowing up bunkers in Berlin when they were being used for desperately needed emergency hospitals.

Others, like decartelization, the breaking up of the vicious German trade and industrial combines, have moved in fits and starts. Although there has been a great deal of criticism of American policy, by and large the Americans have progressed further with this in Germany than any of the other occupying powers.

Some aspects, like the controversial problem of denazification, have proved physically impossible on the scale on which they were planned originally. In the American Zone alone more than one in four adults, a total of 3,400,000, were found liable for trial under the terms of the denazification laws. Very early it was discovered that many of these must be cleared automatically if the program wasn't to collapse of its own weight. Amnesties for youngsters and for "nominal" party members who held no positions released more than 2,400,000. However, trials of the rest were still proceeding more than four years after the surrender, and the appeals processes were clogged.

As in American courts, Germans were reluctant to impose sentences on the planners of Nazi policy and were more prone to convict the streetcar motorman who beat up Jews in his spare time or the guard at the gate of a concentration camp. With the hearings almost finished, in all of the American Zone less than 1,600 persons had been classified as "major" offenders.

When appeals were brought, as they were in many cases, justice very often was tempered. In three out of five appeals the punishments were revised downward. Hitler's dentist, for example, was sentenced to three years at hard labor in the original wave of national purification but was placed on probation for two years when he carried his case higher.

Just as the negative features of the occupation have lagged, so have the positive ones, like turning over responsibility to the Germans. Ever since Mr. Byrnes spoke at Stuttgart it has been American policy "that large armies of foreign soldiers or alien bureaucrats, however well motivated and disciplined, are not in the long run the most reliable guardians of another country's democracy." Yet four years were to elapse before a central government was achieved, and then for only a portion of the country.

Only in the Soviet Zone has anything like the original Morgenthau plan been carried through, and there it has been a twisted, nightmarish caricature. Territory has been shorn away but given to Polish administration instead of international control.

Denazification has been quixotic and arbitrary. So far as can be discovered from the meager records, the percentage of exclusions from public office was lower than in the American Zone. The process was used primarily to strip persons of their property and turn it over to public administration.

At the University of Halle, we learned on a trip through the zone, faculty members suspected of Nazi leanings were easy recruits for the Communist-controlled Socialist Unity party. A party card was as good as a pass from the tribunals.

Demilitarization has been a combination of extreme measures and thinly cloaked evasions. Theaters in Dresden were seized as "militaristic" because they had shown Nazi newsreels during the war, while at the same time returning prisoners were being armed and trained in field maneuvers, disguised as "people's police."

About 125 of the major industrial plants of Eastern Germany became Soviet-owned corporations. They were acquired by book transfers and printing press money and are the most closely held and the largest cartel in Europe today.

Not only was the plant capacity lost to Germany but so were the labor and raw materials which the factories use. Their output goes almost exclusively to the Soviet Union or as exports on the Soviet account.

The Soviets have provided no figures on how much of the rest of German industry was removed, although Mr. Molotov once casually mentioned a total of 676 plants. Certainly it was far more than even the stringent 1946 program foresaw. Current Eastern Zone industrial output has been drained away at the rate of about $500,000,000 a year for reparations, although the Potsdam Agreement required that it be used, in the first instance, to pay for German imports.

Currency reform, when it came on the heels of the reform in Western Germany, was a giant swindle. Soviet corporations and Soviet-sponsored political parties and organizations changed their money one for one while everyone else went through the financial wringer.

Only in land reform has the record been impressive. Almost half a million families have been resettled or permitted to increase their tiny holdings as a result of the break-up of the big estates. The "cow pasture" at least has been divided.

By contrast, in the same period in Bavaria, in the American Zone, only 360 large holdings were affected. They represented about 1 per cent of the area that was seized and parceled out in Eastern Germany.

Political organization under the Soviets has not been training in government but a means of turning over control to the Communist-run Socialist Unity party on the lines of the "people's democracies" of Eastern Europe. The party probably would get less than 10 per cent of the vote in a genuinely free election.

One of the splinter groups which follows the Communist lead caters exclusively and openly to former Nazis. It is the only group of its kind in any of the four zones. Blackmail is enough to keep it in line.

With careful revisions, the elements of the Morgenthau Plan, the "hard" peace, might possibly, but just possibly, have been applied successfully to all of Germany. A fundamental requirement, however, was intimate and continual four-power co-operation of a type the Soviets have never been prepared to give. Once it was plain that this co-operation would not be extended, the Western Allies had only two alternatives. One was the rebuilding of Western Germany with all its inherent dangers. The other was the even more distasteful prospect of an impoverished and disorganized continent in which Soviet influence and control would be extended steadily.

The Western powers have constructed an elaborate machinery to prevent the new and invigorated Germany from jumping the rails. The Ruhr has been given a special status and placed under international control, and a Military Security Board has been established to check on how well Germany abides by the revised regulations.

In the long run the German future will depend on the interest of the Allied powers in maintaining the peace. No amount of checks can be successful without the backing of the governments of the world.

Gustav Krupp boasted openly that he defied Allied regulations after World War I and designed guns under the eyes of the Occupation officials. It will be a little more difficult this time, but it could happen again. Germany is still filled with those who would like to see it done.

Once, at Simferopol in the Crimea, I talked with a group of German prisoners, survivors of one of the most awesome and convincing battles in the world, in which they had been pushed literally off the end of the bleak Chersonese Peninsula into the Black Sea.

Among them was a bandaged major, as tough and unpleasant as they come. His shoulder tabs had been ripped away and he had been slapped around already for his insolence.

"What do you think of the war now?" I asked.

He answered slowly and emphatically. "We are suffering temporary setbacks," he said. "But the next time we come, we'll stay."

I would like to believe, if the major is still alive, that he is a completely reformed individual and is teaching democracy in a school. I'd like to believe it, but I'm afraid he is not.

Perhaps the "hard" peace was the only thing he could understand. I'd like to feel that he has seen the opportunity that has been given to him by the planned and accidental revision of the original Morgenthau Plan. I hope he doesn't think we were suckers. Above all, I hope he was wrong.

Chapter XIV

The Unpayable Debt

By JOSEPH E. EVANS

THE road leading to the dark cavity in the side of the mountain was narrow, and our car halted abruptly to make room for a tractor that unexpectedly chugged out of the entrance to the dim cavern. The tractor was towing a wooden crate on the sides of which were stenciled the Russian letters C.C.P., which means U.S.S.R. We parked our car just inside the gaping mouth of the mountain and then walked through miles of tunnels and chambers, watching ghostly creatures work at a kind of destruction which even then seemed to have little relationship to the sunlit world outside.

But the nightmare was not imagination. The white, colorless workmen were Germans; it was the summer of 1946, and they were tearing apart a German aircraft-engine factory which in happier days had been built inside this mountain at Obrigheim, Württemberg-Baden, in the American Zone of Germany. The workers were obviously not enthusiastic about their jobs, but they were kept busy by nine Red Army officers who were assisting the American supervisor. The Russians were anxious to have the destruction completed. Everything inside the mountain was to be carted off to the Soviet Union.

Like those of almost everyone else, my own reactions were mixed. In one sense what was happening at Obrigheim seemed just retribution. It was here that the Germans had built engines for planes which had bombed towns and cities in Russia, Britain, France, Holland, and Belgium. Now the machines were being removed and sent to Russia, where they would presumably make other aircraft engines. But for what purpose? The Russians had already begun the propaganda cold war, and although it would be nearly two years before the United States introduced an export-licensing system which effectively cut off the Soviet world from American war materials, the question was already there: Should the Western powers, even indirectly, be helping Russia build an air force?

There was also the inescapable feeling that the whole dismantling process was wasteful. True, the Obrigheim factory was a war plant. Practically no one could argue that it should not be destroyed or removed from Germany. But there were, according to unofficial estimates, more than 1,600 other factories in Western Germany which were available for reparations. All of them, or even a large part of them, could not or would not be torn down. And meantime Germany was in ruins, Europe in rags. To dismantle and remove the plants would take years, money, and back-breaking work. If they were reassembled at all, it was doubtful that they could be efficiently operated, and even if they were, the nonproductive job of destruction was occurring at the exact moment when Europe desperately needed production.

At the time I wrote that what I had seen of reparations represented a curious kind of reverse economy and that the whole idea of reparations seemed an inappropriate aftermath of the cataclysm of a modern total war. The principle of an eye for an eye was geared to a simpler economy.

The statesmen who decided that reparations after World

War II should be "in kind"—principally in the form of removals of capital industrial plant and equipment—were reverting to the most primitive type of payment device to compensate for the damages of the most complex war.

The reason the statesmen chose that particular means of payment was that they were disillusioned with others. Monetary reparations particularly had a distressing tendency to boomerang. After the Franco-Prussian War, in 1871, Germany exacted an indemnity of 5,000,000,000 gold francs (about $1,000,000,000) from France. This was a boost to Germany, but it did France little harm; the effort involved in meeting this indemnity, which France promptly enough did, even seems to have strengthened the French economy.

Again after World War I the Allies found out how contrary a device reparations could be. The reparations included money, commodities, and such movable things as armaments, the navy, part of the merchant fleet, and an assortment of rolling stock and motor trucks. Significantly, the means of production were not included.

In 1921 the Reparations Commission assessed the total bill, any part of which could be demanded out of current production, at 132,000,000,000 gold marks (about $32,000,-000,000), to be paid over forty-two years, plus 26 per cent of the annual proceeds of German exports. The Allies had put in claims for a total of 225,000,000,000 gold marks. When the Dawes plan went into effect in 1924, it ignored reparations totals and greatly reduced the annual payments; for the first year Germany was to pay only 200,000,000 gold marks. At the same time an international loan of about $200,000,000, or about four times the first year's reparations, was floated with Germany as debtor. The Young plan, which superseded the Dawes plan in 1930, established a final schedule of payments to end in 1988. The total amount was reduced to about 37,-000,000,000 marks, and another loan was issued.

The depression, and more specifically the banking crisis in Germany, ended reparations. The Hoover moratorium of 1931 suspended payments until June 30, 1932, but except for servicing the Dawes and Young loans, Germany paid no more reparations after July 1931.

From the beginning of the Dawes plan to the Hoover moratorium, Germany paid a total of less than 11,000,000,000 marks. The Dawes period, during which Germany conscientiously met its reparations obligations, was one of unprecedented prosperity.

"How could the 'miracle of reparations' happen?" asked Gustav Stolper in his *German Economy*. "How was it possible that this country, which in the first years after the war had been thrown into the abyss by the load of reparations, now was able not only to maintain reparation payments but at the same time to achieve recovery unprecedented in her economic life, a real reconstruction and modernization?"

Stolper and other observers found the answer in the inflow of foreign funds, mostly from the United States, which far outbalanced the reparations Germany paid. "Hardly one penny of these payments came from Germany's own resources," Stolper wrote. Since Germany had to pay reparations, Germany had to be built up economically to be able to pay reparations. Thus German industry expanded. For example, exports in 1929 were 34 per cent greater than in 1913, and the ceded merchant fleet had been almost completely replaced. In short, reparations had the ironic effect of causing foreign capital to be brought in, capital which contributed to Germany's prosperity and helped make possible the economic groundwork for a new war.

The Allies were determined to avoid repeating this mistake after the Second World War. The way to do it, they thought, was to remove the armament industries and to reduce the metallurgical and chemical industries which were accessories to military production, in that way destroying Germany as a military power. Without heavy industry Germany could never again wage war. In addition, the industry removed would provide tangible reparations. Apart from this was the plan for the return to their rightful owners of identifiable objects looted by Germans and brought to Germany.

Essentially the plan was American, and its chief progenitor was former Secretary of the Treasury Henry Morgenthau, Jr. However, Morgenthau's proposals did not enjoy the blessings of Secretary of State Cordell Hull or Secretary of War Henry Stimson, both of whom regarded it as economically unfeasible; Hull characterizes it in his memoirs as a plan of "blind vengeance." Although it was a complete policy for Germany, I am concerned here only with its reparations aspects.

The plan provided that the Ruhr "should not only be stripped of all presently existing industries but so weakened and controlled that it cannot in the foreseeable future become an industrial area."

For this purpose, "within a short period, if possible not longer than six months after the cessation of hostilities, all industrial plants and equipment not destroyed by military action shall be completely dismantled and transported to Allied nations as restitution [reparations]. All equipment shall be removed from the mines and the mines closed."

That was the genesis of the new version of "reparations in kind." The Morgenthau proposals envisaged capital equipment removals from other parts of Germany as well as the Ruhr. They also provided for reparation through territorial cession, confiscation of "all German assets of any character whatsoever outside of Germany" and "forced German labor outside Germany."

The Russians were thinking about German labor too. In

the same year economist Eugen Varga proposed conscripting a three-million-man German army to work in Russia at reconstruction. As it turned out the Russians found it simpler to get their German labor by hanging on to prisoners of war and by deportations and kidnapings throughout the Soviet Zone.

At the Yalta Conference of January–February 1945, Roosevelt, Churchill, and Stalin distinguished between "reparations in kind" and territorial "compensation." "We have considered the question of the damage caused by Germany to the Allied nations in this war and recognized it as just that Germany be obliged to make compensation for this damage in kind to the greatest extent possible." Reparations were to include capital assets in Germany and abroad, current industrial production, and labor.

The Yalta meeting set up a reparations commission to work in Moscow. The United States representative was Edwin Pauley. The commission was to take "in its initial studies as a basis for discussion, the suggestion of the Soviet government, that the total sum of reparations should be twenty billion [dollars] and that 50 per cent of it should go to the Soviet Union." That the Russians regarded this "basis for discussion" as giving them clear title to $10,000,000,000 was to be made abundantly evident at the postwar meetings of the Council of Foreign Ministers. The reparations commission in Moscow got nowhere, mainly because the Soviets failed to produce any data to support their reparations claim.

Shortly after the arrival of the Western troops in Berlin, a British officer taking over a suburban mansion for quarters found horses kicking up the parquet floor and eating hay from a grand piano with the top up. The Russians who had been staying there thought the piano made a good trough, which is presumably why they left it; they didn't leave much else.

Those of us who lived in Berlin had ample opportunity to observe reparations for Russia. Long lines of barges loaded with machinery steamed up the Havel, northbound to the Baltic to be transshipped to the Soviet Union. Any time we took a train out of Berlin we could see the open freight cars at the sidings, loaded with machinery, headed east. We could also see where the rails had been pulled up, often leaving only a single line. It is estimated that the Russians pulled up some 2,500 miles of track in their zone.

The *Staatsdruckerei,* Berlin's municipal printing plant, which was used both for printing money and for printing books and etchings, was badly bombed but the Russians looted it anyway. In the course of doing so they dumped on the floor its collection of type faces, one of the most complete in the world. It was a labor of many months to restore them.

Few Berlin industries escaped Russian visitation. "What the bombs missed the Russians took" was a common expression. In some cases workers buried machinery before the Russians could get to it. By saving the machinery they could hope to have work later on.

The Russians did not neglect people either. Their two-month unilateral occupation of Berlin was a reign of terror marked by wholesale rape. Often enough German girls were carted off to become enforced prostitutes in Russian military installations in the Soviet Zone. Whether this constitutes reparations or war booty is perhaps a fine point.

That the Russians were exceeding any accepted definition of war booty was not lost on President Truman and his staff when they arrived in Berlin for the Potsdam Conference. In *Speaking Frankly,* Secretary of State James F. Byrnes relates that the "Little White House" in Potsdam had been completely stripped and had to be refurnished for the conference. The statesmen noted the industrial dismantlings as well. Byrnes records that he asked Molotov if it was true the

Russians were removing great amounts of equipment. Admitting that it was, Molotov offered to subtract $300,000,000 from the Soviet reparations claim; seeing that was not satisfactory, he offered to knock off $1,000,000,000. But Byrnes notes that at the later meetings of the Council of Foreign Ministers the bill was back at $10,000,000,000.

The Soviets began taking reparations as soon as they were in Germany, before there was any agreement on the extent of reparations; furthermore, they did it as a matter of official policy. By comparison the depredations of individual Americans and Britons who were not always too particular about sending home bric-a-brac from the houses they occupied appear minor. They were not responsible for denuding Berlin's industry.

Despite Soviet insistence, the Potsdam Agreement set no total reparations sum. After guaranteeing the Germans a bearable living standard, the agreement provided that industrial plant surplus would be available for reparations. This peace economy was subsequently set at approximately 50 to 55 per cent of that of 1938, in effect about equal to the level of 1932, a year of depression and mass unemployment, but "sufficient resources were to be retained to enable Germany to maintain herself without external assistance."

The Potsdam Agreement called for the working out of means to enable Germany to support itself, i.e., "the proceeds of exports from current production and stock shall be available in the first place for payment of such imports." Thus reparations out of current production were not to be allowed until Germany sufficiently recovered economically to be able to pay for its imports.

Although Potsdam did not order the total dismantlement of the Ruhr and the sealing of the coal mines, the Protocol was nonetheless in keeping with the Morgenthau conception of reparations. It looked to the transformation of Germany from an industrial state into one supported by agriculture and light industries. Potsdam provided that a plan be prepared within six months showing how much specific industries would be allowed to produce and consequently how much would be available for reparations. This "plan for reparations and the level of postwar German economy" appeared two months late. It was approved by the American, British, French, and Russian military commanders in the Allied Control Council at the end of March 1946. It prohibited war industries, restricted the heavy chemical, metallurgical, and engineering industries, and exempted those needed for what was thought would be a decent living standard.

According to Potsdam, Russia was to take reparation primarily from its zone; the only limitation made was that there should remain enough industrial capacity to support the agreed-upon level of industry. Since the Russians hermetically sealed their zone, there was no way of guaranteeing that even this modest capacity was left. It is now evident that Soviet Zone dismantlings and removals have been carried out without regard to the level-of-industry agreement.

The signatories of the Potsdam Protocol gave Russia 15 per cent of "such usable and complete industrial capital equipment" as was to be allocated from the Western zones, to be paid for by an equivalent value of food, coal, potash, zinc, timber, clay, petroleum products, and other commodities. It was never made clear whether these products were to originate in the Soviet Zone or the U.S.S.R. Russia was to get an additional 10 per cent of the Western zones' reparations plants without reciprocal payment. Potsdam further allotted to Russia, German external assets in Bulgaria, Finland, Hungary, Rumania, and Soviet-occupied Austria. Two and a half years went by before Russia delivered anything in exchange for the 15 per cent of reparations from the Western zones, and another eighteen months elapsed before the Soviet Union expressed willingness to make a second installment.

Potsdam's failure to define German external assets materially assisted the Soviet economic penetration of the nations which became Russian satellites. Russia took the position that anything which had nominal German ownership at the end of the war was a German external asset, regardless of whether the legitimate ownership had been "co-ordinated" into the Nazi economy. This was the most important single factor which obstructed an Austrian peace treaty for four years.

Reparations claims of other countries were to be met from the 75 per cent of the plants earmarked for reparations left in the Western zones after the Soviet allocation was made and from German external assets in countries other than those given to Russia for the purpose. The Eighteen countries entitled to reparations met in Paris in the latter part of 1945, and in January 1946 established the Inter-Allied Reparations Agency. The members are Albania, Australia, Belgium, Canada, Denmark, Egypt, United States, France, Great Britain, Greece, India, Luxembourg, Norway, New Zealand, the Netherlands, Czechoslovakia, the Union of South Africa, and Yugoslavia. Pakistan became the nineteenth member in March 1948. Poland was not included because, according to Potsdam, Poland's reparation claims were to be met from Russia's share. Whether or not they were was never revealed.

The function of the IARA is to "ensure an equitable distribution . . . of the total assets which are or may be declared available as reparation from Germany, among the nineteen member nations entitled to reparation to compensate in some measure for the loss and suffering caused by Germany." The forms of reparations it has dealt with are industrial capital equipment, external assets, merchant shipping, and captured enemy supplies. The "equitable distribution" is based on a table of shares; each nation is supposed to receive in proportion to its war losses.

The Potsdam Agreement had intended that reparations removals were to begin six months from the time of the conference, or January 1946, at which time the level-of-industry plan was supposed to be ready; the zone commanders could, however, declare some plants immediately available and work on these "advance deliveries" could start at once. The whole program was to be completed within two years from the formal beginning, by January 1948.

Nothing of the sort occurred. A revolution in Allied thinking toward Germany, plus troubles with Russia, intervened.

The IARA was scarcely born before its difficulties with the Western zone commanders began; its history is that of a running battle with them. The level-of-industry plan which finally appeared at the end of March 1946 would have made available some 1,636 plants in the Western zones. But scarcely a month had passed before General Clay, then Deputy American Military Governor, declared a moratorium on all reparations deliveries except for those already approved. There were twenty-four of these in the American zone—three and a half (including the Obrigheim aircraft-engine factory) slated for Russia, the others for IARA nations.

The reason for this stop-order was the failure of the Soviet Union and France to co-operate in the establishment of the central administrative agencies for the economic unity of all Germany envisioned by Potsdam. If a divided Germany was going to have to subsist on imports paid for by the occupying powers, Clay explained to the Allied Control Council, the plants earmarked for reparations could not be spared. Moreover, the agreed ceilings on industrial production had been fixed so as to include production in the Soviet Zone. Without the Soviet Zone both ceilings and removals were unrealistic. The following October, Clay agreed to the resumption of deliveries of specifically war plants. In November the British representative announced the resumption of general-purpose plant and equipment deliveries from the British Zone to the value of 100,000,000 reichsmarks (about $25,000,000). In December the French announced that they would do the same, to the extent of 15,000,000 reichsmarks.

During 1946 and 1947, although the members of the Inter-Allied Reparations Agency pressed their claims repeatedly and bluntly, they were allocated only 250 plants.

In March 1947 the foreign ministers of the United States, Britain, France, and the Soviet Union met in Moscow to work for the first time on a German settlement. None was forthcoming. It was evident that the Soviet Union did not then want a settlement.

At this conference Mr. Molotov repeated his demands for $10,000,000,000 in reparations, to include current production from both the Soviet Zone and the Western zones. The United States was already pouring hundreds of millions of dollars a year into its zone (later, after the assumption of most of the financial responsibility for the British Zone as well, the cost was to soar to more than $1,000,000,000 per year). To have allowed Russia to receive industrial goods currently manufactured in the American Zone from raw materials imported at the expense of the American taxpayer would have meant that the United States was actually paying reparations. It was said that the Russians thought of reparations as a cow which the United States fed and the Russians milked. Mr. Molotov's cow was not admitted to the conference.

When Russia was urging this claim at Moscow it was charged that the United States had already taken $10,000,000,000 out of Germany in the form of German patents and German gold. This charge does not correspond to the facts. The United States made the patents it acquired available to other countries at microscopic cost, and Russia was the chief buyer—an arrangement which was not reciprocal with the German patents which Russia acquired. The gold comes mostly in the category of restitution: it was looted by the Germans and was restored to its legitimate owners. It was some of this gold which helped stabilize the Hungarian currency. None was transported to the United States. Nonmonetary gold, such as that which the SS took from its concentration camp victims in the form of dental fillings, rings, and other items, formed part of a $25,000,000 pool used to aid nonrepatriable victims of Nazi persecution. It needs only to be added that the United States relinquished its share of industrial capital equipment and shipping reparations.

The same basic consideration which made the Russian demand for reparations from current production in the Western zones inadmissible forced America and Britain to revise their attitudes toward the German economy. This consideration was that the Western zones could not support themselves and could never hope to do so unless production and particularly export production were greatly expanded. If Potsdam and the depression level of industry had been literally adhered to, the United States would have faced the alternatives of forever supporting Western Germany or allowing millions of Germans to starve.

A corollary consideration was that Europe was in a very bad way for lack of production and especially for lack of German production. The Netherlands, certainly not the least of Hitler's victims, was one of the first to protest against the restrictive Allied economic policy. It began to seem a little foolish to hold Germany to the production level of 1932 while Europe was desperate for machines and the products of machines. When the Marshall Plan got under way, comprehension of these economic fundamentals had progressed so far that Western Germany was accepted as a member of the Organization for European Economic Co-operation.

Things had begun to move with what eighteen months earlier would have seemed lightning rapidity. The American and British zones of Germany were economically merged in January 1947, pooling all resources and deficite, applying common policies, eliminating trade barriers, and laying emphasis on increased productivity and exports. In the summer of that year the Western nations began to organize themselves for the administration of Marshall Plan aid. In August the American and British military governments publicly acknowledged that Potsdam and the old four-power level-of-industry plan were blunders by supplanting them with a new level-of-industry plan which raised allowable steel production in the combined areas and alleviated other industrial restrictions. In general it aimed at the level of 1936, a "normal" year, instead of 1932, a depression year. This new plan also promised that once reparations were settled, German industry could expand further except for military restrictions.

By very considerably raising the permitted level of industry, the plan necessitated a proportionate reduction in the amount of reparations available. The publication, in October 1947, of the "final" list of plants available from the Anglo-American Zone did not greatly please the IARA claimant countries; and although it greatly reduced the number of plants which would have been taken under the old plan, it did not please the Germans either. In fact it evoked screams from Germans of every political complexion. In view of what was happening in the Soviet Zone, Communist opposition to the list was amusing; the Berlin newspaper *Neues Deutschland,* central organ of the Socialist Unity (Communist) party, said the list aimed "more at clearing the world market of German export goods than at restitution." The American-licensed *Tagesspiegel* perhaps came closest to explaining the source of the unanimous opposition when it said that the psychological time for dismantlings had been missed; they should have taken place in 1945, when the Germans would have accepted them with hardly a murmur. At any rate the two and a half years of waiting for a final statement on reparations gave the Germans opportunity to think about the whole policy, and the evident Allied indecision and dissension during that time did not encourage them to think it was a good policy.

But the "final" list proved not to be final after all. About a score of plants were removed in December on the basis of German recommendations. More importantly, when Congress passed the Foreign Assistance Act early in 1948, it included the following provision: "The [ECA] Administrator will request the Secretary of State to obtain the agreement of those countries concerned that such capital equipment as is scheduled for removal as reparations from the three western zones of Germany be retained in Germany if such retention will most effectively serve the purposes of the European recovery program." A series of missions to Germany followed, culminating in the report of the Industrial Advisory (Humphrey) Committee. This report, which was released in the middle of April 1949, recommended the retention in Western Germany of 167 plants or part plants. The Secretary of State did eventually obtain the reluctant agreement of Britain and France to the retention of 159 of these—144 completely, 15 in part.

These modifications were climaxed late in November 1949 when the Allied powers agreed in the Bonn Protocol to remove eleven important synthetic oil and rubber plants, and eight steel plants, from the reparations list, and to stop all reparations activity in stricken Berlin. Under the terms of the Protocol, equipment already dismantled was to be made available to the Inter-Allied Reparations Agency except in the case of Berlin, and authority was given the Germans to reconstruct dismantled plants only as permitted by the occupying powers. The Germans were reminded that the Allies had made "a maximum contribution" to solution of the vexatious reparations problem, meaning, presumably, that no further concessions would be made. "We are clearly not expecting that this agreement should be regarded as a stepping stone for further demands," said a press statement issued after promulgation of the Bonn Protocol, but this icy warning was not destined to be respected for any length of time.

It is doubtful that the German opposition to dismantling, which mounted during 1948, had much or any influence on these decisions. Not that the opposition was mild. There were strikes and lobbying in addition to constant protests in the press. In August the German governments of South Württemberg-Baden and Baden (French Zone) resigned in protest. In the same month and zone the minister president of Rhineland-Palatinate refused to carry out a dismantling order. At the end of that month the ministers president of all eleven *Laender* of Western Germany passed a resolution demanding the end of dismantling; in February firms earmarked for dismantling were filing writs against Secretary of State Dean Acheson to constrain him to prevent further reparations, and in March and April of this year agitation, fomented by the Adenauer government, reached a new pitch of intensity in the face of mounting unemployment figures.

The reason all this probably had little influence is that, from the point of view of European recovery as opposed to that of reparation, dismantling and removal had long since ceased to make sense to impartial observers. IARA says the "German propagandists employed every sort of argument against the continuance of the policy of dismantling." That is true, but they were only pointing what must have seemed obvious to the American surveyors.

A representative of Vereinigte Stahlwerke (United Steel

Works) whose capital interests are being reorganized with participation of foreign capital and German governmental agencies, showed me lengthy illustrated reports demonstrating why certain steel plants should not be dismantled. Propaganda, doubtless, but I have not heard any refutation of the fact that the dismantling of nonwar plants is economic foolishness, whatever else it may be morally.

It would take an estimated five years and 20,000 freight cars or 400 entire trains to dismantle and ship the August Thyssen-Huette A.G. steel works at Duisburg-Hamborn. The estimated cost of the dismantling alone, apart from production loss and the cost of re-erection, is 63,600,000 Deutsche marks (over $19,000,000). This is one of the steel plants which was withdrawn from the reparations list in the Bonn Protocol.

It would take an estimated 237,000,000 Deutsche marks ($71,100,000) to tear down and rebuild the Deutsche Edelstahlwerke (fine steel works) at Krefeld, including the loss of production during dismantling and re-erection. The reparations value of this plant is 8,000,000 Deutsche marks ($2,400,000). This factory is fortunately on the Bonn list and has been spared. The Krupp works at Borbeck, which was dismantled and sent to Russia, was worth 120,000,000 Deutsche marks; its value as reparations was $9,500,000.

The story of German reparations is thus a sad one. Even if the 1946 level-of-industry plan had not been scrapped, there would not have been enough reparations to satisfy the legitimate claims of the countries which suffered so greatly at the hands of the Germans. As it was, they got very little indeed. The IARA insists that the German equipment parceled out among its member nations has substantially aided their recovery. Yet the IARA had handled only 354 plants and parts of plants, with a total value of 387,000,000 reichsmarks (about

$96,000,000), which isn't much when spread out among nineteen countries.

The Soviet Union doubtless came out best. It has, of course, never given an accounting of what it got, but estimates range from $7,000,000,000 to $10,000,000,000. The latter figure would represent the claim the Russians have been pressing ever since Yalta. Probably not more than one-tenth of the equipment they dismantled and removed was later usable.

The Russians not only stripped industry by dismantling it. They also expropriated industries, forming the so-called Soviet *Allgemeine Gesellschaften* (general corporations). Still other industries they allowed to be socialized and operated under the direction of the communist *Land* governments. In all they seized outright perhaps one-third of the industry of their zone, with ownership of some basic industries as high as 100 per cent. Some of these were required to deliver as much as 90 per cent of their output to Russia, which explains why Soviet Zone exhibitors at the much-ballyhooed Leipzig fairs had beautiful things to display but little to deliver. In Dresden you could not buy a piece of Dresden china though the porcelain factories were working overtime.

The Russians wrecked their zone of Germany in the process of extracting reparations from it, and they finally had to lift the Berlin blockade in order to get materials and goods in. They have had to send things in from Russia to keep industry going at all. It is doubtful if in the end they will be much ahead.

The picture is clear. It was recognizable after the Franco-Prussian War if anyone had chosen to fill in the outlines. The details were painfully sharp after World War I. The full picture now seems clear. Reparations cannot be extracted from a defeated nation unless the victors are willing to destroy the nation and the people in it or rebuild the nation so that it can pay reparations.

The Unpayable Debt

The cumulation of such experience may finally impress upon statesmen that modern war is total injustice. In that totality there can be no serious thought of the guilty one repairing the damage he has wrought.

Chapter XV

Eternal Triangle—The Ruhr

By TERENCE PRITTIE

"THE Ruhr" has become a set phrase in the English language. Today it is spoken of as if it were a long-established geographical fact. Germans are surprised by this. "What do you mean by the Ruhr?" I have been asked. "Do you mean the towns which lie on the Ruhr River, or the distressed area which was given priority in food rations in 1948, or the valleys which the French overran in 1923?" In the past the Germans have never used this phrase. Even today the signposts near Düsseldorf and Duisburg are marked, *Nach dem Industriegebiet,* To the Industrial Area. It is only coincidental that the Ruhr has left its name so clearly imprinted in history.

The Western Allies have today settled on their own interpretation of "the Ruhr." An International Control Authority has begun its task of supervising the economic development of an area roughly fifty miles from north to south and seventy across, with the town of Essen as its geographical and economic center. The area has a population of more than six millions, four-fifths of which is closely concentrated in a central, industrial core. Wisely, the Western Allies have taken in an agricultural hinterland. An obvious German method of evading control in the future could have been the establishment of heavy and "feeder" industries just outside the fringe of the industrial area and beyond the reach of the Control Authority. The Allies have obviated this possibility by simply throwing their net everywhere fifteen to twenty miles wide of the spine of coalfields which runs from Dortmund to Düsseldorf. In planning for the future they have not forgotten the lessons of the past. The Ruhr could all too easily again become the most compact and formidable unit of war production in the world.

This great reservoir of industry has a scenic diversity of its own. It is a mistake to think of it merely as a focus of smoke, grime, and bad smells. Unlike the British, the Germans have a wholesome respect for natural beauty, and in the Ruhr they have been at pains to prevent the evil of "ribbon development" which first constricts, then atrophies the countryside. A mile out of Essen, with its 600,000 inhabitants, the lovely grounds of Krupp's Villa Huegel sweep down to the Ruhr's here unspoiled and sylvan riverbank. Half a mile out of Wuppertal is rolling country and well-kept forest. All the way from Düsseldorf to Solingen are picturesque little valleys with such gaily resonant names as Angerbachstal and Neanderthal. Remscheid is clustered with famous beauty spots, and partridges nest in the very shadow of factory chimney and cooling tower.

The towns, too, have character. Düsseldorf is the "Little Paris" of the Rhineland, splendidly laid out, splendidly situated on the banks of the Rhine, next to Cologne, the home of the Spring Carnival. Solingen and Remscheid were built on the tops of hills and look from across the intervening Wupper River like industrialized versions of the Italian hill cities. Bochum's chimneys are the highest of all, impressively vast in the blue-gray light of a winter evening. Wuppertal has its caterpillar railway, hung between huge, straddling iron pylons and stopping at overhead stations that look like complicated metal pagodas. Duisburg's port has the biggest inland harbor in Europe, and at night the air throbs with the orange heat of a dozen great blast furnaces.

These towns comprise a tremendous potential of industrial power. The Germans linked their industries, first from economic, then from purely capitalistic motives. The hard-coal mines were the basic factor. Iron was the second. Coal and iron, side by side and in great masses in the soil, made the Ruhr what it is. Blast furnaces were sited at appropriate strategic points. Around them was built up the whole complex of steel foundries and rolling mills, then the more widely dispersed associated industries. Krefeld became the "capital" of refined steel, Solingen of cutlery, Düsseldorf of steel tubes and pipes. Today the Ruhr produces three-quarters of Western Germany's hard coal and nearly the same proportion of raw steel. Processing of every sort was begun where a first-class transport system was already in existence and where short "carries" from one type of plant to another saved transport charges. The Ruhr produces everything from razor blades to giant cranes, from wireless sets to tin tacks. It is the industrial hub of Europe.

A third factor in the area's sensational development between 1850 and 1940 was water power. The twelve great dams of the Ruhr area store water for the dry season of June to October. This water is converted into electric power not only to light homes and factories but to supply energy for dynamos, turbines, trams, and railways. Into the Ruhr area flow a large number of sizable streams—Ruhr, Wupper, Sieg, Lippe—passing through narrow valleys, furnishing fine catchments behind easily constructed barrages. Once again geography has worked to develop the Ruhr into an economic concentration unique in Europe.

Tremendous ingenuity and organizational ability have been applied to this economic concentration. Trusts were formed which comprised, first, all the individual parts of a single industry, then ancillary industries, and finally a wide range of capital investments of every kind. The steel barons led the way in this development. Steel firms spread their influence, octopus-wise, into submarine plants, synthetic fuels, coal mines, gas works, tramways, real estate, and hotels and pleasure resorts. When the British authorities began after the war to plan the splitting up of these trusts, they were at once struck with the ramifications of this so-called "horizontal" development. The great German capitalists had spread their net over every field of economic life. It has been said with some truth that they became the real rulers of Germany.

The firm of Krupp provides the classic example of the terrific power and range of the Ruhr trusts. The cast-steel works at Essen were founded in 1811. In 1844 they began to turn out gun barrels for the Prussian army. Krupp guns quickly became famous and by 1879 were throwing 2500-pound shells. In 1902 the firm turned to the manufacture of submarines, later to that of locomotives. By 1939 it owned a controlling share in 110 German companies and large interests in 142 more. Its investments abroad were very large, a controlling interest in 42 firms and a large share in 20 others.

Peacetime turnover was 760,000,000 marks and the profits of the 1914-1918 war nearly 1,000,000,000. Waging war has not always been profitable for the German people, but it was the making of Krupp until British and American heavy bombers peppered the cast-steel works at Essen with 2,100 tons of bombs, and British Military Government earmarked it as a war plant which should be dismantled in the interests of humanity.

Figures are academic but in the Ruhr's case they can be illuminating. Hitler refashioned the Ruhr, for he was the first German who planned war economically. Bismarck fought tactical wars of the old model. Kaiser William II fought a political war with his available economic resources. Hitler planned ahead. Between 1932 and 1939 output of raw steel in Germany more than trebled. A large proportion of it went into Germany's own war industry. Perhaps 25 per cent found its final market, in the form of second-hand armaments, in neighboring European countries. The goods bartered against them went back into the Nazi bomb shop—the tobacco which the German front-line soldier smoked, the leather which made him his durable army boots, the nickel which coated the bullets he fired in "defense" of his Fatherland.

The deliberateness with which Hitler built up his war machine should never be forgotten, particularly by those who today see in the unlimited expansion of German industry a panacea to Europe's present near-bankruptcy. Under the stimulus of a thrift and energy which enabled Germany to take on the rest of the world in mortal conflict with a very fair chance of success, the Ruhr burgeoned into ceaseless activity. Coal production jumped from a daily 240,000 tons in 1932 to 416,000 in 1939, raw steel from a yearly 7,000,000 tons in 1932 to over 22,000,000. Chemical production rose in the same proportion, and important ancillaries were created in the form of synthetic oil and rubber plants.

Germany could more cheaply and more economically have bought the better raw product from export earnings. It is therefore safe to assume that the Nazi intention was primarily not to save foreign exchange but to provide alternative sources of rubber and oil for precisely that time—after war had been declared—when normal channels of trade would be cut. For this reason there was a practical and moral as well as an economic justification at Potsdam for the creation by the victor nations of a category of "forbidden" synthetic industries.

War seemed at first to have paralyzed the Ruhr. The great towns suffered serious bomb damage to nearly 65 per cent of their buildings. Man power was reduced by casualties of up to 30 per cent. The strategic bombing of the Eder and Möhne dams cut off sources of electric power. Transport was crippled by the attacks of rocket-firing aircraft, by wear and tear and the wartime lack of renewals. So disorganized was industry that production of coal and steel, the two essential elements of the Ruhr's economy, ran at 25 and 10 per cent of prewar during the first postwar year.

Western Germany's loss could not, moreover, be measured only in terms of these figures. The prewar counterweight to the Ruhr had been the Silesian-Saxon industrial area in the east. Silesia was now annexed to Poland and probably 80 per cent of the Saxon output began to flow to Soviet Russia by way of reparations from current production or as controlled exports. The Ruhr was expected industrially to supply a population of over forty million in an area which had contained nine million less in 1939.

It is at this point that one of the critical episodes of history jumps out of the pages of the past. The Potsdam Agreement has since been derided and discarded. Certainly the limitations which it—and the subsequent level-of-industry plan—sought to impose on Germany would seem to add up to deliberate economic constriction. A famous statesman once asked, "Can a limit be set to the march of a nation?" Can, indeed, a limit be set to the development of an economic area whose products are badly needed by a war-shattered world? Common sense would, presumably, cry out against what seems a policy of restrictive and obscurantist economic control.

Yet the victor nations had a good reason for limiting what were termed "undue concentrations of economic power." Russia, France, and England know what weapons the Ruhr could forge and just how ruthlessly they would be used against a civilian population. America has had the advantage of approaching a field of battle like a medieval knight— courageous to break a lance, but free to ride away afterward. The European nations have experienced an altogether different kind of war. If the Western Allies have made one serious mistake in their postwar policy in Germany, it has been their failure to convince the Russians that Germany would be speedily disarmed and her power to wage aggressive war strictly curtailed during the generations which must elapse before she learns the democratic way of life. This failure is typified by the explosions of demolitions which still, in 1950, echo across Kiel Harbor and by the retention of concrete air-raid shelters to house the homeless.

The Potsdam guarantees were not enough. When the subsequent level-of-industry plan, with its fundamental clause the limitation of steel production, was agreed upon, it took no account of new economic facts nor of the virtual impossibility of its own execution. Western Germany had to repair the devastations of war; to make good the tremendous losses in skilled labor and in the twenty-five to forty-five age group which is the most productive in industry; to support ten or eleven million refugees from eastern Germany; to quadruple her exports in order to pay for raw materials and for the basic foodstuffs which used to come from the rich agricultural lands lying east of the Oder-Neisse line and now annexed by Poland.

German economists, from Professor Erich Noelting, the Social Democratic economics minister of North Rhine—Westphalia, down to the pundits of the Economic Council of Frankfurt, argued that they were being given a crushing task, with their hands tied behind their backs. No German to whom I have spoken believes that Germany can subsist on a steel quota of 11,000,000 tons yearly, let alone reconstruct her smashed towns and raise her standard of living.

Is there, then, any alternative between condemning Western Germany to economic despair, and raising the level of steel production to a practical minimum of 16,000,000 tons yearly? This question involves the Ruhr so deeply that one must go outside its internal problems to find an answer.

At the moment Western German economy is making a wavering but discernible recovery under the stimulus of the Marshall Plan and of essential imports which America and England pour into the country. These imports are not paid for in the normal way but accumulate on a "deferred" account. Just how uncertain this recovery appears in the Ruhr will be indicated later. But coal production at least has climbed above 330,000 tons daily, 80 per cent of prewar, and steel production to an approximate average of 900,000 tons monthly, or 95 per cent of the "allowed" level. Exports have increased and by the end of 1949 had reached about 40 per cent of the target figure set for 1952 which would enable Western Germany to balance her payments and support herself.

But—and it is a big but—the fulfillment of that target figure must presuppose the re-erection of the Ruhr into that "dangerous" industrial concentration which Potsdam tried to prevent. The immediate implications of this are obvious. France, a senior partner in the Ruhr International Control Authority, must, in order to safeguard her own security, exercise all her influence in that body to retard the industrial progress of the Ruhr. The Russians must see in the recovery of a Ruhr well outside their own sphere of influence the threat of a new invasion similar to that of 1941, which devastated 40 per cent of their European territories. Their foreign policy will be dictated by a desire to secure a part of the control of the Ruhr as well as a part of its fruits. A rejuvenated Ruhr will not, at this rate, have much chance of becoming a factor for peace.

The practical alternative was there, and its implications have been better realized in the American Zone than elsewhere in Western Germany. Instead of bringing the ten to eleven million refugees to centers of industry, it might have been possible to bring industry to the new centers of refugee population. The *Land* of Schleswig-Holstein provides a pointer. It is tucked away in the extreme northwest, bounded by the sea, the frontiers of Denmark and the Soviet Zone, and the River Elbe. About 1,200,000 of its total population of 2,700,000 are refugees. Today the state's virtual bankruptcy is forcing thousands of them into unemployment. In places 40 per cent of the population is being supported by the state. Before the 1948 currency reform, when money was not scarce, the refugees were given some sort of *"Scheinbeschäftigung,"* or "shadow employment," which earned them a bare living wage. Naturally these people became the first to be discarded by employers who found that the present financial crisis cut down the scope of their business and wanted to reduce overheads.

Labor is being transferred from Schleswig-Holstein to the Ruhr. In June and July of 1949 it was planned to effect a first "import" of 29,000 workmen and their families. This makes some sort of economic sense, for the Ruhr still has a limited demand for "selected" labor which can be pushed into factory, steel mill, and coal mine. But what is being done, on the other hand, to develop new industries in Schleswig-Holstein? This would help to disperse industrial effort more rationally over all of Western Germany, would lower the proportion of the heavy industries which France fears and Soviet Russia covets, and would readjust a German economy which was built up in an age of continuously aggressive foreign policy and incipient war effort. The answer is, unfortunately, practically nothing.

Here the Ruhr's problem overflows its own loosely demarcated borders. Her industrial resources have apparently blinded the British to the possibilities of expansion and adjustment elsewhere. Schleswig-Holstein has admirable facilities for the building up of light industries. It has a close approach to the moist Lancashire climate which is best suited to the manufacture of textiles. It is serviced on the west by the port of Hamburg, on the east by its own excellent Baltic harbors of Kiel, Lübeck, and Flensburg. Its narrow body, long from north to south but never more than sixty miles wide between Baltic and North Sea, makes for short carries on land and a natural setting for export trades. It is the halfway point between Swedish iron ore and Durham coal from northern England, and for the Swedish timber which could be worked into paper or cellulose and shipped on to Britain. Only money is needed, and money has not been forthcoming for such projects. Until recently, Schleswig-Holstein was at the bottom of the priority list.

The Western Allies have not worked out a rationalized version of the Morgenthau plan. In many other states besides Schleswig-Holstein refugees cluster in small townships which can maintain and employ them only in times of plenty. The Americans have made some attempts to develop cottage industries, the British none. A large refugee population is being allowed to drift or is being directed to a Ruhr which will become an ever more top-heavy arch to the German economy, an ever more formidable and frightening proposition to the other countries of Western Europe.

It will be argued that fears should be allayed by the creation of the Ruhr Control Authority. This body, intended to be small and compact, will operate the administrative but not the industrial capital of the Ruhr from Düsseldorf. Six foreign nations are at present represented, the United States, Britain, France, and the three Benelux countries. At the end of 1949 Western Germany decided to appoint the delegation to which it was entitled. Its primary tasks will be to supervise the production of coal, iron, and steel and chemicals. The Military Security Board, on the other hand, will see that limitations imposed under the terms of the level-of-industry agreement are faithfully observed.

But will this, in reality, be possible? As German steel production creeps nearer its allowed "ceiling," officials of British Military Government in the Ruhr become increasingly apprehensive. Unless some tripartite or quadripartite integration of a wider nature than thought of at present takes place, they will be only the agents and informants of the Ruhr Control Authority and the Military Security Board, the one a board of directors and a small secretariat and the other a society of ex-officers dispersed in half a dozen headquarters throughout Germany. Will Military Government be allowed to maintain its control officers at Krupp and other great plants? Will industrial intelligence officers be allowed to continue to inspect plants as and when they please? Can these officers rely—as they must, for there is no alternative—on German statistics?

How is a real check to be maintained on the Ruhr when many of its vital records will be kept at Bonn or wherever the Federal Ministry of Economics is set up? Is control, indeed, really feasible when the controllers are an almost isolated collection of foreigners and the controlled include traditional German industrialists, progressive, acute, well informed, ruthless, and dealing with human and industrial factors which they have known intimately for generations? These are only a few of the questions which will have to be settled by a Ruhr Control Authority and Military Security Board, whose brief is very large but whose means of enforcing that brief are likely to be strictly limited. Evasion will not only seem properly patriotic to the Germans but may be unexpectedly easy. German armament firms gained valuable experience in this field after the First World War.

Another factor in the situation is the German attitude toward the Ruhr Authority. When the terms of the Ruhr Statute were published on December 28, 1948, the German reaction was immediate and violent. Professor Noelting, whom I have already quoted, described it as a document bearing the imprint of the victor nations, giving little hint of a wider European co-operation to come. The trade unions expressed themselves to be "alienated" by the lack of consideration for the interests of a working class which "is the strongest protagonist of democratic development in Germany." One newspaper, the *Westdeutche Zeitung*, called the statute politically, socially, and economically unacceptable, ascribed it to the "Monnet Plan," and linked it with "the confiscation of German colonies, the division of Germany into zones, and the destruction of its industry by senseless dismantling."

At Bonn, where German politicians were working on the framing of the constitution for Western Germany, the Social Democratic leader, Professor Carlo Schmid, used the phrase, "the hand at the throat of Germany." He said he believed that the Occupation in general and the Ruhr Statute in particular were conceived with the intention of "manipulating German economy in order to cut out German competition and exploit the German worker." The statute was not designed to obtain security against possible future German aggression but to "prevent any new German competitive prosperity." "The Ruhr Statute," he said, "has disappointed all our hopes. It is another example of victory not making the victor any wiser." The only fruits of the statute would be "the nationalism of a dog on a chain."

All parties combined with Schmid to attack the statute. Max Reimann, the fiery Communist leader, condemned not only the statute but all those who recognized its authority and complied with its regulations. Such people, he declared in a New Year's Day speech in Düsseldorf, would be regarded as quislings by the German nation. British Military Government pounced on him, tried him, and sent him to the mild martyrdom of a cushy prison hospital.

Karl Arnold, the premier of North Rhine—Westphalia, took a more statesmanlike line and proposed the integration of the Ruhr in a wider internationalized industrial area which would include the Belgian coal fields, the Luxemburg iron works, the Saar, and the iron deposits of Lorraine. Many Germans thought the Ruhr Statute might be turned to account as the first step in integrating European economy and promoting European Union. In the Rhineland there were many disciples of the "Europa Union" movement who saw in it a possible instrument for restoring Germany to the comity of nations.

Some of this sound and fury was meaningless. German politicians and organs of public opinion are obsessed with the need to popularize themselves by refusing to recognize the enactments of the Allies. But their words made a deep impression on the average German. Those with whom I spoke honestly saw no advantage in the creation of a Ruhr Authority save the negative one of hamstringing German progress. Such remarks as, "The French wanted this. You've only done this to please them," and, "Do you think you're better qualified to run German industry than the Germans themselves?" were the order of the day.

Although there was no talk of active resistance along the lines pursued by Leo Schlageter in 1923 against the French, distrust was widespread and may be fanned by German governments of the future. The likelihood is that the Allies, in bidding for German co-operation in the rebuilding of Europe and the construction of a new "Roman wall" against the Russians, will be forced to modify the powers of the Ruhr Authority or watch it lapse into impotence while the future of the Security Board remains a mystery. The serious threat is that this latter body will become an overgrown staff of office workers while the numbers of its agents "on the ground" will be so far reduced as to render them ineffectual.

The Ruhr Authority has a significance outside its own functional role. Its workings will mirror the different approaches of the participating nations to the whole German problem. Recently I asked an intelligent German friend to sum up these approaches under the title heading of "What does each country want out of the Ruhr?" He believed that the French would genuinely like to disperse the industrial potential of the Ruhr to Lorraine, Belgium, and even North Africa. The French would brake whatever progress was made, enforce a low level of industry for fear of a successful German economy building up a larger, more successful and aggressive German population, and direct as much German production of coal and steel as possible out of Germany.

Alongside the French, he called the Dutch and Belgians the "small robbers" and "money grubbers," who would probably come down on the side of "economic reason" because they wanted to invest for quick profit and find a German market for their colonial re-exports.

The British, he thought, were actuated by two motives. The first was the "go-slow" complex of a weak and muddle-headed regime. This is typified by a little story. Once a German official in the town of Cologne was asked by a high-ranking member of British Military Government how long it would take to rebuild his battered town. He thought, "Well about fifteen years." "But supposing," he was asked, "the whole weight of British Military Government was put behind you?" "Oh, in that case," he answered, "about fifty." The British have not made more mistakes in Germany than the other Allies. They have not, however, the French aptitude for concealing them or the American flair for explaining them away.

Most Germans think that the second British motive in the Ruhr is fear of competition. They feel that the list of reparations plants has provided the classic example of this. Thus the towns of Sheffield and Solingen have been rivals for sixty years in the world market for refined steel products. The Germans, from factory owner down to humblest operative, think that Solingen plants were scheduled for reparations because of the keenness of the competition they would give their British rivals. I have heard this from the lips of officials of the Economics Ministry in Düsseldorf, cabinet ministers, Communists, and small time capitalists. Why, I have been asked, should production of razor blades be curtailed? By actual weight, they are the most profitable form of steel production. Their lightness makes them cheaply and easily exportable, and they give the quickest and highest returns in export markets. The Germans believe that Britain wants these markets for herself. They realize that during six years of war export markets have shrunk and that countries that once lived off the production of raw materials have had time to develop their own industries—that, in fact, Germany and Britain, who must both "export to live," will sooner or later be thrown into fierce competition with one another. They realize, too, that their own country, with its love of work for work's sake and its greater thrift, will start as the favorite in the struggle. What more natural, then, than that political methods should be used to stultify this desire to earn and produce?

Nothing, therefore, has been more inevitable than the welcome given by the Germans to the Americans in the Ruhr.

The Americans are regarded as apostles of economic reason above political prejudice. German economic arguments will be used to split the Allies in their task of administering the Ruhr, keeping its production to an agreed level, and securing an equitable distribution of its products in the best interests of the whole of Western Europe. From the German point of view the equation is an easy one, to offset Allied political aims with Allied business sense. On the Ruhr Authority the Americans, British, and French will have three votes each, the Benelux countries one each. Germany, however, is now entitled to three votes too, and with the hoped-for support of America and the Benelux countries she will be able first to modify, then to sweep away the principle of Potsdam which states that no undue concentrations of economic power should be allowed to remain in Germany or be created anew.

The Germans are confident that they will get this working majority in the Ruhr Authority. If they do, they can set to work to build up a German power unit which will again be the arbiter of Europe.

In the face of this careful plan the Allied task remains one of controlling and regulating the Ruhr and then easing up on these controls in successive phases, but there must be no relaxing until the Germans have first given sound evidence of progress in democratic self-government and in the development of common sense and democratic thinking. A prerequisite to economic freedom is an orderly, civilized philosophy of life. The Germans can absorb this philosophy only after generations of Allied supervision.

The broad question of the future of the Ruhr is one for endless argument. Easier to focus are its internal problems, covering the whole field of everyday existence. Because it has been perpetually in the news for the last three years, the first of these is the dismantling question. American aid to Europe has so reiterated the need for economic recovery that the original object of reparations has been forgotten. They were intended to provide some compensation for mass destruction which was initiated by Germany. The equipment of the Ruhr steel and chemical plants cannot recompense Germany's victims for the devastation of the Ukraine, the wholesale burning of Polish villages and farmsteads, the flattening of a defenseless Rotterdam, the sinking of hundreds of British merchant ships, and the murder of millions of Jewish citizens of other countries. They were earmarked as a mere token repayment.

At times German opposition to the dismantling of peacetime industry has taken on the appearance of a regular campaign. Propaganda has been produced, such as the pamphlets of the Henkel Soap combine and the magazine *Reparations,* which was freely circulated in the United States and Britain at the beginning of 1949. Appeals to the British Regional Commissioner in the Ruhr, General Bishop, have been made through every possible channel, private and official. Except for the Communists every political party has issued repeated public protests. *Land* economic ministries talk about dismantling by the hour and trot out the same arguments: dismantling is uneconomic; the Germans want to work for Europe; the Allies are taking only the best plants and equipment. Now that the "Petersberg Agreement" of the autumn of 1949 has brought dismantling virtually to an end, it can safely be said that the Allies did their best to initiate and enforce a policy which was historically equitable, but economically embarrassing. Reparations have produced about one-fiftieth of the value of damage done by Germany during the war, one-tenth of the value of postwar Allied aid. The dismantling issue is dead now; it would best be forgotten by all sides.

Another issue which has provoked the extremes of recrimination is the socialization of heavy industry. In 1947 the

British Military Government decided that such a measure could be carried through only by each *Land* individually. The parliament of North Rhine—Westphalia, containing the Ruhr, thereupon passed a moderate socialization measure by a considerable majority. American intervention prevented this measure from becoming law. British Military Government was induced to reverse its policy statement, and the matter went into abeyance. Today it is still not clear whether the federal or *Land* parliaments are qualified to introduce socialization, nor is it clear whether the American High Commissioner would ever be empowered to let such a measure become law.

Yet this issue is not dead. It is the biggest plank in Kurt Schumacher's Social Democrat party's political platform, and Schumacher is the last man in the world to forsake an article of political faith for fear of Allied opposition. Personal inquiry has not convinced me that socialization is a popular demand. When I conducted a small poll on the subject I found that the average coal miner accepted the idea of socialization primarily because his union had told him it was a step in the right direction. Labor history since the war in Germany has been astonishingly placid, and British Military Government officers admit that relations between workers and employers are far better than could have been believed possible, particularly in view of the lack of employers associations. Coal miners and steel workers are far more concerned with obtaining the basic necessities of life than with gaining control of their industries. Their aspirations do not go beyond the *Mitbestimmungsrecht,* or right of joint participation, which they partially exercise in factory and coal pit through their works councils.

The merit of socialization, however, is twofold. It would settle the question of ownership of heavy industry, which has hitherto been readily placed at the disposal of any dictator to be developed as a basis for the German war machine, and it would vest responsibility for peaceful development in the German people instead of the barons of industry.

If it were carried through in Germany, socialization should be a practical measure and not an application of political dogma to economics. The German formula must be a different one from the British. A small body of directors who are truly representative of the nation's initiative should be preferable to the amorphous bureaucracy which can grow up under unlimited state control. The best brains among the Social Democrats seem to me to be working along the right lines in planning for control boards drawn primarily from the industry concerned and representative of both management and labor.

Plans of this kind will turn out to be more practical in the long run than the creation of a new class of coal and steel tycoons who, now that the great combines of the past are being "decartelized," can set to work with a will forming the great combines of the future.

Decartelization, indeed, is a separate chapter in Ruhr history. German trustees were appointed for the new iron and steel and coal companies which were in the process of formation for months. These trustees are approved by the Allied authorities and chosen from men with nominally "clean" political and industrial records. The size of the new companies is limited, and the Allies will still exercise a supervisory right over them. Every possible means of guaranteeing that heavy industry shall not again be a ready-forged instrument in the hands of a political despot has been considered.

There is one flaw in these plans: the component parts of the Ruhr's heavy industry are mutually magnetic, and economic forces will work to bring them together again. Whatever decartelization laws are theoretically imposed, there is nothing to prevent brother and brother, or former partner and partner, from gaining control of individual companies. In ten years' time there may be nothing to stop owners of smaller companies from selling out their interests. Shareholders of companies which are now forming are doing this in advance. Industry will regroup itself. Even the same old families may return to industrial power. Economic fact is stronger than social theory.

Foreign control, dismantling, and decartelization are the major problems of the Ruhr today. Yet they barely touch on the life of the average Ruhr worker, who is the best register of postwar conditions in Western Germany. How far has his life changed and how far is it changing afresh today? Whatever the Western Allies make of the great unit of the Ruhr, whether they overdevelop its economy or stifle its genuine urge to assist in the reconstruction of Western Europe, the man in the street is still the vital factor. A peaceful Germany must first be a contented one.

Today the Ruhr worker is immensely better fed than a year ago. His official food ration is 50 per cent higher and he has ample means of supplementing it. His diet is roughly the equivalent of his opposite number in Britain. He can clothe himself better than was possible a year ago, and the economy has so far stabilized itself as to avoid the incidence of famines in fuel and electric power. But the rest of the "new prosperity" which came to the Ruhr in 1948—the amply filled shops, the gaily lit restaurants and night clubs, the fleets of motor cars, the neo-Parisian modistes and couturiers—is something completely beyond his compass. The workingman still has a struggle for existence, and his standard of living is at least 40 per cent below prewar. The new prosperity is on the surface and is embraced only by a small class of capitalists who invest it with their own peculiar brand of excess.

The average wage in the Ruhr is about 200 marks a month. This has a purchasing value of about $40. Those who draw this or a lower wage are forced by high prices to spend over 70 per cent of their income on food alone. After fixed charges to rent, heat, light, and rates, there is little left to buy the clothes and household goods which are considered basic necessities in any civilized country.

Derationing of foodstuffs was assisted by the inability of large sections of the population to buy even their full legal rations. Its superficial success was less one of good economic planning than an expression of economic need. The cost-of-living index rose in the summer of 1949 to 140 per cent of prewar, and wages still lag far behind soaring prices, the upward movement of which has probably been only temporarily reversed.

The trade unions, the poor man's only mouthpiece, have hesitated to demand wage increases beyond the 15 per cent allowed at the end of 1948 when the wage stop was abolished. Lacking practical experience in planning and bargaining, they are uneasily aware that over-all rises in wages may start prices spiralling upward. The most serious effects of this would be internal inflation, a loss of confidence in the currency, and such a jump in costs of production that the German export program would be dangerously prejudiced. The unions have therefore concentrated on a demand for the lowering of prices. This demand has been satisfied to only a small degree. In the first half of 1949 prices stabilized rather than fell.

The internal economy of the Ruhr is a patchy affair. Here and there are obvious signs of the unhealthiness bred by six years of war and four more of stark economic need. Housing is the greatest immediate lack. British authorities have estimated that housing in the Ruhr must cost 150,000,000 marks yearly for seventy years to restore the situation to normal. The present repair program has been falling short of ordinary replacements for wear and tear. New building may bring 50,000 living quarters a year, but the total deficit is more than a million and a quarter. During the first six months of 1949 work on the vital miners' housing program dropped from 24 per cent of the monthly target in January to 20 per cent in February and 16 per cent in March. Miners' housing is as necessary to industrial recovery as equipment and raw materials.

Electric power has provided another bottleneck in industry. Again the main difficulty has been financial. Roughly 2,000,000,000 marks were needed to re-equip existing power stations in Western Germany and carry out the vast new construction schemes planned for the Ruhr and Aachen coal fields. In February 1949 the first 75,000,000 were forthcoming from counterpart funds in Frankfurt, derived from the sale of American and British food imports. Meanwhile a desperate campaign of mending and patching has just maintained power output at a figure sufficient to supply industry. But the plant is becoming increasingly run down as a result of insufficient maintenance during the war years and allowance must be made for the greater demands of industry as the planned rise in production materializes.

The *Jedermann* program, the production of cheap goods for mass consumption, has not been a real success. In a topsy-turvy economy it was too much to expect that a huge demand could be satisfied with utility goods when a "free" economy was producing luxury and good-quality articles. The *Jedermann* products were largely of poor quality, and the poor man will usually prefer to wait to buy, say, one decent pair of shoes. That is not to say, however, that he has been adequately shod in the meantime. *Jedermann* products have been too few to make any impression on the problem of supplying the workingman at reasonable cost, and many of them remained unsold because of the overwhelming shortage of purchasing power.

The apostles of a free economy should consider two factors. Their economic ideal cannot be suddenly superimposed on the old patchwork of controls which have existed for a dozen years, and in a "deficit" economy such as exists in Western Germany it must lead to a gross disparity between the living standards of different categories of wage earners. The poor man in the Ruhr is today paying for an economic dogma every bit as dangerous as unfettered state control.

Strange contradictions have emerged out of the economic confusions. An unemployment problem has arisen although there is still a demand for labor. A refugee problem comes home to roost as Western Germany tries to move through the later, usually gentler stages of recovery. The refugees have been herded into country districts and there are no houses for them in the industrial centers which need them and no alternative employment near their makeshift homes. The railways are carrying fewer passengers, and the demand for freight cars has declined 30 per cent between October 1948 and March 1949.

Shops are bursting with goods which only a small section of the population can afford. Luxury building flourishes, but ordinary social housing is no longer economic and cannot be so until rents are raised. People still live in attics, cellars, and holes in the ruins. Five million people, many of them in the Ruhr, have no bed to sleep in. Begging, forbidden by law and somewhat alien to the German character, has started again. Money is the first thought in everybody's mind, for with purchasing power so low there is everything here to buy. That is why the appearance of plenty is largely an illusion. A dislocated economy makes an interesting picture, for it contains extremes of riches and poverty, sure evidence of progress and equally unmistakable sign of stagnation.

It is surprising that the Ruhr worker remains so little affected by all this. The toll of the war years has left him not such a deft and prolific worker as before. Output per man shift in the mines and steel works is disagreeably low, partly due to the declining quality of plant and equipment. Even under the urge to feed themselves by their own efforts, German farmers are able to raise agricultural production by only a tiny percentage.

The German farmer has become more acquisitive, but the Ruhr coal miner is still a solid factor in society. Communism has made little headway among men who can remember days when hard work enabled them to live comparatively comfortably—well fed, decently clothed, with their own little gardens, their chickens and, often, their pig. Reimann has won few new followers, and the Communist vote continues to go down in works council, local, and state elections. The Russian blockade of Berlin and despotic control of the Eastern Zone lost the Communists all the ground gained by unremitting propaganda and brilliant organization.

The Ruhr worker is the most important factor in the stabilization of German life. I have found him honest and energetic, naïve but fundamentally sound politically, capable of understanding the democratic way of life. He has not experienced the extremes of nationalism which have racked other parts of Western Germany, and the right-wing Deutsche Partei and the irredentist Committee of Expellees from the East make no appeal to men whose sturdy good sense makes them more capable of learning moderation than the people of any other part of Germany except Berlin.

Yet with any German the same danger exists, that he may become an insensate cog in a machine which is beyond his comprehension or control. For generations the Ruhr workers have made instruments of war under a Krupp or a Thyssen. In moments of national stress they have allowed themselves to get out of the way of thinking. They have been unable to apply the check of ordinary common sense to the greed of their employers and the fantastic designs of their rulers.

The problems of the Ruhr begin and end with these working people. German society is dangerously unbalanced now that the landed class has faded into insignificance and Prussian army tradition and Prussian officialdom are regarded as exploded myths. The greatest task that the nations participating in the Ruhr Control Authority can achieve is the regulation of this tremendous industrial area so that the common man can be educated politically and can regain the self-respect and belief in his own opinion which he lost during the years of Nazi domination. The contribution of American thought will be to help steer the Authority through this task which can help fashion a firm, democratic basis for all German society and make the German into a real European citizen.

Chapter XVI

What Price Co-operation— Resistance and Collaboration in Occupied Germany

By PETER DE MENDELSSOHN

IT IS said that in modern times every people has the government it deserves. Equally well it might be said that every vanquished aggressor gets the occupation he has been asking for, and one is tempted to conclude that every regime of occupation reaps the co-operation or resistance it merits. On the face of it this looks like a truism beyond dispute. Yet in the case of Germany it is very much open to argument.

Judging from the amount of resistance it engendered when it was first imposed in 1945, the Allied Occupation in Germany must have been very nearly above reproach. Measured, on the other hand, by the degree of co-operation it met, its standard and quality would seem to have been less impressive. Moreover, as the years went by the ratio varied; the character of the Occupation changed and German reaction changed with it. There is no doubt that resistance in one form or another, overt and covert, has increased in scope and effectiveness during these years, but should it be concluded from this that the Allies asked for it and deserved no better?

Today there are more and stronger mental reservations to Allied aims and measures than there were in the summer of 1945, and there is considerably less collaboration. As the shackles of foreign rule loosen, the urge to throw them off completely without further delay becomes stronger. Thus the degree of co-operation obtained has become dependent on the measure of latitude and success allowed to resistance.

This development is natural and should have been expected. But was it expected? And if not, why not?

No estimate of any of the four zones of Germany will be correct which ignores the fact that any relationship between occupied and occupant is fundamentally unnatural and that for this primitive reason alone it will not work. No amount of interpretation will get around this basic truth. It is no joke to lose a big war, no matter why and how it was started and how unjust it may have been; and it is not funny to be occupied, however sincerely it is recognized and admitted that this occupation is deserved, justified, and necessary. Nor is it pleasant or easy to be the occupant. It is unpleasant and difficult. It is as humiliating, irksome, and impractical not to be allowed to run one's own affairs as it is the devil's own business to have to look after other people's affairs for them.

If proof were needed for the popular German saying *"Wie man's macht, ist's falsch"* (Whatever one does is bound to be wrong), both sides in a regime of occupation would be supplying it every day and every hour. Military government, it has been said, is in itself a contradiction in terms. No one who has ever been connected with it in any practical way will deny the truth of this, and it is not rendered less true by the fact that in Germany there was no alternative.

At its outset the Allied Occupation of Germany had a double purpose. It was to provide security for Germany's victims against future acts of aggression and to allow them to rebuild their shattered lives without fear of further interference; and it was to orient and educate the German people toward democratic ways of government so as to make them fit to live in peaceful co-operation with the rest of the world.

The two purposes were obviously closely related, but this did not mean that they could be easily harmonized. The first had to be achieved largely through mechanical means while the second called for psychological processes. They were partly contradictory. There was a nonmechanical, psychological side to the security aspect. If it was still about, the aggressive spirit could scarcely be cured with the help of mechanical devices such as disarmament and industrial restriction. But reorientation, if successful, would by itself automatically lead to security and render mechanical measures superfluous. What was more, the simultaneous application of mechanical measures was likely to slow down the psychological process, and that is what actually happened. Finally, the two programs were difficult to synchronize; while the former was essentially a short-term program which, in order to be effective, had to be carried out swiftly, the latter was obviously a long-term project requiring time, patience, and settled conditions surrounding Germany. In practice it was found that these prerequisites did not exist, and as a result the short term program was constantly revised and its execution delayed until it finally led to the head-on clash between the Allies and the Germans over the dismantling question in the summer of 1949. On the other hand, the long-term project was precipitated to a degree which all but nullified the initial effort.

Both programs were finally upset when, halfway through, a third purpose appeared and increasingly moved into the foreground. The rapidly widening gulf between the Western powers and the Soviet Union split Germany and moved her Western half into the Allied camp before it was ready, physically and spiritually, to be received there. The common front against the spread of communism had to be built up and consolidated as quickly as possible, and whether they liked it or not the Western Allies had no choice but to include Western Germany in it.

This meant racing the bewildered and disoriented nation through a course of reorientation at breakneck speed, while at the same time abandoning, step by step and at an ever increasing pace, vital aspects of the security program which began to stand in the way of over-all Western consolidation.

Small wonder therefore that as the Allies, through the force of events outside Germany, became more and more disoriented in their purposes regarding Germany, the Germans themselves saw their chance and seized it. It is all very well for the Western powers to tell the Germans that the Western security system can and will be built without their assistance. What German leaders see is that strenuous efforts are being made by the Western powers to create conditions in Germany which will enable that country to render such help effectively. Their conclusion inevitably is that their co-operation must come at a price, and this price must inevitably be the swift regaining of full independence and sovereignty. Hence the bold, peremptory, and sometimes plainly impertinent language of German politicians. It may be an exaggeration to say that four years after the end of hostilities Germany is blackmailing the Allies. But it is no more than an exaggeration.

No sound and stable relationship between occupant and occupier could possibly develop in these shifting conditions. Friction was bound to increase and not to decrease. It did, and so did opportunity to resist successfully what was left of such Allied aims as seemed incompatible with German aspirations. For instance, the presence of foreign troops on German soil is *not* incompatible at this stage with these aspirations; few Germans would quarrel with the Western powers for wishing to fight a war on their behalf against the Soviet Union; they are quite content to let the American soldier and airman look after their security while they themselves are permitted perhaps to provide the arsenal and stand by with good advice on a matter in which they are experienced. On the other hand, the denial of full sovereignty in the fields of foreign affairs, foreign trade, and scientific research *is* definitely incompatible. Resistance to Allied measures in these fields will increase and attempts to circumvent them multiply in direct ratio to Allied dependence on German co-operation in other spheres.

Opportunities for resistance and circumvention are increasing as victor and vanquished, occupant and occupied move closer together, and they are being exploited with determination if not always with skill. In the summer of 1949 this situation enabled German economists and politicians effectively to split the Allied camp over the question of dismantling prohibited industries and executing the Washington Agreement.

Granting that the relationship between occupant and occupied can only be unnatural, and for the moment leaving aside its historic development over the last four years, on what foundation can this relationship be established?

There are three basic possibilities for the vanquished: hostility, collaboration, and co-operation.

Hostility toward the foreign ruler assumes that "all is not lost" and that the situation can best be retrieved by holding on to this assumption until the course of events turns it into reality. It assumes that a "reversal of fortunes" is still possible and that determined, uncompromising, and implacable hostility will wear down the victor, demoralize him, and finally induce him to throw in his hand. This policy calls for active as well as passive resistance, sabotage, violence, guerrilla warfare, and other methods of attrition.

But it depends on a fluid situation to have any prospect of success. It is the attitude with which the German occupiers were faced in the countries they overran during the last war, and even in the blackest days it was a rational policy on the part of the vanquished while the war lasted. After May 8, 1945, the Germans were rational enough not to adopt this attitude either collectively or individually. But strangely enough, the Allies entering Germany did not credit them with this rationality, and as a result the whole Occupation started off wrong.

There was a visible split running through German military and civilian behavior in the spring of 1945. German soldiers defended their towns until the very last. Cities deep in the heart of Germany, like Leipzig and Halle, had to be reduced by Allied artillery. Yet once the town had fallen, soldiers and civilians emerged with white flags to greet the conquerors as liberators. This did not make sense to the conquerors and future military administrators. The Allies had anticipated the kind of resistance from which the Germans themselves had suffered in their occupations. The Allies appeared fully armed and prepared against guerrilla warfare, "werewolves," uprisings, sabotage, murder, and assassination, and logically enough they established nonfraternization. Most of the Germans, on the other hand, had anticipated the kind of occupational rule which they themselves had inflicted on other peoples. A few visualized themselves as liberated from Hitler and the scourge of war, and anticipated fraternization.

No bridges were blown, no military trains derailed, no attempts made on the lives of Generals Eisenhower and Montgomery. At no time since unconditional surrender has there been anything anywhere in Germany even remotely resembling the activities of the resistance movements in German-occupied lands. That resistance, based on hostility, had been part of the war. Any German resistance would have had to be part of the peace. Wartime resistance was designed to accelerate the war; resistance after the end of the war could only slow down peace.

This was not at first understood by the Allies and their representatives in Germany; many of them would have respected the Germans more if they had shown resistance. In the beginning many Germans received the Allies as liberators whereas the Allies considered themselves conquerors. Today the Allies see themselves much more as liberators or as potential protectors whereas there are few Germans who do not regard them as conquerors deliberately trying to enslave them.

A nation adopting an attitude of abject collaboration has ceased to be a nation; it can hope to survive only by slavishly subordinating itself to the way of life of the victor. In 1945 and 1946, during the early stages of the Allied Occupation of Germany, large sections of the German people found themselves in this frame of mind and acted accordingly. For many of them it became a question of mere physical survival. The prospect of a hot meal or an occasional cigarette determined one's political outlook.

Nevertheless, subservience to Allied plans and concepts, blind obedience to their orders and wishes, went to extraordinary lengths. Few means were too cheap and undignified to use in gaining Allied favor. For example, more would-be agents and informers offered their services than could possibly be used. This form of German collaboration did the Allied armies one particular disservice in helping them to build up the monstrous bureaucratic apparatus of the Occupation.

Allied military bureaucracy in Germany was soon recognized by most Germans for what it was, a cumbersome and ill-functioning machine which often stepped on its own toes and got its hands caught in its own wheels. But the tens of thousands of Germans working in Allied offices and the German civil authorities acting under the supervision of these offices genuinely delighted in making this bureaucracy even more bureaucratic.

With few exceptions, Germans are born bureaucrats, and the ideal position of a bureaucrat is, of course, behind a superior authority, in this case not only foreign but military; there the bureaucrat is quite unassailable. "Allied orders" and "Military Government regulations" were used by German subordinates as an excuse to inflict the most unnecessary tribulations on their fellow Germans. One of the least likable of German national characteristics blossomed forth during this period, a lack of civic sense and solidarity in times of stress. If one German could prosecute another for failing to observe the Allied book, he usually would.

If this was collaboration at its worst, there was at the same time another side to public behavior. This was apathy based on a refusal to shoulder any responsibility for the further course of events. Its main argument seemed to be that since the victorious Allies had taken over the responsibility for the government and administration of Germany, they could carry it and see how far they got. Let us not contradict them, these Germans seemed to say, or point out their errors to them or help them in any way, but let us obediently do whatever they say, no matter how absurd it is. Germany is their responsibility, not ours. Another German saying sums it up: "It serves my father right that I should get frostbitten fingers. Why doesn't he buy me any gloves?"

Co-operation between victor and vanquished assumes that a temporarily unbalanced relationship can slowly but surely be righted by a reasonable give and take on both sides. It

does not demand on the part of the victor that he should forgive and forget all the suffering which the vanquished inflicted upon him; nor does it permit the vanquished to step
forward as a fully respectable partner who has nothing to be
ashamed of. But it recognizes that life must and can go on successfully if, within the limits of the mental reservations which
at the beginning they must necessarily have, victor and vanquished work together.

After a war such as the one the world had just witnessed, it
was probably too much to expect that a relationship based on
genuine co-operation could be established immediately after
the last shot was fired. Neither the Allies as they entered
Germany nor the Germans as they received the Allies were
ready for it, and the desperate economic plight of Germany,
coupled with the total loss of its political orientation, made
the task of establishing it doubly difficult. Yet one feels that
Anglo-American policy was handicapped by a lack of foresight and long-term planning. Time lost in vain efforts to
save and then to restore the four-power façade kept both the
Allies and the Germans in a prolonged period of suspense
which postponed the taking of effective practical measures
such as currency reform and thus delayed the creation of a
genuine give-and-take relationship.

Real Allied-German co-operation dates only from the West
German currency reform and the inclusion of Western Germany in the Marshall Plan. Since then a great deal of progress has been made. During the first two years the anxiety
to be associated and identified with the foreign ruler, if only
for material reasons, dominated the attitude of the average
German. Now the desire *not* to be associated or identified
with Allied measures and concepts is at least as strong.

In the early years of the Occupation there was no specific
German point of view; now the Germans confront every
Allied move or suggestion with a German counterplan. In-

convenient as this is, it is certainly not surprising that "resistance" is at last beginning. It required co-operation to give it a margin within which to manifest itself.

At the beginning of the fifth year of the Occupation, resistance to Allied concepts and measures in Germany springs, on the whole, from an urge to get back to the "German way of life," to do things "the German way." This urge in the common man lends itself readily to exploitation by the politicians, and much of the political resistance is little more than vote-catching window-dressing and plain hypocrisy.

The common man's desire to find his way back to the "German way of life" is genuine enough, and perfectly understandable. There has been a surfeit of foreign blessings in one form or another. They were not refused as long as they filled the vacuum and while the nation itself was physically and mentally unable to produce its own. American films were better than no films, and communal elections according to a strange British electoral system better than no elections at all; French press laws had to be preferred to the absence of newspapers altogether, and land reform along Soviet lines seemed, after all, to contain more elements of progress than the perpetuation of the large estates.

Yet it was never quite clear to the average German why, for purely geographical reasons, accident and expediency should compel him to live the American way of life in one part of the country, the British in another, the French in a third, and the Russian in a fourth. For undoubtedly the four occupying powers went to extraordinary lengths in introducing their own national ways of life into their respective zone of Occupation. The divergencies and discrepancies which resulted were often grotesque, and the upshot of it was that for a long time German national individuality was compelled to express itself through widely different foreign media. German eagerness and ability to pick up and assimilate quickly anything foreign favored this development; but the concurrent streak in the German mental make-up, the inclination to look down on anything foreign and boost the "German way" while turning a blind eye to all its deficiencies, was bound to produce a sharp reaction.

This reaction came as soon as material conditions improved and provided a margin for "freedom of action." The average German now has the feeling that he is no longer at the mercy of the occupying powers but can stand on his own feet again. This feeling may be largely illusion, but where it is, it is a deliberate illusion which gladly ignores the part the occupying powers continue to play in putting him back on his feet. Being back on his feet, he now feels free to reject the foreign way of life, and he is rejecting it in many cases only to demonstrate his independence. Thus German film critics now delight in writing devastating reviews of foreign films which are not nearly as bad as they make them out to be; German economists delight in proving to the Allies that their export-import system does not work even where it works better than anything the Germans could have put in its place; German politicians delight in belittling the Anglo-Saxon electoral system, which has, after all, produced the two most stable parliamentary regimes in the world while their own system is memorable only for the fact that it led them straight into one of the saddest chapters on record in the history of parliamentary democracy.

But is all this "resistance"? Can any agitation rightly be called resistance which develops without involving any physical or material risk on the part of those organizing it or carrying it out? It hardly seems so. It does not require much courage to make bold statements which, in the first place, are sure of applause among large sections of one's own people; which, in the second, cannot and will not, and are not designed to, change anything; and which are highly unlikely to provoke any retributive measures from those against whom they are directed.

This could not be said of an appeal to the people to refuse all service to the Occupation authorities; those obeying it would immediately have to suffer for it; therefore such an appeal is not issued. It could not be said of a German attempt to start an air line or to make atom bombs or to ignore Allied currency regulations; such attempts would have immediate painful consequences, and no one dreams of making them.

Most of the German resistance is more or less academic and costs the resister nothing. For instance, the resistance of German politicians to the Oder-Neisse frontier is mere shadow fighting, since the politicians who agitate against it know that their loud protests will bring no retaliation from Moscow as long as they are made from behind British and American protective walls. Were this resistance to come from Dresden or Leipzig instead of from Frankfurt and Hamburg, it would be a different matter. Resistance against the dismantling of prohibited industries is also largely academic. The workers who barricaded factory entrances against the approaching dismantling squads were fully aware that the barricades were not likely to keep the dismantlers out and that they themselves would not be shot for having put them up.

This sort of resistance almost never involves any actual risk; it has only "demonstration value"—but this value is considerable. Thus during the dismantling controversy a German newspaper stated that "power and might may be on the side of the Allies, but reason is on ours." A French or Polish newspaper which printed the same sentence about the Germans in 1941 would not have survived, nor would its editors. This small but vital difference is the tag on which the price of co-operation is written.

"If the Allies want us to co-operate with them in European

reconstruction, they must take care to treat us accordingly."
This was said by Dr. Konrad Adenauer in June 1949. It was
not resistance, but was it blackmail? And if it was, what kind
of blackmail is this which lets it be plainly understood that
the entire threat consists of mere rhetoric? The speaker knew
as well as the next man that Western Germany has no alternative to co-operation with the Allies, wherever this co-
operation may lead it. What he really asked for was co-
operation from his voters in the impending elections.

The idea of demonstrably dissociating themselves from
anything committing them to the Allies has become important for most Germans; this was made clear during the trial
of Max Reimann, the West German Communist leader. The
psychological significance of this trial was not fully appreciated at the time, yet it marked a turning point in the development of German-Allied relations.

Five days after the announcement of the Ruhr Agreement,
Reimann, speaking at a mass meeting at Düsseldorf, said,
"German politicians who co-operate with the Allies in carrying out the provisions of the Ruhr Statute must not be surprised if they are regarded as quislings by the German nation, and the day will come when they will have to account
for it before the German people."

As a threat, this was the nearest thing to open incitement
to resistance uttered by a responsible German at any time
since May 1945. In the view of British Military Government
it constituted a punishable offense, and Reimann was charged
before a Control Commission Summary Court with having
violated an article in Military Government Ordinance No. 8,
which makes it an offense for Germans to "encourage discrimination against persons aiding and assisting the Allied
forces and the occupying authorities in the administration of
Germany."

Reimann was found guilty and sentenced to three months'

imprisonment, but the significance of the verdict went far beyond the rather humble, humorous, and altogether not unlikable Communist leader who did his best to spoil his own case in court by making an irrelevant propaganda speech. The implications were well set out by his British counsel, Mr. Dudley Collard. Who are persons giving aid and assistance to the Allied authorities? Collard asked. Does this description cover only direct employees of Military Government, such as drivers, typists, waiters in officers' messes, or does it also include German industrialists, civil servants, and politicians?

Mr. Collard thought it did not but the prosecution argued that it did, and the court accepted the argument. But if the case of the prosecution was accepted, defense counsel went on, this must indicate that "German politicians are regarded by Military Government as their agents," and that was the reason why German politicians, whom this ordinance was meant to protect, objected to this trial and therefore, by implication, to this protection. If it were true that German politicians who supported the Allied powers in their policies were subject to protection and those who criticized them subject to prosecution, this would be the "end of democracy, and these politicians might as well pack up and go home." The accused had used words of strong criticism and warning, but they had been addressed to his fellow politicians and could not constitute an offense under the ordinance cited.

The prosecution argued differently. The Ruhr Agreement, it maintained, explicitly "called for co-operation by the Germans in carrying out its provisions." It aimed at the peaceful reconstruction of Germany, and this could not be accomplished without the help of German politicians. It was the view of Military Government that "those co-operating in the Ruhr Statute are doing a noble and patriotic service and are not men who can be said to be traitors."

The implications of this statement were obvious. They

seemed to be that Germans, politicians or otherwise, are not free to determine, according to their own lights, what in their view is a noble and patriotic duty but that their political morals are prescribed to them by the occupying power. Moreover, the West German government was considered by the occupying authorities to be bound to accede to the Ruhr Agreement before it had even come into being; the occupying authorities who are governing Germany's foreign relations had already, in fact, acceded to it on Germany's behalf, and German politicians and statesmen were therefore bound in law to carry out the provisions of the agreement as if they or their government had signed it.

The conclusion was that whether they liked it or not they must now regard themselves as "agents of the Allied powers," since they were so regarded by the Allied powers themselves, and anyone criticizing these "agents" for their actions or inactions—whether he went to the length of calling them quislings or not—was bound to come into conflict with Allied, not German, law.

Events have since traveled well beyond this turning point, and if trials of this kind have not been repeated, it has not been for want of legal opportunity on the part of the occupying powers but in recognition of the fact that this approach is not designed to encourage the "aid and assistance" the Allies need.

Nevertheless, at a critical juncture in German-Allied relations—when the Germans were in the midst of framing their own constitution and preparing for their own government and when the Allies were getting ready to hand back to them large parts of their sovereignty—this trial and its verdict did both parties an important service. It showed them that nothing can be gained by attempts to "naturalize" their basically unnatural relationship and that traditional terms like resistance, collaboration, and co-operation should be used sparingly by both sides at a time when they have largely lost their accustomed meaning.

This situation in Germany is unprecedented, unique, and ever shifting, and so is the relationship between the Germans and their present masters. No simple formula exists for it, and no remedy for its inherent deficiencies. All one can and must hope for, in the interest of all concerned, is that once it has been outlived, it will never produce itself again. For the best one can say of it is that it does no one any good.

Chapter XVII

Obituary of a Government— The Story of the East-West Breakup in Germany

By MARGUERITE HIGGINS

WHEN Soviet Marshal Vasili Sokolovsky stalked suddenly out of the Allied Control Council on March 20, 1948, he shattered finally and completely the greatest experiment in modern government: the attempt of a police state and three democracies to work together in governing a fifth nation, Germany, the heart of Europe.

With the death of the four-power Allied government on that fateful March day, the great struggle for power between East and West for the control of the European continent flared spectacularly into the open. For the walkout of the Soviet Zone commander stripped away the camouflage and restraints of diplomatic negotiation and the latent conflict between the powers exploded. Within a few weeks the Russians had followed through in the Berlin blockade with the use of outright force—everything short of warfare itself—to gain what they had failed to wrest from their wartime allies in four years at the council table.

Why did the great experiment, begun with so much hope

in 1945, collapse in failure? Why could not East and West co-operate in peace as they had in the conquest of Hitler's fantastic dictatorship?

General Clay, America's brilliant, hard-driving Military Governor, considering this question shortly before his retirement, came up with the conclusion: "We could have worked it out at this level, difficult as it was, if there had been agreement at the top. We in Germany only reflected the widening split between the Western democracies and the East."

Despite the infinite number of complicating factors, the split in Germany, in the mind of Clay and other leading statesmen, can in retrospect be pinned down to one central point: Russia, with its distrust of the West, and particularly with its fear of the growing might of America, became increasingly determined to win Germany's resources in order to gain an edge in the world struggle for power, a struggle that all dreaded might burst into armed conflict. The West, having by 1945 already ceded Russia much in Eastern Europe, was equally set against letting Soviet communism expand westward through Germany. These positions proved irreconcilable during the era of four-power rule of this country. And so Germany was split in two, with East and West respectively consolidating what they already occupied.

To Western Occupation chiefs charged with putting into effect the broad and, as it turned out, highly ambiguous policies handed down to them by their heads of state, the first jolt in four-power relations came only a few weeks after the last shots were fired against the Germans.

On a sunny June day in 1945, Marshal Gregori Zhukov, bemedaled chieftain of the victorious Soviet forces, flatly refused to discuss Western Allied entry into Berlin—as provided in the secret London agreement of November 1944—until General Dwight D. Eisenhower had completed the immediate evacuation of American troops from the provinces of Thuringia and Saxony into which they had fought in pursuit of the Germans. All of Eisenhower's assurances that the Americans would be brought back as quickly as possible to the agreed line were to no avail. Zhukov, evincing great suspicion of the Americans, could not be persuaded even to discuss the establishment of four-power government until Eisenhower complied.

As one American diplomat expressed it: "There were several days there when we didn't know whether four-power government would get started at all."

There were other storm signals, particularly at the lower levels of day-to-day negotiations. In the words of Brigadier General Frank Howley, America's colorful, tough Berlin commandant: "Our troubles with the Russians began the second we met them."

Howley, who probably has had more experience in direct dealing with the Russians than any other Allied official in the European theater, encountered the Soviets for the first time at the Elbe River as he was leading a reconnaisance squad bound for Berlin. His opening debate, as to whether the Americans would be allowed across at all, lasted seven hours. This was to be topped four years later, when the argument preceding the breakup of the Kommandatura quadripartite Berlin city government droned on for a record-breaking fourteen hours of futile negotiation.

In those early days harmony was fullest at the top, at the vodka and banquet level, because the world leaders could confine themselves to generalizations and theory. The men who had to put the theory to concrete test found out instantly how hard the four-power experiment was going to be, but it took some time for the upper ranks to grasp that these clashes were not isolated instances but part of a pattern.

The sharp and basic differences between Western and

Soviet ideologies became evident to those on the scene within days after the Americans, British, and French finally reached the city of Berlin. For instance, when the Western Allies found the Soviet-sponsored system of political "block watchers" in Berlin, they immediately denounced this snooper system as a hangover from the Hitler dictatorship and abolished it in their sectors. But the Russians, in what amounted to the first instance of unwillingness to achieve uniformity in Allied rule, refused to end the system. And it should be noted that this was on a political issue, that of civil liberties.

On June 29 General Clay ran head-on into an early example of Russian intractability, a phenomenon with which the world was to become all too familiar. It happened while he was trying to negotiate terms of Western Allied road and rail access to Berlin, which as an island in the Soviet Occupation Zone was separated from the British and American zones by more than a hundred miles. Clay finally settled for a single highway—the now famous Helmstedt-Berlin *Autobahn* —and even at that had to content himself with an oral agreement. He did so because he was under strict orders from his boss General Eisenhower not to push the Russians too hard lest they be provoked and the seed of discord be sown.

For in the first postwar summer, basking in the comradeship and ties of mutual victory, the American leadership ardently believed that if Soviet suspicions and distrust could be dissolved, four-power government could be made to work. So concessions were made and issues—such as the question of access to Berlin—were not pressed as hard as in the light of later history they clearly should have been.

Berlin was the great laboratory of four-power relations and the men on the scene were keenly aware of how much their success or failure would bear on the keeping of the peace. General Clay, especially, as a man accustomed to success, determinedly set out for completion of his assigned mission. But as time went by it became clear to all that the Occupation chiefs had been set an impossible task.

For although the conquerors were determined to remain in Germany, nominally to prevent the vanquished from starting a new war, the blunt truth was that the Allies feared Germany far less than the possibility that one side would use the country against the other.

The bible of the Occupation, the Potsdam Agreement, was an ambiguous and contradictory document that as it turned out could be quoted to support the arguments of both sides. Potsdam, fortunately for the world, was the last of the big four-power meetings where for the sake of surface unity leaders of East and West resorted to generalities to cover up points on which they could not agree. Vagueness in terminology was the instrument used to hide the cleavages which struck at Allied harmony. For the heads of state at that time were not prepared to admit these differences to the world public.

Since the Potsdam Protocol was signed, Western diplomats have learned through grim experience that the same word can mean vastly different things to East and West and that every agreement with the Russians, in order to be workable, must be spelled out almost to the last detail.

But in 1945 top Allied statesmen appeared to think, for example, that in persuading Stalin to transform Germany into a "democracy" they had achieved their primary objective in this country. What Truman and Attlee apparently were not prepared to admit was that by "democracy" the Russians meant something quite opposite to Western concepts of this form of government. For "true democracy," Russian style, means the "dictatorship of the proletariat," which does not need majority approval of the population. In other words, Soviet democracy represents rule by recognized Communist leaders whether or not these people have the approval, as expressed through the ballot, of the people as a whole.

A revealing comment on how dangerous the lack of definition can be came from a British official at a four-power meeting in the fall of 1945. After four hours of fruitless haggling over what democracy meant, he remarked glumly: "Gentlemen, in the light of the conflicting views presented here, about the only definition we seem to agree on is that "democracy" is a form of government imposed by four nations on a fifth."

The definition of democracy is not the only item that the world rulers at Potsdam, being unable to agree among themselves, passed on to their deputies. The unresolved issues included such important questions as how much was to be taken in reparations; the future boundaries of Germany; the severity of the terms of the Allied Occupation; and the disposition of the Ruhr industries which symbolize Europe's industrial heartland.

A host of other complications beset the four-power experiment in the Berlin laboratory; just to name a few, consider the conflicting national approaches with which the occupiers began their task. America, caught in the first postwar years in a sharp split of public opinion, wavered between "hard" and "soft" peace, and only after experience had taught the folly of deindustrialization schemes came out for a "free, peaceful, and *prosperous*" Germany, built upon a basis of a liberal capitalistic economy. Although free enterprise remained the motif of this effort, General Clay insisted that the country could have whatever the majority of Germans voted for, even if it meant socialism.

The British maintained from the beginning of the Occupation that Germany must remain highly industrialized if it was to live. Economically the British wanted nationalization of key industries and a mildly Anglicized form of social democ-

racy. Fears of German industrial competition partially motivated Britain's views on what plants should remain in the
country.

The French, until the advent of Foreign Minister Robert
Schuman, pursued a policy of weakening and dividing Germany by whatever means possible. They looked toward a
loose confederacy of nearly autonomous German states as the
best possible solution. Also partially motivated by fear of
German competition, France had a highly restrictive attitude
toward German industrial revival.

Like the Americans, the Russians had a strong streak of
schizophrenia in their Occupation policies. They were caught
initially by the tremendous pressure to drain Germany of
every possible quantity of capital as well as consumer goods,
machines, tools, etc., to replenish depleted stocks in the
Soviet Union. On the other hand, they tried with desperation
to win Germany for the Soviet camp.

The current pattern in the Soviet Zone tells the graphic
story of Russian economic ambitions: outright Soviet ownership or nationalization of key industries, state control of the
rest, and land reform as a prelude to collectivization of
farms.

The beginning of the four-power attempt jointly to rule the
vanquished foe began formally on July 30, 1945, in the vast,
formidable conference room of the former Prussian law court
that became Allied Headquarters in Berlin. The principal
actors at this historic meeting which took place even as the
heads of state were conferring at near-by Potsdam were Eisenhower for the United States; Zhukov, Russia's war hero;
Britain's Montgomery; and Koenig, the suave, extremely pro-
Gaullist French general. Things went comparatively well at
the outset because the points at issue were largely procedural.
A vast structure of committees—economic, political, and cultural—was erected. Staffs of interpreters rendered into three

languages every word that was uttered; minutes were unanimously approved, as well as produced, in three languages; a modern Tower of Babel was Berlin's newest landmark!

In the early months, General Clay, who sat on the "Coordinating Committee," the meeting place of the deputy military governors, often acted as arbiter between the other Allies. Later, describing his earnest efforts to get along with the Russians, Clay recalled that "in the early months I voted more often with the Russian representative than with any other power." It was the heyday of international good will and the thin cracks which had begun to appear in the structure were hastily covered up.

By October the Allies had run into their first major impasse. This was the refusal of the French, who had not been present at the Potsdam Conference, to accept the provisions for the establishment of central German administrative units. Fearing a new German aggression, the Quai d'Orsay wanted no part of anything that might lead to a centrally organized and unified Germany. France's stubborn defiance of the most eloquent pleadings of the other three Allies struck at the very heart of the Potsdam Agreement. For the administration of Germany as an economic unit was the basic premise on which all the rest of the agreement was based.

But serious as it was, French opposition to central German agencies did not provide the real point of breakdown in four-power harmony. This came over the question of reparations.

The reparations dispute which effectively dug the grave of four-power relations flared to a climax at the meeting of the deputy military governors on April 26, 1946. At this session the Russians made clear that in addition to the outright removals of capital equipment provided for reparations in the Potsdam Agreement they were collecting reparations out of new production—everything from precision instruments to whole bolts of cloth. The Western powers know that the

Soviets were busy absorbing from 60 to 80 per cent of the total production in East Germany without any compensation to the Germans whatsoever. The Western powers labeled this a direct violation of the Potsdam provision that the first call on postwar German production would be for export, the proceeds of which would provide foreign exchange for needed German imports. The West wanted the resources of the Soviet Zone pooled with those of the West so that a common export-import program could be worked out. And they strongly objected to pouring millions of dollars' worth of food and supplies into Western Germany while Russia ruthlessly stripped her own zone.

The de facto end of the Allied Control Council as a government for all Germany came with this meeting, less than a year after hostilities ceased. For from that date forward the four commanders in chief made no important decisions affecting Germany as a whole. The Occupation leaders soon had to admit that they were unable to iron out the unresolved issues forwarded to them at Potsdam by the world's top statesmen. The four-power conferences became forums for mutual and increasingly vituperative recrimination and name calling. Soon the Russians were publicly accusing their former wartime allies of building West Germany into a base for an attack on the Soviet Union.

East and West Germany seemed irretrievably rent in two, politically and economically. The net result was two Germanys so violently contrasting that many wondered whether Humpty Dumpty could ever be put together again. An Eastern "people's democracy" was forming on one side of the Elbe, while on the other a predominantly liberal-capitalist system was emerging.

The year 1946 saw the end of any further Soviet pretense at building a Western-type parliamentary democracy in their zone. And from the evidence it would seem that the debacle suffered by the Communists in the Berlin elections of 1946 was the turning point. The Berlin elections—the only completely free voting ever permitted by the Soviets behind the iron curtain—were followed by an era in which the Soviets set out by force to achieve what they had not achieved previously by propaganda and persuasion.

Political arrests and kidnapings spiraled upward and the twelve principal concentration camps in the Soviet Zone, including the infamous Sachsenhausen and Buchenwald, swelled with so-called enemies of the people, consisting mainly of Social Democrats, the hated political opponents of the Communists. Gradually the Communist-dominated coalition of parties entrenched themselves as rulers in the East, developing as a main instrument of power para-military German troops numbering several hundred thousand and including a detachment of political police.

Actually the story of how the Soviets brought the police state to Germany was in the beginning considerably blurred for the very reason that Western officials on the scene, cognizant of public opinion at home and of the intense desire of the United States to make a go of relations with Russia, hesitated to label by their right names the very tactics that were making East-West co-operation impossible. Such events, however, as the midnight deportation to Russia by Soviet tommy gunners of two hundred skilled Berlin workers, plus their wives and children, accelerated the process of disillusionment of the world about the peacetime tactics of the ally that had been so glorified in wartime. For this was long enough after the war so that the obviously deliberately planned deportation of October 1946 could not be put in the same category with the excesses of the battle-happy Soviet warriors whose deeds almost everybody was willing to pass over with understanding.

It now seems incredible that stories of concentration camps

in the Soviet Zone were often denounced by liberal circles in America as sheer anti-Soviet fabrications. Time has shown that the main purpose of the camps has not been the punishment of the logical victims, the Nazis, but rather of those who resisted the transformation of Eastern Germany into a "people's democracy."

At the Moscow Conference of 1947 and in London in the winter of 1947-48, Secretary of State Marshall made a final pre-blockade attempt to persuade Russia to unify Germany on mutually acceptable terms. Both meetings broke down over Russia's reparations demands.

General Marshall summed up at the Moscow Conference the ominous state of international relations when he declared: "Of all the points in the United States' proposals, primary emphasis is attached to the treatment of Germany as an economic unit as provided for at Potsdam. Our representatives at Berlin have been trying for twenty months to get that agreement implemented. The United States is still trying. If Germany is divided, each half will require strengthening to exist independent of the other. Two halves of Germany may then emerge, later to be fused into a revitalized and militant Germany. The permanent partition of Germany is dangerous to the peace of Europe and the world!"

Rumblings in the Soviet press foreshadowed the blockade tactics of the Russians for more than a year. The Russian argument was that the Western Allies were entitled to their sectors of Berlin only by virtue of the fact that it was the intended capital of a united Germany, and that if a West German state were set up the Western powers had no further excuse for remaining. The Western powers answered that it was Russia's fault, not theirs, that Germany was not united, that they were in Berlin as a result of international treaty and had no intention of being forced out under pressure.

As early as midsummer 1947 the American press corps in

Berlin asked General Clay whether the United States would stay in the Berlin island deep in the Soviet Zone of Occupation if a West German government were created. He answered, "I just planted some seeds this morning in my Berlin garden."

"Annuals or perennials?" General Clay was asked. General Clay's answer then was a broad smile. But there never was any doubt that the American general, if he had his way, would refuse steadfastly to permit the Soviets to push the United States out of the city.

He later said: "So far as the Americans are concerned, the Russians cannot drive us out of the city short of war."

As the American General saw it, Berlin was a better place than most to see if the Russians would risk war to get what they want. Appeasement of the Russians, in the mind of General Clay and his able adviser Robert Murphy, would have been fatal for many important reasons. To name only a few, such a public display of weakness would probably have encouraged future Russian aggression and strong-arm tactics. A United States surrender to the Soviets would have meant a tremendous loss of prestige in Europe. As a high French official in Berlin once asked Robert Murphy when there were rumors that the West might pull out of the Berlin bastion: "If the powerful United States cannot stand up to the Russians, how can you expect Western Europe to resist communism?"

The top men in Germany believed that a retreat under Soviet pressure would eventually mean an American retreat from Europe. And in effect, the decision of the West to make a stand in Berlin was the turning point in the battle for Western Europe: by that decision in the summer of 1948, the westward flow of communism was abruptly halted on the Elbe River, where East and West Germany meet.

The Berlin blockade did not fully answer the question of

whether the Russians are prepared to risk war to achieve domination of Europe and tip the world balance of power in their favor. But in Berlin the Russians did show that they were prepared to come terribly close to conflict.

Berlin's war of nerves was initiated with Sokolovsky's breakup of the Allied Control Council. At the meeting the scene was set with the usual long-winded condemnations of the Western powers. The climax came as Sokolovsky pulled out a prepared statement asserting that the Western Allies by making plans for a West German state "have killed the Allied Control Council." With these words the Soviet Marshal briskly scooped up his papers and to the astonishment of his colleagues added, "I declare the meeting adjourned." Without even waiting for a response, he rose from the table and stalked out with the entire Russian delegation.

There is no doubt that representatives of the three Western Allies were stunned. General Clay, expressing the thoughts of all, exclaimed, "Well, I don't know what this means." It was unprecedented for a single ally to declare a meeting adjourned. For the procedure of adjournment, as with all matters at the Allied Control Council, had to be unanimous.

In the opinion of Washington, the Russians chose March 20 as the time for their walkout because they hoped to throw a spanner into the plans for a West German state, the creation of which was under discussion at that time. The second major objective was to force the Western Allies from their important outpost behind the iron curtain.

Starvation of two and a quarter million people in West Berlin was the threat the Soviets made to win their objectives. And the Russians had every reason to think, when they shut down all road and rail access from the West to Berlin, that the West would be forced to surrender. For nobody, including General Clay himself, envisaged in those early days that food and coal for millions of citizens could be supplied by air.

The day the blockade began, Clay stated flatly to this correspondent, "It is absolutely impossible to supply the city by air power alone." But only four days later, after learning that the United States would make available big four-motored C-54's from bases all over the world, General Clay changed his mind and said: "I may be the craziest man in history, but I'm going to try the experiment of feeding this city by air power."

It was in the early part of the summer of 1948 that General Clay for the first time began to fear that the Russians might be pushing toward a quick war for the conquest of Europe. To evoke the tension of those days of cold war in Berlin, think back on the events. Soviet fighters in the air corridors were harassing and buzzing airlift planes. There was one fatal buzzing already on the record, the smash-up of a Soviet yak and a British transport, and no one knew whether this had been accidental or calculated. The Russians announced antiaircraft fire directly in the path of Allied planes, thus indirectly threatening to shoot them down. Within the city, riots and armed clashes flared between the citizenry and Soviet tommy gunners. And on the East-West border, armed American GI's took up positions several hundred feet across the boundary line from belligerent-looking Soviet soldiers.

This was the headline news. But in addition, Clay had secret intelligence reports of large underground storage of gasoline in the Soviet Zone, of Russian troop movements, of a sudden increase in Soviet air strength.

In early summer General Clay cabled Washington that war had to be reckoned with an as imminent possibility. The top-secret message which caused an international flurry in high places reported that the Soviets might be preparing to grab all Europe in a swift march westward. It is certain that there was no Western force that could successfully have held off the Russians in Europe at that time, though the Americans would probably have put up a token resistance.

It is of course quite possible that the Russians were deliberately bluffing, stimulating the fear of war in hopes that this would prompt Washington to urge an exit from Berlin. And the truth is, as the record shows, that there were many people in high places in Washington who were inclined to retreat. There is no doubt that the firm stand taken by Clay and Murphy more than anything committed Washington and finally London and Paris to holding out in Berlin.

For the American commanders of their besieged island ardently believed that the place to call the Russian hand was in this city and not further westward. To have retreated would have merely postponed the issue until a time when the Russian position had automatically, through the victory in Berlin, become much stronger.

There were many hard decisions to make and sometimes the American General was in a very lonely spot. For instance, he won his contention that American women and children should not be ordered out of the besieged city despite considerable feeling in Washington at one period that this step ought to be taken. But the top men in Washington, many of whom were in considerable awe of the tough and determined Military Governor, were not prepared to go to the length of ordering him to evacuate dependents, not wanting this responsibility on their shoulders.

A typical telecommunications conference between Berlin and Washington on the dependents question shows how much the character and decision of Clay shaped the course of events in those dramatic times.

The tape would come ticking into Berlin, and the conference would open with the words: "here, washington, bradley, marshall, forrestal, royale, draper," and the names of a host of other key public officials. From Berlin would tick back the lone words: "here, clay."

The Washington side came through with obviously prepared statements beginning (to paraphrase rather loosely): "the conferees have recently been subjected to certain pressures regarding the dependents question, etc. etc."

After only a few sentences in this vein, General Clay somewhat wearily, without even waiting to see the rest, sat down to write out his answer.

It went something like this: "Americans here represent the strongest nation on earth. And I don't want them to crack first in the war of nerves. I don't want to have to tell any American that he has to run from Soviet pressure."

All Clay's top advisers shared his belief that it was up to the Berlin community to display absolute steadfastness in the war of nerves. There could be no panic, no sudden departure of dependents, for this would have greatly weakened the United States' position in the dangerous game of bluff. Clay ruled that anyone who wanted to leave could go. The American community in Berlin, realizing its great responsibility, behaved on the whole with admirable calm, and a minute few departed—mainly for reasons which had nothing to do with the blockade.

In the summer fears of a shooting war disappeared as the Russian bluff was called. Airlift planes went through despite Russian threats of antiaircraft fire, repeated buzzings, and every other harassment short of actual hostile attack which the Soviets could think of.

The Russians were now counting on the winter to do what they had failed to achieve against this incredible airlift— namely, freeze the stubborn Allies out of the contested city. But the West German population preferred to endure the cold and the dark than go over to the Russian camp, and by spring the Western counterblockade was grievously hurting the Russian Zone and the satellite countries. It was clear even to the Russians that the Western policy of firmness had paid off.

The Russians lifted the blockade because it had reached the point of drastically diminishing returns. The threat of force had failed. Instead of driving the West out of the city, it had merely succeeded in unifying them as never before.

There are no absolutes in world politics, and the Western Allies undoubtedly made their share of mistakes which increased Soviet suspicions and contributed to their growing intransigence. But the fact remains that in the truly all-out efforts to achieve East-West harmony, it was the West which had made most of the concessions. These included such items as the assignment of some forty thousand square miles of Eastern German territory to Polish supervision, and their willingness to receive into already overcrowded West Germany nearly ten million German refugees from Eastern territories. And every responsible American statesman certainly feels that despite the outcome it was imperative to make the long and strenuous efforts to get along with the Russians, to allay their suspicions and work toward one world. For only through these efforts could the Western world public have come to realize what they had to contend with.

Looking back, American diplomats experienced in negotiating with the Russians believe that the latter deliberately postponed many issues at Potsdam because they expected much of Europe to fall to them by default. There was considerable reason back in 1945 for the Soviets to entertain such hopes, for in that year American troops were in the heyday of the redeployment "I want to go home" agitation. In America, sentiment for getting out of Europe had a new lease on life. In 1945, too, Communist parties in France, Belgium, and Italy were at peak strength. The performance of Communist leaders in anti-Nazi resistance movements everywhere had won them tremendous power. Nor were the Russians likely to forget, in calculating their chances of winning the struggle for Germany, that in pre-Hitler times this nation had had the best-organized Communist movement in Europe. And finally, since Roosevelt and Churchill had conceded so much to the Russians during the war, there was every reason for the Soviet Union to hope for more appeasement in the postwar period.

General Clay and most of the men who weathered Berlin's cold war believe with him that there is only one alternative to a third world war, and that is for the United States and the Western powers to build economically and maintain themselves militarily at sufficient strength to cause the withdrawal of Soviet communism to its own borders in Europe. If the police state recedes from Eastern Germany, the main point of friction between East and West in Europe will disappear. If the police state recedes from Eastern Europe, there will be a new era of liberation, for it is certain that many millions behind the iron curtain have had their fill of tyranny and are eager to return to the freedoms of Western civilization.

A prosperous and free Western Europe and Western Germany will in the coming years exercise a magnetic influence on the iron-curtain area. Economic turmoil in America and Europe will soften up the Western World for new probings by Soviet communism. That essentially is why every American should look at such things as the Marshall Plan in terms of the Western side keeping the edge in the East-West battle and not merely in terms of charity to foreigners. The United States cannot afford to let Western Europe fall to Russia in the era of the cold war any more than we could allow England to fall to the Nazis in the Second World War. In the end Soviet capture of Europe would mean war anyway—a war in which Russia would have just that much more in the way of resources at its command.

It will take strong leadership and great courage to persuade the American people to pour out over a long period large sums for armies and for subsidies to strange lands. And the Russians will do their best to undermine American efforts. Conciliatory talk and a few conciliatory gestures will certainly be used from time to time in hopes of inaugurating a new era of appeasement.

Max Reimann, West German Communist leader, once remarked to me with what appeared to be amazing candor: "If the Russians put on a real peace offensive, will it be possible for a democracy such as the United States to stay armed and to keep on voting huge subsidies for Europe? And if you do not, how can you possibly avoid a depression? And once there is a depression, half our battle is already won!"

No matter how many Soviet "peace offensives" and conciliatory phrases are sprung upon the world in the future, there is one unmistakable lesson that the American people must draw from the Berlin blockade. When the Soviets thought they had the West in a tight corner, they did not hesitate to use blunt and brutal force, including the threat of hunger for millions, to achieve their political objectives.

The first round of the battle for Germany has been won temporarily by the West, but the struggle for Germany and for the world goes on. The outcome will continue indecisive so long as Germany remains partitioned between the Soviet police state and Western democracy. And so long as this division lasts, the specter of war will haunt the world.

It is sad and disillusioning that the magnificent vision of one world disappeared so quickly after the victory of East and West over the common foe. But whatever the mutual guilt involved, the facts are that the Soviets are racing as never before toward air, ground, and scientific strength in arms. This may reflect only a genuine Soviet fear of Western attack and may not be related to any ultimate aggressive aim. But nobody yet knows to what use the dictators of Russia may put the growing might of their country. And until a real time-tested modus vivendi evolves between the Soviet and non-Soviet worlds, Western civilization cannot afford to relax lest the price be its own destruction.

The death of the four-power government of Germany and the partition of the country were but one phase in the great ideological contest between Russia and the West. But as long ago as April 1945, Lucius D. Clay foreshadowed the impact on history of this great experiment when at his first press conference in Europe he stated: *"If the four Allies cannot work together in Germany to rule and punish the common foe, what hope is there for the United Nations?"*

Chapter XVIII

Birth of a State

By KATHLEEN MCLAUGHLIN

FOR three months after quadripartite rule in Germany collapsed, with the exodus of the Russians, four-power control in Berlin itself limped along precariously. Then the final link snapped.

On June 16, 1948, white-haired, pink-cheeked Major General Alexander Kotikov, commandant in the Soviet sector, emulated his superior, Marshal Sokolovsky, and stalked angrily out of Kommandatura headquarters in the United States area. This particular period of attrition had ended. The Western powers stood free.

It took three more months to bring the dream of a West German state to the brink of realization. Ninety days of diminishing tension on the part of the population, and of swelling pride in the skill and stamina of American and British airlift pilots on the part of their contemporaries who witnessed their feat in writing history across the skies above Frankfurt and Berlin.

The first planes of "Operation Vittles" began their clocklike shuttle service on June 26. Western prestige and German determination mounted with every flight. As August faded into September, the RAF and the USAF had the Russians on the run, although we could not perceive it then. By January, they had them licked.

All that we could recognize in those declining weeks of summer was that the Soviets had fumbled. Their blockade had boomeranged and the Germans were overwhelmingly supporting the Western powers, convinced at last that no intention existed of abandoning them to the Eastern threat.

The pace of economic recovery after introduction of the new currency had brought a noticeable stiffening of political spines. Every German longed desperately for reunion with the Eastern Zone, on which the other three had always relied for so large a proportion of their industrial and agricultural products. But self-preservation even at the expense of the isolated East was paramount. Hunger was a powerful stimulus. Temporarily at least, all except extreme Nazis and nationalists gave up hope for a united country. They wanted a state—even a fragment of a state—under German administration, however limited.

No sooner had the airlift hit its stride than the pessimists began to sing lower about the impossibility of finding Germans willing to accept the responsibility of functioning as delegates in the Parliamentary Council which was due to convene at Bonn, on the Rhine, to write a constitution for Western Germany.

Nominees were listed by the Western provincial parliaments. They accepted to a man. They convened as scheduled, on September 1.

With the events of the preceding three years fresh in memory, and full realization of the extent of German terror of Soviet retaliation, this was to some of us on permanent assignment among these people a signal victory.

In the northeast (Bogenhausen) section of Munich the American Press Club had made itself reasonably comfortable in an imposing residence at the corner of Wasserburgerstrasse and Boehmerwald Platz, once the official home of *Gauleiter*

Geisler. Just behind it was the Press Center, erstwhile town mansion of Max Amann, intimate of "Der Führer," who parlayed a modest bankroll into a formidable fortune by picking up and publishing a manuscript of his old crony under the title *Mein Kampf*.

(This neighborhood has a dubious distinction. A stone's throw from the Press Club entrance stood the outwardly unpretentious, inwardly bizarre cottage in which Hitler installed Eva Braun. An American major billeted there after Patton's army took Munich finally had to forbid his housekeeper to admit the droves of sight-seers eager to peer through the secret wall panels that lead to a de luxe underground air-raid shelter, and the Bavarian stove on which each separate tile depicts Eva in the guise of an angel, as Venus, and similar grotesqueries. Hitler himself, in the days of his modest beginnings, had an apartment five minutes' walk distant, on Prinzregenten Platz, and Martin Bormann owned a house at the opposite end of the block.)

At lunchtime on March 20, 1948, I crossed the garden and came into the club lounge by the terrace door. The usual midday gin rummy game was nowhere in evidence. An intent group hovered over the radio cabinet, apparently trying its collective best to crawl inside.

Someone was twirling the dials. In reflex against the raucous growls of the loudspeaker, I clapped both hands to my ears.

Diminutive Sergeant George Mance, announcer in Munich for the American Forces Network, with each individual curl awry on his forehead as always when he is agitated, detached himself from the covey and bawled at me above the din. I took down my hands and cocked an eyebrow in his direction.

"——bulletin from Berlin?" he was asking.

I shook my head.

"Been at OMGB (Office of Military Government, Bavaria) all morning," I reported. "What is it?"

"Mean to say nobody told you the Russians have pulled out of the Allied Control Authority?"

"No!" I gasped, and dived for the radio along with the rest.

Already the needle had found its channel, and the mellow voice of Captain Bruce Wendell, station director, was pouring over the airwaves a flood of supplementary detail. Marshal Vasili D. Sokolovsky, Soviet Military Governor, had flung away from the council table after a brief and bitter interchange, with his aides, interpreters, and secretaries at his heels. He—and they—he had caustically announced, would not be back.

"So this is it," was the consensus at the Press Club.

Across the luncheon tables later, speculation was uninhibited. The crisis had been a long time in the building. Would the next move from the East be a hostile one? No one had the answer. No one except that sinister group in the Moscow Politburo, whom we now realized dictated each move of its subordinates in Germany. One point on which there was complete unanimity was the impossibility of guessing the mental processes of our Eastern "Allies."

Beneath all the banter about the reserve stock of gasoline one would need for a quick getaway, and the distance to the Swiss frontier, flowed a current of excitement and suspense, rather than any real premonition. Most of us who had been based for some time in the country leaped to dissent when a correspondent recently arrived in Germany tossed off the comment, "Well, there goes your ball game. This fries the new German government."

"You're wrong," we told him. "That's what's the matter with the Russians now. They never wanted to come in on it, under the terms set—especially the opening of their zone. Their act today is only a dodge. Unless they actually take the offensive, the Western powers will go ahead with the new state."

And so it happened.

Through wearisome months of dogged and persistent dickering, the Western powers had postponed introduction of a new currency to replace the hopelessly inflated reichsmark, while trying to win Soviet co-operation for its introduction in the East as well as in the Western zones. Withdrawal of the Soviet Military Governor from the four-power administration spelled doom for that project, and symbolized dramatically the splitting of Germany into separate orbits. The end result would have been identical if Sokolovsky had ripped the map of Germany from top to bottom and left it on the table before his vacant chair.

Further delay in the financial muddle meant disaster. It was apparent to all sides, including the German, that the showdown was imminent. When Kotikov made his exit from the Kommandatura in Berlin, the city's population went jittery. A quiet exodus began. Communist newspapers beat the drum relentlessly about impending evacuation of all Occupation troops except Stalin's. In the now silent beer halls and along the length of those pocked and battered streets, the first flutterings of panic stirred.

In the main Berliners credited the Soviet-inspired reports, rather than the firm denials by Generals Clay, Robertson, and Koenig, that evacuation had already begun. Relatively few took reassurance from the trio of banners still fluttering from the four flagstaffs fronting the ACA building, the Stars and Stripes, the Union Jack, and the tricolor of France.

On June 22 came the blockade.

Now the pattern emerged clearly. Soviet aims were, above all, to prevent formation of that separate Western state; and second, to halt rehabilitation in the Western zones by means of the new currency, even at the risk of war.

They reckoned without the airlift. And without the resourcefulness of General Clay, who had both vision and the resolution to implement it.

The Russians lost. Under the powerful impact of the currency reform sponsored by the Western Allies, Western Germany moved overnight into its new era of returning prosperity and ultimate independence.

Placid and as lovely as the river that ripples past, Bonn is a typical university town. On the *Ufer* (embankment) that is the favorite Sunday afternoon promenade for the entire population, the cynosure for Rhine voyagers is not the period-piece architecture of once opulent mansions still dominating the heights on the left bank. Instead, the center of attention is the chunky, ultramodern block of dazzling white masonry that comprises the Pedagogical Academy, which sheltered sessions of the Parliamentary Council through eight months of controversy and compromise.

The gala opening of the assembly, however, was held elsewhere. Its setting was the Museum Koenig on Poppelsdorfer Allee, main thoroughfare connecting Bonn with Cologne on the northwest, and with Coblenz and Mainz to the southeast.

In this stately, pillared, ivory structure beneath towering chestnuts and elms that line the avenue, notables from half a dozen countries thronged balcony and auditorium as the ceremonies got under way that September afternoon.

None of the three Western military governors honored the occasion. Ambassador Robert Murphy for the United States, Sir Christopher Steele for Great Britain, and Ambassador Jacques Tarbe de St. Hardouin for France, each inconspicuous in business suits, represented their chiefs with a minimum of fanfare. Only Josef Cardinal Frings from the See of Cologne, in his swaying crimson robes of office and his broad-brimmed, tasseled hat, surrounded by bishops and monsignori, contributed a touch of pageantry to an otherwise soberly formal scene.

Scarcely had the orchestra conductor lowered his baton, on the flower-banked rostrum, when Max Reimann, the senior of two Communist deputies from North Rhine–Westphalia, shattered the surface mood of solemnity with the first of the long series of discordant episodes which he and his colleague, Heinz Renner, were to launch, obviously under orders from their Soviet overlords.

Briefly, Minister President Karl Arnold of their own province—in which Bonn is located—had voiced regret that due to Russian obstructionism no spokesmen were present from the Eastern Zone. He admonished the sixty-three deputies to consider their task as equivalent to the writing of the Magna Charta. This was not, he emphasized, an Allied but a German gathering. Although it represented only two-thirds of Germany, the "basic law" to be produced in Bonn would hold significance for all Germans, pending the signing of a peace treaty.

Christian Stock, minister president of Hesse, characterized Berlin as the center of the struggle for freedom, and the living proof that Germany was resolved not to bow again before a dictator.

It was then that Reimann, seated only a few feet away from Ambassador Murphy, lunged to the attack. Shouting, gesticulating, ignoring the refusal of the chair to recognize him, Reimann exhorted his fellow delegates to approve a resolution he submitted, asking that the Parliamentary Council be disbanded on the ground that it had been illegally convened. It would, he roared, "torpedo the efforts of the Big Four to reach an agreement at Moscow."

Amid derisive hoots from his colleagues, Reimann invoked the pacts of Yalta and Potsdam. He drew a blank.

"We waited three years for the Russians to live up to those agreements," bellowed his irritated confreres.

Finally Reimann took his seat, still tossing his sleek gray head and snapping retorts to his nearest neighbors. His proposal died without a vote. It was out of order, he was informed.

Doctor Konrad Adenauer, the aging, slender leader of the Christian Democrats in the British Zone, who had been unanimously elected president of the Council, had the last word as he took the platform to dismiss the gathering.

"The German State," he said, directly to Reimann, "must be formed some time."

Twelve days later, at seven-fifteen in the evening, Adenauer called the first working session to order in the moderately spacious hall of the Pedagogical Academy. Its entire south wall is one vast picture window, through which delegates could glimpse the Rhine merely by glancing over their right shoulders. Or could have, except for the barrier of more than a hundred German and Allied correspondents aligned at blond wood worktables which stretched from front to back of the chamber.

At the tap of the presidential gavel Reimann was out of his seat in the second row and had claimed the microphone just below the dais. Pencil slim, tanned, impeccably neat, his black eyes flashing a fanatic's zeal, he was once more dedicated to disruption. None could claim now, he gloated, that he was out of order. Sonorously he intoned again his resolution urging disbandment, in favor of merging with the recently organized "People's Council" in the East Zone.

With the ghost of a smile tugging at his straight lips, Adenauer put the question. The resolution was defeated by a vote of sixty-one to two. As autumn waned and spring came around, it was defeated over and over, always by the same vote.

The initial move in drafting what the Germans call the "basic law"—mainly to emphasize that they hope one day to write a constitution for the entire nation—was the appointment of committees to handle details of the various sections of the document. Here developed the earliest demonstrations of the internal political struggle that was to dominate all succeeding phases down to the final midnight session of May 16, 1949.

Control over the government was bitterly contested by the two major postwar elements, the Christian Democratic Union on the one hand, and the Social Democrats, under dictatorship of the extraordinary Doctor Kurt Schumacher of Hanover, on the other. While Americans, British, and French watched from the sidelines, the battle grew in fury until the possibility became apparent that, in view of the waxing enmities, there might be no coalition administration.

Tactics began with maneuvering for chairmanship of strategic committees. It continued from there. The Social Democratic objective was a strongly centralized government capable of negotiating the socialization of industries. Conversely the CDU was committed to achievement of a loose confederation of *Laender* with greatly restricted powers for the central unit. Such a structure would leave the *Laender* independent in handling their financial and legal affairs.

A powerful factor in the CDU attitude was the traditional separatism of the Bavarians, stimulated during this era to near-frenzy by the influx there of refugees and "Prussians" (a catch-all Bavarian term for non-Bavarians). Not only is Bavaria the largest single province in the American Zone; it is also the most Catholic. In pre-Hitler days a sizable proportion of its membership belonged to the Centrist (Catholic) faction.

Thus the element of religious prejudices and preferences that marked political life in Germany prior to the Nazi era reappeared in Bonn and has figured importantly in events there up to the present time. Broadly speaking, the CDU, which in Bavaria is known as the Christian Social Union, is pro-clergy, and the Social Democrats are anti-clergy in sentiment.

Since the end of the war public opinion in Germany has reflected the tendency to support some form of socialism, including socialization of industry, although visits to the United States by delegations of labor leaders during 1949 revealed that doubts had arisen about the efficacy of this doctrine as a panacea for industrial troubles.

In any case Great Britain tacitly supported the Social Democratic party at Bonn, as most nearly approximating its own contemporary ruling element. However, America and France advocated a course that paralleled the preferences of the stronger Christian Democratic group. French policy was rooted in antipathy to anything that smacked of centralization and consequent future strength for Germany. With the Americans, the doctrine of states' rights was coupled with distrust of any course that might infringe upon private enterprise.

The French were lax in observance at Bonn, but both Britian and the United States, although keeping to the perimeter, maintained a close scrutiny of progress there. Anthony Pabsch, genial and able State Department watchdog, was by far the most diligent of these envoys, and until the end remained persona grata with the Germans.

Yet months of closed committee meetings, with an occasional plenary session in which preliminary drafts were reviewed and rejected, approved, or returned for further work, produced little of significance. The preamble was finished. It guaranteed equality for all, with freedom of worship, of press, of assembly, and of opportunity. It abolished such handicaps of race and creed as disgraced Germany through the so-called

Nuremberg Laws. Equality for women was conceded early and written into the text. So was a more vigorously debated passage protecting the social status and educational privileges of illegitimate children.

By February of 1949 the end was in sight, although the most controversial issues had been postponed and were still to be resolved. Problems of the jurisdiction to be exercised by the federal government, particularly in the fields of finance and of lawmaking, brought the two opposing parties to the crux of their quarrel.

A committee of five, later expanded to seven, wrestled long and acridly over the disputed points. Plenary sessions grew more frequent. Tempers rose. Insults were exchanged. Reimann and Renner ranted exhaustingly at both main antagonists. Deals were put through with the minority parties. The scramble for advantage verged on a free-for-all.

Two at least of the pivot personalities kept their composure: Adenauer "with his flat Mongolian face" (as British correspondent Alan Moorhead described him), and Carlo Schmid, chairman of the Social Democratic faction in Bonn.

Both were indefatigable in their efforts to maintain a united German front in conferences with Allied authorities, against the increasingly assertive attitude of deputies, as improving living standards stimulated their egos and set their nationalist instincts to itching for expression.

The day arrived when by dint of one concession here and another there the committee of seven had sweated out a compromise agreeable to both. It was laid before the military governors at Frankfurt—and promptly vetoed as unsatisfactory to Washington.

The Germans reeled from the shock. In that moment, the Western state all but "died a-borning."

From the outset at Bonn, the voluble, pedantic Doctor

Carlo Schmid stood out as a potential leader of the new government. As chairman of his delegation he merited attention by virtue of his role, but he retained it by sheer ability and personality.

Adenauer inevitably had to be reckoned with as an elder statesman who was also a shrewd political tactician. He had been postwar Lord Mayor of Cologne, resuming by American appointment the office he had held for seventeen years and in which he had made a spectacularly good record. When the Americans withdrew from Cologne after the four-power boundaries had been established, *Oberbürgermeister* Adenauer suddenly found himself banished from the city by an apparently temperamental British Military Government officer, on charges that he had failed to display sufficient initiative in the problem of rehousing the population. He retired again to the house at Honnef which he had built like an aerie, high on the cliffs above the Rhine, as a refuge from Hitler. It proved to be a fateful move, for he turned all his energies into formation of the Christian Democratic Union.

In the ranks of his party his influence extended well beyond the boundaries of his own region, the British Zone. A former *Reichstag* member, scornful of the Nazis and everything they represented, Adenauer is tagged, especially in trade-union quarters, as a "front man" for the industrial interests. But throughout his masterly handling of the sessions at Bonn, he was conceded to be the natural choice for president of the new state, an honorary rather than active role.

Berlin, which had hoped for affiliation with the new Western administration as a twelfth *Land,* was denied that recognition. Although disgruntled, the Western sectors of the city had agreed to send as voteless observers two other possible contenders for eventual honors. They were Jakob Kaiser, CDU leader in the former German capital, and Professor Doctor Ernst Reuter, the former Communist who had won the post of *Oberbürgermeister* of Berlin on the Social Democratic ticket, only to be prevented from assuming office by the veto of his onetime Soviet comrades.

Reuter was then popularly acclaimed as postwar Germany's ablest political figure. After the splitting of Berlin and his installation as *Oberbürgermeister* of the Western sectors, he came less frequently to Bonn. But his prestige still grew. Kaiser's standing, on the contrary, declined despite his assiduous attendance at Bonn. When cabinet appointments were passed out after the August 1949 elections had settled the question of Adenauer's role and he had proudly taken over as chancellor, Kaiser's name was missing. He drew the post of Minister for All-German Questions, created almost as an afterthought, with an assignment to keep contact with the population in the Soviet zone.

Schmid was eternally on deck, affable, intelligent, obviously ambitious. His post was at the front of the auditorium. When the Communist Renner impudently leaned from the podium during his rasping tirades against Schmid, who sat directly in front of that station, the Professor Doctor roared with laughter as often as he simulated deafness. Usually a barbed riposte from Schmid would touch off a counterwave of laughter among the bored delegates.

Born at Perpignan in 1896 of a German father and French mother, Schmid uses both languages with equal facility, but is German to the core. His massive head surmounts a huge torso. His walk is almost a waddle. His complexion is olive, his eyes dark brown under heavy brows, and a cigarette always dribbles, gangster fashion, from the corner of his mouth. He is a brilliant extemporaneous orator, occasionally lapsing into Latin, a trait which reflects his legal background.

In private life, he is professor of international law at the University of Tübingen, near Stuttgart.

During the German occupation of France, Schmid was assigned by his Army superiors as military governor in the Pas de Calais area. Against all American concepts of such German administrators, he left behind so excellent a record of moderation and efficiency that when the tables were turned and France occupied Germany, French officials notified their Allies that they were nominating Schmid as worthy of public office.

The honeymoon did not endure. Schmid was elected and approved as minister president of the French Zone province of Württemberg-Hohenzollern but resigned when French demands for reparations reached a point which he asserted would automatically bankrupt his administration. He returned to the university, emerging again into public life as a deputy at Bonn.

In spite of his meteoric rise, Schmid is handicapped by junior membership in the SPD (*Sozialistische Partei Deutschlands*), which he joined only after its reorganization in 1946. Never one to underestimate his own record, he is careful to defer to older heads of the organization, at least until his personal destiny is more apparent.

Schumacher is a continuous pyrotechnic display in the political scene in postwar Germany. Hitler himself was hardly more of an autocrat, although Schumacher's ruthlessness has been notably free of the viciousness that was Adolf's hallmark and ultimate ruin. As extreme a nationalist as any individual in his native land, Schumacher's honest belligerence was paradoxically almost a relief to the Western Allies, who had quickly become surfeited with German subservience.

In the First World War, Schumacher lost his right arm. Prior to and during the Second World War he spent eleven years in concentration camps as a rabid anti-Hitlerite, sustaining such abuse that on his liberation in April 1945 he had lost most of his teeth and about half of his vision, was afflicted with stomach ulcers, and had contracted tuberculosis. Yet he plunged into the political fray with such vigor of spirit that his appeal to the German mass mind—ever responsive to *der starke Hand* (a strong hand)—remained unchallenged until an infection in his left foot, which began in June of 1948, brought him to bed for thirteen months. After prolonged agony he consented to its amputation only when gangrene made death the alternative.

He was still recuperating when the mounting tension at Bonn threatened the entire project.

The military governors' veto was on.

Essentially this veto meant that the CDU had gone too far in capitulation to the SPD, had permitted too great an encroachment against the powers of the provincial governments and had ceded too much authority to the central unit. Inferentially the SPD had either to back down or accept the onus of having defeated creation of a government of Germans by Germans.

At this juncture Schumacher staged his coup. SPD zonal and regional officials were summoned to the presence at party headquarters in Hanover. An ovation lasting ten minutes greeted his entrance into the session in a wheel chair.

Late that afternoon press and radio representatives swarmed into the same hall to hear whether or not his foes inside and outside the party had succeeded in writing him off as a political power. The encounter was a shock. Heavier by many pounds than we had ever seen him, a rosy flush replacing his usual pallor, more truculent and talkative than before, he seemed completely master of the situation. The opposition, it appeared, had collapsed. He would rule his universe as rigidly as ever, pulling strings in Hanover while his underlings danced. But Schumacher talked too long.

Carlo Schmid, discreetly silent, sat with other functionaries at the green baize table that screened Schumacher's rolling chair and his maimed leg. Gradually we noted that the chieftain who rarely relinquished the limelight was prodding Schmid to bolster his blustering defiance of the Allies on the one hand and the CDU on the other. Schmid was responding dutifully rather than enthusiastically. Was Schumacher placating Schmid, either as a reluctant convert during the preceding session, or because he rated him indispensable at Bonn? In any case Carlo had moved up several rungs on the SPD ladder.

Later events disclosed that Schumacher's performance was largely bravado. The vote, he had asserted, was in. The SPD would not retreat one inch from the compromise arranged with the CDU. If the Western state foundered, the blame could be credited to Allied interference. The Germans had done their part. The Social Democrats would return to the conference chamber only on condition that Allied "meddlers" withdraw and that other pompous rules laid down by the SPD be observed.

Over the next few days the situation continued o be ticklish. Gloom pervaded the atmosphere. The CDU forebore to exult over the veto which implicitly favored its position.

General Clay broke the deadlock. To the patent relief of Schumacher and company, the General released a letter prepared earlier for just this type of contingency, advising Doctor Adenauer that only minor readjustments would be required to bring the final draft of the basic law into conformity with the interpretation Allied authorities held necessary.

Thereafter it was merely a matter of beating the clock, to complete the document on the fourth anniversary of Germany's capitulation, as Adenauer fervently hoped to do to provide a historic antidote for that bitter pill.

The final form of the provisional constitution sufficiently relaxed pressure on the SPD position to permit the party to escape its dilemma with dignity. It somewhat expanded the financial powers of the central government, and contracted a bit the legislative powers conferred on it, in favor of the *Laender.*

The job was finished, and sanctioned by the military governors on behalf of their respective countries.

In a fever of enthusiasm delegates raced back from Frankfurt to Bonn. One midnight session followed another during that first week of May. In plenary meetings the "basic law" was confirmed while Reimann's now habitual resolution was inundated for the last time—sixty-one to two. Frankfurt lost out to Bonn as the future capital of the new government, to the tune of shouts of rage, especially from the Social Democrats who, the story ran, had whispered that Bonn was "too close under the shadow of the [Cologne] Cathedral."

Western German newspapers demonstrated their growing initiative by inserting in their regular editions supplements which carried the entire text of the new constitution, almost as the lights were being extinguished after the last, hectic session.

Ratification by the *Laender* came with a rush. Special sessions were called and the *Landtage* (state parliaments) endorsed it—with one exception. Bavarian politicians, bedeviled by the specter of a new, vociferously separatist Bavarian party whose strength at the polls had never been tested because it had been chartered subsequent to the last previous elections, played it safe in a higgledy-piggledy procedure.

First Bavarian legislators rejected the document—which insured commendation by one portion of the electorate. Then they voted to go along with observance of each separate article, on condition of ratification by a majority of the *Laender.* That took care of the remaining voters.

Within three days the majority was firm. All ten other *Landtage* accepted the document.

The legal successor to the Third Reich, the Federal Republic of Western Germany, was a reality.

Chapter XIX

Beauty and the Beast—France Takes a Slow New Look at Germany

By JAMES O'DONNELL

THE voice of the German officer sounds startling in the soft evening air of Paris. A silver *Wehrmacht* eagle shines brightly from his green-gray uniform, his polished jack boots make the too-familiar click. Stranger still the ringing applause which greets his curtain speech: "Someday our two countries will come together for the good of Europe. I had dreamed that out of this evil, this war, would come the marriage of France and Germany. For who has not heard in his youth of beauty and the beast, *la Belle et la Bête?* . . ." Exit *Oberleutnant* von Ebronnac to die somewhere on the Eastern Front.

Last season Paris audiences applauded a new play, *Le Silence de la Mer,* based on the Résistance novelette by Paul Vercors which became a clandestine best seller during the Occupation. The hero is the proverbial good German, trying eloquently but vainly to drown out the voice of Goebbels with the words of Goethe. The Résistance message was a simple and effective one: Someday indeed France and Germany will come together for the good of Europe, but it will have to be an act of marriage and not rape.

Today the old dream of the union of Gaul and Teuton is no longer the special vision of poets and philosophers, of stage Germans and Résistance prophets. It is the last best hope of Western Europe, the blueprint of a gigantic political tract known as the Marshall Plan.

Was the Paris audience merely applauding good theater, or was there something in the political allegory itself that captured Gallic imagination? If statesmen and diplomats could divine the answer to that one, the road toward the unity of Western Europe might not be so rocky. A German officer on a French stage preaching an end of the ancient hatred—in the years after 1918 the actor would have been hanged and the theatre stormed in a *grande bagarre*.

Nor is this the only anomaly indicating that time-honored textbook approaches to the Franco-German problem, exchanges of stigmas and dogmas and the hammering away at old clichés, belong more to history than to present-day realities. As foreign minister of France we find M. Robert Schuman, who fought in the First World War at Verdun—as a captain in the German Army. Across the Rhine one of the most prominent leaders to emerge in the new West German Republic has been Carlo Schmid, a French-born German who actively aided French Résistance in World War II. Berlin's most colorful and dominant political personality, *Oberbuergermeister* Ernst Reuter, proudly wears a Basque beret at political rallies. These things are small, but they are significant.

This reporter has spent the past five years in Germany and in France, and often in traveling between these two countries. It is impossible in one chapter—or in one book—to give a full, objective account of as hefty and controversial a subject as relations between France and Germany. Let me try rather to give a frankly personal approach to the problem as I have seen it and heard it debated. Sometimes much depends on where you sit, and I have been doing my sitting in Paris and Berlin.

I can remember one such lively discussion last summer when a French friend of mine, a writer, remarked that if we must have clichés on this subject, we ought at least to have some new ones.

Much of the animosity that is often generated on this explosive topic, even among men of good will, comes from the tendency to approach the same subject from different premises. To avoid that, let me state right here the five major premises of my own approach. I am not going to defend them or elaborate upon them. I do feel that most readers will accept them, perhaps not as self-evident truths, but at least as a reasonable frame of reference. Here they are.

1. The Franco-German equation is the psychological key to all prospects of creating a healthy Western Europe. The problem confronting Western European statesmen is not to produce harmony between Denmark and Italy, Belgium and Holland, or Ireland and Switzerland. It already exists. But France and Germany must bury the hatchet or the concept of Western Europe will remain a geographical expression, and an indefensible one at that.

2. The present relationship between these two countries is not the classic victor-vanquished one. This time both France and Germany emerged from the war defeated, France in 1940 and Germany in 1945. This psychology of defeat and occupation is deeply instilled in the present national consciousness of both once-proud nations.

3. Neither country is today a major power in the sense of 1914 or even 1939, and most Frenchmen and Germans are aware that they are pawns between Russia and the United States, *Les deux Super-Grands*.

4. The French approach to Germany today is motivated

less by hatred than by fear—a fear which paradoxically helps to create the very danger it would avoid.

5. And as a natural corollary, there is a very real German danger, although it is not the one that many Frenchmen continually see in their nightmares of memory.

When the average intelligent Frenchman takes a look across the Rhine today, what does he see? More important, what does he think he sees? To anybody who has been exposed to the vagaries of French journalism in handling news in general and news from Germany in particular, it is a wonder that the average Frenchman sees anything. There are not four journals in metropolitan Paris that keep a permanent and reliable correspondent in the Reich. This does not mean that the Paris press is not chock-full of *exposés, enquêtes,* and *exclusivités* so exclusive that they never appear anywhere else. There was more "coverage" of the Ilse Koch travesty than there was of the proclamation of the Bonn Republic, more news on fraternization than there was on the level-of-industry agreement, and a new Black *Reichswehr* is discovered at least once a fortnight by some over-enterprising French journalist or editor.

Despite this, from the few journals that do make an attempt to print and analyze news and policy—*Le Monde, Franc-Tireur, Figaro,* and sometimes *Combat*—the average intelligent Frenchman is able to piece together a reasonably coherent picture of what is actually happening.

He has seen how the currents of world politics have swirled apart the grand alliance of the victors and brought about the unseemly race for the favor of the vanquished, and of course he is not happy about this. But he has a sense of history and of irony and an almost fatalistic acceptance of the fact that while it is difficult to live with the Germans, it is impossible to live without them. And he knows that this is somehow connected with economics, with his own bread and butter. It is Ruhr coal that makes Paris *la ville lumière*.

He sees how his own government, a good deal more reluctantly than the Anglo-Americans, has nevertheless taken sides in the grand showdown between East and West. And here—depending of course on his own private politics—he tends to support his government's policy, but with his fingers crossed.

In fact that government seems often to act as if it had its own fingers crossed. Put bluntly, the French Government and the French people are co-operating with the seeming inevitable, but always with the *arrière-pensée* that it may turn out to be not so inevitable after all, and that maybe the East-West conflict will mellow down and the spirit of the wartime alliance will return to resolve the German problem. In this almost but not quite forlorn hope lies the explanation for the diplomatic double talk which often accompanies France's co-operation with the Anglo-Americans in carrying out a common policy in Germany. "Let us do what we have to do, but let us make haste slowly. In fact, let us drag our feet now and then."

This psychology of hesitation accounts for the very mixed reception that the Marshall Plan has received in France. Support that part of ERP which means five billion dollars for France? *Bien sûr.* But welcome the granting of an equal amount to underwrite the revival of Germany, and specifically the Ruhr? And treat the Germans as equal partners in the new Western Europe? *Ah, non!* French memories of the humiliating defeat of 1940 and the Nazi occupation are still more vivid than their fear of a possible Red Army entry into Paris.

Most of the diplomacy of last year, from the London Agreement of April 1948 to the Washington Accord of April 1949, was given over to a silent clash between the Anglo-Americans and the French within the supposedly grand alliance of the cold war against the Soviet Union. The French called this dispute *la guerre tiède*, the lukewarm war they waged to slow down and weaken formation of the West German Republic. Finally American policy makers, a bit tired of continuing to pay reverse lend-lease to the memory of Lafayette, asked the French to support the full implications of the Marshall Plan or get off the gravy bandwagon. The French wisely chose to stop sticking too many spokes in the wheel.

Much credit for the successful reversal of France's negative policy vis-à-vis the Reich should go to Foreign Minister Schuman, probably the best man France has had in that spot since Aristide Briand. And when one considers the delicate, precarious political equilibrium in which Schuman and his Third Force colleagues have had to create and apply French foreign policy, particularly toward Germany, it is a miracle they have managed as well as they have.

For foreign policy is often, and usually regrettably, merely an extension of domestic politics. This is on phase of the French difficulty that is sometimes less appreciated than it might be among American and British statesmen. I am not referring here to the chronic weakness of the French Constitution, which has already (at this writing) collapsed fourteen cabinets since the Liberation, but rather to the extraneous but nonetheless virulent manner in which the "German question" has become a cloak for skulduggery on the domestic political front.

The present government of France calls itself a Third Force regime. The Third Force is a working coalition of moderate centrists, able to govern only because they have driven a wedge between the two largest political groups in France—the Communists on the extreme left, and General de Gaulle's Rally of the French People on the far right. These two radical wings constitute an estimated 55 per cent of the French electorate (Communists 25 per cent, Gaullists 30 per cent). Fortunately for France and the Western World, a working alliance between these two authoritarian movements on the French domestic front is usually impossible. But extremists often find common ground in the murky realm of demagogy. Whenever foreign policy is up for debate in the National Assembly, Gaullists and Communists pursue identical tactics: embarrass the present government at all costs, and wave the bloody shirt on the German issue.

The Communist strategy is clear. From their own premises the Soviet Union is the friend of France, the Anglo-Americans the avowed enemy. Thus any attempt to reconstruct Germany within a Western Union is doubly anathema—it allies the traditional enemy of France with the new enemy in a vast Marshall Plan conspiracy. And Communist eloquence along these lines is enhanced by the fact that many French Communists (after June 21, 1941) did play a heroic role in the Résistance. They have consciously and skillfully revived the Résistance slogans and Résistance memories. The hated Boche and the now equally hated American capitalist are planning to rape La Belle France.

More dangerous, because it is even more in the patriotic French tradition, is the mystagogy being promulgated by De Gaulle. Le grand Charlie, like the Communists, is still the conscious *résistant,* waging guerrilla warfare against the present Fourth Republic. He does not oppose the Marshall Plan as such. He does not oppose the concept of Western Union on his own terms. But he rejects any conception of the world that does not pivot around France.

How should the Western powers gird themselves against the world-wide Soviet threat? De Gaulle has given his pontifical answer: "France will assume military responsibility for Europe, the British for the Middle East, the United States for the Far East." This is not a policy, it is a fantastic dream.

When asked at a press conference what he would do if this did not fit in with the Marshall Plan, the tall general with the elongated ego had a superpatriotic answer for that one, too: "France has gotten along without a Marshall Plan for centuries!"

De Gaulle's demand that Germany be atomized into a group of petty states and principalities fits into this same pattern of nonrealism and national megalomania. (The General once casually suggested that the best place for the future German capital would be Paris.) French statesmen know that what de Gaulle is advocating has little to do with the realities of the twentieth century, and they are beginning to understand what Winston Churchill meant when he cracked that of all the crosses he had to bear during the war, the heaviest was the Cross of Lorraine. Still, the General cannot be lightly shrugged off.

These two bloc pressures certainly have a continuing braking effect on practically anything French policy makers try to do in Germany. However, the strength of these two mass parties has not been created because of the views they have on Germany but rather the contrary. Communist pulling power at the polls is based on almost purely domestic issues: the class consciousness of the hard-pressed and miserably paid French workers who will continue to vote Communist until conditions in France get a lot better than they are. The vaguer political and economic emotions of discontent behind De Gaulle are more difficult to define and probably more ephemeral. But it is reasonable to assume that many of the *compagnons* who follow De Gaulle do not necessarily share his views on Germany.

There is therefore reason to assume a broader basis of popular support to the present Schuman policy of reconciliation and incorporation of Germany into Western Europe than was at first suspected. And as the Third Force continues to strengthen itself on the domestic front, this support should increase. Already we have evidence of this. When in the spring of 1948 Foreign Minister Bidault returned to Paris after signing the London Agreement (in many ways a French diplomatic victory), he was howled down and voted out of office for having relinquished the French claim to separation of the Ruhr from the Reich. Exactly one year later his successor, Schuman, returned to Paris from Washington after having signed the far more portentous agreement to create a West German Republic. But he wisely brought with him a tangible *quid pro quo,* the Atlantic Pact. This time there was no stormy session in the National Assembly; in fact the deputies went off on their Easter holidays.

"Who does not comprehend the emotional reaction of an invaded and tortured France, of a France of forty millions faced by a Germany of seventy millions? But politics consists in the suppression of sentiment to the imperative of facts. The so-called German danger on which too many of our compatriots continually insist is now no more than a historic souvenir. . . . There is a German danger, but it is not the one one finds in the history books. It is rather a danger one finds written in the pages of the future. . . ."

This statement, titled "The Real German Danger," reads like many editorials of the past year in the British and American press exhorting our French ally to re-examine her traditional approach to the German problem. Actually it is from *Le Monde,* the most powerful journal of informed opinion in France. It is part of the new look that governing circles in France have begun taking across the Rhine. Just what is this danger written in the pages of the future?

It is the very real danger that if the three Western powers do not create, maintain, and bring to a successful conclusion a common German policy, they may yet be faced with: 1. A Germany allied with Russia. The old *ex oriente lux* Bismarckian dream is never dead, in either Germany or Russia. It is the nightmare alliance that would lead as directly to World War III as it did to World War II. 2. A Germany allied with neither Russia nor the West, but able to practice diplomatic blackmail against both East and West, emerging as *Der lachende Dritte,* the Laughing Third. 3. A Germany allied with the West, but so strong and unreconciled that she would become the dominant and domineering member of Western European Union, the arbiter of the Continent. The Western Powers are agreed that this is a threefold danger. The dispute is in the matter of emphasis. The Anglo-Americans insist that the French fear the third prospect so much that they enhance the prospects of the first two. The French retort that the third has become the real danger because the English and Americans are willing to risk it to avoid the first two.

Is there any way to square this vicious circle? Well, let's take a look at political forces emerging within Western Germany itself. Perhaps the pragmatic answer lies there.

A good deal less time need be spent fathoming the German attitude toward France than vice versa. For the past four years it has been a relatively passive and unimportant factor, although it will not always be so. The Germans, with the exception of the fewer than six million who live in the French Zone of Occupation, have had more important problems on their minds than their relations with France. Whatever traditional racial and political animosities linger in the German soul have mostly been transferred to the new enemy on the Elbe.

Nevertheless, among the leaders of the new West German Republic there has been a good deal of effort—and I feel it is a sincere effort—to reach a real and lasting understanding with France. Several leaders of the two major political parties —Konrad Adenauer, Carlo Schmid, Hans Ehard—are convinced Francophiles. They realize that the time for forging real links of co-operation was never better than right now, may never be as good again. French and other skeptics immediately point out that one of the most important voices in Western Germany, that of Doctor Kurt Schumacher, has been caustic if not openly hostile to French policy in Germany. The French ask if they can trust a new Germany in which the voice of Schumacher speaks for millions.

For a reason that this reporter never can fathom, much more time is given over to denouncing Socialist Kurt Schumacher than in listening to him. (I am referring now to the foreign press resident in Germany.) It strikes me that Schumacher, in this as in several other vital matters, has come closer to the heart of the matter than anybody else. Ironic in his utterances, given to wrapping up his policies in phrases a bit too pithy, and lacking many of the smooth graces of diplomacy, still, he does not speak until he has thought things out.

When I first interviewed Kurt Schumacher in the high summer of 1945, he was living in a ramshackle, half-bombed-out house in Hanover's Odeonstrasse. He looked like the ghost of a man—until he started to talk. He touched upon almost every topic, but what lingers most in my mind is his thumbnail analysis of the most important aspect of Franco-German relations: "The French want to internationalize the Ruhr. But the problem today is not the internationalization of a part of Germany. The problem is the internationalization of Europe." Sardonic, abrupt, impatient. But these were wise words for 1945, and from a man who had just spent a decade in Dachau.

What Schumacher was saying then—and the birth of the Marshall Plan two years later only served to underscore his thesis—was that the various schemes for controlling the Ruhr, including the present Ruhr Authority, do not go far enough. Mighty as it is, the Ruhr is only half of the vast industrial Rhineland complex at the heart of Marshall-Plan Europe, a complex which includes Lorraine, the Saar, and Benelux.

It is no accident that this Rhineland valley, the great producer of the coal and iron that forge the steel that is the structural basis of modern industrial society, is the classic area of contention between France and Germany. We do not need the help of the Marxists to discover the primary role of economics in the Franco-German dispute.

Examining the problem in this light, it is easy to isolate the hope and the danger in future French-German relations. Of course the French are right in demanding iron-clad controls over the Ruhr. But have they been wise these past four years in resisting the logical extension of these controls to the whole Rhineland area, bringing it out of the arena of nationalist dispute and into the framework of international control and guarantees? The framework is there: ERP, OEEC, Western Union.

When, in the early months of 1950, French Foreign Minister Robert Schuman made his first official visit to the new Bonn Republic, it was hoped that he and Chancellor Adenauer—two men who quite literally speak each other's language—would come up with a constructive resolution of the Saar question. But from this first meeting on the Rhine came nothing but bitter discord. Schuman insisted on treating the Saar as if it were conquered French territory, which *de jure* it is not. Adenauer retorted that the Saar must be considered a part of the West German Republic, which *de facto* it is not. This road leads nowhere. What is needed is a new approach, within the Western European framework, whereby both nations may move off the barren center of nationalist ambition: a second meeting on the Rhine—in Strasbourg, perhaps—to end the wrangle as to whether the Saar is French or German by announcing that it has become a part of Western Europe.

Many of the best friends of France would like to speed such a development. For they see a very real danger to France in too much hesitation and delay. Today all observers are agreed that the vast majority of Western Germans would enter gladly into such a Western European political and economic entity. But economically revived, politically strong, and psychologically unreconciled, would the Germany of 1952 be so eager to throw in its lot with the West? The reconciliation between France and Germany must take place soon or the opportunity may vanish.

Chapter XX

Germany as Seen by Her Neighbors

By THEODORE H. WHITE

EUROPE is the name of a civilization which for two thousand years has been trying to absorb the wild energy and furious ability of the German people. The Germans are at once the most hated and most needed group on their continent.

And it is the conflict between dread and need in the minds, the memories, and the subconscious of Germany's neighbors which for five years has paralyzed all effort to make peace in Europe.

In the past generation Germany has invaded and sacked every one of her neighbors (with the exception of Switzerland) at least once and usually twice. Germany is thus fringed not by peoples who have learned of her national character from textbooks and the word of returning travelers, but by peoples who have sheltered German orphans after one war to see them return as spies and scouts in the next; by peoples who have heard German spoken in their homes and market places not in friendship and visit but in curse and command; by peoples, finally, who know Germany not from personal experience alone but from the wars of their fathers and grandfathers.

Hate underlies the emotions of Germany's neighbors as

bedrock underlies topsoil; but on every quarter of their compass the Germans have sealed the memory of their acts to geography with physical monuments. Three cities come to mind—Budapest, Warsaw, and Lyons, all of which I saw in a six-month space, as different in texture as in the languages spoken by their citizens and the cultures that nursed them. But they frame themselves as one in memory because a river runs through each of the towns and into each river dip the bridges the Germans destroyed. All these bridges were wrecked not in the high noon of combat but in the ebb tide of defeat when Germans could gain nothing more than the discomfiture of peoples they had already sacked. The broken stumps and girders which dangle in the Danube, the Vistula, and the Rhone all bear the same trademark, and it will be a full decade before the dwellers of these towns can cross their rivers as they did before the German visitation. Whether it is in Hungarian, in Polish, or in French, the words they mutter lining up for crowded ferries have the same sound.

Destruction is monotonously similar on all frontiers of the new, clipped Germany; but the neighbors of Germany all keep fresh the memory of war with new monuments which differ in quality as sharply as the personalities of the bordering states.

In an orthodox Communist state like Poland the wound is commemorated as a great collective hurt by such stupefying monuments as the bronze memorial in the Ghetto or the museum at Auschwitz where the endless silent bins of human hair, the babies' boots, the tons of leather suitcases, the mounds of wrenched eyeglasses testify to the three million people who were butchered there by German officials acting for the German state.

In France, a Western and individualist nation, hate is enshrined more personally and simply and scattered in plaques of marble in every department of the land. It is a marble plaque opposite the grocer's store in the village in Burgundy which always has flowers pinned to it, and the grocer tells how against that wall the Gestapo always shot the local *résistants*. It is something you stumble on when you go on a picnic in the countryside, in the tall grass beyond the apple tree, almost hidden, which says, *"Ici fût sauvagement assasiné par les Allemands Robert Martellau, le 19 Août 1944—Agé de 17 ans."* And fresh flowers grace the plaques from early spring to late fall.

I stress this hate that rings Germany around for many reasons—because the Germans, surrounded by their own ruins and drenched in self-sorrow, have all but forgotten it; because in the United States of America, never occupied by the Germans, people have forgotten that in places like Paris and Warsaw, Germany is a more frightening menace than Communist Russia; because this primordial, remembered dread of Europe's people for their German neighbors must always be balanced by Europe's leaders against that which they can so clearly see from the high vantage point of state-craft, the Continent's aching need of a healthy, functioning German economy.

The need is simple to describe; the last hundred years of industrial development and progress in Europe made Germany the keystone in the arch of European well-being. Germany was a workshop of thriving, ingenious craftsmen who ate the foods of Holland, Denmark, Hungary, Poland, and Rumania and paid back in machines, tools, medicines, dyes, electrical wares, cameras, and all the intricate gadgets without which modern civilization cannot function. Germany was a brute source of prime materials—of coal, of potassium, of steel. Germany was a turntable, a complex of mines, rails, waterways, and transportation facilities that controlled the flow of all goods from the Black Sea to the Bay of Biscay. Dutch ports thrived because German factories smoked and pumped commerce down the Rhine; Dutch artichoke growers prospered because the coal miners of the Ruhr liked artichokes; from Warsaw to Bucharest, when men and women grew ill they turned to German medicines and pharmaceuticals. One-third of French steel production depended on German coke, and the Lorraine ore magnates grew rich on their sales to Ruhr steel barons.

Germany stood halfway between East and West, buying in a good year like 1928 almost 40 per cent of Eastern Europe's exports and supplying 30 to 35 per cent of its imports. It was a broker, merchant, transfer agent, and equalizer between Europe's civilized West and the industrially backward East in much the same way that Great Britain acted as transfer agent and broker between the Continent as a whole and the outside world.

It might have been possible to rebuild Europe after the war by constructing an economy in which Germany played no important part. For example, it is still argued in Paris that with $20,000,000,000 of Marshall Plan aid a European life might have been rebuilt which had no need of Ruhr steel, German coke, Hessian machinery, and Bavarian porcelain. Technically it might have been possible to restore Europe without them—although ten million people might have died of hunger in Germany. But on moral, political, and above all on economic grounds, it was decided to put together the old prewar European jigsaw as quickly as possible. Today the adventure is so far along that it is impossible for Frenchmen, Dutchmen, Danes—and probably Poles, Hungarians, and Czechs—to be reasonably or quickly prosperous unless Germany is too.

The only question therefore, for all Germany's neighbors is: On what terms shall Germany recover, what safeguards shall be taken, what reparations are to be exacted; how, in the present, shall uneasy populations at home be persuaded to accept an economically stable Germany; and how, in the future, will history judge the great gamble with destiny?

No nation in Europe, however, can now think of terms with Germany as a simple variation on the familiar and insoluble formula of hate versus need because they must ponder over the new element in European politics, the power rivalry between the Soviet Union and the United States. It is best to study what these giants want for a moment then before examining the opinions of Germany's neighbors whom they control.

The American thesis, very simply put, is that Germany will be safe only if democratic; democracy can thrive only among people who are well fed, well clothed, and well employed. Finally such prosperity depends on the re-establishment in Germany of free private enterprise as we have known it in America. This is the bold public thesis and, although it is sincere, it carries with it two less elevated footnotes—the first is, "Let's get Germany off the taxpayers' backs as soon as possible"; the second is, "If we've got to fight Russia, let's have the Germans on our side this time."

The Russian thesis is straight Marxist analysis and directly contradictory: Hitler was the creature of German monopoly capital, which (in the Russian opinion) is the end result of precisely that German private enterprise which America seeks to re-create. Ultimately only a Communist revolution can make Germany safe but for the present Russia is willing to settle for two things: first, a sizable share of reparations for the untold billions of German destruction and the millions of murders; second, a cast-iron right of veto over the entire German nation to prevent its people from taking any action contrary to Russian interests. Soviet Russia has sponsored a strongly centralized Germany partly to compete with America in propaganda appeal, principally because a centralized government is the most easily controlled from above.

Neither Russia nor America has been able to sell its ideology to its satellites and a trip around the borders of Germany provides some interesting variants on the two master themes.

The little countries of the northwest, Belgium, Denmark, and Holland, have been all but voiceless in negotiations on Germany. All are bound to America for security and their future is tied up with the Atlantic power bloc. Although these states want protection, they are by far the most dependent on the German economy; their own recovery is virtually impossible without prosperity along the east bank of the Rhine.

France is bound to the Western power bloc by the traditions of democracy, the need of American aid, and fear of Communist Russia. The French, however, fear the Germans far more than they do the Russians and in their eyes America, their patron, has proven itself naïve and unthinking. The French cherish freedom as greatly as do Americans, but they want to protect their own liberties by a few practical limits on the liberty of their traditional enemy and despoiler. They have advanced three favorite ideas since the war. The first was to split Germany into harmless little states, returning it to status quo ante 1870; the second was to internationalize the Ruhr, detaching it from Germany; lastly, to occupy it for a generation while democratic teachers decontaminated the militaristic spirit and tradition, starting their work on the grade-school level. All three have been rejected although French insistence has forced the West to agree to certain technical precautions in the Ruhr arsenal.

The Swiss are probably the only ones of Germany's neighbors who regard her with an attitude devoid of moral judgment. They have fought a bitter rear-guard action against American efforts to confiscate Nazi assets in Switzerland for reparations. They see Germany as past and future supplier and customer and the Swiss do business with anyone who can put gold, dollars, or Swiss francs on the line. The Swiss fancy themselves as the enemy of no one and consequently, are seen by the rest of Europe as the friend of no one.

In Eastern Europe it is somewhat more difficult to find nationalist divergences from the official Communist party line, with the notable exception, of course, of Yugoslavia. In most East European states the leaders are still so insecure and doctrinaire that they can do little more than quote dogma, and beneath the surface in many of them the peasantry and citizenry are only half-converted Axis satellites.

In Czechoslovakia, the regime has found that fear of Germany is the second most important brace, after the party apparatus itself, in welding the country to the Soviet bloc. No one in Prague is allowed to forget that it was France and Britain who sold Czechoslovakia down the river at Munich. "After all," said one official, "a country living between a dangerous Germany and a strong Russia can only make one choice."

Poland, the strongest, most confident, and most successful Communist experiment in Eastern Europe, has deviated sharply from official Marxist dogma, for the Poles are almost as unhappy about Russian policy as the French are about American. They, like the French, want a dismembered, split-up Germany across the frontier—but Russia, like the United States, wants a centralized Germany. The Poles, like the French, favor a long Occupation, but they must be silent as Russia competes with America for German favor. Under the surface, French and Poles are closest to an agreed solution on Germany.

Two facts shape Polish thinking on Germany. The first is the animal dread, the quiver of terror in their memory of the German occupation. Six million Poles—approximately one out of every five citizens alive in 1939—were shot, hanged, cremated, or systematically assassinated by the Germans. The image of this depravity is still so vivid that no emotion of hate for Russia or affection for America can obscure it.

The second fact is that in retracing the map of Eastern Europe, Russia peeled one long sliver off Eastern Poland, tacked it to Soviet soil, then repaid Poland by peeling a commensurate sliver off Eastern Germany to tack on to her Silesian frontier. This operation brought Poland's frontier with Germany to the Oder-Neisse line, gave her the industrial wealth of Silesia and was followed by the expulsion of several million Germans and their replacement by a Polish population.

There was a time, three or four hundred years ago, when the Oder-Neisse line was the real frontier between Poland and Germany, before the expanding Teutons drove the Poles back to the east. But the Germans now regard this lost territory as the ultimate bitter indignity of the present peace and insist on its return, creating a problem which will plague Europe for years to come.

The Polish attitude to all things German rests on the question of the frontier; it is, to their way of thinking, the index of the peace. One devout and realistic Polish diplomat put it this way: "You people are talking nonsense when you speak of your fear of Russian agression. If Russia wanted to make war on the West, whom would she seek as an ally— Germany or France? Germany, of course. What is the most important thing Russia must do to have the Germans with them? Give them back our new territories. This is a situation which you must watch just as closely as we. If they decide to give the Germans any part of Silesia, they are wooing them and there will be trouble. When you think Russia has yielded to you on the Oder-Neisse issue, beware, for that is the moment she will be most dangerous. Up to now the Russians support us, and there will be peace."

Germany is complicated enough when seen at close quarters, across the frontiers and the sentry box. But it is part of the nightmare quality of all things German that perspective, rather than pointing the solutions, confuses them.

Seen in European perspective, the problems of Germany appear something like this: All Europe, of which Germany is only a single part, has been going downhill for thirty-five years. The mounting crisis of readjustment through which Europe is now passing is only in part the result of the war; it is actually a shifting of relationship with the outside world that has been taking place since 1910. The world no longer is dependent upon trade with the old continent, no longer needs to give Europe its foods, ores, and raw materials in return for Europe's manufactured goods. Countries which once shipped their meat and leather in return for shoes, and their cotton in return for cloth, now keep their leather and make their own shoes, keep their cotton and manufacture their own cloth.

Two wars forced the liquidation of the great investments and resources which had paid so much of Europe's food and raw-material bill. First, the United States threw off the tolls of dividends and interest in the 1914-1918 war; South America and Asia liquidated much of their indebtedness in the last war.

To the Germans it seemed after the First World War that the great imperialist powers—France, Britain, the United States—had stripped her of empire in order to profit by controlling the backward raw-material-producing world. The depression that swept all Europe seemed to the Germans the result of indignity and defeat; only Britain and France knew that victory and empire offered no cure for the slow, sad deterioration of industrial Europe's relationship to a world which had outgrown its tutelage.

In the long hard pull back to peace and economic independence, Western Europe now has three major problems: what goods or services to offer to the outside world that will restore its ancient markets on decent terms; how to preserve freedom against communism; and how to persuade the Germans to co-operate.

In the long run, the persuasion of the Germans will probably be the hardest of the three. All Europe will be on an economy of scarcity for years to come and the Germans too will be on short rations. But the rest of Europe will regard its penury as part of a self-imposed austerity while Germany will see it as the penalty of defeat. The Germans must be weaned from the memory of Hitler's crimes to a belief in democracy on rations half those that crime brought them. It is pointless to explain to Germans that war does not pay or that victory on the battlefield brings only impoverishment of victor and vanquished alike; for the Germans did make war pay by looting their neighbors to give butter and silks to the home country.

In perspective, then, here is the counterpoint. Out of the hunger of the early 1930's and the Treaty of Versailles grew a social chaos that ended in national madness, a paranoiac delusion of persecution which Hitler personified. Germany is today an overcrowded dwarf state, far poorer in food resources, raw material, and housing than ever before. Hitler has been removed, but the hunger is greater than ever, and the paranoiac belief in persecution remains.

There is a cure for this ever recurrent hunger—that is, to permit Germany to build a set of industrial muscles more powerful than those ever known before in the Ruhr; with these industrial muscles, perhaps, she can compete and win a large enough share of the world's markets to feed her people as well as Hitler once fed them. But—and here is the question that no Foreign Office or government has solved—who is there to guarantee that the new muscles and new industry will not be controlled by the same diseased minds which brought disaster once before? Yet who can hope that freedom will ever flourish among a starving people?

Last spring, in Paris, the foreign ministers of the occupying powers found themselves unable to agree on any joint solution of Germany's problems, thus, historically, turning Germany's dilemma back to the Germans to solve themselves.

It will be a decade before Europe and the world know whether this decision by default was a blunder; if it is, then civilization as this continent has known it may be doomed.

Chapter XXI

Zone of Silence

By LANDRUM BOLLING

IN THE heart of Europe, between the Baltic Sea and the Czech border, lies a mysterious and troubled region which Western Germans call the Zone of Silence. Its Communist rulers have now named it the German Democratic Republic. It is, in fact, the Soviet Union's super-satellite.

Eastern Germany was formally launched in October 1949 as an independent state and quickly won diplomatic recognition from other Communist-run regimes, from Peiping to Prague. But the Soviets did not surrender in any way their mastery of the economic and political life of this area. They simply undertook to get even more of what they want out of Germany through giving increasing power to their local stooges than they could hope for by continuing their own direct, heavy-handed control. And they want a lot. Just how much has been made quite clear in the years since the Occupation began.

Along with the dog-tired Red Army combat troops who fought their way into Germany in the spring of 1945 came two groups of specialists, sent in to serve two major Soviet objectives. One group consisted of the "booty teams"—engineers, accountants, and assorted other technicians—whose job was to supervise the carting away of whatever kind of wealth the Soviet Union might use. The other group, including top German Communists long resident in Moscow, was composed of propaganda and political experts under orders to win the German people for communism and friendship with the Soviet Union. Understandably, the activities of the first group made life a bit hard for the second.

My own introduction to the work of these experts came in Berlin in 1946, when I hired as secretary a Russian-German girl who had been serving as interpreter with a Soviet finance booty team. Her previous job had been to help with the looting of the banks in the Behrenstrasse, Wall Street of the old Reich.

"It was great fun, once you got used to the idea," she recalled. "My major and his colleagues were very nice friendly people. They would bring along their black bread and sausages and pickled herring, so we had many a jolly lunch on the floor of a bank vault. And they gave me some of the perfume we found, as well as an occasional trinket not valuable enough for the official collections of good jewelry, silverware, money, and stocks."

During that same period other booty teams were dismantling factories and railway yards, seizing stockpiles of food, raw materials, and finished goods before the inter-Allied rules on official reparations could be hammered out at Potsdam and put into effect. To justify these actions the Russians have repeatedly pointed out that collecting booty is a time-hallowed right of victors, a right not very specifically limited or defined. And, anyway, they found more than ample vindication by recalling the enormous destruction Germans inflicted on the Soviet Union.

But whatever the legal and moral judgment of the issue, Soviet booty removals and the subsequent reparations collections have been a great embarrassment to the Communist chieftains, Wilhelm Pieck, Otto Grotewohl, and Walter Ulbricht, and will continue to haunt the promoters of a pro-Soviet Germany for years to come. Moreover, to millions of Germans vivid personal memories of the raping and looting by Red soldiers in the first weeks of victory will remain perhaps forever the best argument against the system under which the Red Army fought.

Yet in the very moment of those excesses Soviet billboard artists were putting up posters and stringing propaganda banners above the rubble of hundreds of East German towns and villages. A favorite one carried a quotation from the wartime speech of Marshal Joseph Stalin in which he said that "Hitlers come and Hitlers go, but the German people remain forever." Another gave a brief extract from the Soviet constitutional provision on freedom of religion. Still others glorified socialism as the ultimate goal of all "progressive democratic peoples." Communism, being a horrid word, was never used at all.

Meanwhile Soviet political experts moved in to organize both their admirers and their political opponents. They hoped that German Communists could win and keep power. But they also hoped that even the anti-Communist Germans could be lured onto the pro-Soviet bandwagon.

Despite the initial bad impression which their undisciplined troops made, the Soviets held certain powerful assets at the beginning of their campaign to win the German people. They had a plan of what they hoped to accomplish in Germany, and they pushed that plan with a sureness and swiftness which contrasted sharply with much clumsy-footed action among the Western Allies. They licensed four political parties in the early weeks of the Occupation, organized a trade-union movement, and quickly reopened the theaters and opera houses, while the Westerners went through the laborious task of "screening" would-be politicians, union leaders, actors, singers, dancers. The Soviets had a group of trusted local disciples to work through; the Westerners didn't. Moreover, the Soviets showed from the beginning a vast confidence in their ability to control Germans of every background—if they were useful. And into mass propaganda they, of course, put massive efforts.

Yet for all of their cleverness, the Russians did not win the German people. They overdid the propaganda. And they could not conceal the fact that month by month their take from the East German economy—however much it might be justified as partial compensation for Soviet war losses—was enormous, and enormously resented.

Since the closing days of the war the men in the Kremlin have been struggling with these two contradictory policies toward Germany. On the one hand they have wanted to get out of the defeated Germans every railway car, every drill press, every watch and shoe and shirt they could haul away. But at the same time they have burned with ardor to woo and win the Germans.

As can now be seen in their relations with other countries in the Moscow orbit, the Soviet leaders are torn between national need and international ambition. Mother Russia must be rebuilt and made stronger. Her patient people must be rewarded from somewhere, somehow, with more clothes and other consumer goods. But the Messianic mission to carry the Marxist-Leninist gospel to all who dwell in non-Communist darkness is equally urgent. In the case of Germany the Soviets have put forth maximum efforts to fulfill both objectives simultaneously. And with reason. Both as a source of the material things Russia needs and as a potential partner in the world revolution, Germany is the top prize.

The postwar story of the Eastern Zone of Germany is the history of those two interwoven Soviet ambitions. It is also in many important particulars a warning of what will happen if all of Germany should ever be united under Soviet control.

When the Big Three fixed the zonal boundaries at Yalta they handed over the granary of Germany to the Soviets, the industry to the British, and the scenery to the Americans. So quipped the late General George S. Patton. Actually the Russians took over a great deal more than the best German farm land. Under their control came vast forests, extensive brown-coal fields, the world's greatest concentration of potash, and numerous important industries. Among these latter were the Jena optical works, the giant Leuna synthetic gasoline works, the famed Meissen china plant, and numerous automobile, rubber, machinery, electrical-equipment, and textile factories.

Stretched across the broad Prussian plain between the Oder and the Elbe, and reaching from the mountainous Sudetenland to the Baltic beaches, the Soviet Zone comprises about 30 per cent of present-day Germany. In total area it is roughly equivalent to Switzerland, Belgium, and Holland, with Luxemburg and Lichtenstein thrown in for good measure.

With 18,400,000, inhabitants, Eastern Germany is the most populous of the iron-curtain countries, save for Poland. It is easily the richest, or soon can be as the Soviet reparations demands taper off. Already its economy, though damaged by war and stifled by artificial separation from the heavy industry of the Ruhr and the Rhineland, has yielded up fabulous treasure to the Soviet Union.

To get the picture of these Soviet collections, their extent, and the comprehensive manner in which they have been organized, you need to make a little list of key terms: war booty, personal looting, requisitioning, dismantling, deliveries from current production, conversion of German plants into Soviet corporations, organization of German-Russian mixed companies. And then you'd have to have a separate, special heading to cover the gigantic uranium-mining project in southern Saxony. Suppose we take them up in roughly that order.

War Booty. The Russians themselves haven't any idea how much they took out of Germany in the form of booty. In the three months prior to the signing of the Potsdam Agreement they removed an enormous amount of industrial and transport equipment and a wide miscellany of other forms of wealth—after helter-skelter seizures on both a personal and an organized basis. Into that giant grab bag also went thousands of Prussian cows which now graze on Ukrainian collective farms, Berlin *S-Bahn* trains which now run on the Moscow subways, and paintings by Raphael and Rembrandt from the Zwinger Museum in Dresden now transplanted to Soviet galleries.

Requisitioning. As is well known, the Soviet troops live off the land, in the traditional manner of most armies of the past. During the years of Occupation they continued this policy. It was not popular. Yet apparently the East Germans found it bearable. During the first two postwar years they were not notably worse fed than the Germans of the Western zones. And there are some who argued they were better fed until the Marshall Plan got under way and pushed Western Germany's recovery far ahead.

As the agriculturally most productive region of Germany, with the lowest density of population, the Soviet Zone's supply of bread, sugar, and potatoes was usually large enough to meet requisitioning demands and to provide the local population with a subsistence diet. But it was a close squeak. Fats and meat were to be had in only the most microscopic quantities. And even potato rations could sometimes not be filled —because of hoarding by the farmers and the Soviet-sponsored expansion of schnapps production. Sickness and mortality rates were the highest for any zone of Germany. From being a food-exporting region, the Soviet Zone was for a time reduced to a level below self-suffiency.

War Plant Production. Eastern Germany is not the Ruhr. Yet its armament production facilities at the end of the war seemed a glittering prize to the Russians. And why not use them?

Despite solemn Allied agreements which called for halting all armament production and dismantling munitions factories, the Soviets made much use of Eastern Germany as an arsenal for strengthening their own military power. Particularly during the first year and a half of the Occupation they kept Germans busy turning out airplane motors, submarine parts, fire-control devices, patrol boats, and artillery shells.

The Western Allies were, of course, well informed about these prohibited operations and throughout 1946 they kept pressing for a joint demilitarization inspection of all zones. The Soviets managed to stall off this proposal for many months. Meanwhile, in the fall of 1946 orders went out for a double-quick dismantling of many of these war plants. Within six weeks an impressive number of them had been picked clean and most of the machinery plus key German technicians had been shipped off to the Soviet Union. When the Allied inspection teams were finally allowed to make their conducted tour the Soviets could proudly show off their demilitarization accomplishments.

Where the Russians acted they did the job with great thoroughness. Coming along behind the official inspectors, I once had a look at some former Messerschmitt and Henkel aircraft factories at Dessau and Halle. Not only had the Soviets removed all machinery, tools, and equipment, but German salvage crews were taking out the window frames and the steel beams and digging up the water pipes—for shipment to the Soviet Union. Yet despite such striking evidence of demilitarization, the Soviets continued to encourage German war material production even further.

As late as 1948, artillery shells were in production at a plant at Kapau. Meanwhile the Neptune shipyard at Rostock was busy turning out speedy patrol boats, incorporating marked improvements over the best wartime German models. And at the GEMA plant in the Soviet sector of Berlin, German engineers and craftsmen built automatic control systems for the growing Soviet fleet of Schnorkel U-boats.

Dismantling for Reparations. At Yalta, as the Russians understood it, Roosevelt and Churchill agreed that the Soviet Union could collect the equivalent of ten billion dollars in kind from Germany as war reparations. Nobody can argue that such a total would cover more than a small fraction of the enormous material losses suffered by the Soviet Union. Yet from the beginning of the Occupation period there was a continual wrangle over the Soviet's reparations demands. That dispute, as much as any other single thing, broke up the planned four-power rule of a united Germany before it ever really got under way. The opposing views are not difficult to paraphrase.

"Look at how much we suffered," the Russians always said. "Morally, politically, legally, we are entitled to collect our ten billion dollars. Why are you Westerners trying to cheat us out of what is rightfully ours?"

"We do not deny your claims," replied the West. "But we want an honest accounting of what is taken, we want the job done according to mutually recognized rules, and we want to make sure that what you remove from Germany is not, in effect, the relief supplies we are pouring in at the other end."

The original demands put forward by the Soviets at Potsdam seemed to the British and Americans so extreme that the conference almost collapsed on this point without agreement. In the end a reparations formula was concocted which allowed the Soviet Union to satisfy its reparations claims primarily out of "surplus" plants in Eastern Germany. Other plants in Western Germany were also to be dismantled for the Soviet account. However, in part these removals would be "paid for" by shipments of raw materials and foodstuffs from the Soviet area to the Western zones. And there was a general statement, inserted on American insistence, that exports from Germany's current production should go in the first instance to pay for essential imports of food and raw materials.

This was a patchwork compromise, and it failed. Within a year after the end of the war the United States military governor announced that no further reparations allocations to the Soviet Union would be made in the United States Zone until Soviet authorities fulfilled their Potsdam obligations. The British and the French followed suit.

The charges pretty much boiled down to this: 1. The Soviet Union had made no accounting of the value of dismantled factories removed or of the "war booty" it collected on a vast scale. 2. Large quantities of manufactured goods from both pre-surrender stock piles and current production, agricultural products, and raw materials had been taken out of Eastern Germany as reparations payments—again without any accounting, and in express violation of the Potsdam Agreement. 3. The Soviets had blocked the economic unification of Germany—thus upsetting all calculations about how many plants would have to be retained in Western Germany, to provide the minimum standard of living agreed on, and how many should be handed over for reparations.

While this squabble raged in the solemn sessions of the Allied Control Authority in Berlin and embittered the meetings of the Council of Foreign Ministers, the Soviets went right ahead. East Germans speak of successive waves of dismantlings. Actually the process was fairly continuous during the first three years of the Occupation, though there were sudden spurts and sporadic slowdowns as the Soviets struggled to reconcile the two policies of stripping the Germans and winning their friendship.

In Berlin the big push to dismantle industries occured during the first two months after V-E Day. The principal reason why the Soviets stalled from early May to mid-July, 1945 on fulfilling the Yalta agreement to admit Western troops to the Reich capital and to set up four-power rule seems clearly to have been a desire to get this hurry-up plant-removal job finished first. Though, naturally, they also used the delay to put a Communist-dominated city administration firmly in the saddle.

Meanwhile factories in other Soviet Zone cities were being taken away, and during the summer and fall of 1945 the major work of stripping the railways was carried out.

Understandably, no dismantling program could be made popular with the Germans. But Soviet clumsiness aroused even greater hostility than was to be expected. The removal of machinery was done so hastily and crudely that great waste resulted, and much valuable machinery was damaged in transport or ruined by weather. Also, German workers got away with a certain amount of sabotage. The Germans liked to tell each other that the whole dismantling program was a kind of dog-in-the-manger madness, that the Soviets were simply destroying wantonly factories they would never be able to reassemble and use.

Moreover, local Soviet commanders and even Marshal Vasili Sokolovsky, the Soviet military governor, provoked additional ill will by trying on occasion to pacify the Germans with phony gestures of generosity.

Once in a bombed-out little town in the Ruhr I came across

a small manufacturer of bolts and nuts who had migrated from the Soviet Zone suburbs of Berlin. His machine shop there had been stripped bare once. He patched it together and started over. Once again it was dismantled. A second time he rebuilt it on Soviet assurances that he would now be left alone. When the dismantling crews showed up a third time, he decided it was time to give up and get out.

On a higher level, Marshal Sokolovsky assured the East Germans in May 1946 that the dismantling of industrial plants had been finished. More than a year later a group of Americans correspondents was taken on a conducted tour of the great Zeiss optical works in Jena. According to statements by the managing director, made to us in the presence of assenting Soviet officers, 94 per cent of all Zeiss equipment had been removed and the work had only just been finished.

In 1947 Marshal Sokolovsky issued another declaration about how all dismantlings had now been ended, though they in fact continued, at least in certain brown-coal open-pit mines and at the Schkopau Buna plant and the Gera Siemens factory, into 1948. That the Soviets had a rightful claim on all the reparations equipment they removed—the things they took in 1947 and 1948 quite as much as what they had shipped off earlier—need not be discussed here. The point is that the attempt to ride two policies simultaneously—to take German wealth to build up the Soviet Union and to curry favor with the German people and convert them to communism—led again and again to awkward situations and to transparent contradictions between words and actions.

Just how much of the Soviet Zone industry remained after all dismantling operations ceased even the economic experts of Eastern Germany find it difficult to establish. The iron, steel, and machinery industries were most severely stripped; the woodworking, paper, cement, and chemical industries were much less affected. The best-informed guess seems to be that by 1949 the over-all industrial capacity of the Soviet Zone had been reduced to about 50 per cent of the 1936 level. But already the zonal German administration, backed by the Soviets, was pushing the expansion of certain key industries, particularly iron and steel.

Reparations from Current Production. At the end of the war the Russian leaders saw quite clearly that one of the most urgent needs of their national economy was for consumer goods. To hurry the rebuilding of destroyed homes and industries Soviet workers would have to be given as incentive a chance to buy more of the simple everyday articles they so sadly lacked and wanted. The same point was underscored by millions of war veterans and liberated Soviet slave laborers, returning from the West, who were bringing home fabulous tales of the high standard of living already attained by the "downtrodden" workers in capitalist states. This naturally created a most serious political problem. Prompt, vigorous action by the party was required, and was undertaken, as informed Communists in Eastern Germany and other iron-curtain countries will testify, off the record. All those areas under Soviet control were called on to help immediately in providing clothes, shoes, bicycles, and other consumer commodities needed by the Soviet population. And in that scheme Eastern Germany was to play a major role.

In the East German factories not dismantled every encouragement was given for full speed toward capacity production, with the goods in large part going to the Soviet Union as reparations. For a time considerable publicity was given to this East German "boom," but it didn't take long for word to get around about where the output went. According to well-informed Soviet Zone sources, reparations quotas ordered the following deliveries to the Russians during the third quarter of 1946: machinery, 90 per cent of total production; textiles, 84 per cent; leather shoes, 90 per cent;

glass products, 70 per cent; paper goods, 49 per cent; vehicles, 90 per cent.

During a period of more than three years it was calculated that between 60 and 70 per cent of the entire industrial production of the zone was drained off to the Soviet Union. Similar deliveries are apparently scheduled to remain high for a good many years to come.

Soviet A.G.'s. To make doubly sure of their collections, and perhaps to establish a long-term basis for direct influence in the German economy, the Soviets issued Special Order No. 167 on June 5, 1946. This was the decree which proclaimed the seizure and official establishment of Soviet ownership of about two hundred key industrial enterprises in Eastern Germany. Each concern became part of a Soviet A.G. (corporation). Russian general directors, deputies, and division heads, were installed, though the German workers and most German supervisors and technicians continued at their jobs as before.

After about six months 74 of the smaller and less important of these enterprises were handed over to the provincial governments as socialized German property. With the reamining 130 A.G.'s the Soviets were still able to exercise a dominant role in the whole economy of the zone. The largest of these corporations put the Soviets into top position in the chemical field, and gave them control of such plants as the vast Leuna synthetic gasoline works at Merseburg, and important film and buna rubber factories.

Other major Soviet A.G.'s brought Russian management into coal mining, and the production of machinery, electrical equipment, potash, optical goods, paper, and transport equipment.

It is conservatively estimated that 20 to 25 per cent of East German industrial production is accounted for in the output of these Soviet corporations. Most of the finished goods from such plants, of course, have gone to the Soviet Union, part of them officially called reparations and bought by the East German government for shipment to Russia.

The financing and administering of these enterprises is a weird affair, compared to which the capitalist cartel is a model of simplicity and propriety. In the first place, when the Soviets took ownership, by decree, all debts charged against the enterprises were assumed by the provincial governments. Operating capital, in addition to whatever reserves were on hand, was furnished by the Soviet-owned *Garantie und Kreditbank,* into which had been funneled large sums of German money acquired in various ways by the Soviet Government. In day-to-day operations the Soviet A.G.'s found the path of business made easy. They were given an absolute priority for labor, raw materials, electricity, coal, and almost anything else they needed. Whatever they required from related concerns they received at low, fixed prices. And yet, according to confidential reports from East Zone economic officials, many of these Soviet enterprises have been operated at a loss. The Leuna chemical works was run at a deficit of about 2,000,000 marks per month in 1946-47, and as late as early 1949 the monthly losses were reported to be even larger. The government budget of the province of Saxony-Anhalt, during 1947-48, carried an item of 60,000,000 reichsmarks as subsidies for the Soviet A.G.'s in that one state.

The reason for this sad showing, it is reliably stated, is the same kind of questionable deal which has on occasion milked capitalist operating companies dry. Above each Soviet A.G. was placed a central administrative body, which for a long time had its headquarters in the Weiseensee district of Berlin. This Communist-style holding company exacted from each subordinate enterprise large fixed sums, regardless of profit or loss. When there have been losses—as has frequently happened—German government taxes have made them good.

East German officials were long ago led to believe that eventually the Soviet Union would arrange a well-publicized gesture of handing back all of these concerns as German socialized enterprises. The precedent was already established, and the Soviets have enough control of Eastern Germany to assure them just about everything they could want from the zone's economy anyway. So why not? Meanwhile the Soviet A.G.'s have served as a highly successful device for getting manufactured goods more quickly and in greater quantity than could have been expected had the factories been taken down and moved to Russia.

The Uranium Mines. Of all the Soviet enterprises and operations in Germany none will ever match the fabulous corporation known as Wismut, A.G. Had it not been for the bomb that wrecked Hiroshima, probably Wismut, A.G. would never have existed.

During their feverish search for the atom bomb the Soviets discovered that in the Eastern Zone of Germany they had fallen heir to possibly some of the best uranium deposits in the world. At the beginning all they had to go on were a few old-fashioned mountain health resorts with their radioactive springs and some long-abandoned silver mines. Careful geological study, however, showed that here, as well as across the border in the Carlsbad section of Czechoslovakia, lay valuable deposits of uranium.

There are two major aspects of the story of what happened next. One involves Comrades Maizev, Mikhailovitch, and Mitrofanovitch, who eventually set up their offices as the Soviet directors of Wismut, A.G., at Niederschlemerweg No. 49, in the little Saxon town of Aue. The other concerns a pasty-faced German blonde, whom we may call Inga.

Understandably, the highly placed comrades were never allowed to talk to a Western journalist. Neither was Inga. But after she ran away, she did anyhow. Scattered across the Soviet Zone are a lot of others who have had just her kind of experience and tell a similar story.

Inga's home was in the once-pleasant resort town of Marienberg. The daughter of a Berlin greengrocer, she had moved away from the bombing during the war to help take care of her grandmother. Like those of many another girl in her early twenties, Inga's thoughts centered around her clerical job and the hopes of finding the right young man.

Then one morning in early 1947 there came a knock on her grandmother's door. It was a notice that Inga should report within two hours to the local labor office for reassignment to the Marienberg mine. She went.

Inga's job was a simple one and so were her tools. Teamed up with another drafted girl worker, she was set to hauling rocks in a crude four-handled box from the refuse dump at the mouth of an old worked-out silver mine to a long inspection table. There stood a Russian soldier with a "machine shaped like a golf club attached to some batteries." With this Geiger counter, or its equivalent, the Russian tested each load, separating the "Soviet rocks" from the "German rocks," as the workers called the process. The "Soviet rocks" were loaded into trucks and hauled away. In time Inga was shifted to the pits, where mining operations had been resumed in the old crumbling tunnels.

"That was a nightmare," she reported. "We had to use makeshift ladders. We had no modern mining tools or power equipment. For want of pumps, workers had to stand much of the time in water. And there was a constant pressure for more speed, regardless of safety."

Frequently sick, and pretending to be in much worse health than was actually the case, Inga finally got a doctor's certificate freeing her from further uranium-mine duty.

In the beginning the vast majority of workers for Wismut,

A.G., were conscripted. And, like Inga, a great many ran away as soon as they could. Others who feared they would be drafted fled to the Western zones as a precaution, and there were sensational kidnapings of some who tried to escape but failed. Rumors of cave-ins, underground explosions, and other disasters at Wismut mines have leaked out of that rigidly blockaded area again and again. How much truth they contain a Westerner finds it hard to judge. Yet workers and engineers who have escaped from the mines have given Western intelligence officers abundant documentary evidence of shocking slave labor conditions there.

Nevertheless, as time went by, Soviet director Maizev and his colleagues were gradually able to make the work attractive enough to draw an increasing number of voluntary recruits. Special "Stalin packages" of food and textiles were given out. Special rations of tobacco and schnapps were distributed, and wages were set at premium rates. Some miners were able to earn between 2,000 and 3,000 marks a month.

By the fall of 1949 it was estimated that approximately 100,000 Germans had been employed on various phases of this vast project—centering around uranium mines operating at Aue, Schneeberg, Lauter, Marienberg, Annaberg, and Johann Georgenstadt. Production results of these operations are of course among the top Soviet secrets. But that they have been quite important to the Soviet bomb program must be taken for granted. And so far as the local economy is concerned, in terms of the Ingas conscripted and the marks invested, Wismut, A.G., overshadows every other enterprise in Eastern Germany. The Russians are in the German uranium mining business in a big way. They probably won't pull out any time soon.

In the beginning the Soviets were reluctant to admit that they were taking any reparations from current production—

since such shipments were prohibited under the Potsdam Agreement, at least until Germany should get on a self-supporting basis again. But at the Moscow and London meetings of the Council of Foreign Ministers, Molotov pressed for agreement that the Soviet Union should be allowed to collect the promised ten billion dollars in goods from Germany over a twenty-year period. The Western representatives, repeating their insistence that Germany be allowed to get off the Anglo-American relief rolls first, rejected the plan for reparations from current production, but offered to consider such a proposal if the Soviets would give the facts about shipments already made. Probably those facts will always be in dispute. Molotov suggested in 1947 that total collections to that date might be reckoned at one billion dollars. Western spokesmen, however, declared that their intelligence reports indicated the real amount was several times as great. In an unguarded moment Marshal Sokolovsky once told one of his top Western colleagues that his country was shipping out reparations goods at the rate of $100,000,000 a month. By the end of 1949 informed experts calculated that at postwar world prices the Soviets in the first four years of Occupation had already collected—in "booty," dismantled plants, and reparations from current production—more than the full ten billions Roosevelt and Churchill promised Stalin at Yalta. Who knows? The truth is that nobody will ever know.

At one time during the first years of the Occupation the big East-West quarrel in Berlin was over Allied Occupation currency. The same engravings had been used by all four of the Allies, and each was to submit careful reports on the number of marks run off and the amount of currency in circulation. These simple statistics were obviously essential if there was to be any adequate planning and control of Germany's finances. In one four-power meeting after another the soviets came up with painful excuses as to why their report wasn't ready. They never did get it ready.

"For a long time," reported the top American finance officer, "we suspected the Russians of some plot, of some deliberate plan to keep the rest of us in the dark. And then slowly as we studied over the whole record of their fragmentary comments on the subject, and pieced together our intelligence reports, we reached quite a different conclusion. The Russians weren't telling us how many Occupation marks they had printed because they didn't have the foggiest notion themselves!"

Much of the mystery about the extent of the Soviet reparations can probably be accounted for in similar terms. But the Russians, the Germans, and the Westerners all know that those collections have seriously altered the face of the East German economy and have helped set in motion political currents the direction of which is still unclear.

What the Russians have taken out of the East Zone has obviously been important—in gains to the Soviet Union and losses to Germany. But the gifts of friendship and communism which the Soviets have sought to bestow in exchange are of far more lasting significance. Long before the war ended Kremlin leaders went to work in earnest on the tactics to win Germany. In the old-time German Communists residing in the Soviet Union, some of them veterans of fifteen years of intensive Moscow political training, and in the Communist underground inside Germany, they had a ready-made nucleus for their new order. Also, in time they were able to draw on the hundreds of thousands of beaten men taken at Stalingrad and afterward.

Wisely, the Russians soft-pedaled at first their interest in exporting Marxism. Instead, they emphasized peace and friendly co-operation between a de-Hitlerized Germany and the Soviet Union. This is still the major theme of their German propaganda, though there have been periods when doctrinaire zeal gained the upper hand.

"There are many steps along the stairway to socialism," an East German Communist once explained to me, "and we have to take them patiently one at a time. The first is that of the antifascist democratic front. The second is the people's democracy. The third is socialism, which has been fully achieved only by the Soviet Union. And the final one is communism, the ultimate goal toward which we all move. Eastern Germany is still on only the first step."

That was the way Soviet Zone leaders saw their local system after four years of struggle and experimentation. But their eyes were still fixed on the far-off goal.

"We are not yet a people's democracy," one of their information directors said in November 1949. "Why do you Western journalists keep giving us credit for having advanced farther than we have? So long as half of the business in Eastern Germany is in private hands and the free-enterprise political parties are allowed to function we have obviously not moved into the ranks of the people's democracies."

These classifications Communists take in deadly seriousness, particularly the orderly, methodical Germans. However, it should be pointed out that the different stages they speak of really represent whole flights of stairs, from one floor to another, not single steps. East Germany may still be barely off the ground level as an antifascist, popular-front democracy, but it has climbed from one step to another to another along the way.

At the beginning of the Occupation, as the Soviets had foreseen, there was a chance to rush their German Communist colleagues into positions of control while the population was still dazed by defeat. This they did with great thoroughness. Out of the 12,236 new *burgermeisters,* appointed in their zone about 8,000 were members of the KPD (*Kommunistische Partei Deutschlands*) or were close fellow travelers. A similar favoritism was shown in filling the controlling positions in other phases of administration.

However, the Russians tried carefully not to overdo it. And here again they quickly got themselves enmeshed in one of those great contradictions of high politics. They wanted to create at least the semblance of a free democracy. They craved the good will and co-operation of the non-Communist elements, who, they realized, far outnumbered the Communists. But at the same time they felt compelled to insure the dominance of the Communist party. A lot of fancy footwork went into the effort to have it both ways.

Official Order No. 2 of the Soviet Military Administration, prepared early in June 1945, provided for the immediate organization of political parties and trade-unions. This was many weeks before the Western Allies were willing to permit similar freedom to the Germans in the other three zones, and, by contrast, it made a generally favorable impression. In addition to the KPD, official recognition was granted to the Social Democrats and to the Christian Democrats. Then the Soviets noted, apparently with some alarm, that this arrangement would split the workers' vote between the SPD and the Communists and tend to bring the rest of the population together in the CDU. Accordingly, good Soviet Communist political liaison officers were sent scurrying around to help organize another "bourgeois" party, the Liberal Democrats.

The Communists, understandably, rushed to the job of reorganizing their party and enrolling members, old and new. The other parties' leaders hung back at first in uncertainty and suspicion; the Soviets had some trouble in finding enough men to take positions of responsibility in the new "antifascist" non-Communist parties.

Once the parties were organized, there was no great rush to hold elections. Rather they became instruments for educating the people for the New Order the Soviets were bent on setting up. Party programs had a remarkably similar ring. Communists didn't say anything about communism and Liberal Democrats didn't say much about free enterprise. They all came out against nazism, war criminals, and profiteers and for democracy, social reforms, and a lasting peace. In the day-to-day work of administration—in which all parties shared on a coalition basis—these fine generalities were in time reduced to a specific program of "bloc policies."

Throughout the zone in the early period of Occupation political activity was largely concentrated in the "Antifa Committees" (short for United Committee of Antifascist Parties). A Central Antifa, with originally twenty members, four from each party, served as a kind of unofficial zonal parliament. Other Antifa Committees operated at state, district, county, and local community levels. Within each such committee the Communists took the lead and usually had their way. They were in close and constant touch with the Soviet Military Administration and held its full support. Actually their proposals frequently came directly from the SMA, so representatives of the other parties knew it was foolish and might be dangerous to object.

"Bloc policy" decisions taken by the Central Antifa were passed down to all the other committees at lower levels and were in turn handed on as directives to the government administrative bodies concerned. After state parliaments were elected and began to function in 1947 the Antifa Committees took no back seat, but instead predetermined what issues the parliaments would consider and how they would vote. Whatever opposition crept up inside the Antifa was quietly smothered, and decisions were almost invariably unanimous. Public actions in the state legislative bodies thus became mere rubber-stamp formalities. The minister president of Saxony-Anhalt, Doctor Erhardt Heubner, a venerable Liberal Democrat, told a group of touring American correspondents once that issues were always talked out fully behind the closed doors of the Antifa, and that unanimous agreements were always reached.

This somewhat incredible *bloc politik* may not be democratic, but it has been cleverly effective in keeping up a fiction of democracy while drawing power into the hands of a totalitarian party on the make. Practically everything that was done toward pushing through the Soviet pattern in Eastern Germany was done with the lawful assent of the anti-Communist parties, whose representatives took part in every decision along the way. They simply found themselves caught up in a system they could not get away from, except by individual flight to the West, so again and again they went along.

After what happened to the Social Democrats in Eastern Germany it was not difficult to see why the two non-Marxist parties should decide to give in quietly. Back in the summer of 1945 certain leaders of the SPD publicly suggested that it might be a good thing to amalgamate with the Communists. After all they were both working-class parties, and they both knew that it was their mutual antagonism in the twenties and early thirties which made it possible for the common enemy, Hitler, to seize power. However, the Soviets frowned on this move as premature. They wanted first to re-establish a trusted simon-pure Communist corps before they started diluting their favored party with Social Democrats.

By the beginning of 1946 the situation had changed. The Soviets and their German Communists now wanted amalgamation; but the rank and file of the SPD did not. In the Western sectors of Berlin the Social Democrats took a vote on the proposal and overwhelmingly turned it down. In the Soviet Zone proper such a plebiscite was forbidden. But by a combination of threats and bribery the Soviets persuaded a bare majority of the executive committee of the East Zone SPD to order a union of its members with the Communists. A number of anti-merger Social Democrats were thrown into concentration camps; and that was that. Thus, in April 1946, was formed the *Sozialistische Einheitspartei Deutschlands*, better known as the SED. This has ever since been the biggest (in terms of card-holding members), strongest, best-financed, noisiest and, for a Westerner's money, most dangerous political party in postwar Germany.

The SED has claimed a membership of close to two millions, though like other Communist parties it expands and contracts with intermittent purges. Its position in Eastern Germany, however, is in no wise dependent upon its numbers. From the beginning it has taken on the role of the "state party." The Soviets backed it openly and ostentatiously. For example, when Marshal Sokolovsky wanted to make a declaration on subjects of major interest—like raising the food ration, releasing German prisoners of war, and promising to discontinue the unpopular dismantling of German industries—he would drag in mention of the SED: "Acting on a request from the Socialist Unity party, I hereby . . ." It was always a pretty corny act. But it always showed even the dumbest East German which party was able to spread a little butter on his bread.

Thanks to the political plums handed out to Communist party members in the beginning, and the forced merger with the more numerous Social Democrats, the SED was able quickly to get a firm grip on all organs of government throughout the zone. A large percentage of the key jobs and the routine administraion posts SED members hold down directly. In other cases, when a representative of another party is put out in front, a loyal SED man is the chief deputy. And, of course, through the *bloc politik* system of hammering out unanimous policy decisions, the SED can call the tune on all significant issues anyway.

So far as party organization and activities are concerned, there is no group in either East or West Germany which can touch it. Moreover, in the familiar totalitarian pattern the SED has set out to organize and run every mass element—farmers, youth, women, industrial workers, intellectuals—and just about every phase of their assorted lives. Specific "non-political" bodies have been created to enable the Communists to do that job, and no competitor groups are allowed. Here is how the system works through the following satellite agencies.

1. The *Freie Deutsche Jugend*. The Soviets don't count too much on their ability to change the deep inner loyalties of Germans of middle age and beyond. But they have a glowing belief in what they can do with young people. Through the so-called Free German Youth they are well along toward bringing up the next generation in the way they want them to go.

The FDJ is the only youth organization allowed in the Soviet Zone. It is strictly, so the saying goes, "above party, above religion, and above class." Its program is designed to appeal to every interest: music, dramatics, dancing, hiking, football, and self-improvement courses in shorthand. There is also more and more opportunity for parading in uniforms and singing marching songs. And along the way the members get generous doses of political education, though of course on an "above-party" basis.

Robert Menzel, a middle-aged Communist serving as state youth leader in the provincial capital of Halle, once explained this phase of the program to a small group of Western visitors. "Our most important objective in the FDJ," he said, "is to lead the youth away from fascism and militarism, to help them understand true democracy, and to give them an organized means to fight against the imperialist forces which want to split Germany and provoke a new war."

"Imperialist forces," as every East Zone schoolboy knows, refers to the United States and other Western powers, but one of Menzel's listeners asked him to define the democracy he was preaching to the East German youth. "It means," he replied promptly, "a system from which monopoly capitalists and big landlords have been eliminated and in which the people's will is law."

Both the Russians and the East German Communists are sensitive about certain obvious similarities between the new *Freie Deutsche Jugend* and the old *Hitler Jugend*. German young people who have been in both say they are practically the same except for the color of the shirts and the color of the political propaganda. Increasingly, veteran leaders of the HJ have found use for their talents in the FDJ, though old-line Communists still hold the controlling hand. And there have been growing evidences of a shift toward quasi-military activities.

The *Freie Deutsche Jugend,* as the principal instrument for spreading SED influence among boys and girls from fourteen to twenty-five, is one of the most important arms of the party. Draped in the robes of nonpartisanship, and possessing a monopoly in the youth field, the FDJ can do its propaganda work in ways the remnant of opposition left in Eastern Germany find it extremely difficult to counteract. It would be unwise for Westerners to play down the long-range effectiveness of such a high-powered youth movement. The Russians know that most Germans hate the Soviet Union and the communism it represents. But they think they know that given time and a free hand they can turn out a new German generation pretty much in their own image. Meanwhile, in the day-to-day political struggle it is quite an advantage for the

SED to have its line "spontaneously" supported by the "non-political" FDJ speaking in the name of all the millions of Soviet Zone youth. Phony? But just the same, a symbol of present and future power.

2. The *Freier Deutscher Gewerkschaftsbund*. This so-called Free German Trade Union Federation is supposed to be the strongest organized association in Eastern Germany. As a labor union it is a shabby fraud. It does not engage in collective bargaining in the Western sense, to win improvements in wages and working conditions for its members. It does not have the right to strike. Its chief function is to educate the workers on the wisdom of the Communist party line, to beat down opposition to the speed-up and the stretch-out in socialized enterprises, and to help soften up the remaining privately owned businesses for collectivization. These duties it carries through with admirable efficiency.

The leaders of the FDGB are mostly veteran Communists. The vast bulk of the membership has lined up behind the Communist-run SED. The chief power in its administration is Moscow-trained Walter Ulbricht, behind-the-scenes strong man of the whole Soviet Zone regime.

As a propaganda agency the Free German Trade Union Federation drums away continuously on all the themes sacred to the SED: damnation of the Marshall Plan, the Western European Union, and the North Atlantic Pact; praise for socialism and the Soviet Union; support for a strong, centralized, united Germany after the East Zone model; scorn for the "quislings" who participate in the West German government at Bonn. Putting out this line day after day in union papers and pamphlets, explaining and elaborating it in factory meetings, spelling it out in wall posters and street-banner slogans, the FDGB must inevitably have a considerable impact on the minds of simple men and women who get no chance to hear any other story about the world around them.

Also, the discipline is firm, and morale, despite the hard life, has held up better than might have seemed possible. As a highly placed former East Zone official who fled to the West once explained it, "If you've got unity of control from the top organ of government, down through various departments and levels of administration clear to the miner working against the coal face, and you can make most of the men involved think they are part of a powerful team, you'll get results—at least so long as that illusion of solidarity lasts."

It is to create and maintain that "illusion of solidarity," to make the little man think he really is an important unit in the great monolithic structure of the East German state, and to enlist his active support for its grandiose plans, that the FDGB has a reason for existence. And, incidentally, the trade unions—as is true in other iron-curtain areas—are the chief source of manpower for the "spontaneous demonstrations" organized periodically to show the people how strongly entrenched the regime really is.

Moreover, on a purely technical level, the FDGB, as one of the mass organizations "above politics," frequently gets official representation on various governmental bodies. It now has thirty of its own delegates sitting in the parliamentary East German People's Chamber. Since the right people are naturally picked for such seats, the result is that the SED is thus able to enlarge its voting majority very neatly—and very innocently.

3. The *Kulturbund*. The conquest of the intellectuals for communism is a top goal of the party in any country. It is particularly noticeable in Eastern Germany. From the beginning of the Occupation the Soviets have showered special attention upon writers, professors, musicians, scientists, actors, and, of course, that always Russian-favored elite, the ballet dancers. Such individuals were assigned the highest "heavy worker" food-ration cards. They were given priority

in getting apartments and clothing. For a long time they kept a considerable degree of freedom; only slowly was Communist pressure to be detected.

Yet from the start a careful effort was made to pull them together into a single, easily controlled and manipulated organization, the *Kulturbund*. This body serves a double purpose: of educating and converting the non-Communist intellectuals and of keeping watch over, criticizing, and "correcting" those who might go astray in their thinking and professional performance.

Strictly "nonpartisan," it is strictly geared to a propaganda line indistinguishable from that of the SED. Members of the SED control the *Kulturbund* and can in turn be counted on for articulate support whenever the party calls. Ten members of the organization sit as special delegates in the East Zone parliament.

4. The *Frauenbund*. The women outnumber the men by a substantial margin in postwar Germany. But even if this were not true, a vigorous political movement, totalitarian or not, would undertake to organize and influence them—as women. In the Eastern Zone the chosen instrument is a thing called the Democratic Women's Union of Germany.

This *Frauenbund* does the usual things: gets out bulletins of interest to women, sponsors lectures, public discussions, and assorted welfare projects, and adopts resolutions. It particularly undertakes to give the timid German women a political education—"above the level of party or class". It agitates for the fullest civic and economic rights for women.

One of the least successful of the so-called mass organizations, the *Frauenbund* had enrolled only about 200,000 members in its first four years. As with the other groups, its policies and controlling personnel are drawn from the SED and it is assigned ten seats in the zonal parliament. Actually the SED can make out a pretty good case for itself as the champion of women. Almost 200 women have been named *burgermeisters* in the East Zone, more than 500 women are members of state legislature, and approximately 21,000 women serve on municipal councils. Among the total 330 members of the first People's Chamber, chosen in 1949, there were 45 women, of whom 12 took their seats with the official SED delegation of 90. A spokesman for the party claims that of all women holding elective posts in Eastern Germany, 80 per cent were put there by the SED.

5. *Bauernhilfe*. The Farmers' Mutual Aid Association (VdGB) is the instrument for the first cautious moves toward applying the Soviet pattern of collectivized agriculture on the people and land once under Junker control. Through its 11,000 local units it is primarily concerned with assigning machinery from the various co-operative tractor stations to individual farmers and with the marketing of produce.

Much of the initial support for the VdGB came, naturally, from once landless rural workers who benefited from the land-distribution scheme. These included not only local farm hands but also peasants who had been driven out of the territories now absorbed by the Soviet Union and Poland. Through this association the SED has labored hard and well to gain a foothold in rural communities, where traditionally Communist ideas have not heretofore had much chance.

All in all, the satellite "mass organizations" in Eastern Germany have proved to be rather effective devices for maintaining SED control and spreading slowly the yeast of Communist ideas. Their purposes seem quite laudable. They do many good and useful services for their members and for the community. They are communism's sugar-coated pills, especially prescribed for the non-Communist masses.

Definitely on the comic side are two satellite political parties. One calls itself the Democratic Farmers party of Germany, the other the National Democratic party. Both profess to speak for non-Communists. Both were got up in 1948 to provide a home for assorted partyless Germans who couldn't be pulled directly into the SED. The Farmers party is headed by Ernest Goldenbaum, a veteran communist who lived for many years in Russia and was brought back to Germany by the Red Army. A pre-Hitler Communist deputy in the Prussian *Landtag,* he withdrew from the SED on the party's orders and is now spokesman for the non-Communist farmers! Minister of Agriculture and Forestry in the East German cabinet is his new official title and party reward.

The National Democratic party is supposed to be a kind of middle-class, nationalist outfit. It seems to pride itself on being called the "party of the little Nazis," for whose forgiveness it constantly pleads. Former National Socialists who have seen the error of their ways should be restored to full rights and good standing—that has long been its chief slogan. Legally that campaign has been won, for the East German government has now come out for a policy of hearty collaboration with all noncriminal elements "willing to join the fight against the Western imperialists and for a strong unified Germany."

The mastermind and national chairman of the party of the little Nazis is no old Nazi, but an old Communist! He is Doctor Lothar Bolz, a bespectacled, scholarly gentleman who once practiced law in Breslau. One of the many Communists who fled to Russia in 1933, he was for several years a teacher of German language and history at Novosibirsk. Later he served as political instructor in German prisoner-of-war camps in the Soviet Union and on the staff of the Free Germany Committee which the Russians organized around Field Marshal Friedrich von Paulus, the defeated Stalingrad commander.

To make sure that the Democratic Farmers party and the National Democratic party should stand forth for the ends of the SED, a number of trusted Communists were infiltrated into them at various levels. To the leaders of the SED all this is a very serious business. Here is the way a highly placed German Communist once explained it:

"We know," he said, "that there is a considerable amount of opposition to the SED and our program among the farmers and in middle-class, ex-military, and ex-Nazi circles. Left to themselves these people may in time organize into a dangerous opposition. We cannot allow that to happen. So what do we do? We send out competent, trustworthy members of our own party to organize these people into new parties. That gives them a kind of outlet for their criticism, but it can be controlled. And it gives us a chance to get the proper viewpoint across to thousands of people we could never reach directly through the SED."

On the surface practically all organized groups in Eastern Germany have by now pledged allegiance to the "proper viewpoint," and have given in to a social and political program which has made over drastically the whole life of Eastern Germany. But even yet that program is only partially finished—and only partially disclosed.

Since the Soviets believe the economic pattern is basic to everything else, they undertook first of all to destroy the strongholds of private property in town and country. Their earliest great reform in Germany called for redistribution of the land. That began in the late summer of 1945. The second was the socialization of industry, which did not begin until June 1946, and which proceeded by fits and starts so that after three years it was only about half completed. These policies, though done in somewhat high-handed fashion, are the Soviets' proudest achievements in Germany. This, they say, is "real democracy" as contrasted with "formal" or voting democracy.

On September 3, 1945, the German provisional administration of the province of Saxony, on Soviet orders, decreed the first land-reform law. In quick succession similar decrees were put out in the other four provinces of the zone. All called for taking over all big estates owned by Junkers and war criminals and subdividing them into small plots of from 12 to 20 acres. Within the first two years of this *Bodenreform* 7,200,000 acres were handed out among about 470,000 families. Of these, 120,000 were previously landless farm workers; 105,000 were small farmers who were considered entitled to more land, and more than 80,000 were refugees from the former German provinces in the East.

The SED has rightly claimed full credit for the land-reform program. Whether all the tales of SED discrimination and favoritism in the original distribution are completely true or not, the election returns show that the greatest gains for the extreme Left have been made in rural communities among people who have profited by land reform.

An enormous amount of publicity at first credited the new small-holder system with drastically raising food supplies in the Soviet Zone. Actually it seems not to have accomplished any such thing. The "new farmers," as they're called, naturally took more interest in raising their own vegetables, potatoes, and pigs than in filling quotas for wheat, rye, and sugar beets to be handed over to government food collectors.

It is widely suggested among both Communist and non-Communist Germans that eventually they must go back to big-scale farming for most efficient production. The SED line has been that through co-operatives and tractor stations, and energetic educational efforts by the Farmers' Mutual Aid Association, the benefits of large-unit farming can be regained. Opponents predict, however, that these are only halfway steps on the road to putting over Soviet-style collectivization. In countries farther east the small-holder reforms have indeed turned out to be mere preludes to experiments of turning little farms into big collectives. And there have been similar straws in the East German wind. In the summer of 1949 various land holdings of the provinces, counties, and individual communities were thrown together into the Union of People's Estates, said to be intended as a kind of administrative body over "co-operative" farms.

The socialization of industry in the Soviet Zone has likewise been a pretty hazy business. Contrary to expectations, the Russians at first encouraged the freest kind of free enterprise. The old rigid Nazi controls on prices and the allocation of supplies were tossed on the rubble heap. The occupying forces were primarily concerned with booty and reparations. Disregarding that small matter, producers were told simply to produce. Scarce materials were worked up as rapidly as possible into the goods which would bring the biggest and quickest returns. It is estimated that in the fall of 1945 enough liqueur glasses and ornamental ironware were turned out to last Germany for three hundred years.

This rampant capitalism was, however, finally brought under control as the Soviets worked out their scheme for economic planning. Then, on June 30, 1946, the die was cast for socialism. Not in a clear-cut way or, theoretically, on a big scale. Still, that was the beginning.

The citizens of the province of Saxony, supposedly the most leftist in the zone, were asked to vote in one of those simple *Ja* or *Nein* elections. The proposition went something like this: "Do you agree that enterprises belonging to Nazi activists and war criminals should become people's property?" There was a good deal of grumbling about the vagueness of the question. Who falls into these classes? And who decides? But the *Ja*'s clearly won. Even a lot of those who had doubts figured this was the best thing to do with concerns which had been run by the old Hitler gang.

The "people's decision" in Saxony was held to be good

enough for all of Eastern Germany. So, by decree, practically all the big business firms in the zone not already directly in Soviet hands were turned over to the states, the counties, or the local communities as socialized property. In some cases factories were given to the workers in the name of the trade-union. And there were also a few co-operatives which got in on this reshuffle of ownership.

Since the original "people's properties" were set up in 1946, East German socialism has crept ahead by piddling little slips and slides. Even so, the movement is getting along, and without ever any formal decision in favor of socialism as such. Anyone who could be classified as a "political offender" —and both the SED and the Soviet authorities were very broad-minded on this matter—had no trouble losing his property. The beauty of the arrangement was that if it wasn't discovered that a manufacturer was a "political offender" one year, he always had a chance to get on the list the next year. Moreover, it turned out that there was a very useful law left over from the Hitler time, a law which authorized the "requisitioning" of any property that might be considered necessary for public use. In addition, the Central Economic Commission—top governmental organ in the zone before the East German state was proclaimed—passed an Economic Punishment Law providing for confiscation of firms that belonged to persons guilty of "economic sabotage." A special commission attached to the Ministry of Economics in each state was authorized to deal with such matters, and there was no appeal from its decision. "Economic sabotage" in the Soviet-controlled world covers, of course, just about everything from stealing the cash box to being late for work.

Thus the legal basis was clearly created for the step-by-step extension of socialism as far as anybody could want to go. In the beginning these "people's properties" were assigned to state and local governments. Later most of them were handed over to central control under the Berlin government. By the fall of 1949 it was estimated that industrial production in the Soviet Zone, by value, was divided as follows: "people's properties," 42 per cent; co-ops and unions, 8 per cent; Soviet corporations (A.G.'s), 25 per cent; private business, 25 per cent.

The German socialized "people's properties" were dominant in mining, metallurgy, and textiles. Soviet A.G.'s had top position in chemicals and were strong in metallurgy, machinery, mining, and electricity production. Free enterprise was strongest in the consumer-goods field, about half the food industry was still in private hands, and the same was true of building supplies, shoes, and textiles.

Even where private enterprise still had a substantial foothold, however, most of the individual firms were small ones, rarely employing as many as a hundred workers. And there could be little doubt that their place in the East German economy was neither secure nor permanent. From the beginning of the Occupation the Soviets showed that they were in no great hurry, that they did not intend to produce a sudden revolution on the Bolshevik model. But they also showed that a revolution was exactly what they were aiming for.

By destroying the large-landowning class and by eliminating capitalist control of industry, the Soviets believed they had cleared the way for the inevitable growth of their kind of socialism and "democracy." In Eastern Germany, as everywhere else, they have seen history "inevitably" working on their side. But, of course, it is the great mission of the Soviet Union to help history out in the clinches.

The Communists have great faith in their ability to shape the history of tomorrow through far-flung educational activities today. In Eastern Germany the Soviets made sure from the outset that the schools and universities should be under trusted Communist control. At first they did not interfere with most fields of academic specialization. They let the theologians, the musicians, the physicists go their own way, wooing them with extra food rations and special privileges. The historians and the economists, of course, were put on the party line. Believing as they do that Marxism as interpreted by Lenin and Stalin is the one true scientific explanation of all social and economic problems, the Communists saw to it that textbooks, curriculum and classroom teaching were reshaped accordingly.

Incidentally, in the public school system the Soviets did a swift and impressive job of revising the textbooks to get rid of Nazi doctrines. From the numerous sample copies I have examined I judge that instructions must have been given to go easy on written pro-Communist propaganda. Only in the teachers' manuals which show how certain phases of history and current affairs are to be dealt with do you get a clear-cut view of how the propagation of the Marxist line has been made a cardinal duty of the East German schools. In the high schools and universities compulsory courses in current events make sure that every student is indoctrinated in that narrow view of the world expounded as "scientific truth" by every Communist organ from Moscow Radio to the *Daily Worker*.

Of two education reforms the Soviets are particularly proud. In the public schools they abolished the double-track system under which traditionally nearly 90 per cent of the German children are shunted into trades training after the age of 10. And in admitting students to the universities they set up special "cram" schools which undertook to prepare the children of workers and farmers to pass university entrance exams despite their limited educational background. Correspondingly, they make it extremely difficult for the children of the upper social classes to get into the universities except with some special political endorsement.

As with the young people, the East German regime has undertaken to remold the thinking of the adult masses as well. The SED runs almost countless party schools throughout the zone, to which the other parties are often invited to send pupils! The radio, the press, the theater, and the movies have all been turned into organs of a monotonous political propaganda line. The newspapers get their news from Tass, the official Soviet agency, and from a Communist-run German news bureau.

It is not difficult to see how an ardent East German Communist can convince himself that all people subjected to this intensive "education" will be persuaded. But at the same time German Communists are not allowed to take their fore-ordained triumph too much for granted. The weapons of control have to be good and strong, and the will to use them has to be unflinching. Those who run Russia's super-satellite can be neither cowards nor sentimentalists. To protect the system and the creeping revolution, both to guarantee the material "take" of the Soviet Union and to push ahead the fight to win the German people, it was necessary to install the machinery of the police state. In Berlin and Eastern Germany the outside observer had a remarkably good chance to watch the gears of that machinery go around.

Once in the lovely old city of Weimar a group of American correspondents spent a pleasant three days as guests of the Soviet Occupation staff. Every day we tried to break away from the banquet and official interview routine and have a look around. One of the places we wanted to see was the Buchenwald concentration camp, a few kilometers beyond the edge of town. Our hosts promised to arrange a visit, but every morning and every afternoon there was some fresh excuse why it wasn't convenient just then. On the last day the Soviet commanding general sent word that Buchenwald was now a "military installation and would be of no interest whatever to the American journalists."

Shaking off our escorts for a moment, I asked a waiter about the camp. "Same as before," he whispered in my ear. "Just the other night a friend of mine, a Social Democrat, escaped from there and as he passed through going toward the American Zone he said . . ." The waiter suddenly checked himself, picked up my empty plate, and walked away without another word.

Going through the nearby Jena Zeiss works on a conducted tour, I fell into step with a German engineer and put the same question to him. He paled quickly and gave me a frigid reply: "That is none of my business. I know nothing about the place and have no desire to find out."

By now the story of how the Soviets used Nazi concentration camps to put political opponents out of the way is well documented. Some of the people who were locked up for being anti-Nazi were put behind the same barbed wire for being anti-Communist.

How many thousands of political prisoners have been held in such East German camps as Buchenwald and Sachsenhausen-Oranienburg the world will probably never know. Moreover, it has been difficult to get a convincingly objective account of how these camps were run. Western intelligence officers have cross-checked the testimony of enough ex-inmates, however, to establish the fact that concentration camps run by Soviet officers and German Communists, though an improvement over the extermination camps operated by the Nazis, are still a revolting spectacle of barbarism in the twentieth century. The arbitrary way in which secret police agents picked up their victims without warrant and threw them into these camps without formal charges or trial, the fiendish interrogations and occasional beatings, the near-starvation diet—these grim and dreary signs of the totalitarian police state the Soviet Zone administration stamped upon itself from the beginning.

Nevertheless, it is only fair to point out that the extermination ovens were not started up again, and that treatment of prisoners apparently improved after the first three years. Bishop Otto Dibelius, head of the Protestant Evangelical Church in Eastern Germany and no friend of communism, was allowed to conduct services in the camps at Christmastime, 1949, and came back to say that the inmates were living under much better conditions than he had supposed. Erich Gniffke, once a member of the SED secretariat, who fled to the West in early 1949, has said that West German accounts of the Soviet Zone concentration camps have been seriously exaggerated. But, however cautiously they may be described, they are still an evil symbol.

To quote Gniffke further, it is not actual, personally experienced terror but the fear of possible terror which keeps people in line in Eastern Germany. An engineer is sometimes waked in the middle of the night and told that he has an hour to pack his bags for a trip to Russia. A university student walking along the streets of Berlin is sometimes crowded into a taxi and disappears into the darkness. A civil servant sometimes goes off for a routine bureaucrats' conference and never comes back. Out of the total 18,400,000 people subject to the East German government these things happen to only a few thousand. But they happen. Word gets around. A "token terror" is all you need. Particularly since everybody knows he is surrounded by spies, anyway.

Using, among other things, Hitler's system of block and apartment-house "leaders" to keep watch over all the neighbors, the Soviet MVD and the local German police combined to create a vast network of informers and spies in every segment of the population, in every factory, school, and office. A favorite way of recruiting such agents was to arrest a person on some trumped-up charge or suspicion, hold him in jail a few days, question him extensively, then offer him freedom and protection if he would turn spy. It was a system that usually worked. Outside that police system, though cooperating, the SED has set up a widespread "information service" which collects detailed private intelligence on everyone who comes under its scrutiny and on their personal beliefs.

Along with the many-faced spy organization of East Germany go a lot of other things frowned on in Western countries: arbitrary arrest, indefinite imprisonment without trial, guilt-by-association reprisals against family and friends. Furthermore, court proceedings have been increasingly brought into line with "positive" political ideas, meaning the interests of the SED. As in Russia and the Eastern European states, lay judges are being used more and more. It is emphasized that their decisions should conform not merely to "static law" but also to the "people's will." When the Supreme Administrative Court of Thuringia seemed at one time too much interested in protecting the rights of individuals, it came under violent attack from the SED, which demanded that it be "reorganized in the public interest."

On the other hand the East German courts have been used at times to protect people who hold the right political views. For example, in Cottbus a Communist functionary named Donath and the local secretary of the criminal police, one Winkler, beat to death a prisoner accused of swindling. Shortly before the murderers were to stand trial, MVD officers sent for the judge and the prosecutor and dictated the charge and the sentence. Donath, who had served as county secretary of the Communist party in the pre-SED days, was acquitted. Winkler got off with three months for assault and battery.

Behind the spies, the secret police, and the courts now looms an increasingly impressive weapon of control, the shadow army which has been slowly formed out of picked units of the so-called *Volkspolizei* (people's police). With officers drawn from top-ranking veterans of Hitler's *Wehrmacht,* it has a significance far beyond the borders of the East Zone.

Organized into "ready squads" of 250 men, it has been armed with machine guns and artillery, and some units have been reported training with tanks. On ceremonial public occasions these "ready squads" have been shown off briefly, to considerable public acclaim. They march as snappily as any German soldiers ever did and have mastered the modified goose step favored by the Red Army.

How large this Black *Wehrmacht* is intended to become is a question of great interest to Germans and the Western Allies alike. Persistent reports in late 1949 indicated that it was expected to reach an effective strength of close to 100,000 by the end of 1950, backed by another 250,000 regular policemen.

Such a force obviously counts for something more than a means of keeping down local disorders. It is a threat to the West German state and a pawn in the East-West struggle for all of Germany.

In that struggle the Soviets and their East German coreligionists are not betting only on physical might, any more than they are counting solely on converting the Germans to communism. Long ago they concluded that their best chance for a quick victory lay in promoting what might be called national bolshevism. They would not give up the ultimate goal of a Communist Germany, but they would disguise it in such heavy nationalist trimmings that it would hardly be recognizable. Vigorously they would hammer away on themes traditionally dear to all Germans: national unity, a strong central government, firm control from the top down, solidarity of the German *Volk*. The East German regime took the lead in embracing ex-Nazis, professional soldiers, and even Junker ex-landlords and industrialists—if they were willing to join in the holy crusade for "national unity." All of them were told over and over again the story of how the long-range interests of Germany intertwined with those of the Soviet Union.

Georg Dertinger, first foreign minister of the new "German Democratic Republic," gave me a thorough briefing on this subject back in the days when he was a minor official of the Christian Democratic party and before he got so chummy with the Russians. As he explained it, then with some amusement, the Soviet courtship line went something like this: "Germany has in modern times produced only one truly great statesman. That was Bismarck. Bismarck understood that the future security and prosperity of Germany lay in an alliance with Russia and the development of the closest trade relations between the two countries. But Kaiser Wilhelm II was a fool who listened to stupid advisers and abandoned Bismarck's wise policies. So, came World War I and bitter defeat for Germany.

"In the 1920's among the fresh crop of German leaders were men who understood the genius of the *Bismarckpolitik,* who sought understanding with the new Soviet Union. During that time the two countries drew close together, as symbolized by the Rapallo Accord. We Russians helped to train a German army when the evil restrictions of Versailles hampered German military revival. Moreover, we were a good market for German machinery and manufactured goods. In turn we supplied Germany with Soviet grain and fodder. We were on the way to building a fine partnership. And then came that madman Hitler. Despite the treaty of nonaggression with Stalin, he attacked the mighty Soviet Union and was destroyed. In the process he destroyed Germany. Surely the German people will not make this same mistake a third time.

"The comradeship of the Germans and the Russians is logical and inevitable. We have the great undeveloped areas where German industries can find a market for all they can produce. We can offer you food and raw material in abundance. What can the Western Allies offer you? Nothing. They fear German competition and they will do all they can to strangle the German economy.

"Moreover, our people have a great deal in common. We are realists. We both understand political and military power. As military allies, controlling the greatest land mass in the world, we are invincible. Think it over."

There is much to what the Russians say. That is what bothers the Western Allies as the uneasy postwar years slip by. They cannot allow the Soviet Union to dominate all of Germany, for they know that would lead easily and quickly to Soviet dominance of all of Europe. They, like the Russians, are committed to the goal of a unified, democratic Germany. But East and West are talking about two entirely different Germanys.

Is there any possibility that the two halves of Germany which evolved out of defeat and occupation can ever be brought together? The answer is clearly yes. But the job can't be done until either the East or the West gives up its ideas about what kind of unified, democratic Germany it can live with. The Zone of Silence beyond the Elbe is no model for a future Germany that any Western democrat is likely to accept. But as the Soviet Union's super-satellite, it can be improved on only by expansion—westward to the Rhine.

Biographical Notes

JOHN ANSPACHER. John M. Anspacher was born in New York somewhat over thirty years ago, and began newspaper work in 1930 when he was a regular contributor to his father's syndicated feature for teen-agers. He graduated from Columbia University in due time and prior to his Army service, which began in 1941, he worked for the National Broadcasting, Columbia Broadcasting, and Mutual Broadcasting companies, and also for the metropolitan dailies in New York, including the *Times*, the *World-Telegram*, and the *Herald-Tribune*. In 1942 he participated as a GI in the invasion of North Africa, was commissioned in the field in 1943, and finished out the war as a psychological warfare officer with the Seventh Army. After a year with U. S. Military Government, during which he assisted in the establishment of a free and democratic press for Germany, he served as public relations man for the war crimes trials at Nuremberg, under both Justice Jackson and General Taylor. He spent two years with United Press in Frankfurt, serving concurrently as news editor and reporter.

JUDY BARDEN. Judy Barden, one-time correspondent for the New York *Sun* and currently for the North American Newspaper Alliance, has held many jobs, from mannequin and free-lance fiction writer to bank clerk. She was born in London in 1911 and was educated in England. In 1941 she joined the *Sun* bureau in England, landing in France on Bastille Day with the first bunch of hand-picked WAACs. Subsequently she joined the Seventh Army and accompanied them through Munich, Nuremberg, Schweinfurt, Salzburg, and Berchtesgaden. At the end of the war she was with the Third Army, and went to Berlin in October, 1945. Since then she has been on the staff of the *Sun*, has covered assignments in Czechoslovakia, Finland, Sweden, Denmark, the Lowlands,

Poland, and France, being on hand in the spring and fall for the Paris fashion openings. In October, 1948, she married David M. Nichol, Chicago *Daily News* correspondent and fellow contributor to this volume.

LANDRUM BOLLING. "Wanderlust, a troublesome curiosity about international affairs, a concern over Germany and assorted other troubles I trace back to Savannah, Georgia, of the year 1918. I was five and much impressed by soldiers and sailors who occasionally marched through the streets, by the war freighters which periodically slid down the ways at the local shipyard amid great rejoicing, and by the hanging of the Kaiser in effigy from a lamp post on Broughton Street. In the *Evening Press* I did my first journalistic dabbling, official reporter for the first grade from Anderson Street school. They gave me a byline, and that did it.

"Somewhat earlier, through no particular foresight of my own, I managed to get born on November 13, 1913, in the small village of Parksville, Tennessee. With a construction engineer father we wandered back and forth across the South while I learned geography firsthand and gained an appetite for still ever more travel.

"We stayed in one place long enough for me to acquire an A.B. at the University of Tennessee (class of '33). Then, at the age of nineteen, with my file of the U-T student newspaper, which I had edited, under my arm, I was ready to crash the world of the grown-up press. I got some beautiful promises, but no job. Instead I went to work for the infant Tennessee Valley Authority writing speeches, news stories, 'progress reports,' and finally wangled a congenial berth as combination housing manager of the model town of Norris, Tennessee, and editor of the weekly newspaper.

"Eventually I married the boss' daughter and had to resign. And so in the middle of Hitler's peace years I came to Europe for some months of looking around and writing. Germany was even then the cheapest and most interesting place for the student of world politics to do some first-hand cramming.

"But I wasn't ready to have a real fling at foreign correspondence, or any other kind of journalism, I decided, and in time settled down for a spell of graduate study in political science at the University of Chicago (A.M., 1938). Afterwards came a total of about five years of college teaching—comparative government, international relations and such things—at Brown University, Beloit College and Earlham College. All along the way I kept flirting with the newspaper trade, and at one very happy, over-worked period, held down practically two full-time jobs: at the Beloit (Wis.) *Daily News* and at the local college.

"In 1944 I went to the Mediterranean Theater as war correspondent for a group of Wisconsin newspapers, soon shifting to Overseas News Agency, for which I have worked ever since. ONA assignments have sent me to spend three months with Tito's partisans, meaning chiefly in the Moskva Hotel in Belgrade, to interview Rakosi in Hungary, Benes in Czechoslovakia, and to wander at length through assorted Iron Curtain countries.

"In early 1946 I was established in Berlin as chief of ONA's Central European office. Most of the following two years were spent in Germany, with lengthy junkets through the Soviet and Western zones and through other sections of Central Europe. At present my job is that of editor of ONA in New York."

JOSEPH E. EVANS. Most newspaper men start their careers in a newsroom, usually in the capacity of copy boy. Joe Evans is one of those rare individuals who started at the top and has remained there. His first newspaper job was as Berlin correspondent for the *Wall Street Journal,* an appointment which he received as the result of a combination of circumstances and coincidences. The Paris Bureau Chief for the *Wall Street Journal* happened to be in the Headquarters Building of U. S. Military Government on a particular afternoon in March, 1946. He needed someone to cover Germany for the *Journal.* Joe Evans had just received his honorable discharge from the Army and was looking for a job with a temporary appointment as a public relations officer with U. S. Military Government in Berlin. The two met and the result was that Joe Evans fell into a job which is the dream of newsmen. He has since graduated to editorial writer, chief editorial writer, special writer on international affairs, and is at present foreign editor for the *Wall Street Journal,* with one of the best-known and most widely respected bylines in the business.

Born on February 5, 1919, in Dubuque, Iowa, Evans attended the University of Southern California at Los Angeles and the State University of Iowa, receiving his Bachelor's Degree in 1939. After teaching English Literature there for two years, concurrently taking an M.A., which was awarded him in 1941, Evans began working toward his Ph.D.

Between 1942 and 1945, he was with public relations, U. S. Army Air Forces. During his tour of duty in Germany as *Wall Street Journal* correspondent, his beat included Central Europe and those countries of Eastern Europe which were accessible to U. S. correspondents. Evans is married to a former member of the Czechoslovakian diplomatic service. Mr. and Mrs. Evans have a son who was born in February, 1950.

ROBERT HAEGER. You cannot pick up a newspaper which subscribes to the United Press without seeing the byline of Robert Haeger, thirty-year-old trouble shooter who has been covering his European news beat since his discharge from the Army in November, 1945.

Bob Haeger is one of the youngest and best known of the press fraternity now covering the Bonn-Frankfurt news axis. Born on August 22, 1920, in what he describes as "super-German Milwaukee," Haeger says that he "wasted" his first year at the University of Wisconsin trying to become a civil engineer. The time wasn't completely wasted, however, for it was on this campus that he met his wife-to-be. Helen Haeger, who is five feet tall as compared with Bob's six feet two inches, was studying journalism and, again in Bob's words, she "pulled him along to graduation," class of 1942. He spent most of his senior year in Madison, covering legislative and other activities for the United Press.

Immediately upon graduation, Bob received "greetings from the President" and he spent the rest of the war as a special agent for the counter-intelligence corps, "a hush-hush outfit that was supposed to catch enemy spies." For twenty months Bob worked in civilian clothes, for twenty more months he was in uniform doing intelligence work in England as well as in France, Germany, and Austria, but he caught no spies.

Back with the United Press in Berlin and Frankfurt after his discharge, Haeger was also given spot-news assignments in Vienna and Paris. He has handled stories ranging from war criminals' trials to conferences on steel production. His direct manner and engaging personality have made him one of the best-liked men in the business. The most notable event in his life, he says, was the birth of the world's most beautiful redhead, Patricia Ann Haeger, on February 7, 1948, in Frankfurt.

RALPH HARWOOD. Ralph Harwood, a native of Indianapolis, Indiana, was born there thirty-three years ago, attended public schools and later the University of Indiana. Before entering the Army in 1942, he did public relations work in his home state. In 1943 he joined the staff of the *Stars and Stripes* in London and wrote its weekly supplement until October, 1945, covering all major combat stories from D-Day to the end of the war.

After returning to the States in November, 1945, Harwood came back to Germany the following spring for the Historical Division of the War Department, where he worked for fourteen months on the history of German military operations. In the summer of 1947 he joined the staff of *Weekend* magazine and continued with that organization after it became independent of the *Stars and Stripes*. He held a post for a time as an editor of the official U.S. paper for Austria, the *Vienna Courier*. He is now a free-lance writer.

MARGUERITE HIGGINS. Marguerite Higgins was born twenty-nine years ago in Hongkong, China, of a French mother and an Irish father who had met during World War I. Educated in France and California, she graduated cum laude in 1941 as the youngest in her class at the University of California. At the age of twenty, having received her M.A. from Columbia University, she joined the New York *Herald Tribune* staff, covering assignments ranging from the Hartford circus fire to the Clare Boothe Luce election. In 1944 she was sent overseas to cover the American Air Force Headquarters in Europe and later the deGaulle government. Before the end of the war she went to the front with the Third Division, saw the capture of Cologne, Frankfurt, and Berchtesgaden, and the liberation of Buchenwald and Dachau. In 1945 she received the New York Newspaper Women's foreign correspondents award as well as a citation from the Army. She has covered the Petain and Nuremberg trials and the Polish elections, and from 1947 to 1950 was in charge of the *Herald Tribune's* Berlin office. She is now Tokyo Bureau Chief for the *Herald Tribune*.

RUSSELL JONES. Russ Jones is best known to the Fourth Estate in Europe as one of the original founders of *Stars and Stripes,* which is still the principal medium of communication between the rest of the world and the G.I.'s who are stationed in various European countries.

Born on January 5, 1918 in Minneapolis, Minnesota, Russ was educated in the public schools there and later began his newspaper career on small-town dailies until 1938, at which time he joined the St. Paul *Dispatch* as a reporter and radio columnist.

In 1941 he enlisted in the Army, was assigned to the infantry and, when it was discovered that he could not only read but also write, he was assigned to help launch and edit *Stars and Stripes,* on which he served as a combat correspondent until 1945.

Jones worked for a year in the New York bureau of the Associated Press before returning to *Stripes* for duty in New York, Frankfurt, Berlin, Vienna, Munich, and Wiesbaden.

In 1948 he resigned to do free-lance work. He became part owner and associate editor of a magazine called *Now,* which enjoyed only a brief existence and then folded for lack of financial —but not want of moral—support. Russ Jones subsequently went to work for the UP London Bureau, where he is now stationed.

ERNEST LEISER. "Born February 26, 1921, in Philadelphia. Brought up in milltown of Gary, Indiana. Attended University of Chicago, edited student paper there. First newspaper job was as police reporter for the City News Bureau in Chicago, from which I went to the Chicago *Herald-American.* There held various jobs from reporter, through copyreading and caption-writing, to acting as picture editor. Thence into the Army, where after nine months in the infantry and a year in military intelligence, I joined *Stars and Stripes.* I was U.S. Ninth Army combat correspondent from the winter campaign until the end of hostilities (I sneaked into Berlin as one of the first American correspondents to reach the city—illegally, of course—while the Soviets were still fighting for it). Remained in Germany through the Potsdam conference, subsequently went back to the U.S., got out of the Army, and returned to the *Herald-American.* After six months, rejoined staff of *Stripes* as civilian, returning to Vienna to join two-man bureau there. Other staffer who came over with me was Caroline Camp, whom I met on *Stripes* in Paris during war. We were married in Vienna on arrival. After six months in Austria, returned to Germany in spring of 1947, where I have been based since. Left *Stripes* in summer, 1947, and have subsequently been working for Overseas News Agency. Been in Germany, except for such outside assignments as French general strike in winter of 1947, Prague coup in February, 1948, Italian elections, spring 1948, and a couple of swings through the Balkans. Nancy Monroe, newest addition, is eight months old. Contributor to *Collier's* and *Saturday Evening Post*.

ROBERT LEWISON. Robert Lewison is the nom de plume of the Central European correspondent of an American magazine of national circulation. He has been stationed in Germany since 1948 and previously worked as a correspondent for American newspapers and magazines in Washington, Moscow, and Eastern European countries, including Yugoslavia, Bulgaria, Romania, Hungary, and Austria. During the war, he was chief of psychological warfare in Burma for the Office of War Information, attached to the staff of General Joseph Stilwell. He also served in OWI posts in India, Australia, New Guinea, the Philippines, and Honolulu.

RICHARD LOWENTHAL. Forty-two-year-old "Rix" Lowenthal is a legend in the community of newspaper correspondents covering Germany. It is well known that when certain German political leaders come to Frankfurt, they drop in for a chat with Rix in his private quarters before venturing into the "Little Pentagon" which houses the Office of the U.S. High Commissioner and his staff. No one has ever been able to find out what the peripatetic German officials and Lowenthal say to each other, but reports have it that they come away from their séances better informed and perhaps better men than when they went.

Lowenthal came to Germany as correspondent for the largest news agency in the world, Reuters, which services newspapers throughout the British Empire and scores of other publications in North and South America, Europe, Asia, and Africa. Born in Berlin, Lowenthal studied economics and sociology at the universities of Berlin and Heidelberg, receiving his Ph.D. at the latter institution in 1931.

Rix was forced to leave Germany soon after Hitler came into power. He lived by his pen—in Prague, Paris, and London. He survived the Blitz in London, participated in a radio propaganda program directed at Germany, and in 1942 joined the Reuters News Agency, first as an analyst and monitor of German broadcasts, and subsequently as a staff writer specializing in German affairs.

After the war, Lowenthal worked as a labor specialist for Reuters, reporting on the British labor movement with particular emphasis upon its role as the Government party. Early in 1948 he returned to Germany as a correspondent for the London *Observer* with the special assignment of covering political and economic developments.

Rix's wife is a writer too, and acts as correspondent for the *Financial Times* of London. The couple enjoy an enviable reputation for their intimate knowledge of the complex issues of present-day Germany.

DENIS MARTIN. Denis Martin has been the chief correspondent in Germany of the London *Daily Herald* since the end of the war. His newspaper, the official journal of the British Labour Party, has a predominant interest in the political, social, and economic aspects of the German problem and Martin has written widely on these topics from Berlin and the Ruhr. Martin, who saw active service in the Middle East Command of the Royal Air Force, was released to become a war correspondent in 1943. He covered the Allied campaigns in North Africa and Northwest Europe and entered Germany with the British Second Army.

KATHLEEN McLAUGHLIN. A New York *Times* staff correspondent since 1935, Kathleen McLaughlin first broke into newsprint in her home town of Atchison, Kansas, where she worked for E. W. Howe's *Daily Globe,* once considered the best small-town newspaper in the U.S. While on vacation in Chicago, she joined the staff of the *Tribune,* covering assignments ranging from visits of European royalty to violent gang wars, until in 1933 she became women's editor. In 1935 she went to New York, began work for the New York *Times,* and from October, 1941, to November, 1943, organized and directed its women's news department. Thereafter she was assigned to the *Times* Washington Bureau as a Capitol

Hill correspondent and in November, 1944, was accredited as a war correspondent.

As a result of the Battle of the Bulge, Miss McLaughlin arrived in England in late February, 1945, and reached France only one week before the German capitulation. There she saw Paris begin celebrating on May 7, flew to Brussels, and motored through the low countries, witnessing, along with the hysterical celebrations, the withdrawal of beaten German forces and the retribution visited on Dutch collaborators. From July, 1945, on, she covered various phases of the occupation from Munich, Frankfurt, Berlin, and from Nuremberg during the trials of Göring, et al. Beginning in January, 1949, she reported on the Ruhr and the Bonn constitutional assembly. Twice winner of the New York Newspaper Women's Club award for best coverage of general news, she holds an honorary Doctor of Laws degree from Mt. Saint Scholastica's College, Atchison, Kansas.

PETER DE MENDELSSOHN. Born in Munich, Germany, in 1908 and educated in Dresden and Berlin, Peter de Mendelssohn was correspondent in Germany for the London *Observer* in 1948 and 1949. After studying political science and modern languages at Berlin University, he worked as a junior editorial assistant on the *Berliner Tageblatt* and later for UP in Berlin and London, going later to Paris as a free-lance for German and foreign papers. In the fall of 1932 he returned to Germany, but left after the outbreak of the Hitler regime. After free-lancing in Paris, Vienna, Zurich, and Amsterdam, he settled in London and was from 1936 to 1938 the London correspondent for Czechoslovak newspapers.

Following a brief visit to the U.S. in 1938, he held the post of foreign editor from 1939 to 1943 and later was chief of the foreign department of the *Exchange Telegraph*. In 1941 he became a British subject, and as British deputy to the news and press branch, Psychological Warfare Division, he entered Germany in the spring of 1945. Until October, 1945, he was Press Control Officer of the U.K. Military Government in Berlin. His further positions include coverage of the Nuremberg trials for the London *Observer,* London *New Statesman,* and the New York *Nation* during the winter of 1945-46, and chief press advisor to the British Control Commission in Germany. He has published fiction, non-fiction, and numerous translations. His book, *Japan's*

Political Warfare, was used by the British Admiralty and War Office as a textbook for Military Government officers in the Far East.

LYFORD MOORE. The author of "The Man in the Goldfish Bowl" tells his own story:

"To begin with I was born. This happened in Portland, Oregon, in 1910. I then grew up in Detroit, which is situated in the lower Michigans. With this auspicious beginning, I proceeded rapidly to Ohio Wesleyan University, in the heart of the Bible belt of central Ohio. My professors all contended that I was one in a billion—destined for *le grand success.* I proved this immediately after college by going on to the Ford Motor Company, where I worked in the glass plant at stamping name-bugs on windshields, obviously a job calling for the best in intellectual prowess and training.

"During that long-lost star-struck period I fluctuated for several years between Detroit, New York, California, and Western or pre-war Europe, whittling away at short stories the while. I had the great good fortune of having enormous success, with the first story which I wrote being published, and thereafter was unable to break into print.

"After that I served time in the studios. Luxury at last! I wrote for Republic in a stable that was part of a set, and in ladies' dressing rooms, and in a motel. And I had a most weird job at Universal. Then I went to the state of Washington as continuity director for a couple of NBC (don't tell ABC) radio stations in Spokane.

"Somewhere in here I wrote a play called "Sleep it Off with Ann Corio" but without inner punctuation. This quickly soured me on play writing and its audiences as well. In time I found myself back on the scene of my early triumphs, pastoral old Detroit, now converted into the arsenal of democracy. Here everyone was busy breaking the neutrality laws. I found myself a stranger in my own street, so I got a job on the *Free Press* and learned to know all the other streets in town.

"When I looked up from my work bench after four years I found the war was on. I got a job with the OWI, presumably to come to Germany after the war and guide its press into the ways of democracy. Instead I was transferred into a film unit in London, then switched into Psychological Warfare Division of SHAEF, and found myself at Radio Luxembourg at the start of 1945. In the guise of a war correspondent for this American propaganda station, I entered Germany with Patton's Third Army and by the end of the war was in Prague, where I celebrated V-E Day aboard a Russian tank as a prisoner during their triumphal entry into town.

"I switched to Reuters (British News Agency) to go out and cover the end of the Pacific war, but the atom bomb blew me right back to Frankfurt, Germany, and I spent the next years there and in Berlin for Reuters. Last autumn I switched over to ABC (American Broadcasting Company) and am still with them."

DAVID M. NICHOL. Ever since his graduation from the University of Michigan in 1933, David M. Nichol has been doing newspaper work. Born on December 29, 1911, in Dundas, Ontario, he is now a U.S. citizen and got his first job on the staff of the Iron River (Michigan) *Reporter,* remaining until 1936, when he joined the staff of the Chicago *Daily News.* Since 1940 he has been a foreign correspondent for the *News,* with assignments initially in Berlin, and subsequently in London, the Middle East, and Moscow (1943-44). Since 1946, Nichol has been covering the Berlin story. He is married to Judy Barden, Berlin correspondent for the North American Newspaper Alliance.

JAMES PRESTON O'DONNELL. At present a roving correspondent for the *Saturday Evening Post,* living in Paris, James Preston O'Donnell was born in Baltimore, Maryland, in 1917. He attended public and private schools in Maryland and Massachusetts. In 1939 he received his A.B. in classics and literature from Harvard and was the same year a traveling fellow at the University of Jena, Germany. Following receipt of an M.A. in modern European history in 1940, he became a graduate fellow in the history department at Harvard, where he assisted a professor of German history. In 1941 he worked in the Washington Bureau of *Newsweek* magazine until he joined the Army as a private. Between 1941 and 1945 he participated in the liberation of France and the entry into Germany. He was a captain in 1945 when he separated from the Army and became chief of *Newsweek*'s Berlin Bureau, remaining there until 1948.

TERENCE PRITTIE. The son of Lord and Lady Dunalley, the Honourable Terence Cornelius Farmer Prittie has been the Berlin correspondent for the Manchester *Guardian* since October, 1946. Born in London, December 15, 1913, he attended the Stowe School and later Christ Church, Oxford, where he held an exhibition scholarship for modern history in 1936. During the war, where he served with the Rifle Brigade, he was mentioned in dispatches and also received the Medal of the British Empire. Later he joined the staff of the *Guardian*, serving both in the London office and as cricket correspondent before taking up his Berlin assignment. His publications include *South to Freedom, Mainly Middlesex, Lancashire Hot-Pot,* all published by Hutchinsons, London.

JACK RAYMOND. "I've been working for newspapers since the age of fifteen, starting as stringer and assignment reporter in sports in New York, working my way through police and court reporting and joining the New York *Times* in June, 1940, doing education assignments.

"I was in the Army for four years, two at home and two abroad with *Stars and Stripes.* I've covered baseball and football games, home building and bombing, murder and war crimes trials, public parliaments and secret meetings, barroom and front-line battles, big and little and in-between shots in the United States, North Africa, Sicily, Italy, France, Austria, and Germany.

"I am in the midst of satisfying my greatest ambition, to be a newspaper man. I met and married my wife within four months, the wedding taking place on the anniversary of my birthday, October 6, 1918. She joined me in my trip to Berlin from the United States, November, 1946, a month after the wedding. Our son David Alan was born in Frankfurt, April 30, 1949—and he crossed the ocean twice within the first seven months of his existence."

ARTHUR SETTEL. The editor of *This is Germany* has spent the past ten years in public relations work, most of that time with the government. But he considers himself primarily and always a newspaperman.

Art Settel was born in Brooklyn, New York, on November 26, 1911. He attended public schools in that treeless section of Brook-

Biographical Notes

lyn known as East New York, was graduated from Columbia University in 1932 and remained an extra year on a Sackett scholarship to do graduate work in English literature. He spent three years in Jerusalem as an editor and feature writer for a tabloid-size, English-language daily, *The Palestine Post,* writing articles for magazines and feature supplements in Great Britain and the United States. Later, in 1937, he left for Cairo, Egypt, to join the staff of *The Egyptian Mail* as managing editor. He resigned to spend full time as correspondent for the British United Press, with the entire Levant as his newsbeat. He contributed to the *Tatler,* the *Sphere, Toronto Star Weekly, Variety, Living Age, Current History and Forum,* New York *Herald Tribune* etc.

In 1942, Settel enlisted in the Army as a private. As soon as his literacy was discovered, he was assigned to the Public Relations Office of the Air Forces Technical Training Command in Miami Beach, Florida, where he edited a weekly called "Keep 'Em Flying" which was read by 500,000 more or less homesick GI's. He was sent to Officer Candidate's School, also in Miami, was commissioned a second lieutenant in February, '43, then assigned to Air Intelligence School in Harrisburg, Pa. Somebody heard about him in the Pentagon Building and soon he was off for Army Air Force Headquarters in Washington, where he sweated out the war as a "chairborne paragrapher," despite his protests and pleas to the contrary.

In August, 1945, Settel was finally given overseas duty and flew to Berlin where he was assigned to the Office of Military Government as Economic Information Officer. He remained with OGMUS until it was supplanted by the Office of the U.S. High Commissioner for Germany, and he is now Director of the Public Relations Division. He is the author of a number of brochures and special studies published, including *AAF in the Pacific, The Role of AAF in Strategic Warfare, Strategic Mission of the AAF in Europe, One Year of Potsdam,* etc.

THEODORE H. WHITE. Born in Boston in 1915, Teddy White's first practical break in the newspaper business came when he won a newsboy's scholarship at Harvard. There he concentrated on the study of the Far East, taking, among other courses, three years of Chinese. He graduated summa cum laude, arrived in China in 1939, and in the ensuing seven years, during most of which he was with the Chunking Bureau of *Time,* he traveled 200,000 miles through the Orient. During the war he covered the Indian uprisings of 1942, the Honan famine, flew with the Fourteenth Air Force and the Hump Command, saw the relief of Stilwell, the last battles of the Burma Road, and its reopening in 1945. He was present when the Japanese signed the surrender.

After the war, White resigned from the staff of *Time* and devoted himself to free-lance writing until 1948. His first book, *Thunder Out of China,* which he co-authored with Annalee Jacoby, was published in 1946. It was a selection of the Book-of-the-Month Club. His close relationship to the late General Stilwell led to the publication in 1948 of *The Stilwell Papers,* which he selected and edited. His articles have appeared in numerous publications.

Since 1948, he has been roving European correspondent for the Overseas News Agency.

J. EMLYN WILLIAMS. The most frequently-heard comment on the work of J. Emlyn Williams, chief Central European correspondent for the *Christian Science Monitor,* is that he knows more about the economic and political problems of Germany than the experts and specialists employed by the Occupying Powers.

And it is probably true. When Emlyn attends a press conference, his questions are like pointed darts and they often have the same effect. He has been known to trip up men who are on the inside looking out and who know their stuff. He keeps his sources strictly to himself and, unlike many of his colleagues, Emlyn reaches down to the grass-roots level for the background and color which are well-known characteristics of his dispatches to the *Monitor.*

Born on February 6, 1896, at Pontypridd, Glam., Great Britain, Williams received his education at the University of Wales, where he subsequently served as a "One Time University Fellow." He received his Ph.D. at Charles University in Prague and joined the staff of the *Christian Science Monitor* in 1926. For the next five years he was stationed in Vienna as the chief European correspondent for the *Monitor,* worked out of Germany from 1932 to August, 1939, returning to London in September to take up his duties as European diplomatic correspondent for the same paper.

Biographical Notes

During the war, Emlyn Williams was in the Political Intelligence Department of the Foreign Office and in December, 1944, he re-entered his own profession as a war correspondent. Since July, 1945, he has been with the *Monitor* as chief Central European correspondent with headquarters in Germany.